FRIENDS
OF ACPL

Perversion of Power

Sexual Abuse in the Catholic Church

Perversion of Power

Sexual Abuse
in the Catholic Church

Mary Gail Frawley-O'Dea

Vanderbilt University Press
NASHVILLE

© 2007 Vanderbilt University Press
All rights reserved
First Edition 2007

10 09 08 07 1 2 3 4 5

Printed on acid-free paper.
Manufactured in the United States of America
Text designed by Dariel Mayer

Library of Congress Cataloging-in-Publication Data

Frawley-O'Dea, Mary Gail, 1950–
Perversion of power : sexual abuse in the Catholic Church /
Mary Gail Frawley-O'Dea.—1st ed.
p. cm.
Includes bibliographical references (p.) and index.
ISBN-13: 978-0-8265-1546-9 (cloth : alk. paper)
ISBN-13: 978-0-8265-1547-6 (pbk. : alk. paper)
1. Child sexual abuse by clergy. 2. Catholic Church—
Clergy—Sexual behavior. I. Title.
BX1912.9.F74 2007
261.8'3272088282—dc22
2006029442

To My Family

Dennis, Mollie, Sally, and Martha

Contents

Acknowledgments

There is a paradox to writing. It is a very solitary pursuit yet it cannot be accomplished without others. Those others deserve recognition and giving it is one of the more pleasurable aspects of writing a book.

In April 2002, Therese Ragen, Ph.D., a fellow psychoanalyst, piqued my interest in the Church sexual abuse scandal and prompted me to use my expertise to educate the bishops about the long-term impact of sexual abuse. I am grateful to her for many reasons.

I have been treating adult survivors of sexual abuse for almost a quarter of a century. My life has been enriched through my relationship with survivors from whom I have learned much about suffering and triumph. Since I began working on this book, I have been supported by many survivors of priest abuse. Kathy Dwyer of Boston is a woman of great integrity who has become a colleague and a friend. Arthur Austin, Ann Hagan Webb, Steve Lewis, and David Clohessy all have modeled courage and persistence in pursuing personal recovery while insisting on restorative justice. There are other survivors who cannot be mentioned by name for whose encouragement I am deeply grateful. Survivor advocates like Anne Barrett Doyle, Paul Baier, Paul Kendrick, Terry McKiernan, Marge Bean, Lori Lambert, and Steve Sheehan also have welcomed me into their midst and cheered on my work.

Bishop Paul Bootkoski allowed me to interview him and opened a window to his thinking and to his heart. I appreciate his confidence, his generosity, and his honesty.

A number of priests read all or sections of this book or have helped me in other ways. Before I even spoke in Dallas, Rev. Richard P. Mc-Brien, theologian at the University of Notre Dame, encouraged me to share with the bishops my knowledge about sexual abuse. He has been responsive to various questions I have had over the years. Rev. John L. Franck, A.A., and I agree about little that appears in this book yet John has been generous with his time and knowledge. We both have learned from our differences and I treasure our "odd couple" friendship. Rev. Paul Berube of Newburyport, Massachusetts, read the manuscript and made valuable suggestions, especially about my understanding of the theology of the Crucifixion. I am particularly indebted to Rev. James Martin, S.J., associate editor of *America* magazine, whose comments on Chapters 3–7 improved them greatly. Jim did not necessarily agree with all I had to say but was willing to comb the manuscript to improve my theological discussions. Rev. Michael Papesh also read much of the manuscript and was generous with helpful comments. Rev. Thomas P. Doyle, O.P., has sacrificed much to support victims and survivors of abuse. I am honored that he has become a friend who read the manuscript when he did not have the time to do so and made very valuable suggestions. Msgrs. John Allesandro and Peter Pflomm of the Diocese of Rockville Center, Msgr. Lawrence J. Breslin of Ohio, Revs. Ken Mich and Michael Erwin of the Archdiocese of Milwaukee, Rev. Robert Bowers of Boston, and Rev. James Scahill of East Longmeadow, Massachusetts, all were generous in sharing their perceptions about the crisis and the Church with me. Rev. John Bambrick of New Jersey is a survivor and a priest. He has spoken out courageously about the scandal in the Church and was kind enough to share a dinner and many helpful insights with me. Through my conversations with these priests, I developed an appreciation for the dedication and long days of decent priests throughout this country. In addition to these Roman Catholic priests, I am grateful to Rev. Armand LaValle, an Episcopalian priest, who also read the manuscript and provided helpful comments.

There were a number of Catholic laypeople who encouraged this project. Historian and author Garry Wills read a very early outline of the book and encouraged me to find a publisher. Paul Kellen of Massachusetts opened up speaking opportunities for me and has been a steadfast friend despite my lack of availability much of the time. Theologian Elizabeth Johnson and I spent a wonderful evening breaking Italian bread together on Arthur Avenue, the Little Italy of the Bronx. She shared her incredible intellect, generous spirit, and playful humor and I learned a lot in one night. Eugene Kennedy, psychologist, author, and inactive priest, urged me early on to pursue this book. He has been a regular correspondent who injected his wonderful sense of humor when I was most in need of a lift. Psychologist and inactive monk A.W. Richard Sipe's work was important to me as I developed my thinking about the crisis and he also has been generous in corresponding with me. Kathleen McChesney, first director of the Office of Child Protection for the United States Conference of Catholic Bishops (USCCB), and her associate Sheila Horan both have taken time to answer questions about the data generated by the John Jay College of Criminal Justice study of sexual abuse in the Church, and by audits conducted by the bishops' conference. Tom Roberts, editor of *National Catholic Reporter*, provided an empathic ear on various occasions when I felt overwhelmed with sadness or anger about a new development in the scandal.

Outside the Church, I have been fortunate to have the support and insight of colleagues. Virginia Goldner, Ph.D., psychoanalyst and associate editor of *Studies in Gender & Sexuality*, gave me the opportunity to coedit two issues of the journal devoted to the Catholic sexual abuse scandal. Reading those articles sharpened my own thinking about a number of issues covered in this book. More important, Virginia became a friend with whom I have been honored to work and play over the past few years. Jack Drescher, M.D., distinguished fellow of the American Psychiatric Association and chair of its Committee on Gay, Lesbian, and Bisexual Issues, read and commented on portions of the chapter on homosexuality. Similarly, author David France reviewed the homosexuality chapter and offered excellent insights. Irwin Hirsch, Ph.D., psychoanalyst, former supervisor, mentor, and friend, read the manuscript and made a number of important suggestions. This is the second book of mine he has read and I am grateful for his stamina as well as for his willingness. Joan Sarnat, Ph.D., psychoanalyst, friend, and coauthor with me of *The Supervisory Relationship: A Contemporary Psychodynamic Perspective*, also read the manuscript and applied her considerable intellect in providing feedback. It is comforting to know that she is a reliable and competent critic as well as a friend. While I was codirector of the Manhattan Institute for Psychoanalysis, I was in absentia more than I should have been, in part because of the demands of the book. My fellow directors, Jim Traub, M.S.W., and Ann de Armas, M.S.W., were endlessly understanding and filled the gap for me. Sandra Green, M.S.W., director of the institute's Trauma Treatment Program, also tolerated less support than she was entitled to and I appreciate her sensitivity and kindness.

This book could not have been written without Kathy Shaw, religion reporter for the Worcester, Massachusetts, *Telegram & Gazette*. In her "spare time" and as a volunteer, Kathy collects the articles appearing daily on the *Abuse Tracker* (www.ncrnews.org/abuse). The *Abuse Tracker*, managed from 2002 to 2003 by the Poynter Institute and since then by the *National Catholic Reporter*, posts summaries of articles from all over the world concerning the abuse crisis and provides links to the original news pieces. Kathy *is* the *Abuse Tracker*. She facilitates research on the scandal that simply would be impossible without her dedication and thoroughness.

Michael Ames, director of Vanderbilt University Press, has been a skilled and patient editor. When he and I dined at a Nyack, New York trattoria to discuss Vanderbilt's involvement in this project, I had no idea how long it would take to complete the manuscript or how difficult it would be to find the most effective voice. Michael was persistent in challenging me to produce the best work I could in a voice that would invite readers into the story. To the extent that I succeeded, he deserves a great deal of credit. Any failure is my own.

Throughout my adult life, I have been blessed with wonderful friends. While "working on the book" for almost four years, I often did not hold up my end of my friendships. My friends were patient, encouraging, and understanding. Love and appreciation are heartfelt for Judy and Howie Brown, Ellen and Ran Rubinstein, Jane and Richard Gartner, David Friedman and Suzanne King, Tony and Sally Sapienza, Sunny Lee, and Sandy Crapanzano. It's your turn now! I am also grateful for the humor, intellect, independent-mindedness, and generosity of spirit of the members of my book group: Sylvia Ann Beyer, Betty Brown, Diana Congdon, Robin Curlin, Jane Golz, Karen Hartfeil, and Julie Nussman.

Finally, my family. My cousin, Fred Frawley, read the manuscript as it developed and has already been marketing the book to his extensive network of family and friends. Other cousins, Anne and Leo Panas, read the final product and were kind enough to call and write with compliments and support. For several years, my husband and friend, Dennis O'Dea, has been patient about my immersion in a subject that truly sickens him. His love makes my world work and enriches my intellect and my soul. I am fortunate to have the most loving stepson in the world. Mollie and Sally, my delicious daughters, always remind me by their presence what really is important in life. I cannot imagine my life without their love and joie de vivre. Finally, my aunt, godmother, and godsend, Martha Quinn, lives with us and kept things running when I was locked up with my computer for hours on end. Thank you with all my heart to my family—I love you dearly.

Personal Preface

I was born in 1950 and raised in the Irish Catholic culture of Lowell, Massachusetts. Catholics were known and located in the cultural landscape as much by their parish affiliation as by their street address. I was baptized and made my First Communion at St. Patrick's where many years later Fr. Dominic Spagnolia would successfully stare down sexual abuse allegations only to resign over a homosexual affair.[1] For most of my childhood and adolescence, though, I was a Sacred Heart girl, a parish recently closed by Boston Archbishop Sean Cardinal O'Malley.

A public school kid through eighth grade, I attended high school at the Academy of Notre Dame in Tyngsborough, Massachusetts, run by the Sisters of Notre Dame de Namur. There, I was challenged intellectually, supported emotionally, and enveloped spiritually by the nuns. After high school, I followed the S.N.D. sisters to Emmanuel College in Boston for two years where Rev. William Murphy, cited by the attorney general of Massachusetts as complicit in the cover-up of sexual abuse in Boston and now bishop of Rockville Centre, New York, taught my freshman theology course.[2] As a junior, I transferred to St. Mary's at Notre Dame, run by the Sisters of the Holy Cross and sister school to the then still all-male University of Notre Dame. While I was a student, there were rumors about Fr. James Burtchaell, Notre Dame's provost, who supposedly had "wild" parties in the penthouse of the library. In 1991, Burtchaell resigned from Notre Dame amid allegations of sexual misconduct with students.[3]

Like many St. Mary's women, I married my Notre Dame honey two weeks after graduation. Children of the '60s, we had a sometimes relationship with Catholicism as we went to graduate school, moved to New York City, and started business careers. Then, in 1983 we separated and eventually divorced. I went back to school for a doctorate in clinical psychology and a certificate in psychoanalysis, and began working with survivors of childhood sexual abuse. In 1994, Jody Messler Davies and I coauthored a book on treating adult survivors of childhood sexual abuse. We were among the first psychoanalysts to refocus the field on the importance of early sexual trauma in the lives of substantial numbers of our patients.

Until 2002, I rarely thought about religion. After I remarried, I knew that I could not come to the table at a Catholic Church unless my first marriage and my current husband's first marriage were annulled. It seemed shabby even to think about annulling what was to me a very meaningful marriage, despite its ultimate dissolution. Although a number of priests over the years urged me to use my conscience in terms of receiving the Eucharist, I always ended up feeling guilty and ashamed or defiant in an adolescent sort of way if I partook of the sacrament. Neither is a graced state in which to take Communion.

In April 2002, Therese Ragen, Ph.D., a colleague who had grown up in a Chicago Irish Catholic family and also attended St. Mary's for a time, suggested we write an op-ed piece about the Catholic sexual abuse crisis for the *New York Times*. We did, it was not published, and I figured that was it. She had a friend at the United States Conference of Catholic Bishops (USCCB), however, and in May, I was invited to address over three hundred bishops at their semiannual meeting in Dallas. The meeting that year was dedicated to discussion of the sexual abuse crisis and the topic of my talk was the long-term effects of sexual abuse. After I spoke, some bishops thanked me personally for helping them grasp more deeply the impact of abuse on survivors. Others, like Edward Cardinal Egan of New York—my home bishop—seemed to choose not to speak or make eye contact even when I was just a few feet away. Back home, I felt an itch about the scandal. I began reading and then I began writing. This book started to take shape.

Many reporters and other commentators on the scandal have told me how painful it has been for them to be immersed in this material. It has been for me as well. As a clinician working for almost a quarter century with men and women who were raped or sodomized, sometimes even tortured, by family members, neighbors, teachers, or the fathers of friends, I thought that I had heard it all and was almost too hardened to what is done to minors by people they love and trust. But priest abuse was different. To someone raised a Catholic, priests essentially are God-on-earth, so their crimes were even more upsetting to me than the "usual" sexual abuse stories. Like others, I also found it particularly disturbing to come to terms with the reality of bishops presiding over depravity and not being motivated to move heaven and earth to stop it.

In the next chapter, I advise that one must dance with evil in order to "get" more fully sexual abuse by priests and its cover-up by bishops. I have tried to do that, and therefore it has been an emotionally intense experience to write this book. For almost three years, my last act of the day has been to check the latest postings on the *Abuse Tracker*, a website that collects media articles on the scandal. Sleep has not always come easily.

As I wrestled with the facts of the abuse crisis and its meaning, including its potential meaning for me and my relationship with Catholicism, however, a curious and lovely thing happened. I stumbled across St. John's-in-the-Wilderness, an Episcopal church nestled at the foot of New York's Harriman State Park, and I decided to spend a Sunday there. When Fr. William Dearman, the rector, announced after the offertory that anyone who was baptized was welcome to receive the Eucharist, I teared up and realized how much I had missed the rituals and sacraments of Christianity. Now living in Charlotte, North Carolina, my family and I attend St. Martin's Episcopal Church, where we have found a welcoming and challenging spiritual home. The Anglican Church is imperfect and has its own contemporary internal struggles. I do not idealize it as a flawless religion. For me, however, it is a good fit.

CHAPTER 1

From the Bayou to Boston

A Developing Pattern

Bayou Beginnings

Most writers agree that the Catholic Church's contemporary sexual abuse crisis began in Henry, Louisiana, in 1983 when molestation allegations were made against Fr. Gilbert Gauthe.[1] The Gauthe case, set in the deeply Catholic bayou country of Louisiana, was the first nationally publicized narrative of sexual abuse by a Roman Catholic priest. In addition to being first, it contained within it all the factors that became routinely associated with the Church scandal as it unfolded over the next twenty years.

Gilbert Gauthe was the charming pastor of Henry's St. John parish.[2] Gauthe's parishioners appreciated his availability, his empathy with the economic and social concerns of his rural flock, and his involvement with the parish youth. Fr. Gauthe spent much of his free time with the kids in his care, especially the boys, and even took them on regular Friday night sleepovers at a parishioner's island camp house. One night, however, nine-year-old Craig Sagrera told his parents that Gilbert Gauthe had been molesting him.[3] Stunned, the boy's father approached his fifteen- and twenty-nine-year-old sons with Craig's story only to learn that the priest also had sexually abused them. Further, they gave Wayne Sagrera the names of other boys sexually victimized by the pastor.

Mr. Sagrera contacted Paul Hebert, a local attorney, to figure out what to do next. Hebert in turn placed a call to the diocesan chancery in Lafayette, Louisiana, and spoke with Monsignor Henri Alexandre Larroque. Hebert and Sagrera were astonished when Larroque told them that Henry was Gauthe's sixth assignment after the bishop learned in 1973 that Gauthe had molested children. After Gauthe sexually victimized children in his first parish assignment in Broussard, Louisiana, he was told by his bishop to sin no more and was moved to a new parish. New complaints were made against him there so he was moved to two different assignments in Abbeville, Louisiana, where he was reported to be sexually active with minor boys. The diocese responded by appointing him chaplain to the Boy Scouts. Finally, he was made pastor of the Henry parish. No one there had been apprised of their priest's previous crimes.

Under pressure from Sagrera and Hebert, Bishop Frey eventually instructed Monsignor Larroque to remove Gauthe from the parish in Henry. Various representatives of the Church then began to exhort Paul Hebert and the Sagrera family not to make a fuss about Gauthe's sexual exploitation of boys. One priest in a neighboring parish, Monsignor Richard Mouton, told Wayne Sagrera that if anyone were injured from the Gauthe case, it would be Sagrera's fault for making the facts public. When Paul Hebert suggested to the monsignor that civil lawsuits might be filed against Gauthe and the Church, Mouton reminded him that he was a good Catholic high school boy and a good Catholic boy would never sue his Church.

Paul Hebert did file nine lawsuits on behalf of victims in six families, but he also attempted to work with the chancery to avoid publicity. In June 1984, the insurance carriers for the Lafayette diocese paid $4.2 million to settle the nine civil suits. Settlement documents were filed in court under seal by agreement of both parties, but a court clerk alerted a local reporter and the press began investigating the case. In the meantime, other Gauthe victims launched civil suits. Four families settled out of court with the diocese and their insurance carriers but one family, the Gastal's, did not want to be bound to secrecy and instead sued the Church in court. A jury eventually awarded the Gastal's $1.2 million, a sum reduced by settlement to $1 million.

In addition to civil litigation brought against Gilbert Gauthe and the Lafayette diocese, the local district attorney brought criminal charges, including rape and possession of child pornography. In October 1985, Gauthe was sentenced to twenty years in prison. He was released from prison after ten years but reoffended by molesting a three-year-old boy in Texas and was returned to prison. Released again, his whereabouts as of 2002 were unknown.[4]

As civil and criminal proceedings developed in the Gauthe case, press coverage picked up and eventually included both the secular and Catholic print and TV media. Press interest also spread from the bayou, where sexually abusive priests other than Gauthe were being identified, to the national scene, and one reporter, Jason Berry, wrote the first book on the Church scandal in 1992.[5]

Most of the players in the Gauthe case moved slowly at first, wanting to believe that Fr. Gauthe's sexual violation of minors and the diocese's apparent complicity in tolerating repeated sexual offenses by a priest were aberrations. Reporters and lawyers involved in the case were Catholics who expected their Church willingly to make right a terrible but unusual situation.

While those Catholics involved in the Gauthe case were frightened and conflicted about challenging the Church they loved, they began to shatter previously sacred relationships protecting the Church from scandals associated with sexually abusive priests. Laypeople, who at one time would have done what they were told by priests and bishops, stood up to the clergy and demanded accountability for the crimes of a priest and the complicity of his ecclesiastical superiors. Newspaper publishers and editors, once deferential to the Church, stayed on the story and made it national news. Police, prosecutors, plaintiffs' attorneys, and judges who years before might have colluded with secrecy went forward with the Gauthe case. Mental health professionals who once would have known little about the impact of sexual trauma on children and adolescents testified about the damage inflicted on Gauthe's young victims.

Over the next two decades, sexual abuse of minors by a priest and the concomitant cover-up of his crimes by his diocese or religious order were exposed as a repetitive pattern lived out within the Catholic Church for decades across the United States.

Typically, a priest arrived in a parish or other Church setting sometime between 1950 and the early 1990s. Often energetic and charismatic, he focused his ministry on youth activities. Gradually, he developed close relationships with the young people entrusted to his care, frequently—but not always—boys between the ages of ten and fourteen. Sometimes the children or adolescents were from difficult homes and needed attention from an adult who had concern for them. Others hailed from stable and loving homes. All had been taught from birth to honor and trust with their souls priests who were viewed as Christ's representatives on earth. Kids and parents all were thrilled when Father played sports with the youngsters, took them to the movies or holiday carnivals, came to the house for dinner, organized weekend car washes, chaperoned dances, helped with homework, chose a son as an altar boy, or took children on weekend trips to the shore or to an exciting city.

Successfully insinuating himself into the hearts of the families and minors in his care, Father at some point introduced sex into his relationships with young people. Sometimes, it was "just" fondling as when Fr. Edmond Lemire of New Hampshire allegedly befriended a parish boy through a shared interest in magic and stamp collecting, and then groped him under his bathing suit on a swim outing in 1963.[6] Sometimes, fondling or kissing progressed to oral sex. Fr. James F. Hopkins, for example, allegedly forced Jonathan Norton to perform oral sex from ages eight to ten when Norton was an altar boy at St. Peter's parish in Merchantville, New Jersey.[7] In still other instances, a priest's sexually abusive behavior was entwined with bizarre distortions of tenets of Catholic faith that were deeply disturbing to the victims. Fr. Robert V. Meffan of Massachusetts, for example, allegedly engaged teenaged girls who were preparing to be nuns in sexual unions with him by describing himself as the second coming of Christ who could help them experience what it would be like to have sex with their future spiritual bridegroom.[8] Similarly, victims of Fr. Larry Brett of Stamford, Connecticut, report that he told them that performing oral sex on him was a special way of receiving Holy Communion from a priest.[9]

Sometime during the career of an abusive priest, a fellow priest, a parishioner, a victim's parent, or a victim complained about Father to the pastor, diocesan representative, bishop, or religious superior either when the abuse was occurring or later. When an accusation was made, there were a couple of likely outcomes. Years ago, the complainant may have been scolded for daring to "bring scandal to the Church," an overused term connoting an offense that historically too many clerics considered more grievous than anything Father may have done.[10] In this case, the chastened individual was sent home, and, as rumors of the accusations surfaced in the gossip mill of the parish or institution, he or she might end up shunned by both priests and fellow faithful.[11]

While priests and parishioners were rebuffed by clerical officials when they reported sexually abusing priests, back at the rectory, chancery, or provincial house, Father was confronted about his behavior and, not always but in a remarkable number of cases, acknowledged the accuracy of the allegations. Having confessed, he promised not to sin again and was sent back to ministry, often in a new setting. As the decades passed, it became increasingly likely that Father would be sent off for psychological evaluation and/or treatment. After that, he sometimes was returned to ministry with access to children; sometimes he was placed in a ministry ostensibly removed from young people; sometimes he was laicized; sometimes he resigned. When priests were reassigned, the receiving clergy and community typically were not informed about the priest's background and therefore there was no particular supervision of his activities.

By the mid-1980s and into the 1990s, another scenario often played out when a priest was accused of past or present abuse. Here, the complainant was taken seriously. She or he was assured that Father would be removed from any ministry involved with children. The Church offered to pay for the victim's counseling. As accusers became more aggressive in their demands for redress, sometimes engaging attorneys to help them, secret settlement agreements were reached in which money was given to plaintiffs.

This was more or less the characteristic pattern of sexual abuse and the response to it enacted by the Catholic Church for decades. From the Gauthe case onward, however, the Church's handling of the sexual victimization of children and adolescents by its priests became more publicized until it grew into the scandal that spread out from Boston in the first years of the new century.

Boston and Beyond

> Since the mid-1990s, more than 130 people have come forward with horrific tales about how former priest John J. Geoghan allegedly fondled or raped them during a three-decade spree through a half-dozen Greater Boston parishes. Almost always his victims were grammar school boys. One was just four years old. . . . There is no dispute that Geoghan abused children at Blessed Sacrament in Saugus after his 1962 ordination. . . . Cardinal Bernard F. Law knew about Geoghan's problems in 1984. . . . [I]n 1998, the church "defrocked" Geoghan. . . . Why did it take a succession of three cardinals and many bishops 34 years to place children out of Geoghan's reach? . . . Donna Morrissey, a spokeswoman for Law, said the cardinal and other church officials would not respond to questions about Geoghan. Morrissey said the church had no interest in knowing what the *Globe*'s questions would be.
>
> —*Boston Globe*, 6 January 2002[12]

By publishing a detailed account of John Geoghan's serial abuse of children, the Archdiocese of Boston's repeated transfer of Geoghan even after many chancery officials knew about his crimes, and the ongoing efforts of the Boston hierarchy to cover up the extent of Geoghan's crimes and their complicity in them, the *Boston Globe* swung wide open a door first cracked in the Gauthe case twenty years earlier. After that *Globe* article, survivors, reporters, lawyers, and laypeople focused more closely than ever on the repetitive pattern of crime and cover-up detectable in Catholic priest sexual abuse cases across the country. As judges ordered previously secret documents to be released from chancery vaults, the public was both morbidly fascinated and dismayed by what emerged.

By 2004, we knew that more than forty-three hundred priests were alleged to have abused almost eleven thousand young people between 1950 and 2002.[13] That number of victims, recorded in a study of abuse conducted for the United States Conference of Catholic Bishops (USCCB) by the John Jay College of Criminal Justice, reflects only those victims who came forward to report abuse to Church authorities. Studies indicate that at up to one third of female victims and a greater percentage of male victims never disclose their violations to anyone.[14] Even more never report sexual abuse to authorities, including Church officials, disclosing instead only to friends or to a therapist. Not all dioceses or religious provinces kept accurate records of alleged abuse, nor did all bishops or provincial superiors participate in the John Jay Study. It is therefore reasonable to estimate that over fifty thousand young people were abused by priests over the fifty years encompassed by the study.

Much more than by the sexual abuse itself, heinous though that often was, Americans were shocked that Catholic cardinals, archbishops, and bishops had failed repeatedly to respond well to abusing priests, victims, other priests, and laypeople. Catholics felt betrayed and non-Catholics were surprised by the hypocrisy perceived between the moral rectitude portrayed by many in the Church's hierarchy and the apparent immorality practiced by certain prelates nationwide.

In 2002, few would have predicted that the story of sexually abusive priests would "have legs." Yet, over four years later, the press still is churning out articles about priest abuse and cover-ups in dioceses across the United States, and the Catholic Church has paid out over $1 billion in sexual abuse lawsuits.[15] At the same time, victims/survivors, accused priests, other priests, Catholic laypeople, and observers continue struggling to understand how the Church managed itself into a crisis of this magnitude. Many Americans continue to ask a more general version of the question posed by the *Globe* in January 2002. They wonder: "How could the officials of the Catholic Church allow young people to be sexually violated by priests and do so little about it for so long?". This book suggests some answers to that question.

The Catholic Crisis in Context

Sexual abuse of young people has been a larger social problem than many Americans are comfortable knowing. Fathers, uncles, grandfathers, brothers, teachers, scout leaders, bus drivers, camp counselors, and even mothers sexually violate children and adolescents in numbers that surprise many people. In fact, we now know that almost one third of all girls and up to one fourth of all boys experience some form of sexual abuse before they reach eighteen years old.[16] Some researchers state that up to 10 percent of children in public schools will be sexually mistreated by teachers before they graduate.[17] For example, sexual abuse of students is the primary reason public school teachers in West Virginia lost their licenses between 2000 and 2005.[18]

Until the 1980s, sexual abuse was kept as secret in the wider society as it was within the Catholic Church. Institutions like schools or camps often protected abusers, allowing them to resign after a complaint was made and even providing positive recommendations for their next job. Families rarely turned an abusing relative over to authorities, and too often victims who disclosed abuse by a family member were blamed, ignored, or reabused.

Sexual abuse of minors also occurs in other Christian denominations and non-Christian religions. The Anglican Church in Australia has been scandalized by clergy sexual abuse and by the allegedly uncaring responses of bishops there.[19] Sexual violation of minors has been reported in Protestant denominations[20] and among Jewish rabbis,[21] Islamic clerics,[22] Buddhist monks,[23] and Hare Krishna officials.[24]

If sexual abuse happens in every religion and in every sector of secular society, why are we so captivated by the Catholic sexual abuse scandal? I think a partial answer lies in the hypocrisy it bespeaks. The Catholic Church tells us that it knows the truth and lives the truth of moral principles deriving directly from Jesus Christ. The Church is particularly certain and stringent about what is morally correct in the area of human sexuality. At the same time that popes and other officials spoke with conviction about how human beings should lead their moral lives, however, they were and still are presiding over a moral scandal of the worst kind—the sexual abuse of children and young people by priests and the ecclesiastical cover-up of those crimes. The juxtaposition of manifest moral rectitude offset by evidence of underlying moral corruption captures the human imagination. We watch and wait to see if, in the end, the good guys will win or if the bad guys will get away with it.

The activities of the American Catholic Church include much more than the sexual mistreatment of the young, though, which complicates the good-versus-bad scenario. Over 90 percent of Catholic priests never have violated a minor in that way. To the contrary, many Catholic priests provide excellent role models and effective mentoring for children, adolescents, and college students all over the world. In 2005, Catholic elementary and secondary schools educated almost 2.6 million young people.[25] Close to 30 percent of these students were minorities and over 13 percent were non-Catholic, many of whom were from disadvantaged families. In

2003, Catholic colleges and universities enrolled over 700,000 students, about a third of whom were non-Catholic.[26] Catholic hospitals treated almost 84 million patients in 2002[27]. In 2003, Catholic Charities agencies throughout America served over 6.6 million individuals without regard to religious, social, or economic backgrounds.[28] Almost one quarter of the population of the United States—over 63 million people—are Catholics who are served in more than 19,000 parishes by over 40,000 priests, most of whom never would harm a young person in their care.[29]

When one considers how vital and effective the Catholic Church is for many people in spiritual, educational, economic, medical, and social need, the tragedy of the sexual abuse crisis becomes clearer.

"Experiencing" the Crisis

Sexual abuse challenges our faith in the basic goodness of human beings. It is disturbing to think about little girls and boys having penises shoved into mouths too small to accommodate them without gagging. It is disorientating to stand in the reality of ten- or eleven-year-old girls and boys finding tongues swabbing the inside of their mouths, hands rubbing their penises or clitorises, or penises forced into their vaginas or rectums. It is sickening to imagine adolescent boys and girls plied with alcohol, pot, or porno films then groped, raped, or sodomized. It is even more distressing to visualize any of this occurring on altars, in confessionals, or on rectory beds with crucifixes hanging over them. We want to turn away from mental images of priests violating young people in this way. We do not want to believe that cardinals and bishops who knew what priests were doing could have transferred these men again and again, putting them in contact with more potential victims and then dismissing victims who managed to work up the courage to come forward. It is too much—too sad, too frightening, too close to what we think is evil.

Psychoanalyst Leonard Shengold entitled his book on the consequences of childhood sexual abuse, *Soul Murder*. Similarly, William Cardinal Keeler, archbishop of Baltimore, equated the sexual abuse of minors by priests with murder.[30] Cardinal Keeler, in fact, in a statement to his diocese in September 2002, said, "Child sexual abuse, regardless of any other factor, is evil."[31] Columbia University humanities professor Andrew Delbanco, in his book on evil, refers to Milton's devil. "He [Satan] invades his prey, as Milton tells it, by a rape . . . 'in at his Mouth the Devil Enter'd.' "[32] Milton's description is uncanny in its evocation of sexual abuse. Uncanniness is scary, but Delbanco comforts us. He tells us that this "nighttime burrowing into human bodies" represents Satan's power, but it is borrowed power and limited.[33] Christianity, he says, reassures us that, ultimately, the devil will be defeated, "driven out of his playground world" by God and goodness.[34] But, what happens when you are young, still visit playgrounds, and the devil is a priest?

Psychoanalyst Sue Grand further chills us when she addresses the role of silent bystanders in the perpetration of evil: "Secrecy, concealment, denial, ambiguity, confusion: these are Satan's fellow travelers, requiring elaborate interpersonal and intrapsychic collusion between perpetrators and bystanders. The operations of silence potentiate evil and remove all impediments from its path."[35] Keeping evil secret begets more evil. Silence about evil; minimization of evil (it was only a few priests; the bishops made mistakes but it's time to move on); obfuscation of evil (no one really knew how bad sexual abuse was for a child; I, the bishop, refuse to turn over the records that would make clear what sexual abuse took place in my diocese); and projection of evil (the doctors gave the guy a clean bill of health; the whole crisis is overblown by the anti-Catholic media; our critics are dissenters from the faith pushing their own agendas) allow evil to reproduce itself.

It is important to use our heads to devise intellectual conceptualizations about the Catholic sexual abuse scandal. But, first, before we apply our minds to the problem, we owe it to the victims to enter the discussion with our bodies, our souls, and our emotions. We need to take up a tango, a *danse macabre*, with evil for just a few moments. To really "get it," we have to let go for just a little while and try to experience viscerally the sights, sounds, smells, tastes, touches, and feelings of being betrayed by a priest and then betrayed again by his bishop or provincial superior. The victims are due at least that much.

Starting at the Top

Sexual abuse in the Church assumed a regular pattern in dioceses across the country and in countries throughout the world. When a phenomenon is replicated so seamlessly by very different people in multiple locations, it suggests that something systemic is at work. We must therefore consider the possibility that something is inherently wrong with the umbrella under which all these people are gathered. In the case of the Catholic Church, it seems important to identify teachings and traditions that may have contributed to the crisis. Further, since sexual abuse is first and foremost a crime of power, it is also helpful to examine power relationships within the institutional Church that are potentially implicated in its scandal.

Chapters 3 through 7 take on this task. Sexual abuse and its cover-up occurred at the intersection of power, sex, and suffering. These chapters therefore unpack Catholic teachings about bodies, gender, desire, sex, mandatory celibacy, and sexual orientation. It is my contention that Catholic theological renderings of these aspects of human experience are often stultifying to human psychological and spiritual growth and even can be unethical. Dualistic views of the body; misogynistic views of women; the inability of priests to fulfill stereotypical masculine gender norms; the oppression of lust; the straitjacketing of condoned sex into marital sex, open to biological procreation, between a man and a woman in a sacramentally blessed marriage; the imposition of celibacy on all priests; and the Church's relationship with homosexuals all contributed in some way to the sexual abuse of minors and, even more, to its cover-up.

In this section of the book and in others, I suggest possible psychological, even unconscious, motivations for the behaviors of priests, laypeople, victims, and Church officials. My intent is to offer these interpretations as tentative possibilities to be considered and, perhaps, to be operationalized and empirically tested by others. Here, I assume a certain amount of knowledge and authority based on training, experience, and professional recognition of my expertise in assessing human behavior in general and the dynamics of sexual abuse in particular. Because I do not know personally the people about whom I comment, however, my suggestions are intended to be just that and should not be mistaken for intended proclamations of truth.

The Cover-Up *Is* the Scandal

Roman Catholic cardinals and bishops, the group of churchmen most responsible for the scandal, continue to resist acknowledging how much of it was their fault, and they remain unwilling to be held accountable for it. Just before the bishops' 2002 spring meeting in Dallas, the *Dallas Morning News* reported that about two thirds of the bishops then leading American dioceses had allowed priests accused of sexual abuse to continue working in ministry.[36] Yet, when the bishops passed new norms for diocesan management of sexual abuse at that meeting in the form of the Charter for the Protection of Children and Young People, they avoided calling for any censure of bishops who violated the norms. Although the norms call for ecclesiastical participation in diocesan audits of compliance with the norms, Fabian Bruskewitz, bishop of Lincoln, Nebraska, refuses to follow some provisions of the charter and he declined to participate in the John Jay Study on the prevalence of sexual abuse in the Church.[37] In 2004, he and other bishops, including Edward Cardinal Egan of New York and

Howard Mansell of Hartford, Connecticut, expressed dismay that the National Review Board, appointed to work independently of the bishops, was working independently, and these bishops argued against conducting further audits of diocesan compliance with sexual abuse norms. They suggested they could audit themselves. In 2005 the president of the United States Conference of Catholic Bishops, Bishop William Skylstad, expressed his disappointment that a few abusive priests had tarnished the image of the Church and its good priests.[38] Given the long-standing collaboration of many bishops with abuse, juxtaposed with the seeming desire of some bishops to divest themselves of lay monitoring and immersion in the crisis, it is little wonder that many commentators and laypeople feel the bishops still do not "get it" when it comes to the sexual abuse scandal.

In addition to refusing to accept responsibility for the sexual abuse crisis, many bishops were publicly willing to embrace and claim brotherhood with those who had most disregarded the welfare of children. During a coffee hour at the Dallas meeting of the USCCB, I saw one bishop walk over to Bernard Cardinal Law, already infamous for his mismanagement of sexual abuse in Boston, grasp his hand, and tell Law how proud he was of all that the cardinal was doing in Boston. A year later, at the June 2003 USCCB meeting, after Law had resigned in disgrace as archbishop of Boston, he was welcomed by his fellow bishops, not one of whom publicly suggested that his presence there was an offense. Quite the contrary, Daniel Reilly, former bishop of Worcester, Massachusetts, Theodore McCarrick, then cardinal archbishop of Washington, D.C, and Rev. C. J. McCloskey III of the Catholic Information Center in D.C. all welcomed Law's presence at the conference and suggested that he still had much to offer the Church.[39] Apparently the Vatican agreed. In May 2004, Pope John Paul II appointed Law archpriest of St. Mary Major basilica in Rome, and he still serves on several Vatican congregations.[40]

The bishops continue to act in deference to one another rather than holding themselves and each other to account. It is frustrating for observers who know that the dynamics underlying the scandal cannot be changed unless the hierarchy acknowledges the primacy of their roles in the crisis. As the *National Catholic Reporter* put it, "Any other institution in this society . . . would rightly show these men the door. Enron was a catastrophe, but Ken Lay is now unemployed; Howell Raines no longer edits *The New York Times*. It's called accountability."[41]

In Chapters 8 and 9, I examine the bishop's lack of pastoral sensitivity during the sexual abuse crisis and the influence of clerical narcissism on the dynamics and behaviors of the episcopacy. These failures of leadership were egregious, yet it is also true that many bishops presiding over the sexual abuse of youngsters brought great good into the world through other aspects of their work. There are two demographic factors that may shed light on their particular inability to respond pastorally or effectively to sexual abuse. Explanations are not exculpations—ultimately, each bishop was responsible to care well for his priests and laypeople. It is worthwhile, however, to put the bishops' actions into a psychosocial context.

Catholic Victorians

More than 80 percent of bishops leading dioceses between 1983 and 2003 were born before 1940; almost 50 percent before 1930. They were men born and raised, therefore, in an era in which sex, much less sexual abuse, was barely mentioned in most social circles, especially Catholic milieus.

Throughout the first half of the twentieth century, American social and sexual mores were derivative of Victorian sensibilities.[42] Here, genteel social customs coexisted with sexual acting-out that was known about but not acknowledged openly. Irish critic Fintan O'Toole expresses it well when he says that the Victorians concocted a "cocktail of do-gooder moral activism and sexual hypocrisy."[43] During the Victorian era, the dissociation of sometimes outlandish sexual behavior from socially acceptable lifestyles was for the most part effective. Historian Getrude Himmelfarb, in fact, states, "The Victorians thought it no small virtue to maintain the appearance of good conduct even while violating some moral principle, for in their demeanor they affirmed the legitimacy of the principle itself."[44]

The majority of bishops who led dioceses during the last half of the twentieth century were steeped in these Victorian attitudes about sexuality and the privileging of manners over meaning. Even as the rest of twentieth-century America began to shed Victorian manners and sexual trappings in the 1960s and 1970s, the hierarchy remained embedded in them, enhanced as they were by Catholic teachings about the status of bishops and the narrow range of sexual behaviors acceptable within Catholicism. In addition, for many bishops, Victorianism intersected with an Irish cultural heritage that perhaps rendered many in the hierarchy even less equipped to confront effectively the sexual abuse crisis.

The Irish Factor

In 1900, 75 percent of American bishops were Irish or Irish American; as late as the 1990s, over half the hierarchy still could claim Irish heritage.[45] The majority of bishops presiding over the sexual abuse crisis as diocesan leaders, therefore, were freighted with the status insecurities and sexual repressiveness endemic to that culture.

Because of their long experience with second-class status, the Irish in America craved respectability.[46] Until at least the 1970s, the road to respectability most cherished by Irish families, especially by mothers, was to send a son to the priesthood.[47] When that priest/son became a bishop, a Lord of the Church, he brought spiritual and social salvation to his family and to his ethnic group, alleviating some of the cultural shame instilled by years of discrimination against those Irish who came to America. Acknowledging and confronting the shameful sexual crimes of his priests, many of them also Irish, might be literally unthinkable for an Irish bishop upon whose scarlet-caped shoulders rested ecclesiastical duty and, perhaps more to the point, responsibility for both familial and cultural redemption. Rather, a profound tribalism influenced the Irish bishop to do everything possible to keep sexual abuse a secret. As author Thomas Keneally says, "Even today, the attitude (among the Irish) in the face of villainy on the part of the Church is: 'Don't do anything to make bullets for the enemy. Leave it to us to look after the problem.'"[48]

Irish American bishops were additionally burdened by a cultural heritage so outwardly sexually repressive that, despite the large families produced by the Irish, it was cliché to consider Irish sex an oxymoron. The Irish Catholic Church adhered to a harshly moralistic theology that viewed sex as a distasteful act unfortunately necessary for procreation; sex thus became colloquially known as "the lack of the Irish."[49] It is not surprising, therefore, that Irish bishops may have been paralyzed by their personal discomfort over anything sexual, much less sexual abuse. In addition, the peculiar use of language inherent in Irish culture supported a bishop's defense against knowing fully the dimensions and meaning of the sexual victimization of minors by his priests.

Conditions of life were so harsh in Ireland that, over the ages, the Irish developed a creative imagination to cope with and escape from the cold realities of life.[50] Convinced beyond a reasonable doubt by the climate, endless wars, British occupation, and Church teachings that life on earth mostly was about suffering, the Irish wove imaginative alternate realities that were expressed through poems, sagas, humor, and literature.[51] In the process, they achieved a high tolerance for nonrational thinking and for language that is intricate but conveys little information about the real-time life, especially the interior life, of the speaker.[52] Novelist Mary Gordon captures the essence of Irish language when she says, "[T]he Irish believe that language is at least as much an ornament as a telegrapher, and one can be astonished at how many words one has heard at an Irish gathering without having learned the slightest thing about the speakers' lives."[53]

Within the pre–Vatican II Latin-speaking Church, language also was employed as much to create an impression as to communicate meaning with clarity. Irish bishops, brought up in households in which speech often was used as much to obfuscate as to convey meaning and trained in a Church in which the multilayered meanings of the language used (Latin) were often inaccessible, may have fallen easily into using words to talk about sexual abuse that were not grounded in reality, clarity, and stark meaning. Rather, the words were catchphrases recited in a metronomic litany that dulled the senses and lulled the listener, as well as the speaker.

To the extent that they remained embedded in Victorian social and sexual codes, reinforced by Irish cultural mores, many bishops were psychosocially unprepared to confront sexual abuse by priests directly. The Gospels might have saved them, but many seemed to lose track of those books, which, if nothing else, are exemplars of words laden with meaning and of a man portrayed as caring little for manners and much for truth. Instead, the bishops seemed to push sexual abuse and its victims out of their minds much as they pushed offending priests into new parishes or other settings.

Priests, Laypeople, and the Cultural Milieu

Abusive priests, other priests, and Catholic laypeople share responsibility with the bishops for the sexual abuse scandal. Chapter 10 describes what we know about priests who abused minors in the Church. I also address the powerful priestly tradition of "omertà" that kept most priests silent about abusive brethren and that punished those who broke ranks to speak up. Finally, the chapter looks at the contribution to the scandal of laypeople who were trained by the Church to "pray, pay, and obey," to remain silent even when they suspected or knew for sure that a priest was abusing a minor.

Catholic priests, like men from other walks of life, have sexually abused children for many centuries. Why did the Church's secret come out and stay out in 2002? In Chapter 11, I list and briefly expand on the social and cultural forces both outside and within the Church that resulted in sustained public scrutiny of sexual abuse by priests. Finally, in Chapter 12, I suggest that while much has changed since the hierarchy began to confront sexual abuse more forcefully in 2002, too much also remains the same.

Responses to sexual misconduct by clergy can be clear-headed yet pastoral. Clerical leaders and parishes can protect young people and the community while leaving room for transformation of the perpetrator; they can be mindful of legal liability while attending first and foremost to those suffering. Crimes can be named and confronted without a loss of compassion. This can be done, at least most of the time, when there is leadership that insists on it. The Catholic Church is not there yet, but the people depending on it deserve for it to get there. The outcome depends on the will of the people—bishops, priests, and laypeople—to make it happen.

CHAPTER 2

Surviving Soul Murder

For thousands of men and women, the Catholic sexual abuse scandal is not just a newspaper story or a fascinating psychosocial study; rather, it is a central thematic strand of their lives. They live, or try to, with the physiological, psychological, and spiritual wounds inflicted upon them as children and adolescents by men they loved and trusted. Sometimes the wounds heal over and are remembered only when the scars are unexpectedly revealed; at other times, they fill with pus and suppurate, requiring the victim to attend to nothing and no one else; at still other times, for some, they turn gangrenous from lack of care and infiltrate the victim's whole being with a sickness unto death. Because of the effect of sexual abuse inflicted by priests and vowed religious on victims/survivors, it is crucial that we understand this story. To do so, we must begin with their experiences.

A True Crime Story

Let us begin with a true crime story, a story told in my consultation room by a thirty-something-year-old man.[1] Since we all want to distance ourselves from the tumultuous internal states evoked by intimacy with sexual abuse, I ask the reader to engage the following as much with your body, guts, feelings, and imagination as with your intellectual prowess. Your feelings and bodily states reflect the meaning of sexual abuse as truly as your mind does.

Imagine, then, that you are eight years old and have just become an altar boy. Your parents, struggling with marital problems and alcoholism, are not very available to you, so you are especially proud to have a place in the family of your parish. It is a bright, cold February Sunday and you have just finished helping Fr. Bill, your favorite priest, serve Mass. As you enter the sacristy, Fr. Bill tells you that you did a great job at this last Mass of the morning and you can feel the pride and happiness filling you up. The priest—your priest—offers to help you pull the cassock over your head, joking that he still can't get used to wearing dresses. But, as Fr. Bill lifts the cassock up, he holds it over your face with one hand, unzips his trousers with the other, and pushes his erect penis into your back. You sense him moving back and forth against you. Blindfolded by the cassock, you can only stand still until, after moaning and leaning into you one more time, Fr. Bill loosens his grip. You feel moisture on your back but, as he pulls the cassock all the way off, he is wiping your back with a towel and mumbling about the steam radiator heat making you sweaty. He pats you on the back and tells you to turn the lights off before you leave for the day. Not a word is said about what just happened. What did just happen, you wonder? You feel funny—scared but not really sure if you have any reason to be. It's Fr. Bill after all. Can you imagine?

For the next three years, Fr. Bill repeats these acts in many places at many times. Empty classrooms, the sacristy, the small school chapel, the nurse's office, the rectory—all become sexualized spaces. He asks your parents if he can take you to his summer place at the beach and they are relieved not to have to worry about you. There, the abuse, during which you always are blindfolded, meshes with fishing expeditions, movies, riding the ocean waves, clam digging, and other activities a lonely child living in a city apartment building with drunk and arguing parents finds amazing. That fun and adventure fills your days. Your nights, on the other hand, find Fr. Bill rubbing his penis between your buttocks, caressing and sucking on your now erect penis, tongue kissing you, and pushing your blindfolded face onto his penis. You clench your teeth tightly and, as far as you can remember, never let him get inside your mouth. It is a small but important act of defiance and self-protection. Imagine.

You are now eleven and prepubertal acne is spurting on your face. On the first day of sixth grade, Fr. Bill pulls you into a storage room and, as he tries to kiss you, he tells you that your "badness" is coming out all over your face. This time, you push him off and run. He never touches you again.

Can you imagine the life of this young boy from ages eight to eleven? And afterward? He never spoke of the abuse until beginning treatment. Shortly before beginning therapy, he had read in the paper that Fr. Bill was accused of sexually molesting boys thirty years ago in another parish. Although removed from ministry, Fr. Bill denied all the charges and was quoted in the paper saying that he was being scapegoated in the Church scandal and had never even known his accusers when they were boys. At that point, my patient contacted other men that he suspected had been molested by Fr. Bill in their parish, and a number of them went to the papers with their stories. My patient is not suing anyone nor does he plan on suing anyone. He does say the following:

> It is something that I have thought about every day of my life, yet have always been far too ashamed to talk about. I am still ashamed. After reading Fr. Bill's denials in the papers, though, I decided I couldn't hide my story any longer. I was robbed of my youth and my faith at a very young age. If I can prevent this from happening to other children, then perhaps I am on the right track. I am not a practicing Catholic, and I certainly don't need the Catholic Church to teach my children morals and values and right from wrong. In fact, it will probably be years before I have to answer the question, "Hey, Daddy, what's a priest?"

Can you imagine?

The Victims

Usually, the victims of abusive priests were children or adolescents yearning for adults who saw them, heard them, understood them, made time for them, and enjoyed their company. Many were minors from families with a parent missing, or they were youngsters coping with alcoholism, spousal abuse, or other forms of violence and neglect in their environments. They may even have been physically or sexually abused by someone else and were therefore especially vulnerable to further exploitation by a trusted figure.

Other victims from intact, well-functioning families were abused at developmental stages, like pre- and early adolescence, when it is normal for minors to find mentors outside the family as they begin a process of separation and individuation from parents. This is a stage at which teachers, coaches, youth group leaders, and other adults involved with them are idealized and sought out for advice or companionship. Often, these relationships are tinged with eroticism as young people develop "crushes" on adults they look up to. This erotic component exists no matter the gender mix of the dyad. In other words, girls have crushes on older women, boys develop crushes on men, and each gender has erotic strivings toward members of the opposite gender.

Crushes like this are erotic but not frankly sexual, and they occur regardless of the sexual orientation of either the young person or the adult involved. Because they represent the first shoots of emerging sexuality for the adolescent, adults idealized by these young people must walk a fine line. It is important that they value, validate, and treat tenderly the affection, even worship, offered to them by starry-eyed girls leaning toward womanhood and gawky boys trying to find their way into manhood. If adults react with anxiety and distancing, they can engender shame and discomfort in young people about their sexuality. If, on the other hand, an adult transgresses against the preadolescent or teenager, exploiting youthful sexual strivings, the young person is compelled prematurely into engagement with a sexuality that is just beginning to show itself, and the results can be devastating.

Whether the victims were prepubescent children, pubescent youth, or teenagers, sexually abusive priests often ingratiated themselves into the lives of their targets, evoking trust, respect, and dependency long before the first touch took place. In eighteen cases of priest abuse reviewed by the *Toledo Blade*, reporters concluded that in twelve of them the offender was close to the families of his victims; in the other six instances, he had a close relationship with the victim.[2] Fr. Bruce Ritter, for example, preyed on some of the troubled boys he took into New York City's Covenant House.[3] Rather than providing the pastoral care, mentoring, boundary modeling, and impulse control these street boys needed, he took advantage of their already disrupted lives by sexually exploiting them. Fr. John Geoghan from Boston often sought out fatherless children, cultivating their mothers' reliance on him as a compensatory father figure and as a relief from their own overwhelming task of single parenting.[4] Altar boys, like my patient described earlier, often felt a special bond with "their" priests and were therefore particularly vulnerable to clergy who betrayed that respect and trust by transgressing against them.[5]

In 1992, for example, Allen Vogel told his father that Fr. Cosmos Dahlheimer of St. Augustine's Church in St. Cloud, Minnesota, had molested him when Allen was an altar boy.[6] Dahlheimer seduced both Vogel's devoutly religious family and Allen by telling them that the boy was special and could become an important person in the Church under the priest's guidance. Eventually, Fr. Dahlheimer introduced sex into the relationship with Vogel, exposing himself and masturbating in the sacristy, his room, and his car. Ray and Arlene Vogel had taught their children that priests were the closest beings to God and, devoted to the priests at St. Augustine's and nearby St. John's Abbey, never suspected that a priest would hurt their son. After Allen revealed his abuse to them, two other sons reported that they too had been sexually assaulted by priests, one by Fr. Dahlheimer and another by Fr. Richard Eckroth. Although both priests denied the allegations, St. John's Abbey found the accusations to be credible and removed the priests from ministry.

Keeping the Secret

There are those who devalue survivors of childhood and, especially, adolescent victims, for not disclosing their victimizations when they were occurring. Secrecy, however, is the acknowledged cornerstone of sexual abuse. Some perpetrators extract silence by suggesting that victims will be blamed for the abuse, taken from their homes, and placed in an orphanage, or worse. Jonathan Norton said Fr. James H. Hopkins warned him that if he told anyone about the oral sex Hopkins engaged him in, God would hate the boy, who would burn in hell along with his family.[7] As in this case, perpetrators often threaten the victim's family as well as the minor in order to ensure that the young person will not disclose the abuse.

Sexual abusers may also blame the victim, accusing him or her of seducing the predator, effectively ensuring secrecy by filling the victim with the shame and self-loathing more appropriately experienced by the victimizer. Priests abusing girls may have been particularly inclined to blame their victims. There is a long tradition in the Catholic Church that views females as seducers capable of making a man lose his mind, as Adam sometimes is depicted as doing when he succumbed to Eve's plea that he eat of the forbidden fruit.[8]

In addition, female victims were predisposed to feel guilty for their own abuse. First, as Catholics familiar with stories of saints like Maria Goretti, who died rather than submit to rape, girls may well have experienced themselves as sinners rather than as victims. Further, victims generally believe that they must have in some way invited their own victimizations. It is preferable for all victims, male or female, to believe that they had some control and power in the abusive situation rather than to acknowledge utter powerlessness. Or, as psychoanalyst Ronald Fairbairn put it,

> [I]t is better to be a sinner in a world ruled by God than to live in a world ruled by the Devil. A sinner in a world ruled by God may be bad but there is always a certain sense of security to be derived from the fact that the world around is good . . . and in any case there is always hope of redemption. In a world ruled by the Devil the individual may escape the badness of being a sinner; but . . . he can have no sense of security and no hope of redemption. The only prospect is one of death and destruction.[9]

When the abuser is "God-on-earth," it would be difficult for any Catholic youth to believe that he or she was not the devil—the sinful person in the sexual situation. This predisposition to take on responsibility for sexual abuse by a priest would be even stronger when the priest in fact blamed his victim. Silence in almost every case would be assured.

In a more covert covenant of secrecy, the abuser provides the victim with gifts, praise, and special privileges that both buy silence and instill terrible and long-lasting guilt. Many sexually predatory priests took their victims to vacation cottages, on camping trips, to sporting events, and to other venues where the fun and excitement to which they were exposed came with a heavy price. Fr. Larry Brett, for example, took his victims to see pornographic movies in Manhattan and let them drive his hot car.[10] Allen Vogel says that Fr. Cosmas Dahlheimer told him that their sexual relationship would help Allen become a man in the Church, that he was a special person whom Dahlheimer would help advance within the Church when Allen grew up.[11]

Other minors maintained their silence because they perceived, accurately or not, that no one in their environments would believe or help them if they did disclose. It is much more hopeful for traumatized young people to preserve a fantasy that, if they told, someone would protect them than it is to reveal the abuse to others who might ignore, blame, or reabuse them. Wayne and Rose Sagrera, parents of one of Fr. Gilbert Gauthe's victims, report that other members of the Henry, Louisiana, community failed to believe their own children when they came forward with accusations that Gauthe had also molested them, even after it was clear that the priest had numerous victims.[12] William Claar, allegedly abused along with two of his brothers by Fr. Bernard Kokocinski, did not tell anyone about the sexual victimization until the scandal broke nationwide in 2002.[13] He said, "I never told my parents. I never told anyone. He [Fr. Kokocinski] was like a member of the family. I didn't think anyone would believe me."[14]

Finally, children and adolescents do not disclose the sexual abuse secret because they care for the perpetrator. Especially when the abuser is a beloved figure in the young person's life, the victim is likely unconsciously to detect the man's inner brokenness and lovingly try to heal the person. A central cruelty of sexual abuse, in fact, is the perpetrator's trampling of the victim's freely bestowed affection and respect.

Long-Term Consequences of Sexual Abuse

The victim of early sexual violation simply cannot reconcile the respected figure who helps him with his homework, teaches him how to throw a curve ball, takes him to the local hockey game, and, after turning bread and wine into the Body and Blood of Jesus Christ, uses his hands to administer the nourishment of Holy Eucharist, with the sexually overstimulating man who uses those same hands to fondle the victim or to present his own penis for the victim to suck. It is simply too much for the mind to bear and organize. Sexually abusive experiences thus often lead to a debilitating posttraumatic stress disorder that affects every domain of the victim/survivor's functioning and lasts for years after the abuse has stopped. While some victims are resilient and emerge into adulthood functioning well in most if not all domains of living, they are the exceptions. They tend to be people whose abusive experiences were limited in time and severity, and whose perpetrators were not figures with whom they also were emotionally close. Much more common is the survivor who suffers in various ways for many years after the abuse stops.

Let us now take a tour through the corridors of a psyche and soul twisted by sexual transgression. It is a trip through a psychological house of horrors in which experiences of self and other often are grotesquely distorted, and terrifying images pop up unexpectedly from seemingly safe places. The first stop is the organization of the victim's images of self and other.

Dissociation and the Victim Self

Often what brings adult survivors of early sexual trauma to treatment is that their lives are wracked by unexpected regressions to their victimized selves triggered by seemingly neutral stimuli. Much as the Vietnam vet who hits the floor during a thunderstorm screaming about incoming artillery is, in a very real way, back in the Mekong Delta seconds before his buddy's skull is blown off, so too sexual abuse survivors may be thrown into a regression by something or someone reminiscent of the earlier traumas. No longer firmly located in the present, survivors dissociate—they think, feel, experience their bodies, and behave as the victims they once were, badly confusing themselves and those around them.

For victims of priest abuse, the scent of incense, light streaming through stained glass at a certain time of day, organ music, or, most certainly, interacting with clergy about their abuse may well evoke the appearance of usually dissociated self-states. One sixty-seven-year-old man, abused by a priest decades ago, fears being alone with another man in a car; when he goes fishing with a friend, he sweats the whole ride, plagued by the irrational fear that his friend will molest him.[15] Mark Furnish, a lawyer in Albany, New York, reports that for years he would cry and become ill when asked to take long car rides, had panic attacks, screamed if another person disturbed his sleep, and fell apart emotionally during certain TV programs or movies.[16] He eventually was able to connect these symptoms with being sexually abused from ages twelve to fifteen by Fr. Robert O'Neill, who often took Furnish on weekend car trips to a cabin in the woods where he reportedly molested him. Newspaper reporter Doug Mandelaro likened Furnish's dissociated experiences to living with an internal masked demon who was unnamed but wreaked havoc all the same.[17] This description is remarkably similar to Fairbairn's depiction of the role that internalized traumatic relationships play in the inner world of the survivor: "[H]e is internalizing objects [traumatic relationships] which have wielded power over him in the external world; and these objects retain their prestige for power over him in the inner world. In a word, he is 'possessed' by them, as if by evil spirits."[18]

Dissociation is a function of the human mind that exists along a continuum from the very normal to the extremely pathological. The normal operation of dissociation allows, for example, each of us to drive ten miles and then "come to" with no memory of the time just past. While one state of self was driving, attending to the road, other cars, even weaving in and out of lanes, another state of self was planning the weekend's events, choosing outfits, and perhaps even engaging in imaginary conversations with others. For the victim of child or adolescent sexual violation, however, dissociation is often a more dramatic phenomenon that is both a blessing and a curse.

On the one hand, by entering into an entirely different state of consciousness while being abused, the victim preserves a functional and safe self who is removed from the trauma and is therefore able to learn, grow up, play, work, and even form relationships incorporating some degree of intimacy. This is the self-state that grows into adulthood and usually is recognized as "I." On the other hand, the curse of dissociation condemns the state of self who experienced the abuse to a trapped existence in the inner world of the survivor, a place dominated by terror, impotent but seething rage, and grief for which there literally are no words. Often the "I" self remembers the abuse but the split-off, victimized self carries the emotions associated with it. This leads to the unsettling experience of having sexual abuse survivors describing in treatment the most horrendous experiences with absolutely flat affect, as if they are reading them from a newspaper. At other times, the victimized self seems to take center stage and the previously well-functioning, articulate patient is speechless, curled up in a ball, trapped in raw emotional storms.

The Abuser Self

Coexisting with victim states of self, adult survivors of childhood sexual abuse have within them self-states that were forged in relationship with the abuser. These aspects of self preserve an attachment to a once-loved figure and have become like him in some ways. When threatened by experiences of helplessness, vulnerability, or anticipated betrayal, survivors may unconsciously access this self-state to gain a sense of empowerment. Often subjectively experiencing themselves as righteously indignant, survivors may at times enact boundary smashing, cold contempt, and rage. While some survivors of childhood or adolescent sexual abuse become sexual victimizers themselves, most do not.

One survivor, who was sexually abused by her grandfather and a priest, could become verbally contemptuous seemingly out of nowhere. If I could not remember one of her dreams or could not recount portions of a previous session verbatim, she would castigate me as stupid and just in the "therapy business" for the money. She ridiculed my outfits, hair, make-up, and shoes, accusing me of spending more time on myself than I did on my patients. At these times, my patient experienced herself as victimized by me—her self-centered, greedy therapist—and felt justified in letting me have it. It was a long time before she could work with the idea that she could be abusive and unfairly demanding.

Not surprisingly, survivors are sickened by the thought that they resemble in any way their perpetrators and therefore avert their gaze, for long periods of time, from these aspects of their personalities lest they fragment even further at the sight of their own abusive tendencies. At the same time, their sometimes shocking capacity to inflict psychic pain on others can evoke in those others disorganizing and unpleasant reactions of counterrage and dismissal.

It is delicate therapeutic work to introduce survivors gradually to their disrespectful, sometimes abusive selves. While doing so, it is crucial for therapists to model setting limits on what they will tolerate in a relationship with another person, while holding in mind an empathic recognition that the clay of the survivor's abuser self was molded quite literally by the hands of a master—the sexual victimizer.

One difficulty in the current Church crisis is that relational patterns forged amid violation have been endlessly enacted by various parties in the scandal, with no one to interpret or contain them. For example, a survivor, subjectively experiencing himself as wounded and in need, may present himself to a bishop's chancery or Mass and aggressively demand instant access to the bishop. The bishop and his staff, experiencing themselves as invaded by a hostile survivor, summarily refuse to see the survivor and may even call upon others to have him removed. Both the survivor and the bishop end up feeling self-righteous and badly abused by the other. Mistrust, anger, and fear increase on both sides.

The Entitled Self

Finally, sexual abuse survivors commonly have aspects of self that can be greedy, grandiose, and insatiably entitled. There are two sources of these islands of self.

First, there are often identifications with the insatiability and greed of the perpetrator who took what he wanted when he wanted it and never seemed satisfied with what he got. The sexually predatory priest's desecration of the most sacred spaces—altars, sacristies, chapels—by sexualizing them as he imposed himself on minors he had vowed to protect testifies to his sense of unlimited entitlement. Psychoanalyst and sexual trauma expert Richard Gartner offers an example of the ongoing grandiosity of one priest who abused Gartner's patient, Julian.[19] When Julian encountered the priest at a funeral in his hometown years after the abuse ended and Julian had moved away, the priest took him aside and whispered, "You may feel better than the rest of us now that you've left town, but you and I know that all I have to do is rub your belly and you'll squeal like a puppy!"[20]

Both the insecurity and entitlement of the abusive priest illustrated in Gartner's vignette are often both internalized and later enacted by victims/survivors. As with their abuser selves, survivors are horrified that they possess and are "possessed" by these identifications and refuse to face them for very long periods of time. In treatment, survivors' entitlement sometimes is enacted by excessive demands for between-session phone contact, refusal to leave the room at the end of a session, rages over the clinician's vacation, or unnecessary requests for a lower fee or no fee, as all the while they experience themselves as simply asking for what is their due. While therapists specializing in trauma work are prepared slowly to bring to awareness the survivor's capacity for entitled greed and grandiosity while holding in mind its relational roots, others in the survivor's life often react to his or her entitlement with rage, self-protectivness, and the very rejection that the survivor most dreads.

The survivor's entitled state of self also is likely to emerge as a way to stave off mourning. There comes a day in the lives of most survivors on which they fully comprehend their losses. Further personal growth and healing requires that, at that point, survivors mourn the childhood and/or adolescence that never was, the defensively idealized caretakers who never existed, and, perhaps most poignantly, the self that could have been had hope and possibility not been shattered. One patient, at this point in treatment, cried,

> This is too much. I can deal with the abuse . . . I think . . . maybe I can. But the idea that this is all there will ever be. That when I think of being little, all I will feel is pain and terror . . . that's too much . . . I can't live with that. I want to feel what I see in the eyes of little children. You [therapist] say I deserve this . . . so why can't I? The sense of safety, I want a place that's safe. I want to get into trouble and be mischievous . . . safe trouble . . . usual trouble. I want someone else to do the worrying and the punishing. I'm tired. You say I can feel some of these things as a grown-up . . . you tell me about them. But how can I feel them when I'm not sure what they are . . . words. It's like trying to describe a color to someone who was born blind.[21]

Quite understandably, sexual abuse survivors may act to avoid the mourning necessary to move on from the abuse and all that was stolen from them. It is often at this point in treatment that the survivor is able to give full reign to fantasies of revenge in which the abuser and his protector(s) are forced to pay, to make restitution for the lost childhood. Launching a lawsuit against the perpetrator or against those who abetted him may be one strategy tried by survivors in the Church abuse crisis. No matter the amount of the ensuing financial settlement, a residue of emptiness and lost hope often will persist. At the core of the survivor's being, the worst has happened once again; he or she has been paid to go away while life goes on relatively unscathed for the perpetrator and, even more, for those who shielded him. Only when the suit is over, the lawyer has moved on to other cases, and the media has bigger news to report may the survivor realize that, in all the ways that count, nothing has changed.

After receiving her settlement check from the Archdiocese of Boston, sexual abuse survivor Alexa MacPherson said, "This money means nothing to me. . . . I thought I'd feel light-hearted. Instead, I feel weighed down. . . . I feel like a price has been put on my head. That's not what I wanted."[22] As a clinician, my concern is that many survivors, stimulated by unrealistic hope and perhaps avoiding mourning a childhood gone forever by chasing the Church in court, may one day face even more depression and despair when their checks have been deposited and they still are visited by ghosts in the night.

On the other hand, it is important to note that a lawsuit, when all requests for pastoral responses have failed (as they did for so many victims), may represent a healthy effort by survivors to become agents in their own lives. Further, lawsuits put into action an understandable demand that the truth be told one way or another. Bringing the names of accused priests into the public, when Church officials refused to remove them from contact with children, also sometimes marked very adaptive attempts on the part of survivors to protect children from suffering at the hands of these priests and to reach out to other victims of the same perpetrators who might then feel free to come forward. Finally, Susan Archibald, former president of The Linkup, a survivors' group, was quoted as saying that lawsuits can help survivors psychologically return their guilt and fear to the rightful owners of those emotions—their perpetrators and Church officials who covered up crimes.[23]

Whether involvement in lengthy and often frustrating litigation with the Church promotes growth and healing or impedes it will differ from one survivor to another. For Scott Gastal, one of Gilbert Gauthe's victims, the jury award of $1 million did little to alleviate his suffering.[24] The money was given to his parents who lost it all in bad business ventures. Working at a horse ranch in bayou country, Gastal tries not to feel much of anything at all, stays away from people most of the time, continues to be haunted by his abusive experiences, and suspects that he never will really recover from them. Ryan Di Maria, however, settled with the Church for $5.2 million and a series of reforms in the dioceses of Orange County and Los Angeles, California, to provide more effective and pastoral responses to victims coming forward with reports of sexual abuse by a priest.[25] In June 2003, recently married and expecting his first child, he was sworn into the bar as an attorney in Orange County by Superior Court Judge James P. Gray, who mediated the settlement between Di Maria and the Church. Di Maria now uses his legal talents to help other victims of childhood sexual abuse.

In the end, whether survivors of sexual abuse by priests sue or not, the chance of maximum recovey is usually increased by mourning the youth that can never be. Finally, the abuse takes its proper place as a truly past part of life, as when incest survivor Louise Armstrong responds to a question about early childhood trauma:

> So it doesn't go away?
> *Armstrong:* It recedes.
> I don't like that.
> *Armstrong:* You don't have to like it. You just have to live with it. Like a small, nasty pet you've had for years.[26]

The Interpersonal World of Survivors

One patient of mine was sexually abused and physically tortured by her stepmother many years before she entered treatment. After working with me for several months, she began to look at me suspiciously when she came in the room and became more and more withdrawn. Then, she accused me of working with sexual abuse survivors because I "got off" on the stories; she imagined that I masturbated after sessions in which she thought I became uncontrollably aroused at the material. Sometimes after saying these things, she then crumbled on the couch and cried, telling me she did not mean those terrible things and begging me not to hate her. Eventually, this patient tearfully confided that she snorted cocaine in my bathroom before coming into the consultation room because it was so unbearable to be in my presence. Yet, she also felt that it would be unbearable to leave me.

This young woman and I worked together for some time to try to understand her reactions to me but made little progress. Outside the treatment, she functioned reasonably well and I became concerned that her seemingly inexplicable, terrified yet dependent response to me would begin to infiltrate her extratherapeutic life. She agreed to transfer to a colleague, also an expert in trauma, to see if she could work more effectively with another therapist.

A year or so later, this survivor called and asked to see me for one session. When she came in, she told me that she and her therapist had been able to unpack her extreme reactions to me, which had confusingly coexisted with a more mature appraisal of my skills and personality. She always had remembered that her stepmother had blonde hair and blue eyes, as I do, and was named Mary Ann (I am Mary Gail), but she had not made the connection that working with me evoked relational expectations derived from her abusive relationship with that woman. In addition, my green office couch was somewhat similar in color and texture to the bedspread on which her stepmother would tie her up and perform oral sex on her.

At the same time that she hated and feared her stepmother, my former patient had been dependent on her for the little physical care she received, since her biological mother was dead and her father was in the military and away much of the time. There were enough superficial similarities between me and the stepmother that self-states and interpersonal expectations embedded in the relationship with the stepparent literally came alive in the treatment with me. The therapist to whom I referred this woman did not trigger the same kinds of reactions so, although their work was volatile in its own way, they could sustain a working alliance that carried them through the rough spots.

Working from a template of relational possibilities imprinted amid abuse and calcified by ongoing posttraumatic stress reactions, the sexual abuse survivor often exhibits rapidly shifting relational stances. In many cases, adult survivors lurch from periods of dependent clinging to those marked by vicious rage aimed at the same person. Terror and tears can switch in an instant to cold aloofness, while warmth and vivacity may turn kaleidoscopically to paranoid suspicion. All this, of course, leads to many chaotically unstable relationships, often alternating with stretches of the loneliest isolation.

Not surprisingly, until well into the recovery process, normal sexual functioning is almost impossible for most people who were sexually abused as minors. Too often sex, even with a trusted and loved other, triggers disorganizing flashbacks during which survivors sometimes literally see the face of their abuser superimposed on the visage of their sexual partners and begin to relive their sexual traumas. A sexual encounter can be unfolding in a lovely way when a sound, a change in the way the moonlight filters through the curtain, a word or phrase uttered by the lover, a touch to a certain spot on the body, or an unexpected shift in the pressure of body meeting body engenders a dissociative episode in which the survivor is no longer located in the present but rather is experiencing again his or her abuse as if it were happening right in the moment. Gone temporarily is the adult man or woman, replaced for now by a paralyzed abused child.

In addition, survivors frequently are disgusted by and ashamed of their own bodies and sexual strivings. Unfairly blaming their abuse on their own physicality and sexuality, they often insist that the victimizations never would have occurred were it not for their self-perceived seductive bodies and deplorable sexual desires. Especially when they reacted to the abuse with arousal and even orgasm, survivors believe that they must have wanted, brought on, and enjoyed the abuse. It is a long process for them to realize that their biological response to the stimulation of nerve endings does not connote free-flowing desire. In fact, the criminality of abuse lies in part in its disruption of the victims' ability to be freely desirous as they struggle with guilt and shame about *wanting* much of anything sexual.

Boys abused by men are additionally tormented, wondering what it was about them that attracted the perpetrator. For sexually traumatized minor males, doubts are raised about both their masculinity and the strength of their sexual orientation. It is culturally unacceptable for a male to be sexually victimized; unfortunately, only women and girls make culturally appropriate victims. Thus, the sexually abused boy wonders about his maleness. Does his abuse make him a girl in some way, or a girlish boy, both often devalued by the wider society?

To reinforce his masculine gender identification, the sexually abused boy may resort to a hypermasculine persona, displaying aggressive, macho behavior toward others.[27] Further, although there is no convincing evidence that premature sexual activity with a man changes a boy's sexual orientation, sexual abuse of a boy by a male is disturbing for boys no matter their sexual orientation. The heterosexual minor male may be plagued with doubts about his "real" sexual orientation and may compensate through compulsive sexual activity with women in order continually to reassure himself that he is straight.[28] Homosexual boys may blame their sexual orientation for their abuse, developing a destructive homophobia about their own sexual strivings.

Sexual abuse survivors of all genders and sexual orientations are deprived of their right to grow gradually into a mature sexuality and, instead, are forced or seduced into premature sexual encounters they are emotionally ill equipped to handle. As adults, therefore, these men and women often spin between periods of promiscuous, compulsive, and self-destructive acting-out and times of complete sexual shutdown during which, like burn victims, they experience the gentlest physical contact as excruciatingly painful.

Finally, there is a characteristic relational stance assumed by many sexual abuse survivors that is particularly germane to the Church scandal. It involves others who did not abuse them but also did not protect them.

If it takes a community to raise a child, it also takes a community to abuse a child; whenever a minor is sexually violated, someone's eyes are closed. Throughout history, the most common response to the suspicion or even the disclosure of sexual abuse has been denial and dissociation. Elective blindness, deafness, and muteness are reactions endemic to many people confronted by a victimized child, an adult survivor, or a perpetrating adult. To the extent that sexual victimization of a minor depends upon the silence of adults who knew, suspected, or should have known about the abuse, then, the burdens of shame and guilt reach beyond the individual abuser. In the case of the Church, it is particularly the members of the hierarchy who contributed to the suffering of thousands of children and adolescents by keeping abusing priests in ministry where they had contact with children in case after case, year after year, decade after decade.

Sexual abuse survivors often are even angrier with adults who failed to protect them than they are with their direct perpetrators. Because the survivor's internal relationship with the abuser is organized around paradoxical feelings of attachment and hate, and because the survivor may have sensed the woundedness of the perpetrator, he or she may feel freer to turn the full blast of long pent-up rage or bitterness on those who failed to protect and who, in addition, failed to provide for the victim in ways the perpetrator seemed to, albeit at an unholy cost to the exploited child or adolescent.

Cognitive Confusion

One survivor patient worked as an investment banker in the competitive New York world of finance. She was so intellectually gifted and her ability to think strategically under pressure was so incisive that she was considered a Wall Street whiz kid. When beset by psychological or interpersonal stimuli linked to her uncle's sexual abuse, however, she became, in her own words, "stupid minded." At those times, she literally could not think at all or could access only immature, disorganized, and panicky ways of thinking. At times, for instance, she had to attend meetings with a former law school classmate of her uncle's who would reminisce about "the old days" and speak of meeting her for the first time at her uncle's home when she was nine years old, two years after the sexual abuse had begun. After those meetings, colleagues tended to ask her if she was feeling okay; they noticed that she had become uncharacteristically inarticulate, vague, and confused when speaking, forgetting facts and decisions that had been at her fingertips just hours before.

Part of what is overwhelmed during sexual abuse is the young person's cognitive ability to contain, process, and put into words the relational betrayal and physical impingement with which she or he is faced. It is striking and often bewildering to observe in adult survivors the coexistence of contradictory thought processes that ebb and flow with little apparent predictability. One moment, you are speaking with an adult capable of complex, flexible, abstract, and self-decentered thinking. Under sufficient internal or external stress, however, or in situations somehow reminiscent of the abuse, the cognitive integrity of the survivor shatters and the individual becomes locked in rigid, irrational, self-centered thought patterns; simplistic black-and-white opinions devoid of nuance; and an immutable conviction that the future is destined to be both short and unalterably empty.

Affective Functioning

When a young person is sexually traumatized, hyperarousal of the autonomic nervous system and the body's subsequent attempt to restore order disrupt the brain's neurochemical regulation of emotion.[29] In addition, recent studies indicate that attachment relationships also influence the brain's ability to modulate feelings, with traumatic attachment relationships interfering with effective neuropsychological regulation of affect.[30] The brain of the sexually abused minor thus suffers a double assault. Both the sexual traumas themselves and the betrayal of an important attachment relationship assail the flow of affect modulating neurochemicals.

As adults, survivors shift—sometimes quite rapidly—from states of chaotic hyperarousal to psychic numbing. This inability to modulate emotional arousal often leads to interpersonally inappropriate verbal or motoric responses. Further, autonomic arousal becomes a generalized reaction to stress, in the midst of which sexual abuse survivors are unable to discern realistically the severity of perceived threats. Instead of reacting at the actual level of psychological danger, survivors may engage in seemingly irrational behaviors like temper tantrums, terrified withdrawal, or profound depression. These behaviors do not fit the present-day situation but are perfectly complementary to the now affectively revived earlier trauma.

My former patient's reactions to me, described above, are an example. When she was with me, she unknowingly was triggered to experience me as her stepmother, which evoked paranoia about sexualized responses to her followed by equally strong abandonment fears. While her extreme emotional arousal did not fit the current situation or resonate with my actual feelings about her, it was congruent with her relationship with her stepmother, now revived in the therapy with me.

Intense and unpredictable emotional swings contribute to the apparent "possession" of survivors by internal processes over which they experience little control. They are frightening for survivors and for those around them and, in fact, become retraumatizing phenomena. Adult survivors often need psychotropic medications, like antidepressants, mood stabilizers, or antianxiety medication for some period of time during recovery.[31] For some, their psychological and neurobiological impairments are sufficiently intractable to require lifelong medication.

Self-Abuse

Kevin and Barry McDonough were identical twin sons in a devoutly Catholic family in Canton, Massachusetts.[32] When Kevin was thirteen or fourteen, he changed from a happy, joking kid to a brooding and withdrawn teenager. While Barry went to college and became a film editor, Kevin joined the Marines after high school but came home after two months because he could not make it in boot camp; eventually, he became a car salesman. He struggled with alcohol and drug abuse, depression, a suicide attempt in his teens, and psychiatric hospitalizations. Early in 2001, Kevin told his niece that he had been molested as a child by a priest, Fr. Peter J. Frost. He also shared his sexual abuse history with his girlfriend who said, "He was so angry, upset, and ashamed. I know it affected his whole life. It turned into everything he became. I think he felt people could look at him and know. . . . He had a lot to offer . . . but it was just too many de-mons."[33] Kevin McDonough, thirty-six, died 1 May 2001 after overdosing on cocaine, just months short of the exposure of priest abuse in Boston.

Also partly due to disrupted brain functioning, sexual abuse survivors often display a wide array of self-destructive behaviors. They may slice their arms, thighs, and genitalia with knives, razors, or shards of broken glass. Jonathan Norton, Fr. James Hopkin's alleged victim, bloodied his arms with a box cutter and attempted suicide more than once before the age of seventeen.[34] A teenaged male victim of Fr. Michael Hands of Long Island, allegedly abused for eighteen months, also cut his arms.[35]

Survivors burn themselves with cigarettes, pull hair from their heads or pubic areas, walk through deserted areas alone at night, play chicken with trains at railroad crossings, pick up strangers in bars to have unpro-tected and anonymous sex, drive recklessly at high speeds, gamble com-pulsively, or further destroy their minds and bodies with alcohol and the whole range of street drugs. Of thirty-two adult survivors of sexual abuse by a priest interviewed by the *Toledo Blade,* 50 percent had abused drugs or alcohol until confronting their traumatic histories, usually in therapy.[36] Studies suggest that between 60 and 80 percent of male and female pros-titutes have histories of child or adolescent sexual abuse.[37] Survivors also are two to three times more likely than adults without abuse histories to make at least one suicide attempt in their lives.[38]

Survivor self-abuse performs a myriad of functions. A quick inventory of survivors' motivations to act self-destructively includes punishment for the abuse they blame themselves for; mastering victimization by taking charge of the timing and execution of harm; attacking the internalized abusers by whom they are "possessed"; and self-medicating turbulent af-fective storms. Engaging in dangerous or self-destructive acts also repre-sents an unconscious attempt to reach states of hyperarousal that then trigger the release of brain opioids, providing a temporary sense of calm.[39]

At an even more deeply unconscious level, self-destructive sexual abuse survivors often want to turn the tables on present-day stand-ins for those who violated and neglected them. Here, they long to see their own terror, helplessness, impotent rage, and shocked recognition of betrayal reflected now on the faces of others in their lives.

Both male and female sexual abuse survivors often act out self-destructively. In addition, male survivors may act out aggressively toward others, getting into fights, committing crimes, or, rarely, even abusing others sexually. Masculine gender norms make it difficult for men to acknowledge victimization. Experiencing themselves as demasculinized or even feminized by sexual abuse, some male survivors develop compensatory aggressive personas through which they frighten and even harm others.[40]

Two of Fr. Larry Brett's sexual abuse victims went on to sexually violate others, passing the baton of suffering to another generation.[41] Another, Mark Frechette, died in prison at age twenty-seven in an apparent gym accident.[42] Soon after Brett began to perform oral sex on him, Frechette turned from a straight-A student to a high school drop-out who started to burglarize homes. Before his death, he had spent time in a psychiatric hospital as well as in prison.

Spiritual Sorrow

Unlike other forms of sexual abuse, the sexual exploitation of a Catholic child or adolescent by a priest directly assails the minor's religious faith and broader spiritual functioning. This assault on faith historically has been exacerbated within the Catholic Church by the failure of many Church officials to provide a pastoral response to victims coming forward with their stories. When a young person is victimized by a man purporting to represent the living Christ and when that man's crimes are tolerated by cardinals, bishops, provincial superiors, or other officials, the individual's ability to believe in a just and merciful God often is dismantled. Even more assuredly, trust and belief in Catholicism, instilled early on in the victim, is shattered.

Many victims of priest abuse have turned away from Catholicism. Of 128 plaintiffs suing the Archdiocese of Louisville, 84 no longer consider themselves Catholics; 75 of the 84 feel they lost their faith because of their abuse or the Church's response to it.[43] Some survivors develop a cynicism about all religion. Dr. X, a patient of trauma expert Richard Gartner, says the following:

The fact that it was a priest [who abused him] was cataclysmic. It taught me that there is a lie in the world. I developed a slowly evolving cynicism. As I got older and gave up on my piety, I grew to hate the smells, sounds, feelings of Church—the incense, the collars, the robes. My spirituality and ability to believe in a higher power were destroyed.[44]

Other survivors continue to feel a great hole in their life where practicing Catholicism or some other spiritual devotion should be. Julian, another patient of Dr. Gartner's, reports that he is a religious man without a church:

I went to seminary because Catholicism means something to me. But, now, I can't go into a church without feeling I will vomit. My wife says, "Let's go to an Episcopalian Church—it's almost the same!" But it's not the same. I'm not an Episcopalian, I'm a Catholic. And there's nowhere I can go to be one.[45]

Teachings and Traditions
Implicated in the Scandal

Elisabeth Schüssler Fiorenza, in fact, states that the central theme of Jesus' life and ministry is not ultimate suffering but the ultimate celebration of life lived by whole, healthy, strong people and symbolized by the festivity of a banquet feast.[1]

Despite the celebration of temporal, historical life portrayed in the Gospels, some within the Church came to emphasize the suffering and death of Christ as central iconographic and narrative themes.[2] It is important to note that veneration of the crucifix developed gradually. Crosses were not part of public Christian symbology until Constantine abolished crucifixion as a means of capital punishment.[3] Crosses after that were elaborately carved or gemmed and were intended to represent the Resurrection rather than the Crucifixion; veneration of a crucifix was not introduced until the fifth century.[4] The realistic crucifixes found in American churches prior to Vatican II began to appear only in the thirteenth century and were not customary at church altars until 1570.[5] At that point, it had become Christ-as-crucified—crowned with thorns, nails piercing his hands and feet, blood dripping from his wounds—that dominated the center space of worship as an idealized icon of pathos and pain. In addition to the dominance of the crucified Jesus over the altar, the Stations of the Cross (a sequence of wall art placed on both side of a church) drew the faithful to reflect on Jesus as he was condemned, scourged, burdened with the cross, nailed to the wood, ridiculed, died, and was buried. (Think how the psychological culture of Catholicism might have developed differently had churches featured, for instance, the gloriously risen Christ and the Stations of the Beatitudes [Matt. 5:3–11], which emphasize the human qualities Jesus valued.)

In addition to emphasizing the Crucifixion over other aspects of Jesus' life, ministry, and Resurrection, the Roman Catholic Church developed a theology of atonement through which it taught that Jesus died for the sins of all humankind, past, present, and future. Author and inactive priest James Carroll says that St. Anselm (1033–1109) solidified the Crucifixion as the central Christological and salvific event:

> The first result of Anselm's theology of salvation was to solder the faith to the cross, and to make the death of Jesus more important than . . . his having been born, having lived as a Jew, having preached a gospel of love . . . . having opposed the imperium of Rome, even having been brought to the new life of the Resurrection.[6]

Theologian Richard McBrien points out that this meaning of the Crucifixion developed gradually and was joined by other interpretations

CHAPTER 3

Suffering, Submission, and Sadomasochism

The Valorization of Suffering

Until Vatican II, themes of suffering dominated much of the
and narration of Catholic theology. Some Catholic thinkers
to idealize suffering. This valorization of suffering may have s
behavior of abusing priests while influencing other Catholi
many bishops and the Vatican, to minimize the suffering of
victims.

Jesus spent thirty-three years among his fellow human
Gospels tell us little about his life between the ages of twelve a
thirty, Jesus began his public life as an itinerant preacher. The
tell us that, during his three years of ministry, he enjoyed good
drink, and good company (Matt. 7:10, Luke 5:33). He went f
the Apostles (Luke 5:6–10) and visited close friends like Lazar
and Mary (Luke 10:38). Jesus worked hard to lift the psycholog
cal, and spiritual torments of a host of men, women, and chilc
of them objects of the social prejudices of the day, like lepers (N
Luke 5:12–13) and the mad (Matt. 4:24). Nowhere in Matth
Luke, or John is it suggested that suffering is a good thing in an
to be sought out. Rather, the Gospels imply that Jesus realized t
ing, while both inevitable and potentially transformational, also
an impediment to living a full, rich, productive life in relation
others. Often after curing someone, for example, Jesus sent ther
their lives without requiring greater repayment than living life v
love and respect for self, others, and God. Similarly, Jesus did
ebrate death but rather restored temporal life to a number of inc
including his friend Lazarus. The Gospels understand physical
and death to be symbolic of soul sickness, or sin. It is significant, l
that Jesus lifted sin by alleviating bodily suffering and death. The

of the cross.[7] In addition, McBrien insists that the salvific nature of the Crucifixion can be understood as the ultimate triumph over sin and temporal death only in conjunction with the Resurrection and not as an independent event.[8]

Some theologians disagree with atonement theology entirely. Elizabeth Johnson, theologian at Fordham University, cites a variety of other theologians when she repudiates the institutional Church's interpretation of Jesus' death as required or even willingly permitted by God as atonement for sin.[9] Rather, Johnson asserts, "Jesus' death was an act of violence brought about by threatened human men, as sin, and therefore against the will of a gracious God. It occurred historically in consequence of Jesus' fidelity to the deepest truths he knew."[10] Johnson's illustration of the Crucifixion as an exemplar of state terror has a meaningful contemporary impact:

> Jesus' death included all that makes death terrifying: state torture, physical anguish, brutal injustice, hatred by enemies, the mockery of their victorious voices, collapse of his life's work in ruins, betrayal by some close friends, the experience of abandonment by God, and of powerlessness in which one ceases to be heroic.[11]

There are analogues to the sexual abuse of minors within Johnson's description of the Crucifixion. Physical anguish, brutal injustice, betrayal by trusted others, the experience of abandonment by God, and the sense of abject powerlessness all are aspects of sexual abuse by priests *and* of the paradigmatic response of many within the Church to victims.

It is important to note that valorization of suffering was not predestined by the teachings of Jesus. Rather, the emphasis on the crucified Christ—instead of on the risen Christ or Jesus, the teacher—developed over the first two centuries of Christianity, times during which the early Christians were persecuted, first by the Jewish hierarchy and then by the Romans. Jesuit psychoanalyst W. W. Meissner suggests that the centrality of the Crucifixion in Christian symbology derived in part from the early Christians' identification with Jesus as a persecuted scapegoat.[12] In other words, the phenomenological experiences of the early Christians rendered it psychologically likely that the representation of Jesus with which they were inclined to identify most was the brutalized, scorned, and crucified man-god. In order to withstand their own suffering as something leading to a greater good, the early Christians may have idealized their travails by valorizing the horrible suffering of the final day of Jesus' human life.

Meissner's work also helps us understand why themes of suffering continued to predominate as Christianity grew.[13] He suggests that the persecuted early Christians embraced Jesus' teaching to turn the other cheek in the face of aggression as a way of emulating Jesus' own response to his arrest and torture. Aggression then was projected outward onto others who were perceived—often correctly—as hating, fearing, and wanting to destroy the new religion. By having external enemies to stand in unity against, intragroup aggression and conflict were minimized, allowing Christianity to become ever more universal and codified. Over the centuries, sufficient numbers of external enemies surfaced enough of the time to facilitate a continued narrative of a suffering Church courageously staring down her enemies.

With so many actual enemies, it became difficult for the Church to recognize itself as the instigator of gratuitous aggression and suffering as it was, for instance, during the Crusades or the Inquisition. Rather, it developed an organizational defense of projection, which became fossilized and through which the Church blamed external forces for its own shortcomings. Even during the sexual abuse scandal, many Catholic officials focused on the suffering of the Church at the hands of the media, lawyers, or anti-Catholics rather than on the suffering of children at the hands of abusing priests and facilitating prelates.

In addition to the centrality of the Crucifixion in the iconography of the Church, Catholics at least until the 1970s were raised with stories of many saints who were martyred for their faith and sometimes, in the cases of women, for preserving their virginity. St. Agatha, for example, was given to a brothel by a Roman magistrate.[14] When she refused her customers, she was beaten and imprisoned, her breasts were cut off, and she was rolled on live coals in prison.[15] Surviving all this, Agatha died in an earthquake in jail.[16] St. Blase was tortured for his faith with hooks and iron combs tearing at his flesh and then was beheaded.[17] St. Cecilia was locked in a bath by Romans after her Christianity was discovered.[18] Emerging unscathed from the bath, she was partially beheaded and died three days later.[19] Many stories of the saints are now recognized as legends woven around sometimes historically verifiable figures and designed to inspire the faithful at various times in history. During the faith formation of most bishops, priests, victims, and other laypeople involved in the contemporary sexual abuse scandal, however, these stories of the saints were taught as truths.

Even in 2004, when Rev. Arthur J. Serratelli became bishop of Paterson, New Jersey, he referred to Maria Goretti in his installation address.[20] Serratelli called Goretti, killed during an attempted rape, a "martyr for purity."[21] He said that "her holy life and tragic death challenge us to renew our efforts to safeguard our young—to protect them from insidious evil that would rob them of their innocence and scar them for life."[22] Although emphasizing the need to protect children, Serratelli must have been aware that Maria Goretti was presented to young Catholic girls as a model not just because she died rather than sacrifice her virginity, but also because she forgave her attacker before she died. The new bishop pointed out that the killer went to prison, was reformed, and attended a communion service with Maria's mother who also forgave him. Here, Serratelli, perhaps unintentionally, seemed to be instructing victims and their families to forgive molesting priests, rather than expressing outrage about the sexual abuse of minors by priests or vowing as a new bishop to hold abusing priests and himself accountable for the protection of minors in Paterson. He also seemed to edge toward suggesting that good girls would die rather than submit to rape, which essentially blames the victim for living through sexual abuse.

In addition to iconographic and literary valorization of suffering, Catholics—especially prior to Vatican II—were taught that temporal suffering could be accepted as a way to move closer in spirit to the crucified Jesus. Life on earth was but a prelude to eternal life in heaven. The implication was that the more graciously one suffered on earth, the more sure one could be of reaching heaven with no side trips to purgatory. The living, in fact, could "offer up" their earthly pain and tribulations for the souls in purgatory, thus shortening sentences there and building up enough goodwill in the next world to obviate or at least truncate their own stays in purgatory.

It can be spiritually sound and transformational to accept life's inevitable tribulations and to engage with them as a way to grow spiritually and psychologically by patterning oneself after Jesus. Here, it is not suffering itself but faith in the potential "resurrection" offered through mature work with suffering that gives meaning to the pain we all encounter in human life. When suffering becomes isolated as a good in itself, however, spiritual health and transformational potential can erode into a pathological valorization of suffering devoid of anticipated triumph. St. Paul (Col. 1: 24) illustrates this overvaluing of suffering when he claims that suffering can benefit the Church by filling in for what was lacking in Christ's suffering: "I am now rejoicing in my sufferings for your sake, and in my flesh I am completing what is lacking in Christ's afflictions for the sake of his body, that is, the church."

As Paul seems to anticipate, at various times in Church history suffering was not just accepted but sought out. In the Middle Ages, for example, some Christian men and women pursued enhanced holiness by employing ascetic practices that today would be considered pathologically self-abusive. Some ascetic women fasted so vigorously that menstrual bleeding ceased, a symptom we associate with severe and life-threatening anorexia.[23] Self-flagellation was common in the Middle Ages among monks and some holy women.[24] Well into the twentieth century, some seminarians were expected to engage in what historian Garry Wills terms "masochistic asceticism."[25] For some Jesuits, for example, the "discipline" included flogging oneself with a small whip in the dark at night and wearing prickly chains around the waist at certain times.[26] Jesuit seminarians also were encouraged to walk with pebbles in their shoes, eat foods they particularly disliked, and see how long they could function with their eyes lowered.[27] Legionaries of Christ seminarians, some of them just boys, whipped their legs and thighs and wore a leather strap studded with hooks around their thighs.[28] All this suffering was intended to bring the individual closer to Christ, a man whose life had been dedicated to lifting humans beings out of suffering.

Given the Church's idealization of suffering, it is not surprising that many Catholic children complaining of the usual childhood and adolescent hurts and betrayals were frequently told by their elders to "offer it up" and were thus caught in a conflict. On the one hand, suffering was among the best ways to emulate Jesus and the saints and thus should be welcomed. On the other hand, no one ever could suffer as horribly as Jesus did *for us*, so any earthly suffering was barely worth mentioning. Suffering greatly in silence therefore was the most virtuous response to bodily, emotional, and spiritual pain.

The valorization of suffering that marked centuries of Catholic teachings, traditions, and much iconography is implicated in the sexual abuse crisis. Rev. Mark Roberts, for example, admitted to whipping his male victims and pouring hot candle wax on them while they stood with their arms outstretched as if they were on a cross, perhaps enacting a perverted and sexualized version of the Crucifixion.[29] Other clergy and laypeople, steeped in the belief that temporal suffering brought closeness to Christ, were often unattuned or insufficiently empathic to the suffering imposed on sexual abuse victims and survivors. One priest, in fact, told me that he had heard a few other priests suggest that survivors of sexual abuse had been given the opportunity to share the cross with Jesus and should graciously shoulder their burdens. In this scenario, survivors "should" accept their suffering as an opportunity for enhanced identification with the crucified Jesus instead of demanding earthly restitution at the expense of the Church.

After Vatican II, the iconography of Catholicism shifted toward emphasizing more the hope and glory of the risen Christ than the torturous sacrifice of the crucified Jesus. Renditions of Jesus on the cross became more abstract in a move away from the blood-drenched plaster figures of earlier art. Many Catholics under Pope John Paul II, however, began turning back to the Crucifixion as the central Christological event. John Paul II, for example, stated in his theology of the body that the Crucifixion represented the moment of Christ's nuptial with the Church; according to the pope, it was on the cross that Christ became the bridegroom of the Church.[30] The pope's own years of public agony from Parkinson's disease concretely illustrated his belief in the salvific role of human suffering. In 1994, as he became more demonstrably incapacitated, John Paul II said: "I must lead [the Church] with suffering. The pope must suffer so that every family and the world should see that there is, I would say, a higher gospel: the gospel of suffering, with which one must prepare the future."[31]

Whatever may be the theological merits of this construction and others like it, the psychological symbolism is a gruesome conflation of unspeakable suffering, nuptial union, and holiness that, if internalized, could result once again in a troublesome refusal by some Catholics, including priests and bishops, to accept personal responsibility for pain and suffering inflicted on individuals by members of the Church. Here, complacency about and even valorization of suffering substitute for dismay, and the wounded are administered even more pain by those ostensibly dedicated to pastoral care.

Dominance, Submission, and Sadomasochism

Centralized Authority and Submission

The Catholic Church's exercise of power through models of dominance and submission, sometimes devolving into sadism and masochism, began with the early Christian construction of the Crucifixion and continues into the twenty-first century. The centrality assigned to the Crucifixion in Jesus' life, the theology of atonement that grew around it, and early Christian life under Roman law and government forged a template for a religion organized by relationships of domination and submission. As the Church developed, the institutional structure became ever more hierarchically and kyriarchically organized.* By the end of the first century,

---

*Kyriarchy, as defined by Elisabeth Schüssler Fiorenza, is "a social-political system of domination and subordination that is based on the power and rule of the lord/master/father" (*In Memory of Her: A Feminist Theological Reconstruction of Christian Origins* [New York: Crossroad, 2000], 329).

Pope Clement claimed divine approval of a hierarchical Church structure and demanded that bishops and priests close ranks around it. By the time of Thomas Aquinas (1225–1274), obedience to God was conflated with obedience to the Catholic Church, which in turn merged with obedience to the pope, as Aquinas proclaimed that obedience (submission) to the pope was necessary for salvation.[32]

Today, those power relationships continue in one of the few remaining kyriarchal monarchies. In a world in which democracy is idealized and theories about egalitarian power arrangements dominate thinking, at least in the West, institutional Catholicism still operates through a power system based on sworn obedience to superiors. Here, the papal regent, cardinal princes, and bishop lords retain the hierarchical relationships, secrecy, and political intrigue of royal courts of old. Ecclesiastical power is conferred by the pope and assumed by bishops; there is little room for power that is authorized and reauthorized over time by other bishops, priests, and laypeople.

Vatican expert Rev. Thomas J. Reese, S.J., cites an Italian with years of Vatican experience: "In this court, the closer you are to the throne, the more important you are. Becoming a bishop or cardinal is like entering the nobility or royal family, and it is for life. Great deference is given to titles and hierarchy."[33] Once ensconced within their chanceries, cardinals and bishops historically wielded ultimate power and authority over their priests and laypeople. Having usually spent thirty years or more taking orders from others, often swallowing personal opinions that diverged from those of a superior, it is perhaps not surprising that many bishops expected the same deference from subordinates that they had extended to others over decades. Too many were unwilling to hear bad news about the sexual abuse of minors by priests and too few subordinates were wiling to speak up. Thomas Reese, for example, conveys one Vatican consultant's rules for surviving in the power structure of Church:

> Don't think.
> If you think, don't speak.
> If you think, and if you speak, don't write.
> If you think, and if you speak, and if you write,
>   don't sign your name.
> If you think, and if you speak, and if you write,
>   and if you sign your name, don't be surprised.[34]

Successful adherence to this adage simply is not compatible with effective responses to sexual abuse. Rather, the saying itself is reminiscent of the instructions explicitly or implicitly imposed by the perpetrator on the sexually abused minor. In general, power arrangements within the Church are symmetrical with those embedded in sexual abuse. Strict hierarchical and patriarchal power structures, pervasive secrecy, and speech that is dissociated from truth in order to preserve relational bonds are factors inherent both in sexually abusive families and organizations and in the Catholic Church.

While Vatican II began to move the Church away from relational grids based on dominance and submission, Pope John Paul II, whose papal term (1978–2005) encompassed almost all the years of the contemporary sexual abuse crisis, once again centralized Church power, resuscitating an emphasis on dominance and submission. Far from supporting democratic debate and the free flow of theological and doctrinal perspectives, John Paul is said by many commentators to have governed autocratically, refusing even to entertain discussion about Church teachings he considered irrefutable.[35] Many topics the pope considered unspeakable were not related to dogmas historically deemed unchangeable by the Church, but rather included teachings that indeed could be modified if there was the will to do so. Moreover, John Paul attempted to strengthen teachings he favored, like the ban on the ordination of women, by labeling them definitive or irreversible.[36] Rather than encouraging theologians and lay experts from various disciplines to air, fully delineate, and energetically debate controversial exegeses of Church teachings, especially those related to gender and sexuality, John Paul clamped down on anyone he judged to be in dissent from his view.[37] Further, life could get nasty for anyone who was tagged as a dissenter.

During John Paul's pontificate, theologians, teachers, priests, brothers, and religious women determined by Vatican officials to be in dissent were silenced by the Congregation for the Doctrine of the Faith, headed by Joseph Cardinal Ratzinger—now Pope Benedict XVI (2005–)—through processes experienced as humiliating by those censured.[38] German moral theologian Bernard Häring, for example, was persecuted as a young man by the Nazis.[39] After being investigated and ultimately silenced by the Church for his views on contraception, Haring said, "I would prefer Hitler's courts to another papal interrogation. Hitler's trials were more dangerous, but they were not an offense to my honor."[40] Lavinia Byrne, a vowed religious woman and popular British religious radio personality, wrote a book on the possibility of ordaining women to the priesthood.[41] In the book, she also recognized contraception as a liberating development for contemporary women. After Byrne and her supporters haggled with the Vatican for some time over their insistence that she publicly disavow her work and submit to Church teachings on birth control and female priests, the Vatican ordered her publisher, the Liturgical Press in Collegeville, Minnesota, to destroy all remaining copies of her book, which they did.

In addition to stifling speech on matters he considered essential, John Paul II centralized power even further by diminishing the authority of national conferences of bishops to develop policies uniquely suited to their country's needs and character.[42] Likewise, the synod of bishops, theoretically a quadrennial opportunity for bishops worldwide to advise the pope, became under John Paul a forum where bishops vied to quote the pope in their presentations, thereby demonstrating their familiarity with his voluminous documents and proving their personal loyalty to him.[43] The late Joseph Cardinal Bernadin of Chicago once complained that the pope treated his bishops like altar boys, certainly a relationship historically based on a boy's adulation of and obedience to the priest.[44]

Dominance/Sadism and Submission/Masochism

The paradigm of centralized power organizing Church relationships sometimes devolves from dominance and submission into sadomasochism, as evidenced in the treatment of once-respected theologians like Hans Küng, whose ideas became suspect at the Vatican and as witnessed in the sexual abuse of minors by priests and its cover-up by bishops.

Sadomasochism carries, in the popular imagination, a variety of definitions and connotations that tend to evoke strong emotions like disgust or morbid fascination. It is also simplified and misunderstood, as when the sadist is perceived as experiencing pleasure in administering pain and the masochist as taking pleasure in receiving pain. While pleasure of some kind and pain may be conflated in certain sadomasochistic enactments, they are more complicated than that. Moreover, sadomasochism rests on the dynamics of power relationships much more than on concretized pain and pleasure.

Contemporary views of sadomasochism recognize it as a relational phenomenon or pattern in which each individual engages in a perverted* attempt to find a true representation of himself or herself and another.[45] Psychoanalyst Emmanuel Ghent adds that sadomasochistic relationships frequently incorporate corrupted channels through which individuals seek

---

*Psychoanalyst Emmanuel Ghent defines perversion as "something akin to distortion, corruption, diversion, misconstruction" (Ghent, "Masochism, Submission, and Surrender," *Contemporary Psychoanalysis* 26 [1990]: 108).

to satisfy a deep longing to surrender, a concept replete with meaning in any religious tradition.[46] It may be, in fact, that the Church's conflation of surrender and submission generated patterns of sadomasochistic relating that have rigidified over two millennia to color the relational ambiance of the Church and to support the sexual abuse of minors, which also is often embedded in sadistic and masochistic dynamics.

Ghent suggests that the adaptive longing for surrender is a force drawing the self to discover "one's identity, one's sense of self, one's sense of wholeness, even one's sense of unity with other living beings."[47] Discovery of one's unity with God might be added to Ghent's list. In surrender, according to Ghent, there is no domination or control.[48] Surrender is passionate, joyful, filled with Eros. It also can be marked by fury and dread because surrender often involves the temporary chaos of breaking down the false and the petrified in order to embrace authentic and fluid experiences of self and other, including God.[49] Surrender results in growth, transformation, and acceptance of self, others, and the world. The capacity for surrender is promoted by developmental relational environments in which children and, later, adults are encouraged to play, to express a wide range of feelings about themselves and others, to risk knowing and being known, and in which they are accepted for who they are and who they are becoming through relationship with self and others.

Not all early and later relational contexts are conducive to safe surrender. Some parents and elders refuse to honor children in their fullness and paradoxical facets; adults can experience similar relational dynamics with superiors. In these cases, caretakers or elders in power are willing to recognize only those elements of another's subjectivity that are in alignment with their own or that in some way comply with what the elder needs to experience in order to support his or her own often insecure self-system. Surrender in that relational surround is unsafe, and submission or masochism becomes a corrupted and corrupting substitute that ensures ongoing attachment but at the cost of authenticity.[50] While surrender involves discovery and liberation from falseness, in submission, individuals experience themselves as puppets of another's power.[51] Self-knowledge, self-discovery, and self-recognition atrophy as one becomes a compliant false self, serving another's psychological or material needs.[52] In submission, resignation replaces acceptance and weightedness takes over joy.[53] Ghent depicts submission this way:

> Submission, losing oneself in the power of the other, becoming enslaved in one way or another to the master, is the ever available look alike to surrender. It holds out the promise, seduces, excites, enslaves, and,

in the end, cheats the seeker-turned-victim out of his cherished goal, offering in its place only the security of bondage and an ever amplified sense of futility.[54]

Once a submissive/masochistic relational stance is routinized, the search for recognition of self is turned toward another who is perceived to have the power to bestow that recognition.[55] Psychoanalyst Jessica Benjamin says, "This other has the power for which the self longs, and through this recognition she gains it, though vicariously."[56] And ephemerally, necessitating the serial reenactment of the masochistic relational position.

Sadism, suggests Ghent, represents the corruption of a deep longing to know the true self of another; to find, penetrate, and recognize the authentic other in all his or her fullness and inner diversity.[57] When early and later caretakers defend or retaliate against being probed and known by their charges, the latter may pervert adaptive seeking of another into a determination to control and dominate the other. For the dominator/sadist, others are valuable primarily as reflections of his or her own power. Power conflates with being so that the sadist is reassured about her or his existence only when there is another from whom submission is extracted. Ultimately, loneliness prevails for the sadist.[58] He or she cannot truly be known because that requires ceding power to the other. Nor can she or he truly know another who has, through submission, become objectified and dehumanized.

As we saw earlier, some interpretations of the Crucifixion are encrusted with sadomasochism. They dictate that God the Father sent his only son to earth to die for the sins of humankind. Knowing what would happen to Jesus and witnessing it when it occurred, this God had Jesus submit to his Father's plan. In real life, only a dangerously psychotic or viciously sadistic father would engage in such madness. Any parent approaching normalcy would throw himself against his son's tormentors and die trying to save the life of his adult child. Elizabeth Johnson, for example, says: "One can imagine a loving mother or father suffering the grief of the loss of a son due to an unjust death; how terribly often this happens in our world. But to think that the parent takes the initiative in arranging the sacrifice—here imagination reaches its limits and humanistic values rise up in protest."[59]

When the Crucifixion is emphasized as a solitary event, it can appear to the human imagination that God the Father choreographed infanticide; that he produced and directed a snuff film in which he cast his son in the starring role. It is difficult to imagine a more sadistic scenario. This one, unfortunately, sometimes became the iconic image of fatherhood passed down through generations of Church "fathers," an image formed to valorize the suffering of the Crucifixion over the rest of Jesus' temporal life and resurrected presence.

We have also seen that alternative theologies of the Crucifixion are offered by contemporary theologians. Interestingly, these provide a relational paradigm antithetical to sadomasochism, one anchored instead in surrender and mutual recognition. If Jesus, in fact, died for his most deeply held beliefs, he surrendered to experiences of self and others through which he remained heroically aligned with his truest self and his love for others. Here, Jesus could not betray the fullness of his being nor his unity with this world and God's by compromising love and truth as he knew them. Similarly, his Father recognized his son and his integrity and therefore could not subvert Jesus' journey by changing the course of events. God the Father only could offer himself to his son to be accessed and known and, in that way, hold up Jesus throughout his horrific suffering.

In this reimagining of the meaning of the Crucifixion, father and son surrender to the experience of knowing and being known by one another. Their relationship is embedded in mutuality, respect, and reciprocal surrender. Had this version of the Crucifixion become mainstream theology, it might have been more difficult for clerical "fathers" to dehumanize and demand submission by children in their care or for the father's fathers, the bishops, and provincial superiors to behave so callously toward the victims of their priests.

However, such a version of the Crucifixion was not predominant. As victims of sadistic persecution, the early Christians may have failed to recognize Jesus, rather imposing on him a submissive/masochistic relational stance that, in turn, provided them with a figure with whom they could identify. Unknowingly, they perhaps confounded surrender and submission, infusing the early Church with themes of domination and submission rather than recognition and reciprocity.

It is not unusual for an abuser who enacts dominance/sadism to experience himself subjectively as a victim. We have seen this throughout the Church scandal as bishops and Vatican officials blame the media, greedy lawyers, and dissenting Catholics for the scope of their problems. In other instances, the sadist enacts his violence without compunction because he perceives himself to be justified; so successful has been the dominance of another that the individual is seen more as a threatening thing than as a three-dimensional human being. We have witnessed this dynamic as well in bishops who castigated victims or their families for coming forward, ordering them into silence rather than embracing them as fellow travelers in need. Masochists, on the other hand, sometimes feel that they are "bad" even when they are being victimized and therefore collude with their further dehumanization. The sexual abuse crisis generated stories of victims who allowed themselves to be silenced by bishops or who were continually surprised by the Church's hardball legal tactics. These people, trained to submit, hoped against all hope that their Church would recognize them and voluntarily make efforts to heal them.

Dominance/sadism and submission/masochism are rooted primarily in the dynamics of power, and power often is an aphrodisiac. When Eros and its expression are suppressed or oppressively regulated, as they have been for much of Church history, power can become even more eroticized. The more that power is exercised through organizational relational structures that mitigate against surrender hued with Eros, the more likely relationships will be configured through sadomasochistic dynamics. Psychologist and inactive priest Eugene Kennedy bridges the concepts of power, sadomasochism, and eroticism when he discusses the silencing of theologians dissenting from Catholic teachings important to John Paul II:

> To this day, men and women who wish to remain in "good standing" . . . are forced to reenact what we may call the Galileo Myth. They must surrender [*author's note: I would say submit*] themselves—mind, heart, will—to their accusers, disown their creation, forsake their potency by giving up what they can bring forth from themselves and, therefore, maim themselves intentionally and suicidally at the command of, and to gratify, the Institution. . . . Men and women must *submit* and accept the conditions that . . . desexualize them by numbing their creativity, forcing them to abort what they beget through their generativity. . . . This profound humiliation is sexual in its intent and erotic in its gratification, as it aims not just to correct but to wound offenders in their generativity, in the sexually striated core energies of their being.[60]

As Kennedy implies, the sadomasochistic relationship is moribund; it kills off the hope of genuine surrender in both parties. Authenticity is corroded until it becomes a false-self masquerade. Here, arousal, nerve-jangling excitation, and ultimate exhaustion play perverted understudy roles to transformational erotic excitement, sensuality, and reimagined life. Despite the erotic (really pseudo-erotic) channels through which sadomasochism often is enacted, Benjamin insists that the sadomasochistic relationship "metaphorically . . . and sometimes literally . . . tends toward death or, at any rate, towards deadness, numbness, the exhaustion of sensation."[61] That death has walked amid the sexual abuse crisis is disturbingly evident in the multiple suicides among accused priests and alleged victims, as well as in several murders in which priests or former priests are the primary suspects.

A number of priests and ex-priests have committed suicide after being accused of sexual abuse. Former priest Sigfried Widera, for example, faced charges of molesting three Wisconsin boys and four California boys.[62] He fled to Mexico to avoid arrest and took his life by jumping off a hotel balcony there. Accused molester Rev. Richard Lower of New Hampshire allegedly committed suicide one week after a man accused Lower of sexually abusing him years ago.[63] Former priest Andrew Burke of Colorado shot himself while being investigated for sexually abusing a teenage boy in the 1970s.[64] Rev. Ryan Erickson of Hudson, Wisconsin, hanged himself in 2004 while he was under investigation for murdering two men.[65] In 2005, a judge concluded that the evidence against Erickson was overwhelming and that he killed Dan O'Connell and a student visiting O'Connell because O'Connell was going to report Erickson for sexually abusing minor boys.[66] At the trial, evidence was entered that Erickson also carried a handgun that he pointed out a church window at people he disliked, beat his dog, placed firecrackers in the mouths of fish and blew them up, and had hardcore child pornography on his computer filed under "holy Mass prayers."[67]

In 2004, Janet Patterson had a list of 145 alleged victims of priest sexual abuse who had killed themselves.[68] One was her son, Eric, an alleged victim of former priest and convicted child molester Robert Larson.[69] Eric shot himself when he was twenty-nine years old; four other alleged victims of Larson also have committed suicide.[70] Dennis Brown of New Jersey was the lead plaintiff in a suit against Rev. James Collins; Brown drank antifreeze in what was ruled a suicide attempt one week before the case was to go public.[71] James Kelly, thirty-seven, also of New Jersey and an alleged victim of former priest Robert Hanley, killed himself by stepping in front of a train.[72] Three alleged Oregon victims—Larry Lynn Craven, forty-nine; Peter Ryan, forty-four, and Steven Colvin, forty-three—all committed suicide, prompting the plaintiffs' attorney to request that funds be freed from the bankruptcy proceedings of the Archdiocese of Portland to provide counseling for victims.[73] Kevin McDonough, alleged victim of Rev. Peter Frost, and Patrick McSorley, alleged victim of Rev. John Geoghan, both of Boston, died of drug overdoses; both victims had made previous suicide attempts.[74]

The Magdalene homes, Irish laundries that housed about thirty thousand girls and women during a period of 150 years before the last one closed in 1996, are particularly gruesome example of sadomasochism deriving in part from the relational power structure of the Catholic Church.[75] Unwed mothers or young women who were judged to be too "loose" were placed in the laundries by their families and/or their priests.[76] Other residents included orphans, the retarded, and illegitimate children who were thought to be in potential moral danger.[77] The babies of unwed mothers were taken from them at birth and given up for adoption without the birth mother's consent. The laundries were

> virtual slave labor camps. . . . [The girls] were put to work without pay. . . . They were completely cut off from their families, and many lost touch with them forever. . . . [T]he girls were given numbers instead of names. They were forbidden to speak, except to pray. If they broke any rule or tried to escape, the nuns beat them over the head with heavy iron keys, put them in solitary confinement, or shipped them off to a mental hospital.[78]

Mary Norris, a former laundry resident, was taken from her mother by the local priest who decided that Mary's mother was unfit because she had begun a relationship with a man.[79] Arriving first at an orphanage, she says that one nun, Sister Laurence, responded to her frightened tears by saying: "What are you crying for? You know your mother is a tramp, an evil woman."[80] Later, Mary was placed in a Magdalene laundry in Cork:

> Her hair was chopped short. She was given the name Myra and made to dress in a long gray shift, thick stockings and a white cap that marked her as a penitent. . . . Once, when she refused to work or eat . . . . she was made to lie prostrate on the floor at bedtime, endlessly repeating, "Through my fault, through my fault, through my most grievous fault."[81]

The Magdalene laundries, brought to life in the 2003 film *The Magdalene Sisters*, were exemplars of the Church's organization of relationships through dominance and submission. This model was carried to a sadomasochistic extreme in the Irish laundries, where the girls were stripped of their identities and could survive only by complying perfectly with the sadistic demands of the nuns and priests running these institutions. The nuns' and priests' apparent paradoxical obsession with and hatred of erotic beauty and youthful sensuality, much less frank sexuality, were enacted through erotically charged humiliation of the girls in their "care."

These examples of sadism and masochism bespeak, at least in part, the emphasis on submission and dominance prevalent within many Church relationships. The majority of priests and almost all of the bishops involved in the scandal were trained when such pathological practices and relational templates were accepted and even at times idealized, rather than viewed with skepticism, much less abhorrence. Under these relational circumstances, it may not be so surprising that the sexual abuse of minors evoked such little outrage within the Church until the early twenty-first century. The kind of sadomasochistic power dynamics inherent in sexual abuse were ingrained in the relational patterns of the Church. The body must submit to the mind/spirit, and juniors must submit to the most inhumane demands of superiors. The laity must submit to the clergy, and children must submit to parents, including their clerical "fathers." Who in this chain of submission could raise their voices against the abuse of the Church's young?

CHAPTER 4

Embodied and Gendered Souls

The perversion of power relationships often characteristic of the Catholic Church sometimes was eroticized and expressed sexually. It is therefore necessary to unpack Catholic teachings about bodies, gender, desire, sexuality, and sexual orientation to illustrate the links between the Catholic theology of sexuality, the valorization of suffering, sadomasochism, and the sexual abuse crisis. We begin with bodies and gender.

Embodied Souls

The human body is the foundational imprint of the human story. Whether one turns to Genesis or to Darwin to discover the origins of humankind, it is clear that intelligent life is embodied. Bodies are so central to the human story that, according to Christian beliefs, God sent his offspring to spend time on earth as a particular body, a fully human body.

As a body, Jesus must have experienced all the stages of human development. When he was a little boy, Jesus likely had stomachaches, fell and skinned his knee, cuddled with Mary and Joseph, liked certain foods better than others, and perhaps hit his hand with a hammer from time to time while learning to be a carpenter. He probably got his feelings hurt when kids fought with him and may have felt competitive with other children when they played together. As an adolescent, Jesus would have experienced nocturnal emissions, unpredictable erections, and the need to accommodate to a newly deepened voice. His stomach may have gone on elevator rides when Nazarene girls or boys he had crushes on passed by. In adulthood, Jesus enjoyed eating and drinking, surely in part because of the bodily sensations arising from those activities. Certainly, he danced at the weddings of family and friends, and he undoubtedly sweat doing carpentry in the heat of Middle Eastern summers.

Throughout the Gospels, the health of the body and the soundness of the soul are connected. During the three years of his public ministry, Jesus healed others primarily by alleviating physical symptoms, often using his hands to minister to other bodies. Even if we view the physical conditions healed by Jesus as symbols of soul sickness, it is relevant that the Gospels portray Jesus using his body to reach through the bodies of others into their souls. Finally, during his torture and crucifixion by the Romans, Jesus almost certainly vomited, urinated, and defecated while hanging naked on the cross.* Here, he suffered bodily before attaining spiritual *and* physical transcendence through the Resurrection.

God's decision to incarnate divinity through the body of Jesus might have influenced Christians to honor the body as a sign of divine approval of the human body and *all* its functions. In such a view, the body would be on equal footing with the mind and the soul. In fact, each human could be considered a symbolic representation of the trinitarian nature of the Christian deity, incorporating three divinely inspired elements none of which were idealized or devalued at the expense of the others. Within this paradigm, the full life of any one of the trinity would be mutually dependent on the full life of the other two, as body, mind, and soul continually inscribed and were inscribed by one another.

Instead of this holistic view of human beings, Christianity, influenced by Neoplatonist and Stoic philosophical trends and by the relational context of dominance and submission already taking hold in the Church, developed within its first two centuries a theology in which the body, particularly the sexual body, was placed in antagonistic relationship with the spirit.[1] Bodies, which were thought to need taming, became equated with sex organs and were imbued with shame instead of reverence. St. Paul (Rom. 7:23) says of himself, "I see in my members another law at war with the law of my mind, making me captive to the law of sin that dwells in my members." Bodies and especially sex organs were said to be potentially dangerous distractions from an individual's spiritual quest. St. Paul (Rom. 8:10) captures this splitting into "bad" body and "good" soul when he says, "But if Christ is in you, though the body is dead because of sin, the Spirit is life because of righteousness."

It is important to remember that the shame and potential danger were man-made, not God-given, attributes of the body.[2] Mark Jordan, professor of religion at Emory University, reminds us: "Certainly it is not God who is ashamed of human genitals—or God who pulls back from the

---

*The Romans hung their prisoners naked on crosses to be crucified. Although he is rarely portrayed this way, Jesus would have been crucified naked as well.

shame meant to be inflicted on Jesus by crucifying him naked. We are the ones ashamed both of our human bodies as created and of what we do to human bodies when we want to humiliate them."[3]

As the iconography of the Church developed over centuries, Jesus' body was usually distorted to omit his genitalia. Hanging on almost every crucifix was not a naked man, but rather a body whose genitalia were covered by a loincloth. Some crucifixes did not even have genitals carved or cast under the loincloths, rendering the body of Jesus that of a prepubescent girl or a eunuch from the waist down. The loincloths covered an absence where a presence once was, a presence exposed during the Crucifixion. Whereas God allowed Jesus' full body to be known by humanity, man (and it has been primarily men) deprived Jesus of his bodily fullness in artistic renditions of him. Further, as Jordan points out, talking about Jesus' genitals usually is considered irreverent:

> [T]he genitals of Jesus are typically and normatively excluded from speech. To talk about them is indecent or provocative or blasphemous. To meditate on them would be obscene. We are urged to meditate on Jesus' acts and sufferings. We are asked to gaze on imaginary portraits of him and picture for ourselves his height and weight, the color of his skin or the length of his hair. But if our meditation should drift down toward his pelvis, we are immediately rebuked and then condemned as perverted or pornographic.[4]

The obsession with covering genitals, betraying perhaps an underlying obsessional interest *in* genitals, reached the Vatican where it was at one time ordered that loincloths be added to Michelangelo's nudes in the Sistine Chapel.[5] Pope John Paul II had the art restored to its original form when the Sistine Chapel was renovated during his papacy.[6]

Dualistic views of a shamefully provocative body seducing an idealized soul to fall away from Christ continued to influence Catholic iconography and traditions until Vatican II. Until then, priests customarily wore cassocks that resembled long, tailored dresses; some priests still favor this garb. At Mass, they were covered in layers of vestments. Similarly, vowed religious women's bodies were invisible, encased in habits. While this attire was consistent with the culture in which it was first worn, it outlived its social surround. These garments, however, continued to reflect the Church's problematic view of bodies. They rendered bodies invisible and caused bodily discomfort, a daily dose of small suffering (or not so small, teaching in June in a classroom without air conditioning) that could be graciously accepted and offered up.

Most of the priests and all of the bishops involved in the contemporary sexual abuse crisis up to 2002 were trained when seminaries maintained a dualistic view of body and soul. The genitals were again the emphasized concern. In some seminaries, men had to wear bathing suits when they showered lest their genitals be noticed by them or others.[7] In other seminaries, the students were required to tuck their shirts into their trousers using paddles so that their hands would not "accidentally" brush their genitals.[8] This kind of profound dissociation of body, especially genitalia, from mind and spirit may have created within many priests an odd relationship with their own bodies.

Despite the demands of the body, body experiences, and particularly forbidden sexual body experiences, were likely to take on a "not me" quality. The "I" most acceptable to many a priest and to those around him was a peculiarly disembodied "I." Further, too many messages from the embodied self were likely to be infused with fear and shame, ensuring that dissociative barriers between the body and "I" were maintained. Finally, as an "other Christ," a priest strove to emulate Christ and, as we have seen, Catholic iconography most often offered a body of Christ that was feminized or eunuchized, certainly not a helpful body image for a priest to internalize and with which to identify.

Few around the priest were likely to value his genitals, and Jesus' genitals were not available as icons to meditate on, pray about, or identify with for guidance. Within the Church, many priests could not turn to their spiritual fathers, bishops, or provincial superiors for reassurance about their genital adequacy since those men were likely to be living in the same kind of body-soul dissociation. Youngsters, especially pubescent or slightly older male adolescents, may have been sought out by priests unconsciously looking for a male who knew what to do with genitalia and who could reassure the priest about the presence, value, and adequacy of his own genitals and thus his body. In a peculiar reversal of Oedipal dynamics, therefore, some fathers/priests may have searched for their lost body parts by merging with their sons/victims. Further, many of the boys abused by priests were around the same age that the priest was when he began to consider seriously a vocation or entered the seminary and "lost" his body/genitals. For the priest, the abuse may have represented an unconscious attempt to re-find his body where he last fully experienced it—in adolescence—and to jump-start stalled stages of psychosexual development.

When and if the priest recognized the abusiveness of his behavior, the inherent shamefulness of his body would likely be confirmed and even greater defensive dissociation might ensue. To that extent, the subjective experience of the priest may well have been a vague sense of his body doing something separate from the self identified as "I." Why would "he" be too concerned or feel badly since "he" had done nothing? Similarly, when a bishop learned of his priest's sexual abusiveness, his own shame about the unruliness of his body, as well as the priest's, may have caused him to avert his gaze from the situation and hurry to restore the status quo. "Looking" meant seeing bodies/genitals—the bishop's, his priest's/son's, the victim's. Few bishops were prepared for those sights, so bureaucratic blindfolds were often used to create an absence where indeed there was a presence. When victims, the media, plaintiffs' attorneys, and others demanded that Christ's suffering and nakedness, now represented by the victims, be engaged, bishops—perhaps anxiety ridden and ashamed—looked away.

Pope John Paul II attempted to restore the body as the essence of humanity and insisted that it should be revered and honored.[9] He emphasized that the experience of embodiment is fundamental for every person, even more fundamental than the gender of the body.[10] John Paul echoed anthropologist and psychoanalyst Muriel Dimen in stating that the body is the signifier of the person's individuality and interiority.[11] In rectifying the Church's historical devaluation of the body, John Paul welcomed the body as a God-designed expression of creation and spirit. In the process, however, the pope moved to an opposite extreme in which the body became an overvalued emblem of sacredness.

Bodies—how they are dressed, portrayed in art and advertising, nourished—symbolize culture and the power relationships within that culture.[12] To that extent, it is not only the Catholic Church that has yet to construct a paradigm of flesh that neither overvalues nor denigrates the body. In much of today's Western culture, the body dominates the iconography. In diametric opposition to the Church, much of society equates the perfect body with the perfect life. While John Paul insisted that the subjectivity of the body must never be compromised, many aspects of twenty-first-century culture dis-grace the body by glorifying its ultimate objectification. It is perhaps only when holistic views of the body acquire cultural acceptance, including within the Church, that bodies will be integrated with psyche and soul sufficiently well to reduce the likelihood of bodies becoming the instruments and inscriptions of sexual abuse.

Gendered Bodies

Contemporary studies and theorizing about gender have significantly altered the ways in which gender is understood in society.[13] Today, gender is not considered fixed, even within one individual. Rather, there is within each man or woman a multiplicity of more or less intense experiences of maleness *and* femaleness as well as nongendered experiences of being. In addition, implied in the terms "man" and "woman," "masculine" and "feminine," are politically mediated ideas about dominance versus submission, active versus passive, subject versus object, taking versus taking care of. Muriel Dimen says: "[G]ender is not an essence but a set of relationships[14] Masculinity and femininity are a sort of cultural code signifying not only (anatomical and representational) sexual differences, but other qualities, entities, and relationships that have nothing to do with it."[15]

Despite contemporary scholarship on gender and progress in the area of gender equality, the genders still are not valued equally in our culture. Rather, biological males and females are pressured to conform to certain socially and politically determined aims. The Catholic Church remains even more firmly rooted in dualistic paradigms of gender that are implicated in the sexual abuse crisis.

Can Real Men Be Priests?

Although this may seem like a specious question, it is not, and the answer is, well, yes, but often no. While male is the favored gender within Catholicism and priests are the favored males, Church doctrines and traditions offer contradictory and confusing constructions of maleness for priests. Not only does the Church present its clergy with internally inconsistent messages regarding clerical genderedness, but priestly maleness is (and always has been) meaningfully divergent from culturally stereotypical male gender characteristics and roles. While many priests attain a maturity through which they can honor their differences from culturally normative secular men, others may become increasingly insecure about their own masculinity when culturally stereotypical gender roles are unavailable to them.

The Church takes a concrete approach to gender and insists that since Jesus was a biological male, his priestly representatives must also be male. Further, the Church argues that the twelve Apostles were male, shoring up teachings that only biological males can be priests. In order to do this, the institutional Church has had to close its eyes to contemporary biblical scholarship and feminist theology indicating that early texts suggest the presence of female disciples who served in ministry.[16] Here, the Church accepts some biblical and historical texts and their exegesis at the expense of others, which helps to preserve both kyriarchy and patriarchy.*

---

*Patriarchy is seen as the domination of men over women. Patriarchy is subsumed into kyriarchy, a term that includes the dominance of some men over other men, as well as over

The Church, while requiring priests to be biological men, then places many of them in a situation in which they are prevented from conforming to most of the roles by which society judges manliness. Perhaps even more important, priests are proscribed from achieving some culturally norma- tive markers of *adult* manhood—marriage, children, family support and care responsibilities. In addition to priests' inability to follow the wider society's acknowledged routes to adult manhood, they are conditioned to play some traditionally feminine roles. For example, until Vatican II priests wore cassocks, which not only hid their bodies but also resembled dresses. Especially during the formative years of many priests and almost all bishops involved in the sexual abuse crisis, at Mass and other ceremo- nial functions clergy were clad in "women's" fabrics: satins, laces, silks, and fur.

There are, of course, exceptions to this presentation of priestly life. Some priests, like Rev. Theodore Hesburgh, former president of the Uni- versity of Notre Dame, shouldered challenging responsibilities. He sat on a number of U.S. presidential commissions and built Notre Dame into an expanded and world-recognized institution of learning. Other, less-re- nowned priests, serving in underprivileged urban areas or in foreign mis- sions, worked manfully with often limited resources to serve the limitless needs of their pastoral families. Yet, the stereotype described above was also real and could become particularly problematic for immature men who were already unsure of their masculinity.

After leaving their seminaries, especially before Vatican II, some priests lost even the sense of masculinity, albeit adolescent, provided by intramural sports and the camaraderie of other young men. Further, while in the seminary, their divergence from their agemates in terms of norma- tive gender roles may have been obscured. Once in parishes and schools, however, priests were confronted immediately with male parishioners living out society's prescriptions for male behavior. Taught that priests lived out a calling spiritually superior to these men; sensing that many other men would not agree with that assessment; perhaps needing to cen- sor proscribed feelings of inferiority, envy, or competitiveness with other priests—much less laymen—some priests may have experienced anxiety about their masculinity.

Comparisons with men outside the priesthood may have been one potential source of gender anxiety for some priests. Within the priest-

---

women and, I would add, children. For a discussion of kyriarchy, see Elisabeth Schüssler Fiorenza, *In Memory of Her: A Feminist Theological Reconstruction of Christian Origins* (New York: Crossroad, 2000), 329.

hood, as well, stereotypical feminine traits sometimes were most rewarded. Although some priests were very ambitious and worked hard to climb within the political structure of the Church, the ethos cultivated the idea that priests were not *supposed* to be overtly ambitious, aggressive, or competitive—all traits culturally associated with men. Submission and cheerful obedience were often most likely to earn affection and advancement. Open competition for promotions or self-promoting ambition were often viewed with disdain, perhaps in part because those characteristics threatened superiors who had habituated to their own stereotypically feminized genderedness and, indeed, had been recognized and rewarded for it. Rather, to get ahead, some priests had to please their bosses and lobby for promotions in a more stereotypical female manner, using flattery and guile and accepting a fundamental oppression of their independent thinking, sense of agency, and creativity.

A number of writers suggest that, to the extent a priest could embrace his masculinity at all, it was difficult for him to progress beyond the psychosexual stage of an adolescent boy.[17] Boys become men, in part, by gradually relinquishing their primary relationship with their mothers and identifying with their fathers and other adult male role models. When things go well, boys test out their emerging manhood both by becoming like and by establishing difference from these older men, especially fathers, who (we hope) are sufficiently secure to celebrate the "like me" and the "very much not like me" aspects of their sons.

Psychoanalyst Ruth Stein describes the "possible primal ferocity between father and son, an underside of their great love."[18] She suggests that the battles between father and son end well for the son when the father, as a representative of life-giving law and order, makes room for his son's unique subjectivity and difference rather than imposing an arbitrary or cruel will posing as law.[19] Within the priesthood, many men could not easily work through a "very much not like me" with their superiors or spiritual fathers, because only "like me" behaviors and attitudes were permitted by most bishops. Further, it would be challenging for a priest to differentiate himself from the bishop to whom he had sworn obedience and apart from whom he had no shelter, food, health insurance, or career. Many a priest, therefore, was caught in a "deeply problematic Oedipal triangle of father-bishop, mother-church, and son-priest."[20]

Andrea Celenza, a psychoanalyst who has worked clinically with numerous priests, also describes the priest as forever the less-powerful son of God, a male figure who never can be delimited in the psyche of the priest.[21] One cannot easily go "mano-a-mano" with God, much less successfully compete with or defeat him. Therefore, the priest was not free to try on "not God" attributes, even in a temporary process characteristics of the son's struggle to dis-identify with his father long enough to consolidate an independent and unique sense of manhood. Never able to equal, must less exceed, the power and accomplishments of the God-father and his earthly ecclesiastical representatives, some priests may have experienced themselves as eternally needy, always admiring and never admired, demasculinzed sons yearning for paternal approval. When expectable periods of disillusionment in God or superiors occurred, more immature priests may have experienced themselves as held in contempt and scorned by their heavenly and earthly fathers to whom they were nonetheless required to submit.

Stein suggests that men in this position dread their implied feminization and the concomitant regression to dependency on the mother.[22] One possible coping mechanism is for a priest to avoid the downward slide to mother's engulfing embrace by soaring upward into ecstatic contemplation of an idealized heavenly Father.[23] Here the priest identifies in an immature way with cultural law and masculinity as represented by the Almighty. That identification becomes the priest's source of personal, even entitled power.[24] Unconsciously, however, the priest knows that he is borrowing the power of a figure—God—with whom he cannot both identify and do battle. This priest's power and masculinity is ersatz, and, somewhere, he knows that and can become self-hating and angry. Consciously, the priest is one with God and can demand anything of anyone; he is entitled to whatever he wants. At the same time, unconsciously, some priests "know" they are contemptible and weak; their manly power literally lives on borrowed time. Finally, the priest's emulation of Christ too often required him to relinquish his genitals both in his internal fantasy life and in the external world. As an *alter Christus*, as we have seen, the priest was offered icons of a castrated Christ whom he was supposed to become like.

All these factors may have created for some priests a myriad of maturational and gender problems. One vowed religious man working with Celenza said, "The Catholic Church is a very castrating hierarchy. . . . It removes the opportunity for initiative. . . . [For vowed religious priests], there are three vows: chastity, in Latin castitas, which means "to be made impotent"; obedience, submit your will; and poverty, surrender ownership."[25]

Sexual potency, dominance rather than submission, and ownership of property historically have been key elements in cultural definitions of manhood. All were difficult for some priests to attain or even to imagine themselves having. While Celenza's patient may have internalized a model of priesthood that is not fully descriptive of all those available, for the man vulnerable to doubts about his masculinity, the Church's power structure and organization of the priesthood can make maturation even more difficult to achieve.

Former seminary rector Donald Cozzens suggests that the Catholic priest can achieve both adulthood and manhood only when he becomes both a man of the Church and his own man.[26] As a man of the Church, Cozzens says the priest is

> blessed with a deep and abiding sense of the Spirit's presence, directing, sustaining, and renewing the Church. . . . He possesses the courage to stand in loyal opposition should official Church policies appear unfaithful to the Gospel of Christ.[27] . . .

> The wisdom generated is of the ancients in "thinking with the Church; [while] he is also fearless in thinking for himself. His theological reflection on his own pastoral experience and the events of the world, while done in communion with his companions in ministry and his parishioners, transcends 'group think.'"[28]

Cozzens posits that the path to adult manhood is obscure and cluttered with obstacles for the priest. Too many priests have dissociated the quest, instead developing personae as "sycophant ecclesiastics and pious, effete clerics or the less common but equally destructive path of the maverick."[29] In gender terms, the first accepts his castration and implicit feminization while the other becomes a hypermasculinized rebel, challenging superiors just to reassure himself of his own identity.

For some priests, sexual abuse of minors may have represented one way to express emotions, like rage and the lust to dominate, which unfortunately were culturally associated with masculinity but unacceptable within the priesthood. It was one immature and destructive way to individuate from bishops/Christ who forbade use of the genitals. Further, abusing boys, for some priests, may have represented a temporary identification with domineering superiors. Here, the powerlessness and impotent rage perhaps experienced by the priest in submissive relationship with his bishop and even with God was projected onto the minor male over whom the abusing priest held omnipotent sway. At the same time, the priest could experience, at least for a time and albeit in a distorted way, a sense of genital potency and masculinity denied to him as a priest. He could not only be the boss, demanding obedience from another, he could be the sexually successful master of another submissive, feminized male.

A boy also becomes a man by loosening dependency ties to his biological mother. As the boy matures, his needy dependence on an objectified mother transforms into a relationship with a maternal subject resting on mutual recognition, respect, affection, sameness, and difference. Historically, many Catholic priests faced significant impediments to accessing a manhood that implicated an internalized autonomy from their mothers. Cozzens points out that many priests have had enmeshed, mutually dependent relationships with their mothers.[30] It is an old saw that a mother whose son is a priest never really loses him.[31]

While many priests negotiate healthy relationships with biological mothers, many others remain bound to their mothers, who depend on their sons to fill their own emotional needs.[32] When that occurs, priests may transfer their adolescent relationships with their biological mothers to their new mother, Holy Mother Church. For some immature priests, biological mother, Holy Mother Church, and Mary, the Mother of God, merged into one sacred, untouchable, yet demanding maternal configuration. Here too, the priest was trapped in an eternal boyhood, unable to consolidate a sense of adult manhood. Cozzens explains: "This maternal Church, while supportive and pointing to his dignity as a priest, is also demanding and controlling. His sexuality is restrained, his dress determined, his residence assigned. This mother wants him for herself."[33] For priests whose sense of manhood was stunted and who unconsciously were in thrall to mothers who were experienced as both demanding and idealized, sexual abuse may have represented an unconscious attempt to free themselves from attachment bonds to insistent women. In these cases, choosing an adult woman, or even a minor girl, as a sexual partner may have felt unconsciously too much like an attack on a potentially retaliatory female figure. Here, the selection of a minor male may have represented a psychological merger with a boy who could help the priest rebel against his controlling mother(s).

Women in Catholicism

Because women and children are culturally merged, the Church's attitudes about women influence its treatment of children. It is therefore important to delineate institutional Catholic views of women.

As Christianity grew from a movement within Judaism into a separate religion during the first two centuries C.E., early Church fathers were influenced by misogynist Neoplatonist and Stoic philosophies.[34] They engaged with the canonical Gospels (Matthew, Mark, Luke, John), already culturally and politically mediated selections of all available Gospel material, as well as with texts attributed to St. Paul, to develop a theology suited to the social and political climate of the times.[35] Theologian Schüssler Fiorenza cautions that the New Testament "should not be misunderstood as abstract, timeless theological ideas or norms, but should be understood as faith responses to concrete historical situations."[36] According to Schüssler Fiorenza, through the selection and subsequent processing of Scripture, woman was constructed by kyriarchal language systems as "other" to the man/lord of the house.[37]

Until the papacy of John Paul II, the dichotomization of womanhood between virgin or mother, on the one hand, and the evil seductress or whore, on the other, prevailed in Catholic teachings. In 386, St. John Chrysostom wrote: "What else is woman but a foe to friendship, an inescapable punishment, a necessary evil, a natural temptation, a desirable calamity, a domestic danger, a delectable detriment, an evil of nature painted with fair colors."[38]

In 1486, Pope Innocent VIII, ironically named given his several illegitimate children, authorized a book, *Malleus Maleficarum* (Witches' Hammer), which was used as a seminary text until the 1600s.[39] A view of woman is presented that possibly suggests the writer's terror of female power, defended against by vitriol: "When a woman thinks alone, she thinks evil. . . . She is a liar by nature. . . . She is more carnal than a man as is clear from her many abominations . . . the mouth of the womb is never satisfied.[40]

These man-made paradigms and others like them continued to influence seminarians and priests well into the twentieth century.[41] Non-virginal, assertive, intelligent, ambitious women consciously or unconsciously became, for some priests, dangerous daughters of Eve, intent on distracting men, especially priests, from their service to God.

Historically, the Church's construction of a respectable and loveable woman was Mary, the virgin mother of Jesus. Over the centuries, Mary became an increasingly man-made character, as she was declared free of original sin, kept a perpetual literal virgin, and determined to have ascended bodily into heaven. Men within the Church constructed a Mary further and further removed from the experiences of womanhood.[42] In Mary, men of the Church recreated a very daring Jewish woman as their own safe, endlessly nurturing, sexless female protector.[43] The female saints, some of whom sacrificed their lives in defense of their chastity, also were acceptable role models for women and prayer objects for men. Women, therefore, who never fed the mouths of their wombs, or who opened those mouths only to bring forth children, were idealized by the institutional Church while other women were feared, degraded, and marginalized.

Attitudes have not changed all that much, at least within segments of the hierarchy. In 1989, for example, the Vatican radio supported the comments of Giacomo Cardinal Biffi of Bologna, Italy, who echoed earlier churchmen in equating modern women with Eve, denoting them to be "squalid" and "a collector of death":

> The splendor of the Immaculate Madonna allows us to see with biting clarity how great is the misfortune of our era, in which the prevailing image of women . . . is one that appears to be the deliberate contradiction of that of the Virgin Mary; a woman who even if externally refined is substantially squalid; who appears to detest virginity and maternity in equal measure; a woman who does not say to God, "Here I am, I am yours" but who cries hysterically, "I belong to myself"; a woman . . . who claims the right . . . to decide the existence or nonexistence of the fruit of her innards.[44]

Similarly, in 2004, the Vatican issued a letter attacking feminism, which, it said, diminished the differences between the genders thereby threatening the natural two-parent family and rendering homosexuality and heterosexuality morally equivalent.[45] Earlier that year, Archbishop Sean O'Malley (now Sean Cardinal O'Malley) of Boston refused to wash the feet of women on Holy Thursday, allowing only men to participate in the traditional Easter Week ritual.[46] In a Holy Week sermon, O'Malley blamed feminism, along with the sexual revolution and divorce, for baby boomers' spiritual deficits.[47] The *Southern Nebraska Register,* the newspaper of the Diocese of Lincoln, headed by Bishop Fabian Bruskewitz, has published diatribes against a number of contemporary Catholic women.[48] Sr. Jeannine Gramick, advocate for homosexual Catholics, was called an "apostle of sexual perversion" while renowned theologian Rosemary Radford Ruether was named an advocate of "witchcraft."[49] Finally, Judge Anne Burke, chair of the National Review Board of the United States Conference of Catholic Bishops (USCCB), said that bishops hostile to the board had dubbed her "Mother Superior," a contemptuous and immature term perhaps suggesting that, more unconsciously, they were intimidated by her.[50]

Within Catholicism, then, some clerics consciously devalue the smart, sexual, independent woman while perhaps unconsciously both fearing and desiring her. At the same time, they may have consciously idealized the virgin and mother while perhaps unconsciously despising her as a controlling, sexually punitive, ultimately unavailable tease, or holding her in contempt for her submissiveness and passivity.

Certainly, idealization itself is a form of objectification and oppression. The idealized person becomes an object, not a subject, and is not free to move out of the positions that render her able to be idealized. Clinically, one learns that idealization usually veils feelings and attitudes that lurk below the patient's awareness, including envy, fear, rage, competition, and devaluation. The greater the idealization, the more it is likely that it covers coexisting but unconscious negative feelings. It is likely, therefore, that the idealization and adoration of Mary, significantly enhanced by the motherless Pope John Paul II, hides other, more complicated and ambivalent feelings about women, as well as covert yearnings to be perfectly mothered. In the end, idealization of a woman created by man is no less misogynistic than hatred of a woman who defines herself through reciprocal, rather than submissive, relationship with others.

Children historically were perceived as occupying their mother's life space. To the extent that minors were consciously or unconsciously viewed as extensions of degraded women, it may have become easier for some priests and bishops to degrade the child as well. Once again, the abusing priest could launch a rebellion against oppressive internal maternal images by oppressing those individuals he thought mothers held most dear. Sexual abuse could render the woman wounded and impotent in the mind of the abuser since she was unable to protect her child from harm. Thus, the priest motivated by this kind of destructive dynamic temporarily triumphed over and humiliated a woman, at least in his perhaps unconscious fantasies. Selection of a male victim protected the priest from recognizing that he was assaulting the taboo woman; he could consciously protect an idealization of women, including Holy Mother Church, while enacting more unconscious feelings of rage and impotence.

Pope John Paul II drew the Church away from a dualistic version of women as either virgin–mother or evil seductress–whore into a better-sounding but equally forlorn and misogynistic paradigm of separate but equal.[51] The pope began well by insisting that before we are gendered, we are humans all made from the same stuff.[52] He then defined complementarities between the sexes that privileged maleness. For example, theologian Christopher West explains the pope's consideration of the nuptial meaning of gendered bodies: "The nuptial meaning of the man's body calls him to image God's initiation of the gift, whereas the nuptial meaning of the woman's body calls her to image humanity's receptivity and response to the gift."[53] Turning to the sexual relationships between spouses, West says that, based on John Paul's teachings, "if a husband loves his wife 'as Christ loved the Church,' he says: 'This is my body which is given for you (Luke 22:19).' And if the wife responds in love to her husband as the

Church responds to Christ, she says. . . : 'Let it be done to me according to your word (Luke 1:38).' "[54]

Elizabeth Johnson states that the pope's gender theory of "equal in dignity but separate in social roles" stamps this new version of gender with just another kind of dualism.[55] It is in fact a regurgitation of historically stereotypical gender roles, ones Johnson says have been potentially dangerous for women (and by extension, children) who are rendered unable to say *no* to abuse and oppression.[56]

Despite some advances in the pope's construction of women, he still left the Church with a "father/papa/pope knows best" configuration of gender. One can legitimately ask, however, what particular knowledge or expertise a Catholic pope brings to the study of gender, especially female gender, a project that is vibrantly underway in other fields. Moreover, it should be distressing that a celibate Catholic patriarch, especially one raised after age eight in a womanless home, experienced himself qualified, even exceptionally gifted, to say anything authoritative about the experience of women (and thus children). One would at least expect that a pope hoping to say something meaningful about gender would submit his work to other experts in the field, including women, who would provide feedback and even vetting of the final teaching. John Paul's promulgation of a theory of gender, therefore, in and of itself enacted the kind of kyriarchical processes described by Schüssler Fiorenza and reflected more hubris than wisdom. Hubris about clerical power over women and children, combined with objectifying attitudes about both, significantly mediated the sexual abuse of minors and, especially, its cover-up.

At the same time that Catholic teachings and traditions about gender, and about women in particular, are deficient, it is also a mistake to assume that merely filling diocesan lay review panels or other consultative groups with women will enhance the Church's approach to sexual abuse. This attitude also betrays stereotypical views of women as ultimate mothers who never would stand by in silence about abuse. Unfortunately, however, many women who know their children are being abused by individuals with whom those mothers have attachment relationships collude with the abuse by remaining silent. They may even turn on a child who reports abuse to them. Surely, over the years, many parish housekeepers and other laywomen, including mothers, knew or suspected that some priests spent too much time with children. Some spoke up; most remained silent. Further, many religious women also knew or suspected that priests were violating the children entrusted to the care of these nuns for schooling, and few intervened. Finally, nuns also have been accused of sexually violating minors, although the percentage of abusive nuns seems to be significantly lower than the percentage of abusive priests.[57] Women who depend on kyriarchal systems for their physical and emotional sustenance or who adhere to the values permeating patriarchy are not likely to raise their voices against the men around them.

CHAPTER 5

Degraded Sexual Desire and Theologized Sex

The sexual abuse scandal cannot be understood apart from the Catholic Church's broader teachings about sexual desire and sex.

Degradation of Sexual Desire

Outside Catholicism, sexual desire and lust have a number of connotations:

> *Desire:* 1. Conscious impulse toward something that promises enjoyment and satisfaction in its attainment. 2. Sexual urge or appetite.
>
> *Lust:* 1. Intense or unbridled sexual desire. 2. An intense longing. Craving, enthusiasm, eagerness.
>
> *Lust:* In German, both the desire for pleasure and the experience of its satisfaction. The meaning is ambiguous, doubled. Both/and, not either/or.[1]

Despite the breadth of potential perspectives on these human yearnings, sexual desire and its first cousin, lust, have had troubled histories within Catholicism. In fact, they have been the victims of oppression, confined to narrowly defined channels of officially sanctioned expression wholly limited to heterosexual marriage. Like ants at a garden party, sexual desire and lust have evoked shivers of horror throughout the body of the institutional Church, which has done everything possible to exterminate them. Sexual desire and lust, however, like those determined, playfully persistent ants, are not so easily dispelled and return again and again, invited or not, to surprise and upset the planned and the peaceful.

For all of Catholicism's legislation about sexuality, Jesus had little to say about it.[2] The early Church fathers, heavily influenced by Stoicism and writing from the end of the second century to the middle of the fifth century C.E., emphasized the dangers of sexual passion and the concomitant need to regulate it.[3] Tertullian and Jerome insisted that willpower could and should control sexual desire.[4] Origen (185–254) exercised ultimate extermination of his passions by castrating himself.[5] It was Augustine (354–435), however, who set the tone for centuries of Catholicism's degradation of sexual desire.

Augustine postulated that the Fall of Adam and Eve proceeded from the original couple's failure to quell sexual desire.[6] Here, sexual concupiscence became the core obstacle to oneness with God's will.[7] Augustinian theorizing thus placed sexual desire at the epicenter of sinfulness. In wedding sexual desire and sin, Augustine provided justification for the Church to regulate an individual's relationship with passion. During the medieval period, the Church developed a penitential code used by confessors to evaluate the seriousness of sin.[8] Sexual sins were elaborated according to their category, their frequency, and the penitent's degree of malicious intent.[9] Penances for sexual sins could be long and severe, such as fasting on bread and water for several years.[10] Here we see sadomasochism channeled through the confessional to keep Eros where the Church thought it belonged.

St. Thomas Aquinas (1225–1274), a Scholastic thinker, introduced the idea that sexual desire was natural and could be legitimate as long as it was guided by reason and not experienced as pleasurable.[11] Catholic moral manuals, influenced by Aquinas, recategorized sexual sins into those that accorded with nature and those that were contrary to nature.[12] Using these criteria, adultery and incest were considered less serious sins than masturbation or homosexuality, because the former remained open to procreative possibilities while the latter did not.[13] Within Catholicism, moral teaching still is said to rest on natural law, understood as human reasoning reflecting on human nature to discover wisdom regarding the Creator's intent for human behavior.[14]

Augustinian sexual teachings, Scholastic categorization of sexual sin according to natural law, and an elaborate sex-centered penal code ensured that few Catholics would be able to stop thinking and feeling about sex for very long. It all put Catholics in a terrible bind. Most sexual desire was forbidden, and, as French philosopher Michel Foucault tells us, the forbidden becomes both more enticing and even more eroticized.[15] Regular confession required Catholics to search their memories for instances of sexual desire, thereby providing the necessity of reliving those moments, while trying again to suppress the initial arousal. Now perhaps with another sin to confess, the penitent disclosed it all to the confessor. The confessor, the only person able to mediate God's forgiveness, spent Saturday afternoons listening to erotic material, perhaps experiencing instances of sexual arousal that would have to be shared with his own confessor. In the process, the Church gained enormous power to govern and discipline the lives of Catholics. Religion and psychology expert Gillian Walker says:

> The more central sexuality became in Catholic teaching, the more power a sexually pure clergy had over the economy of sin and salvation. As Marina Warner put it, "For if desire, as natural as breath or as sleep itself, is sinful, then the Christian, like the man in the grip of a usurer, must always run back to the Church, the only source of grace which can give him a reprieve."[16]

Most of the priests and all of the bishops involved in the contemporary sexual abuse crisis were taught that sexual desire was inherently sinful. Their own holiness could be measured in part by their success in quelling lust. Sexual desires that did not respond well to reason and prayer would be sources of shame for most priests, especially since struggles with desire and celibacy were not normalized and discussed until the late 1980s either in seminary or as a part of ongoing formation. At the same time, the priest hearing confessions each week, while perhaps struggling in silence with his own forbidden surges of sexual desire, was presented with sexually stimulating material shared by penitents. Here again, priests were confronted with their differences from other men and boys who confessed not just thoughts but actions that must have seemed dangerous and shameful yet titillating.

Many priests were able, at least eventually, to sublimate their sexual desire through passion for God and for their ministries. One can imagine that for other priests, however, the dam of pent-up desires broke and they sought to experience what they only heard about in the confessional. While some men became involved with adult women or men, more insecure, immature, or pathologically organized men may have turned to young people who provided gratification of sexual desire and would not be likely to criticize the priest's sexual skill. For some of these priests, minors became a habitual outlet for the satisfaction of desire.

Pope John Paul II constructed a new Catholic theology of sexuality, which he promulgated in 129 general audience sessions between 1979 and 1984.[17] The pope moved the Church beyond a purely mechanical notion of permissible sex, emphasizing the sanctity of sex and even sexual pleasure occurring between married heterosexuals, open to procreation and recognizing each other's subjectivities. His formulation of lust, however, kept it enthroned as humanity's primary sin. Christopher West paraphrases John Paul: "Nonetheless, in a way sexual purity lies at the basis of all moral good since all moral disorders, according to John Paul, stem from the impurity of a lustful heart."[18] The pope taught that lust is always evil since, according to him, lust must objectify another person in order to obtain its gratification. It is an all-or-nothing perspective on lust: "This 'flaming up in man,' the Pope says, 'invades his senses, excites his body, involves his feelings, and in a certain sense takes possession of his heart.' . . . In other words, because passion aims at satisfaction, 'it blunts reflective activity and pays not attention to the voice of conscience.' "[19] Lustful sexual union, even within heterosexual marriage, was counseled against, and married couples were instructed by the pope "progressively to conquer lust in order to relive an original virginal experience of unity."[20]

John Paul envisioned lust as dichotomously opposed to love, as "a primordial plagiarization of love."[21] Here, despite the pope's emphasis on the importance of relationality—the interpersonal, intersubjective entanglement—between sexual partners, he decontextualized lust. It became the same sin regardless of the relational context in which it occurred. In addition, the pope's teaching continued the conflation, common in Catholic tradition, of thinking, feeling, and fantasizing with action. The thought or the emotion becomes the thing for which it stands, leaving little room for play, illusion, or symbolic creativity.

The traditional Catholic position on sexual desire and lust contradicts what we know from biology, anthropology, and psychology about the reality of appetite. Because lust is "as natural as breath or as sleep," it is *un*natural to banish those longings from the body, psyche, and soul of the individual.[22] Those who try to comply with the teachings of the Church are likely to divide against themselves, storing unacceptable desires in unconscious regions of their minds. Rather than having erotic desires available to process, play with, and even act on with integrity, such desires work on the individual from the storage room of the psyche. Already considered shameful and sinful, when and if they break into consciousness, they may lead to enactments that are also shameful and sinful—like sexual abuse of a minor—rather than to mature, creative, and modulated actions *or* to a choice not to act at all.

In describing lust, John Paul, like centuries of poets and philosophers before him, compared lust to a burning flame.[23] The metaphor of burning passion offers another perspective on lust, one that is both/and rather than either/or in relationship to love and holiness. Author Karol Jackowski, for example, reminds us that flame and fire long have been symbols of sacredness, of passion for God, of an insatiable burning for spiritual fulfillment.[24] Rome's highly honored Vestal Virgins were responsible for ensuring that the sacred fires of the temple were never extinguished; the Romans believed that if the fires went out, disaster would ensue.[25] God appeared to Moses as a burning bush whose flames would not extinguish (Exod. 3:2); Deuteronomy speaks of God as a jealous, consuming fire (Deut. 4:12); 1 Kings (18:24) advises that the god who answers by fire is the real God; Song of Solomon (8:6) asserts that love "burns like a blazing fire, like the very flame of the Lord"; Matthew (3:11) has John the Baptist prophesying that another will come to baptize with the Holy Spirit and with fire. Finally, Jackowski recounts that, on the first Pentecost, the Holy Spirit is said to have descended on Jesus' disciples as tongues of fire, endowing them with the ability to speak in many languages.[26] The Pentecostal flames ignite a passion for spreading the word of Jesus, "of having a new spirit rise within, bringing . . . new ways of thinking, feeling, living, and loving."[27]

Unlike the Church, contemporary secular theorists of sexual desire insist on giving the vagaries of lust their due. Muriel Dimen tells us that in German, *Lust* connotes "both the longing for pleasure and pleasure itself."[28] It rests on the erotics of early sensual experiences with caretakers and reaches up and down and out for *more*: more love, more life, more experience, more self, more other, more God, more of what cannot be found without it. To live love and love life to the fullest, we need our lusts. They keep us alive and not just living, restless in ways that open us to possibility—to the "yes" of life as well as to the necessary "no." Desire, including sexual yearning, fills the inner spaces where soul, psyche, and body intersect, negotiate, quarrel, tease, play, and look for true love. Lust defies limits in imaginative ways that result in the never before envisioned. What happens with lust depends not on lust itself but on what the individual decides to do with it.

While lust is limitless and free, at least in fantasy, Dimen insists that it also and paradoxically is a reminder of loss, finiteness, and mortality, about what never can be as well as what can be touched.[29] When sexual desire is acted on and quenched, the sensations of pleasure subside and we see the walled perimeters of possibility and play in the moment and throughout our lives. We are reminded of temporality; we glimpse what never was and what may never be. When, on the other hand, lust is processed and sustained but not acted on, we also are exquisitely reminded of what we may not have if we wish to live with integrity. Psychoanalyst Jody Davies, quoted in Dimen, says:

We all have sexual desires on which we do not act—places in which such action would be inappropriate and wrong. As adults, we can desire without the promise of satisfaction; we can want without having to possess. Perhaps this is the true legacy of Oedipus—the capacity to sustain desire for what we can never have.[30]

A vital phrase in Davies' passage is "as adults." One task of parents and the symbolic parents found in seminaries, chanceries, parishes, and analysts' consultation rooms is to model healthy lust in work with children, the immature, and the broken. Adults must bear and negotiate with their lusts rather than banish them and must tolerate the grief inherent in both refused and satisfied sexual desire. Sexually abusing priests and their enabling superiors failed in that task.

The traditional Catholic approach to lust, including John Paul's, does not treat Catholics as adults who can know, be filled with, name, and express or restrain their lusts. And, although Pope John Paul II insisted that lust is a neon-lighted manifestation of a contemporary culture of death, a theology of sexuality that degrades lust generates its own culture of the living dead. For some people, the deadening self-seriousness of faux adulthood replaces the confidence, spontaneity, and humor about self that mark the mature adult lustily dancing with life. The sacred flames of possibility and poignancy—for self, other, and community—are snuffed out. As the Romans protecting the flames of the Vestal Virgins knew, disaster may well ensue when sacred fires are allowed to go cold. The disaster of the sexual abuse of minors by priests and its cover-up by bishops is a neon-lighted sign proclaiming, among other things, the failure of the Church's theology of sexual desire.

Sex in the City of God

Sexual desire encodes what you *want* to do; sexuality represents what you *do*. Catholic teachings on sexuality are easily summarized. Every thought, word, desire, or action outside heterosexual marriage, sanctified by a priest and always open to biological procreation, is gravely sinful. Inactive priest and psychologist Richard Sipe emphasizes the gravity of sexual sin as theologized by the Church: "Sexual misbehavior constitutes grave matter in every instance. No other area of moral life, including murder, is treated with the same moral rigidity."[31]

Until the papacy of John Paul II, Catholic sexual teachings were focused exclusively on *acts*. The imagined or enacted sexual act itself, rather than the relational context in which that act was fantasized or took place, constituted holy or sinful sex. It was only when a man's penis filled his wife's vagina, and the possibility of conception was not frustrated, that sex could be considered spiritually sound.

While it was encouraging that John Paul expanded the Church's perspective on sexual union to include real persons and not just body parts, the bottom line on acceptable sexual activity remained essentially unchanged and grounded in potentially procreative acts between a man and a woman in a marriage sacramentally endorsed by the Church. Even those sexual unions were confined within a limited repertoire of behaviors. Married couples sinned, for instance, if any of their sexual encounters focused only on oral sex or mutual masturbation since those acts are not open to conception.

Contracepted genital sex, of course, is banned. Christopher West summarized John Paul's emphasis on the sinfulness of contracepted sex:

> As John Paul affirms, the spouses' dignity cannot be divorced from their potential to be parents. . . . In contracepted sex, the language of the body is akin to blasphemy. It speaks not the symbolic word but the diabolic word. . . . Contraception is to be judged so profoundly unlawful as never to be, for any reason, justified. To think or to say the contrary is equal to maintaining that in human life, situations may arise in which it is not lawful to recognize God as God.[32]

Catholic couples wishing to limit the size of their families are allowed to do so only through total sexual abstention or abstention during the fertile days of a woman's monthly cycle.

The Church's singular focus on proceation, interpreted in the most concrete biological terms, fostered a theology of sexuality that is internally consistent but impervious to most twentieth- and twenty-first-century findings about human sexuality generated by biology, epidemiology, anthropology, psychology, philosophy, some theology, and most human experience. It leads inexorably to blanket, and I will argue unethical, prohibitions against artificial birth control, abortion, the use of condoms to prevent the spread of AIDS, and same-gender sexual unions. Further, as the twentieth century progressed, increasing numbers of lay Catholics and priests diverged privately, and sometimes publicly, from their Church's teachings on sex. Although the Church decries this dissent as embedded in cultural decadence and narcissism, the historical and scientific factors actually at work comprise some of the data the Church refuses to integrate into its theology of sexuality.

Contemporary society has learned that sex, in most cases, is not just an act but is an expression—for good or ill—of the relational context in which it occurs. No matter what the sexual *act* is, the meaning of it, the motivations for doing it, and the degree to which it is symbolically procreative vary greatly across coupling individuals and within couples across time. Depending on the day and the status of a relationship, sex can be about reproduction, recapturing romance, playing or playacting, comforting friendship, humiliation and degradation, lifeless going along to get along, giving, getting, dominance, submission, negotiation, reparation, love, hate, or love and hate dancing together under the sheets. Or, as Muriel Dimen states, "Any sexuality may be symptomatic—or healthy."[33] I would add that any expression of sexuality can be transgressive of another's dignity or spiritually sound, it can be impressively procreative although no egg is fertilized or dangerous and anti-life even when a child issues forth nine months later. Within the Church's theology of sexuality, however, there is room for little variety and not much spice. Garry Wills says of it: "In sex, you see, it is all or nothing. Unless the act expresses all values possible to it all the time, it is immoral. It would be hard to find a parallel in the moral world for this principle."[34] Wills here refers to the Catholic proscription against all sex that is not open to biological procreation and that takes place outside a sacramental marriage between a man and a woman.

Long before the "sexual revolution" and "women's revolution" of the late 1960s and early 1970s, historical events cited by the official Church as partially causal in the Church crisis, American Catholics and many of their priests tacitly agreed that Catholics, at least heterosexual married Catholics, could remain in good standing with the Church while living out a sex life that reframed the Church's teachings on procreation in metaphoric rather than concrete terms. Thoughtful, pastoral priests evaluated their parishioners' sexual activities in terms of the relational qualities and exigencies of life within which the activities took place. These priests counseled family kindness and mutual love and respect rather than upholding rigid rules.

Lay Catholics and priests alike expected that Vatican II and the deliberations of a fifty-eight-member commission appointed to study the birth control issue would result in an end to the ban on artificial contraception. Instead, Pope Paul VI (1963–1978), negating the majority report of his own commission, issued the 1968 encyclical *Humanae Vitae*, which reaffirmed the Church's birth control prohibitions. Garry Wills asserts that *Humanae Vitae* was based on a minority report from the commission that emphasized the need for continuity in Church teachings.[35] The teaching could not change because it had been the teaching for so long, and, if it changed, the Church would have to acknowledge that it had been in error about the teaching, and how would they explain what had happened to all the souls supposedly in hell for using artificial birth control?[36]

While the continuity-of-teaching argument might have contributed significantly to the pope's thinking, it is also true that over the centuries the Church changed other long-standing teachings like those about slavery, usury, the earth's relationship to the sun, the use of the vernacular during Mass, and the theory that unbaptized babies went to limbo rather than heaven if they died. What seems to have differentiated the birth control debate from other changes in doctrine wrought by Vatican II were the accompanying implications for power relationships within the Church. What was different about birth control?

Had Pope Paul VI lifted the ban on artificial birth control, there also would have been an implicit decentralization of power within the institutional Church. Once sex was disconnected from procreation, individual Catholics and individual priests would have to be trusted to work separately and together to evaluate the spiritual soundness of the sex lives of Catholics. Power and authority regarding sexual matters necessarily would become democratized with influence and wisdom moving up from the laity as well as downward from the hierarchy. The very reversal of the prohibition against artificial contraception, in fact, would signal the ability of lay Catholics and even women to affect Church doctrine since the commission considering the issue had been staffed with thirty-four laypeople, including five women.[37] Bishop John Heaps advocates such a shared sexual authority and argues that a contextualized rather than legalistic approach to sex derives directly from the teachings of Jesus:

> With regard to the law, Jesus did not observe any law which contradicted love. The Pharisees and lawyers spoke of cases in law, but Jesus responded in terms of persons, loved by God and deserving of the respect which that love implied. . . . In a personal, intimate Church, we can have the same attitude. We would not be dealing with cases, but with friends whose qualities we would know. As those in community speak to people and know them, they are no longer cases to which unchangeable principles are applied as though no person existed, but they are human beings with responsibilities to each other and to the community.[38]

It apparently was not conceivable, however, that Pope Paul VI and the Roman Curia would allow centralized power to dissipate on an issue long considered vital to the economy of sin and grace. Rather than share power with the laity and lower clergy, Paul tried instead to maintain kyriarchal power. His refusal to follow the recommendations of the majority of his advisors, however, constituted a misuse of papal authority; within five years of the promulgation of *Humanae Vitae*, 60 percent of American priests disagreed with its position on birth control.[39] By 2002, only 27 percent of American priests and 12 percent of the laity believed that birth control is always wrong.[40]

Humanae Vitae has been likened to the Church's Vietnam War.[41] The Vatican put its moral authority on the line by rebuking science, psychology, human experience, and the recommendations of its own counselors. Catholics worldwide responded with wholesale rejection of *Humanae Vitae* and therefore of the Church's authority to instruct them about other aspects of life considered central to the institutional Church. Catholics increasingly refused to accept the Church's authority over their sex lives; the Church refused to be moved by the voices of its people. As the American government did in Vietnam, the hierarchy of the Church clung to an essentially corrupt position and, in the process, lost the hearts and minds of its people, not only about the contraception issue, but about the Church's trustworthiness to teach Catholics how to lead spiritually sound lives, especially in the realm of moral sexuality. Catholic commentator Peter Steinfels points out that while the United States eventually got out of Vietnam, the papacy of John Paul II tried even more strongly to emphasize the centrality of *Humanae Vitae* in the life of the Church.[42]

Astonishingly, at the November 2003 meeting of the United States Conference of Catholic Bishops—only the third meeting since 2002, when the group had for the first time focused exclusively on the sexual abuse scandal, which was still raging in 2003—the American bishops voted to oppose homosexual unions publicly and to develop a booklet instructing the laity about the Church's position on artificial contraception, linking it to abortion.[43] Given the impact of the sexual abuse of minors by priests and the cover-up of those crimes by many of the bishops attending the conference, it was incomprehensible to most observers that the bishops thought they should spend their time developing new brochures on artificial contraception. Their desire to reassert themselves as moral instructors apparently was sufficiently overwhelming that good judgment and a wise sense of priorities eluded them. Instead of continuing to examine themselves and each other in terms of their commitment to protect children and respond pastorally to victims/survivors, the Catholic hierarchy tried to get back to business as usual, with "usual" being to focus on the sexual sins of the faithful rather than on their own sexual harmfulness.

The Ethics of Catholic Sexual Teachings

The pope, most Vatican officials, many bishops, and some conservative commentators within the Church cited external factors operating in a contemporary, sex-obsessed, morally relativistic culture of death as the etiology of the divergence of lay Catholics and many clergy from Church teachings about sex. Further, they suggested that the sexual abuse crisis had its roots in lay and clerical disobedience to those teachings. There are, however, alternative perspectives linking official Catholic sexual theology and the sex abuse scandal. One is that the Church's sexual teachings are inherently unethical and that priests and bishops lost their moral compass when confronted by the criminally unethical sexual abuse of minors and its cover-up.

Vanderbilt University professor and community psychologist Paul Dokecki casts the Catholic sexual abuse scandal in the context of gross violations of professional ethics.[44] Ethics can be examined from many viewpoints and Dokecki's is just one. Since he focuses particularly on the ethical lapses inherent in the Catholic sexual abuse crisis, however, it is useful to extend his paradigm into a discussion of the ethics of the sexual theology on which the sexual abuse scandal rests.

Dokecki roots professional ethics in a larger ethic of human development and community: "Ethical practices or policies: . . . ought to enhance the human development of persons (their growth and wellness) and to promote community and thereby the common good."[45] Ethical practices depend on principles of "caring; telling the truth; treating persons as persons, not things, and respecting their autonomy; doing no harm, doing good; and being just."[46]

Caring, in this configuration of ethics, connotes promoting growth and development in individuals and community.[47] It requires that professionals, including popes, bishops, and priests, establish empathic relationships with others in their care through which each person's experience can be grasped—not just intellectually but emotionally and spiritually—from *within* that person's life.[48] Caring also entails promoting self-determination through mutually respectful and influential relationships with others, rather than through one person's conformity with or obedience to another.[49] Here, Docecki emphasizes invitation and surrender over the kind of dominance and submission often marking relationships within the Church. Dokecki claims that caring by the institutional Church has been more absent than not in its response to the sexual abuse crisis. I suggest that this is not surprising if the sexual abuse of minors and its cover-up rests on a theology of sexuality that is itself uncaring.

Popes Paul VI, John Paul II, and now Benedict XVI refused to enter empathically into the life experiences of Catholics to discern the wisdom, ethical care, and grace woven through the approaches of these men and women to sexuality and love. Instead, the official Church, through these popes, spurned the life experiences of millions of men and women in order to preserve a moribund theology of sexuality that the vast majority of their people respond to as uncaring and of little value in helping them to grow as individuals, partners, parents, or Christians. Far from encouraging relationally based self-determination and surrender, Catholic sexual theology requires submission to tenets formulated by celibate men and received as untenable the world over.

Dokecki's second ethical principle is to tell the truth, and he discusses how little truth telling occurred within the Church regarding the sexual abuse of minors.[50] Again, however, the sexual abuse scandal is but one manifestation of a theology of sexuality that negates many truths about human sexuality. The Church's stonewalling against incorporation of much philosophical, psychological, historical, sociological, anthropological, and biological data into its theology, coupled with its rejection of the recommendations of its own commission on birth control, render the theology of sexuality full of half-truths. When a theology so privileged within the institutional Church is based only on partial truths, other untruths flow effortlessly from those supporting the larger lie. It was, in part, the comfort and familiarity of Church officials with compromised truths about sex that allowed cardinals and bishops to transfer abusing priests from parish to parish or to punish priests who complained about abusive brethren. The latter dynamic, in which whistle-blowing priests were poorly treated while their abusive colleagues remained in ministry, particularly highlighted the degree to which truth telling was experienced as threatening to Church officials. Once truth begins to emerge, it is difficult to keep it under wraps or to limit it to one area of institutional functioning. So Vatican officials and bishops, seemingly shamelessly, told more untruths to explain away the sexual abuse crisis, like blaming the media for the crisis, understating the number of victims and perpetrators, and pretending it was an American problem only.

The third ethical principle espoused by Dokecki is treating persons as persons, not things.[51] Despite John Paul II's insistence that his theology of the body was based on preventing objectification of sexual partners by one another, he, like his predecessors, in fact objectified *all* sexual beings by assuming that he knew what is best for every one of them all of the time, regardless of data to the contrary. By dismissing Catholic dissent from Catholic sexual theology as always embedded in self-centered refusal to take up the cross with Jesus, the pope appeared to devalue the unique lives of individuals, couples, and communities.

It is not difficult to see how this theological approach to sexuality resulted in the degradation of individual victims and families who reported abuse or sought redress from the Church. For a very long time, they were not viewed as unique, suffering individuals but rather were objectified as threats to the good name of the Church and may even have been regarded with suspicion as having deviated from Catholic sexual norms. This objectification of sexual beings also encouraged bishops to treat all abusing priests in the same way, first by returning them to ministry again and again and, then, by applying the zero tolerance removal from ministry regardless of the unique circumstances of each priest. Throughout the crisis, then, and within the realm of sexuality in general, Catholics were theologized as objects of doctrine, not subjects of their own spirituality and sexuality.

Finally, Dokecki asserts that professional ethics demand a resolve to do no harm, to do good, and to exercise justice.[52] Clearly, the institutional Church and individual priests, bishops, and provincial superiors inflicted harm and voluntarily rendered little justice to thousands of sexual abuse victims, their families, abusing and decent priests, and the wider Catholic community. In effecting its theology of sexuality, moreover, the Church denies justice and fails to prevent harm in too many instances.

Insight into the seamlessness of the sexual abuse crisis with other aspects of the Church's sexual attitudes is gained by examining the potential impact of the theology of sexuality on Africans suffering from HIV and AIDS. The Catholic Church insists that the only theologically sound way to avoid contracting the HIV virus is to abstain from sexual relations. The Church refuses to endorse the use of condoms, the second-best defense (after abstention) against the communication of HIV. Alfonso Lopez Cardinal Trujillo, president of the Vatican Pontifical Council for the Family, shocked the world's scientific and medical community when he misrepresented the efficacy of condoms in preventing the spread of AIDS, saying, "[T]he spermatozoa can easily pass through the 'net' that is formed by the condom."[53] (UNAIDS and the National Institutes of Health conclude respectively that consistent and correct condom use reduces the risk of HIV by 90 percent and that condoms are "essentially impermeable" to even the smallest sexually transmitted viruses.)[54] Priests and bishops who, following these official teachings, counsel African Catholics against the use of condoms, potentially do harm. The flip side of the harm done is the passively homicidal and unethical refusal to do good. The World Health Organization, for example, rebuked the Vatican for Trujillo's remarks, asserting, "These incorrect statements about condoms and HIV are dangerous when we are facing a global pandemic, which has already killed more than twenty million people."[55]

When the Catholic Church insists that it is more sinful to use condoms in the midst of a sexually transmitted epidemic than it is for the same Church to withhold approbation of the use of condoms, it is less surprising that the sexual abuse of minors was handled unethically.

The theology of sexuality has been a key spoke of the Catholic theological wheel for centuries. No matter how much attention is directed to solving the "sexual abuse crisis," it does not seem likely that the Church can reestablish moral authority unless the pope and other officials develop an ethical theology of sexuality. Or as Tom Fox, former *National Catholic Reporter* publisher, asks, "Are we ready to baptize the erotic in our lives? Are we capable of cultivating and sharing the male and female in each of us? Can we see our endless and seemingly uncontrollable desires for intimacy and physical union as mere foreplay to total union, male and female, in God?"[56]

CHAPTER 6

Celibate Sexuality and Sexually Active "Celibates"

Many commentators on the scandal focused on mandatory celibacy as a cause of the crisis. Some felt that required celibacy contributed to the sexual abuse of minors by narrowing the field of candidates for the priesthood to an already unusual slice of men—those willing at least to try to refrain from sex for a lifetime.[1] Others insisted that it was not celibacy itself but, rather, lapses of celibacy, tolerated by superiors and fellow priests, that supported the sexual abuse of minors.[2] What became evident is that some number of clergy worldwide live active sexual lives while other priests and prelates—some of them sexually active as well—turn a blind eye to the chasm between celibacy as mandated and celibacy as lived.[3] It is the secrecy and hypocrisy about celibacy that supported other sexual secrets like the abuse of minors by priests.

History of Celibacy

Rev. Thomas Doyle defines celibacy as proscribing "not only marriage but also any kind of romantic or sexual relationship or sexual contact with any other person in any degree."[4] Despite its centrality in official views of the priesthood, mandatory celibacy is a relative newcomer to Catholic discipline.[5] The Apostles were married, including Peter, and priests and bishops continued to marry throughout the first millennium of Christianity. St. Paul even emphasized that it was an apostolic prerogative for Christ's disciples to marry, and he refused to impose celibacy on priests, even though he thought it preferable to marriage.[6] In fact, it was not until the Second Lateran Council in 1139 that celibacy was declared mandatory for Catholic priests.[7] This twelfth-century decision symbolized the culmination of strong sociopolitical concerns within the Church involving perceptions of priestly spirituality and, according to Richard Sipe, progeny, property, and power.[8]

As Christianity developed over its first thousand years, substantial numbers of men and women experienced themselves as called to a freely chosen life of perpetual chastity. These were the early ascetics who were revered by many Christians for their perceived spiritual wisdom and healing powers.[9] Further, the assumed correlation between virginity and spiritual power was common in the pagan society surrounding Christianity, where sex, women, and the material body were devalued as impurities interfering with an individual's spiritual enhancement.[10]

By the fourth century, the height of the ascetics' popularity, purity rituals were imposed on the priesthood in part to render it more spiritually powerful in the minds of the Christian populace—to bring the priesthood into closer alliance with the ascetics.[11] Priests, for example, were instructed to abstain from sex for at least twenty-four hours before consecrating the Eucharist so that they would be free from the contamination connected with sexual relations with a woman.[12]

As celebration of the Eucharist became more frequent in Christian communities, priests were required to refrain from sex for longer periods of time.[13] Eventually, they were directed to abstain entirely, even if they were married. The purity impositions were unpopular and many priests failed to comply with them. Up until the twelfth century, in fact, popes, bishops, and priests married and/or produced offspring who, in some cases, inherited their fathers' offices. For example, Pope Anastasius I (399–401) was succeeded by his son, Pope Innocent I (407–417), and Pope Hormisdas (514–523) was followed in the papacy by his son Pope Silverius (536–537).[14] Pope Sergius III (904–911) bore an illegitimate son who became Pope John XI.[15]

Inherited priesthood or bishoprics left the Church vulnerable to the corruption or incompetence of heirs. Further, children required support, depleting the potential coffers of the Church and offering additional opportunities for financial mismanagement. Mandatory celibacy promised childless bachelors whose offices remained in the hands of the Church.

Closely related to progeny was the issue of property. Married men might own property that was passed on to widows and children rather than to the Church when a priest or bishop died. Obligatory celibacy ensured that property was retained in perpetuity by the Church. This focus on property did not simply represent a lust for additional wealth but also solidified the continuity of parishes, monasteries, and abbeys. Property ownership provided the Church at least a modicum of protection from the vagaries of history, politics, and the relative financial or pastoral competence of its priests.

Finally, mandatory celibacy enhanced the power of an increasingly centralized Church. Priests sworn to perpetual chastity became more materially and emotionally dependent on the Church, the primary source of all their physical, psychological, and spiritual succor. Indeed, mandatory celibacy created, for centuries, legions of priests and bishops who were available to serve their parishes and dioceses twenty-four hours a day. A priest on a given day could celebrate early morning Mass, participate in a funeral, pay parish bills, pray his breviary at the appointed hours, work on his Sunday sermon, attend a late afternoon Catholic Youth Organization basketball game, preside over an evening novena (nine days of prayer) service, and roll out of bed at 2:00 A.M. to administer the last rites to a dying parishioner. In addition, when priests were plentiful and rectories full, priests could count on a certain amount of camaraderie and conversation with fellow priests, somewhat assuaging the loneliness associated with celibate lives.

It is important to note that even the harshest critics of mandatory celibacy acknowledge the potential grace and fulfillment attainable through a life of elective celibacy. For those who are truly called to that life, celibacy offers what is experienced as a graced opportunity to live in the image of Christ. Richard Sipe, a critic of obligatory celibacy, describes the truly celibate priest as transcendent, even mystic. He says: "The awareness of the transcendent in themselves and others, past and future, come together in them and their work. . . . They have a spiritual transparency—they indeed are what they seem to be. . . . These men point to 'life beyond' and to values not yet achieved. They are what they set out to be: men of God."[16]

For the true celibate, chastity is not an accoutrement of the priesthood, worn externally with more or less comfort and regularity, but is an essence of the priest's being. Even if this man struggles during his lifetime to achieve and preserve perpetually celibate behavior, he *is* a celibate. Celibacy here is an invitation and a gift from God, not a requirement of the Church, and the true celibate is a gift to his Church and its people.

Theology of Celibacy

A theology of celibacy gradually was constructed to support what originally seems to have been a pragmatically and sociopolitically motivated discipline. Once obligatory celibacy was theologized and institutionalized as a requirement for the priesthood, it was also idealized as spiritually superior to marriage. Thomas Fox reports that the Council of Trent (1545–1563) asserted, "If anyone says that it is not better and more godly to live in virginity or in an unmarried state than to marry, let him be anathema," that is, cut off from the Church.[17] Eugene Kennedy points out that when men left the priesthood to be married, the Church referred to them as "reduced" to the lay state, suggesting a status demotion rather than a lateral move.[18] Still today, the documents granting laicization to a petitioning priest wishing to marry direct the man to locate with his wife to a new parish where his "previous condition" is not known.[19]

Vatican II and, more recently, Pope John Paul II attempted to develop greater equivalency between marriage and celibacy but continued the idealization of celibacy as a superior state. In his exegesis of John Paul's theology of the body, Christopher West states:

> John Paul points out that if marriage "is fully appropriate and of a value that is fundamental, universal, and ordinary," then it makes sense that continence for the Kingdom "possesses a particular and exceptional value." . . . Marriage certainly has great value as an earthly sacrament of the eternal communion of heaven on earth. Because it anticipates the eschatological [*referring to the ultimate destiny of humankind*] reality, it [celibacy] *is* "heaven on earth."[20]

Previously, I noted that idealization tends to represent a psychological defense against conscious awareness of more negative feelings and perceptions. Conversely, devaluation often defends against conscious recognition of envy and desire for what one cannot have. Devaluation, in other words, frequently is an unconscious reaction: "I can't have it, so it can't be much good anyway."

Sexually Active "Celibates"

Some priests who are faithful celibates believe that few other priests are sexually active and claim to know none themselves. It is likely that these priests attract as friends and confidantes other priests who also keep their celibacy promise. In addition, faithful priests may not recognize or assign appropriate meaning to signs of sexual misconduct among their peers, superiors, or charges because their perceptions are filtered through their personal experiences and expectations of celibate compliance. Finally, it is possible that some groupings of priests develop a culture in which active sexuality is more genuinely taboo than in other diocesan or religious communities. Still other priests, however, learn to maintain silence about sexually active brother priests because they fear, with good reason, that speaking the truth could alienate and marginalize them with both bishops and peers. When Christian Brother Barry Coldrey prepared a report for his order's superior general on sexual abuse and other violations of celibacy, he felt shunned by other members of his order: "It's fair to say I was marginalized—There was a lot of bitching and bickering about what I was doing."[21]

Despite the perceptions of these priests, there is evidence that throughout ten centuries of obligatory celibacy, substantial numbers of priests were sexually active. Many almost assuredly continue to be. In fact, in 1971, Franjo Cardinal Seper told a synod of bishops, "I am not at all optimistic that celibacy is being observed."[22] Inactive priest Paul Dinter comments, "I was never an eyewitness to misdeeds, but I knew more than I wanted to know about sexual acting out among priests."[23]

Some sexual exploits of priests with adults have been publicized. In a memoir published after his death, Rev. James Lex, who entered the seminary at fourteen years of age, related years of romantic relationships with women, one of which became sexual.[24] An Argentinian priest, Rev. Jose Mariani, wrote a similar memoir of his sexual relationships with women and one man.[25] He said he felt that Catholics needed to know about the sexuality of priests in order to understand more fully their clergy and the issues of celibacy. In 2005, a popular French priest, Abbe Pierre, published a book in which he talked about priests he knew who lived with common-law wives, and he acknowledged having broken his own promise of celibacy.[26] Abbe Pierre wrote, "I'm convinced the Church needs married priests and celibate priests who can devote themselves totally to prayer and to others."[27]

Richard Sipe conducted an ethnographic study of celibacy in the priesthood that spanned forty years (1960–2002) and included data on 2,776 active and resigned priests.[28] Sipe concluded that, at any given time, 50 percent of the priesthood is living out a commitment to celibacy; their intention is to become a celibate even if they experience occasional lapses along the way.[29] Another 28 percent of priests are sexually active with adult women; 11 percent are homosexually active with adult men; and 5 percent engage in other sexual pursuits like cross-dressing, pornography, masturbation, or exhibitionism.[30] Sipe estimated that the remaining 6 percent are sexually active with minors, a percentage consistent with the results of the John Jay Study of abusive priests between 1950 and 2002.

Some commentators disagree with Sipe's numbers. Priest and sociologist Andrew Greeley is most critical. Using data from two *Los Angeles Times* surveys of about 2,000 active priests, Greeley estimates that 82 percent of priests honor their promise of celibacy.[31] Somewhat similarly, sociologists Dean Hoge and Jacqueline Wenger found in a 2001 survey of over 1,200 priests that only 11 percent of active priests cited celibacy as a serious problem for them.[32] In another survey of priests who had been ordained less than five years, however, Hoge found a clear difference between active and resigned priests.[33] While only 30 percent of resigned priests had been satisfied living celibately, 87 percent of active diocesan priests and 74 percent of active religious priests reported satisfaction with celibate life. This may suggest that celibacy is not problematic for a priest until it is and that, sometime after it becomes problematic, many priests for whom it is a problem resign, perhaps after a period of active sexuality.

Sipe's data are disadvantaged in being drawn from clinical samples of active and resigned priests in psychotherapy. In addition, some of his data are derived from third-party sources rather than a celibate or sexually active priest himself. On the other hand, Sipe collected his data over forty years. He was able to develop a sense of celibacy lived or not over many years. The *Los Angeles Times* survey (available at www.latimes.com), Hoge's, and Hoge and Wenger's research all asked respondents about their relationship with celibacy at the time of the survey. None of these polls asked specifically about a priest's current or past sexual activity. It is conceivable, therefore, that a priest could report not having a problem with celibacy because he no longer lived it. Of particular note is that 55 percent of respondents to the 2002 *Los Angeles Times* poll and 54 percent of those who responded to Hoge and Wenger's poll were over sixty years old. It is possible that most of these men had arrived at a stage of life at which they had come to some peace with their relationship to celibacy. In fact, in the *Los Angeles Times* survey, 43 percent of priests over forty asserted that celibacy was not a problem and that they did not waver from their promises, while only 22 percent of priests twenty-two to forty years old endorsed that statement. Twenty-one percent of that age group acknowledged that celibacy was neither relevant nor observed within their priesthoods. For all these reasons, this book uses Sipe's numbers on celibacy.

Sipe's work indicates that celibacy remains experientially optional for many priests. Officials, however, deny or minimize that reality while paying lip service to the centrality of celibacy in the Catholic priesthood. Even when there is some acknowledgment of the activity itself, the meaning of the sex—for the Church, for the priest's brethren, for his parish or ministerial community and, especially, for his partner(s)—is kept at bay. Rather than open discussion, analysis, and confrontation of the paradox inherent in sexually active sworn celibates, secrecy and denial prevail. The same paradigm characterized the sexual abuse of minors.

Sexual activity in the priesthood extends both vertically through the hierarchy of the Church and horizontally throughout each of those ranks. Nine American bishops who led dioceses have resigned since 1990 amid allegations of sexual misconduct. In 1990, for example, Archbishop Eugene Marino of Atlanta was forced to resign after he was found appropriating Church funds to support his mistress with whom he had traveled openly for over a year.[34] It is notable that the pilfering was responded to with greater urgency than was the archbishop's affair.[35] Likewise, the sexual abuse of minors by priests was seriously addressed by the official Church only when victims/survivors began to sue for damages.

Priests and bishops whose sexual behaviors are known but unspoken in their communities are vulnerable to overt or covert blackmail by other clergy, including child molesters. Br. Barry Coldrey is quoted by Jason Berry and Gerald Renner as saying: "[Those] who abuse minors and commit criminal offenses have been able to hide within a sympathetic underworld of other clergy and Church workers who are merely breaking their vows by having heterosexual or gay sex with consenting adults. . . . They share an unstated capacity for mutual blackmail."[36]

Even without an amorphous threat of blackmail hovering over them, priests and bishops hiding their own shameful sexual secrets undoubtedly experience conflict about confronting, exposing, or appropriately censoring priests who abused minors. In a culture in which *all* sex is "bad" sex because it transgresses the promise of lifelong celibacy, moral distinctions between categories of "bad" sex may have become blunted by priests and prelates who had their own "bad" sexual histories. Potentially lacking both the moral sensibility to fully appreciate the criminality and consequences of sexual abuse of minors and the moral authority to confront abusing priests forcefully, the priesthood, including the hierarchy, turned the same blind eyes to sexual abuse that they did to other forms of active sexuality among their brethren.

Heterosexual Activity in the Priesthood

In this chapter, only heterosexual activity by priests and its influence on the sexual abuse crisis will be addressed. Sexually active homosexual priests are discussed in the following chapter on the broader issue of homosexuality in Roman Catholicism.

Richard Sipe estimates that, at any point in time, 28 percent of priests are involved in heterosexual activity with adult women; two-thirds of them are in stable relationships or in stable patterns of sequential relationships, one-third of them in experimental or exploratory encounters devoid of relational commitment.[37]

Some priests may feel that their ministerial work is enhanced by their involvement in a relationship infused with love and continuity. Thomas Merton, a revered monk and spiritual writer, engaged in a short-lived but passionate and loving relationship with a younger woman and wrote about it in his journals.[38] Merton believed that his relationship with "M" was a God-given blessing that changed him forever and brought him closer to God. Rev. Donald Cozzens quotes Merton: "I do not regret at all my love for her and am convinced it was a true gift from God and has been an inestimable help to me. . . . There is a certain fullness in my life now, even without her. Something that was never there before."[39]

Certainly, a long-term or deeply felt love relationship may open a man's soul and even allow him to continue as a more effective priest or to remain in a priesthood he might otherwise leave from loneliness. Unfortunately, however, even these warm and consensual relationships are embedded in dishonesty and secrecy. That alone deprives both the couple and the priest's community of relational integrity and, in the end, detracts from the potential fullness of both relationships. In addition, there is often a disregard for the impact on the woman after the priest ends the affair and returns to his former life or seeks a new partner. "M," for example, never spoke of her side of her time with Merton, but Cozzens perceptively wonders "whether the relationship was ultimately a graced experience for 'M,' who was thirty years Merton's junior and engaged to be married at the time of the affair."[40] Sipe picks up that theme:

> Even saints who opted for celibacy after they sowed their wild oats— Ignatius and a myriad of others—leave no bold trace of gratitude to their former partners or a sense of the injustice done by their use of women. They lamented *their* sins, but have left no history of model for reparation to the woman involved in their development.[41]

The disconnect between the experience for the priest and the effect on the sexual "partner" was also a hallmark of the sexual abuse scandal.

Except in situations of long-term, mutual commitment, women involved with priests are always vulnerable to abandonment if the priest is transferred or decides to resume a celibate existence. Seldom does the priest or his Church show much empathy for the jilted woman, often perceiving her as a temptress who led the priest astray in the first place. Sipe puts it this way: "What about the woman? The unspoken explanation within the system persists that: (1) she is to blame for the priest's dalliance; (2) she should be grateful and silent for the privilege of such selection or closeness; (3) it is part of the special grace and gift of a woman to be able to save a priest by her love."[42]

While it is true that an adult woman entering into a consensual relationship with a priest should be aware of the emotional perils involved, it is also true that she deserves comfort and recognition of her loss if the affair is ended by the priest. Instead, the institutional lack of empathy for the voluntary lovers of priests became part of the Church's response pattern to any sexual partner of a clergyman, even if the "partner" was a child or adolescent who was violated by the priest.

When a priest enters a sexual relationship with a parishioner or employee (often the same), the power differential inherent in the relationship represents an ethical violation of the priest's fiduciary obligations as well as a breach of his celibacy. As the sexual abuse scandal burgeoned, numerous adult women came forward to report sexual experiences with priests who were pastors, spiritual directors, pastoral counselors, or employers. In 2003, for example, the Archdiocese of Boston held records of forty-one priests who had been accused of sexual misconduct with women, many of them likely to have been parishioners.[43]

In another instance, a New York judge ordered the Diocese of Brooklyn to reinstate Barbara Samide, a Catholic school principal, who had been placed on leave after she reported to the diocese that Rev. John Thompson, pastor of her school's parish, sexually and physically assaulted her.[44] Samide also told the diocese and the Queens District Attorney that Thompson had embezzled funds from the parish. Thompson admitted stealing $95,940 from the Church but denied the assault charges. New York Supreme Court Justice Duane Alphonse Hart was quoted as saying: "The way I am following the facts . . . after she turned Fr. Thompson in to either the Diocese of Brooklyn or the District Attorney, her services were no longer needed by the diocese." Here, breaking silence and making public a priest's alleged sexual and financial crimes were deemed by the judge to have incurred punishment, rather than gratitude and reparation, from a Catholic diocese. During the sexual abuse crisis, Church officials often responded with the same ire to victims/survivors or their family members who spoke up to report the abuse of a minor.

In San Antonio, the diocese awarded $300,000 to Julia Villegas Phelps, who alleged that her pastor, Rev. Michael Kenny, had forced her to have intercourse in front of her two sons during their two-year affair.[45] Kenny acknowledged that he had sex with Phelps, as well as with other women, and admitted to fathering two children. Kenny also alleged that he divulged his sexual activity to at least six other priests. After the settlement, Archbishop Patrick Flores announced that Ms. Phelps's sins were as damaging to her faith as Kenny's were. While that may be true in some theological way, Flores's comments suggest little compassion for a young woman in a relationship with an enormous power differential built in. Nor do they at all address the pain, overstimulation, and confusion the two boys experienced if indeed they were exposed to their pastor engaging sexually with their mother.

Because Catholic priests until the late 1980s received little or no training in sexuality—their own or anyone else's—they had no template for appreciating the idealized, eroticized transferences the priesthood often evokes in women (and children, especially adolescents). In psychoanalysis, transference connotes the human tendency to experience feelings, fantasies, and expectations about another person that are not really reflective of the current relationship but rather bespeak relational strivings formed in earlier relationships. Oftentimes, the intensity of the transference reactions is related to the level of anonymity of the other person—the more anonymous, the more intensely felt.

As a representative of the Divine, the priest unconsciously draws erotically tinged yearnings for intimate, even sexual, communion with the Divine. If he is not aware of the erotic power of his status, he easily can mistake flirtations and sexual attractions for "the real thing." Rev. Ann Richards, Episcopalian priest and former Canon for Ministry Development for the Episcopalian Diocese of New York, addresses this issue so well that it is worth quoting her at length:

> A priest—male or female, married or single, straight or gay—attracts sexual energy and generates sexual energy in a unique way. This aspect of being a priest is rarely discussed in the formation process or in the seminaries. A priest is a numinous figure, representing God in the religious tradition. . . . It is simply a fact that the concept of a priest holds great power. . . . The writings of the mystics in every religious tradition testify that spiritual energy and sexual energy are the same energy, and thus the priest is—by virtue of his or her vocation—a sexual icon. The priestly garb, the black clothing and white clerical collar, intensify the sexual mystique. Like the uniform of the firefighter or police officer, the collar invests the priest with an allure that has nothing to do with who he is as an individual. . . . [F]or lay persons, the collar represents a glamour that is for some extremely enticing. . . . Intensifying this aura of charged sexuality is that priests do not simply draw sexual energy toward them; rather, sexual energy flows between

lay persons and priests in a way that may never reach awareness. . . . If not handled respectfully, reflected on, and integrated, however, it can degenerate into sexual transgression. When sexual energy is handled wrongly, when the priest is not equipped to respect a layperson as "off limits" for him personally, he no longer functions to represent God. He acts as God.[46]

Richards refers to the abuse of power inherent in sexual engagement with a layperson, especially a person with whom the priest has a fiduciary relationship. For Catholic priests who are trained to believe that they are "other Christs," acting as God is not always a foreign idea and may generate additional erotic stimulation for both the priest and the woman. Further, for women who are disempowered in their life stations or in their primary relationships, sexual union with a priest may offer an illusory promise of status, a fantasied empowerment as consort of the Divine.

The Sexual Victimization of Nuns

The perversion of power inherent in sexual abuse also has been evident in the sexual victimization of religious women by priests. In a 1996 study of more than eleven hundred nuns from 123 different orders conducted by St. Louis University researchers, more than 6 percent of the women reported having had sexual liaisons with priests or vowed religious men.[47] The rape of some religious women serving in Africa by priests and bishops was publicized in late 1995.[48] Nuns were considered to be safe sexual partners for priests and prelates fearful of contracting AIDS from African natives.[49] Superiors of communities of religious women were asked to make their nuns available for sex with clergy; some young women aspiring to religious life had to submit to sex in order to obtain permission from priests to further their vocations; and nuns were impregnated by priests in substantial numbers—twenty-nine in one community alone.[50] Priests brought nuns and other women to abortion clinics to dispose of the fetuses they had conceived, and, in one case, a nun died during her abortion only to have the priest who impregnated her preside over her funeral Mass.[51] Although the Vatican claimed that priests raping nuns was confined to Africa, researchers noted the behavior in twenty-three countries, including the United States.[52]

Sex between priests and nuns, even if it is consensual, represents incest. Religious women and priests are members of the inner family of the Church and address each other in familial terms: "Sister," "Brother," and "Father." Their sexual unions not only break the promises or vows of chastity each made, but also symbolically violate the incest taboo. When sex is imposed by a priest on a nun, a woman who by status always is in a less powerful position than the priest, the incest morphs into incestuous abuse. Like so many victims of rape and sexual abuse, religious women have been loath to come forward with their stories of exploitation by priests, preferring to confront the issues internally and therapeutically.[53]

Silence and secrecy thus prevailed about sex between priests and nuns. It was one more category of shameful sexual secrets pressing against the moral integrity of the Church, enhancing the dynamics of incest, denial, and secrecy evident in the sexual abuse of minors.

Fathers, Not Dads

In Illinois, under questioning in a 1995 deposition that came to light in 2002, Joliet Bishop Joseph Imesch was asked about his decision to invite a priest into the diocese even though the man had been convicted and sentenced to six months in prison for sexually abusing an altar boy at a Michigan parish. Imesch had worked at the same parish and had known the priest before becoming Joliet's bishop. When the priest, Fr. Gary Berthiaume, arrived in Illinois, Imesch assigned him to a busy parish with lots of children. "If you had a child," the lawyer recalled asking Imesch, "wouldn't you be concerned that the priest they were saying Mass with had been convicted of sexually molesting children?" "I don't have any children," Imesch replied.[54]

Paradigms of Fatherhood

One aspect of the sexual abuse of a minor is its inherent corruption of the parental role symbolically embedded in any relationship between a child and an adult who has authority over that youth. Incestuous abuse by a father is particularly heinous because it perverts the essential caretaking responsibilities of parenthood and the trust that children place in parental figures. Sexual abuse by a priest *is* incest; it is a betrayal of the paternal authority assumed by priests and bishops and invested in them by the laity. Sexual abuse and its cover-up perhaps were fueled, in part, by emotions and attitudes associated with the paradoxical demands on Catholic clergy to be fathers to communities of faithful while at the same time being proscribed from experiencing parenthood within a nuclear family. To that extent, priests have been expected to be fathers to all and dads to none.

Catholic priests are called "Father" and are the symbolic patriarchs of their parishioners' families. Especially during what Eugene Kennedy calls the "Brick and Mortar" phase of American Catholicism (roughly the late 1800s to the late 1960s), children and adults alike looked to their priest for the moral and spiritual guidance traditionally associated with paternal roles within a family.[55] Especially salient was the priest's position as the living icon of the Law—the Law of God, the Law of the Fathers. As representative of the Law, the priest served as an embodied reminder that Catholics in his care were to regulate their actions to conform to the cultural demands of their faith.

There are psychological constructions of this regulatory aspect of parenting, especially as it applies to fathers. Freud, for example, credited the father as the major influence in the development of the child's super-ego, the seat of conscience and ideals.[56] Inherent in the Freudian perspective is the father's responsibility and authority to represent the demands and traditions of the culture into which the child is born. The Freudian father also warns his children about the consequences stemming from failure to conform to the cultural demands he carries into the family. The grating adage, "Just wait until your father comes home!" captures the image of father as Law that was stereotypically played out in many families, especially those of the "Brick and Mortar" era.

This view of father cast him as a potential wedge between an endlessly nurturing mother and a child yearning for freely given feedings. Within families, it was the father who ensured that the child gradually was trained to earn access to mother's goodness and generosity by conforming to the rules of the family and the culture. Although many past families were never perfectly congruent with this stereotype and although the configuration of a substantial number of contemporary families has changed dramatically, the role of the father as transmitter of the Law prevails in the unconscious of human beings and in the systemic patterns families put into operation to regulate themselves.

Certainly, pre–Vatican II views of the function of priests were consistent with these perspectives of the father as guardian and conveyer of laws, morals, ideals, and values. No matter how paternal a priestly Father might be, it was he who heard a parishioner's confession and meted out the penance befitting the sins. In that role, a priest controlled a Catholic's ability to partake of the nourishment of Holy Communion, the sacramental meal lovingly provided by Holy Mother Church but served by Fathers. Since a Catholic had to be in a state of grace, with all sins confessed and forgiven, to receive the Eucharist, the priest stood between the supplicating parishioner hungry for sacramental food and the table laden with mother's nurturing meal. Further, through his reading of and commentary on the Gospels—the Word of God—at Mass, the priest taught the children of the

Church the laws and cultural mores of Catholicism. He represented the love and forgiveness of the Divine as well as the punishment and deprivation experienced by those who strayed too far from cultural mandates.

Over the last decade or so, social scientists have recognized that fatherhood can be described in other terms. Calvin Colarusso, a psychiatrist studying the experience of fathering, postulates that a man's identity begins to change with the impregnation of a woman.[57] Through that act, the man is confirmed in his anatomical and procreative adequacy; he is assured that his sexual equipment functions as intended and, in that process, transits more completely into a generative adulthood. After the birth of his child, the father, through cocreating with his spouse and child an intergenerational family, experiences himself more as an adult father and less as a child and son of his own father. When things go well, vestiges of adolescence are transformed as the father cares for his partner and child.

Particularly emphasized in contemporary views of male development is the importance of the father's ability to provide what psychoanalyst Michael Diamond calls "watchful protectiveness" over his child and its mother.[58] In this role, the father mediates between the external world and the mother-child pair, freeing the mother to engross herself in her baby's care, especially right after birth. In so doing, the man relinquishes remaining claims to more adolescent notions of limitless freedom and narcissistic omnipotence—a macho sense that he can do anything. Rather, Diamond says, "the selfless generosity, sacrifice, and servitude required by such early forms of fathering strengthen a man's sense of 'real manhood,'" in part because the new father fulfills at that point cultural definitions of men as providers for women and children.[59] Donald Cozzens agrees that "the sobering realities of marriage, fatherhood, and mortgages . . . often shake an emotionally adolescent male into maturity and manhood," and he notes that these experiences are not available to seminarians and priests.[60]

The watchfully protective function of the father is particularly relevant to a discussion of sexual abusiveness. The man who successfully assumes this role is unlikely to violate a child or to stand by while someone else does it. For example, when Wayne Sagrera learned that Fr. Gilbert Gauthe had sexually abused three of his four sons, he called the office of Lafayette, Louisiana, Bishop Gerard Frey and was told by Church officials there that Gauthe would remain in his parish because they had no one with whom to replace him.[61] Sagrera told *60 Minutes II* that, at that point: "I called and cussed and told him you either take him out of here or someone's gonna kill the son of a bitch and it might be me. He's gonna die. The relationship between a father and his son is a powerful thing. And you just best get him out of here."[62]

While this may seem excessively macho, it also portrays Sagrera's intense determination to protect his sons from further abuse. Other men, like priests or bishops who have not experienced the developmental milestone of providing early and primary material and emotional provisioning for a partner and child, may not forge a fully empathic recognition of a child's vulnerability to betrayal by trusted adults.

In becoming a father himself, the man also learns to acknowledge his capacity for "mothering." Psychoanalyst Chasseguet-Smirgel suggests that, as a nurturing, maternal father, a man identifies with the nourishing Father in the Lord's Prayer, a maternal father who provides daily bread while his stereotypical paternal side forgives sins and asserts his will, hopefully in negotiation with his partner.[63] Ideally, as the father tries on roles historically associated with women, particularly mothers, he broadens his identity to include emotions, attitudes, and behaviors previously experienced as located only in the "other," usually "woman." Damon Linker puts it well when he says:

> Would my life be easier if, in premodern fashion, my wife took on almost all the responsibility of caring for our son? Perhaps. . . . For all the stresses and strains of life as a new man, there's no substitute for the act of devoting oneself to another person, especially one so helpless and needy. It—and arguably it alone—grants a gift of spontaneous, unconditional love that every human being, and not just women, should experience.[64]

Fatherhood also allows a man to mourn lost opportunities with his own father. Here, the father stops looking to his father or to substitute father figures to fill unmet childhood needs. Rather, by loving and caring for his child, the adult father identifies with his young child and is able to parent his internal child through fathering well his own child. Priests are deprived of this particular potential to rework internalized relationships with their fathers. Given that many priests appear to have had troubled relationships with fathers, or were actually or symbolically fatherless, it may signify a real loss.[65]

Dean Hoge suggests that the priesthood is overrepresented by sons of alcoholic fathers.[66] Andrea Celenza, a psychoanalyst who treats priests, finds that many of these men had fathers who died early, left the family, were emotionally unavailable, and/or were degraded by the future priest's mother.[67] Paul Dinter reports that few of his fellow seminarians or priests had close relationships with their fathers.[68] Priests may also have had mothers who idealized the parish priest at the expense of their husbands.

Some of these sons, deprived of a role model in their fathers, learned that the best men were priests who had no families and no sex.

Becoming a priest, at one level, can be seen therefore as an unconscious attempt to become the man the mother really loved while finding a new father in the Church—God, bishops, pastors. When inevitable relational disappointments occurred, some priests may have felt abandoned by the people they turned to for love and recognition. Having received little empathy from paternal figures, these men perhaps were ill-equipped as priests/fathers to develop empathy for children in their care. As they or other priests sexually transgressed with minors, they did not feel compelled to protect the young.

Priests and Progeny

Scores of priests have become fathers through sexual relationships with adult women,[69] and most were unwilling to take responsibility for their paternity, much less to engage in watchful protectiveness over anyone involved.[70] In late 2003, for example, two adults received confirmation that Fr. James Foley is their father.[71] Foley, who had a long-term affair with their mother, left her one evening in 1973 after she ingested a drug overdose and he did not return to her home in time to save her life.[72] Richard Cardinal Cushing, former archbishop of Boston, was aware that Foley had been involved with women as early as 1968.[73] Although Foley had been removed from a diocese in Canada because of his affairs with women, Cushing assigned him to a new parish in Haverhill, Massachusetts.[74] In 1993, Bernard Cardinal Law and Bishop John B. McCormack, now head of the Diocese of Manchester, New Hampshire, and a seminary classmate of Foley's, learned that Foley had left the mother of his children to die.[75] The priest was then sent to a treatment facility whose staff deemed him unstable and "highly charged sexually."[76] Cardinal Law responded to the assessment by placing Foley in another parish, and Foley remained in ministry until the record of his affair became public in 2002.[77] Foley never attempted to locate or provide for his children, one of whom bears his first name.[78]

Fr. Gerald John Plesetz reportedly acknowledged impregnating a fourteen-year-old girl and also allegedly fathered the child of a twenty-two-year-old woman; he had nothing to do afterward with either his children or their mothers.[79] Alabama Fr. Adrian Cook confessed to having fathered a child with one woman after he was accused by another woman of sexual assault; Cook termed the latter relationship consensual.[80] Bishop Hubert O'Connor of British Columbia left office in 1992 after being indicted for raping two women, one of whom, a seamstress for priests, bore a child whom O'Connor, the alleged father, arranged to have adopted immediately after she was born.[81] Similarly, Bishop Eamon Casey of Ireland resigned when it was learned that he had fathered a child in 1974.[82] When the mother refused Casey's request that she place the boy up for adoption, he siphoned Church funds to help her raise their son in America.[83] Sipe reports that one priest had an ongoing relationship with the parish housekeeper during which he impregnated her twice; both times, the couple chose to abort the child.[84] In these cases and others like them, the Fathers apparently felt little or no need to *be* fathers: to care for, provide for, or even meet their offspring. Sometimes, in fact, they reportedly preferred to abort them despite the Church's strong teaching about the grave sinfulness of abortion.

In another part of the world, Ricardo Cardinal Vidal of the Philippines announced a 2003 misconduct policy that automatically leads to the defrocking of any priest who fathers two or more children but imposes less serious penalties on priests who sire "only" one child.[85] It appears to be a somewhat inexplicable policy for an ostensibly celibate organization to propagate but sets in relief the apparently common reality of priests siring children.

Although within the Church, celibacy and priesthood were considered above, rather than different from, active sexuality and fatherhood, most priests would know at least unconsciously that the wider world celebrated as ultimately potent a man who produced progeny. Throughout history, for example, kings only attained legitimacy as regents after they had delivered an heir into the kingdom. The king or emperor appearing on his palace balcony, holding his child—especially his son—high in the air for all to see, was showing off his genital accomplishment as much as the embodied being of his new heir.

Before celibacy was required of the priesthood, we have seen that popes, bishops, and priests had children to whom they even passed on their holy offices. Long after celibacy became a requirement for the priesthood, at least one pope's yearning to parent overcame the limitations of his clerical state. Historian Garry Wills relates the story of Pope Pius IX, the late nineteenth-century pope, who "adopted" Edgardo Mortara, a Jewish child baptized secretly by the family's Catholic servant and then kidnapped by men associated with the Vatican.[86] It is a story of "fatherhood" that paradoxically underscores the lack of appreciation some priests, bishops, and popes have had for that parental role.

Deciding that a "Catholic" child literally could not be raised in good faith by Jewish parents, Pius took the child into the Vatican and raised him as his son. The pope's perversion of parenthood and his disregard for Edgardo's suffering parents are detectable in Pius's reactions to criticisms generated around the world by Edgardo's kidnapping. Pius blamed Christian-hating Jews for questioning his "adoption" of Edgardo, apparently dissociating the probability that the kidnapping was prompted in part by Jewish-hating Catholic prejudices. When Jewish delegates in Rome pleaded with Pius to return Edgardo to his parents, Pius lambasted them: "Lower your voice. Do you forget before whom you are speaking? I suppose this is the thanks I get for all the benefits you have received from me. [Pius had freed Rome's Jews from earlier anti-Semitic restrictions.] Take care, for I could have made you go back to your hole."[87]

The pope perhaps perceived that his emancipation of the Jews from discriminatory laws entitled him to kidnap one of their children in a kind of bizarre blood tribute. Later, Pius felt satisfied and vindicated in his parenting when Edgardo followed in his "father's" footsteps and became a priest. Pope John Paul II beatified Pius IX. The decision to send on his way to sainthood Pio Nono, "a man who today in any civil society would have faced a jail sentence for . . . kidnap, was sending entirely the wrong signals" to the world, especially in view of the sexual abuse scandal.[88]

Pius's kidnapping of Edgardo deprived the boy's father of his parental rights and opportunities. Similarly, in any parish or church setting, a young person represented living evidence of his or her father's sexual potency and competency in impregnating a woman. These men often were parishioners and thus spiritual sons of the abusing priest. In the unconscious of the priest, the male parishioner's fatherhood may have challenged the sexual adequacy and manliness of the childless and supposedly celibate "father" who was expected to have a paternal relationship with both the adult male and his children. In a clerically distorted enactment of the classic Oedipal configuration, the symbolically castrated priest/father may have, in fact, symbolically castrated his parishioner/son by abusing the parishioner's child, thereby assaulting the parishioner's virility and capacity to fulfill his culturally mandated role to protect the young.

Adopted or Fostered Children

In a series of investigative articles published in 2004, the *Seattle Post-Intelligencer* found another disturbing course some priests pursued to obtain "sons" who allegedly also were used as sexual objects by their new fathers.[89] In these situations, priests formally or informally fostered or "adopted" boys, often telling them and their parent(s) that they would care for them as sons. Once ensconced in the priest's rectory, the boys—usually from situations of poverty in foreign countries or violence and abuse here in the United States—learned that their new Father/father demanded a high price for his provisioning.

Albert Green, for example, claims that he lived with Rev. Ed Olszewski on and off for almost thirty years, beginning at age eleven.[90] He recalls being thrilled with the grand size and fine appointments of the rectory when he first moved in. His first night with his new parent, however, allegedly established the sexual nature of the bond. Green reports: "Olszewski took out some Vaseline and he was rubbing it on me, my front and back. He put it up into my rectum. I felt something really weird. I just turned over and felt something else go inside of it."[91]

Olszewski reportedly did provide Albert with a luxurious lifestyle, which the previously impoverished kid loved. In addition, Albert was recognized by the priest and the parishioners as special, even powerful, nothing he ever had experienced about himself before. For a long time, he tried to reconcile the two sides of his life:

Church members would ask him to serve as an intermediary with "Father Ed." He was somebody and he liked it that way. "I knew what he was doing. I just felt like he was my father, he was the president, whatever he says, goes. I never really had nothing, now I'm rich and famous. . . . I felt special," he said. "It never clicked that you were being abused. He was my dad. I was in love with him. I was so happy to be there. I didn't care about the sex. Who cares about this? Look what I got in return."[92]

Part of what Albert got in return was a life reportedly marked by drug abuse, alcoholism, and drifting. Although Olszewski denies any wrongdoing, a Michigan jury found him guilty of taking indecent liberties with Green, and he lives as a registered sex offender. For a time prior to his conviction, he ran a licensed foster home in Florida.

The Seattle reporters investigated eleven cases and note that 120 other accusers, described in the 2004 John Jay College of Criminal Justice study of the prevalence of priest abuse, asserted that they also were living with their abusers at the time of the sexual molestations.

In these cases, the sexual abuse of minors became concretely incestuous, with the priest claiming to be both father and lover to his acquired son. It represented not only an attack on the minor, but also a betrayal of the parents or social service organizations that entrusted a child to the priest for protection and nurturing.

Churches traditionally have been places of refuge and sanctuary for the hunted and forlorn; metaphoric wombs that contain, nourish, heal, and protect those who have nowhere left to go. By taking a minor into a rectory as a son and keeping him a state of concubinage, the priest also desecrated Holy Mother Church, sullying what should have been prayerful and safe sacred space.

The Bishops: More Childless "Fathers"

When victims or their families complained to members of the hierarchy about an abusing priest, they were turning to men who also were childless Fathers/fathers. Many of these men, like Bishop Imesch quoted at the beginning of this section, had difficulty appreciating the pain and damage inflicted by the sexually abusive priest. They had never served as watchful protectors of their own children nor directly shielded a mother-child dyad from premature impingements from the outside world, even though they may have had pastoral responsibilities within a community.

In addition, paternal feelings that might stir within a bishop confronted with sexual abuse by a priest would likely be directed toward the priest, positioned by the Church as the bishop's spiritual son. To acknowledge fully the transgressions of the abusing priest might evoke shame in the bishop for having produced a "bad seed" son. Further, bishops and priests, as has been seen, were formed to think of their station as spiritually above that of a married man, woman, and child. If one can imagine a baker in a feudal village seeking redress from a nobleman whose foster son had raped the baker's daughter, one can better understand the contemptuous response so many victims and their families received from the Church's hierarchy.

Sublimated Fatherhood

It is important to note that there are men, including priests and bishops, who can grow into a mature manhood without fathering children. Sipe, for example, rightly points out that many priests work with minors and do great good through a healthy sublimation of their generative strivings.[93] These men provide invaluable guidance, education, emotional support, and recreation for young people who become better human beings for having known their priest. In the process, the priest successfully develops into a true spiritual father.

Perhaps most emblematic of this successful fathering are the legions of young men and women educated by Catholic priests and brothers. These youngsters, often from underprivileged backgrounds, were given a foundation for a life they would not have had without these clergy, most of whom never harmed a child. I myself remember the many Catholic priests who lived for most of their priesthoods in the dorms at the University of Notre Dame and who were available almost every hour of every day to provide paternal listening, guidance, and, yes, discipline to college students struggling with the challenges of growing into adulthood. This book is about the priests who failed their communities, but it is important to remember and respect the many priests who succeeded in being appropriate and loving "fathers" to young people.

It is most often through mourning the family that never will be constituted that a man is able adaptively to redirect generative strivings, including those to watch over and protect a child in whom a man sees his own reflection. One priest, for example, told me about a year-long depression, occurring in midlife and stimulated by the full recognition that he never would be a husband or father. Similarly, disappointment and pain remaining from the man's relationship with his own father must be acknowledged and psychologically addressed without access to the "second chance" inherent in parenting a child in whom one may refind and repair an earlier version of self.

The priest or bishop who believed that the priesthood was an elevated state perhaps could not mourn openly because he had been taught that he had lost little in becoming a priest. During his priestly formation, and later in his life in the rectory, school, or chancery, there were no words, no syntax given to him for symbolizing the pain of childlessness. And even if he formed the words, there were few people available to listen to them. Rather than grieving the pain of relinquishing the chance to become fathers, some priests may have dissociated these emotions, perhaps even unconsciously replacing them with an indifference or hardness of heart toward that which they lacked in their own lives. Sexual abuse, in this case, partly represented an adolescent denial of impossibility; an impulse-driven insistence that the priest could "have" a child whenever he wanted one.

The Future of Celibacy

Most priests and laypeople believe that celibacy should be optional, at least for diocesan priests. In a 2001 survey commissioned by the National Federation of Priests' Councils, 56 percent of the priests surveyed felt that celibacy should be optional for diocesan priests.[94] Another survey of priests, conducted by the *Los Angeles Times* in 2002, found that 69 percent of respondents favored the ordination of married men to the Roman

Catholic priesthood.[95] Laypeople long have favored a married priesthood. Surveys indicate that more than 70 percent of laypeople believe in a married priesthood and almost 80 percent would like to see former priests who left to marry welcomed back as priests.[96] Even some bishops agree. Bishops from Asia, Oceania, Latin America, and Africa all have asked Popes John Paul II and Benedict XVI to allow the ordination of married men, knowing that in many cases that decision would simply legitimize what is happening anyway among their priests.[97] There already are about two hundred married priests serving in American parishes because Pope John Paul II allowed married Episcopalian priests to convert and enter the Roman ministry.[98] It is a situation that makes mandatory celibacy even more unfair to Catholic men who enter the priesthood and are required to remain forever unmarried.

The end of celibacy would not signal the end of child abuse. Married men throughout the world sexually violate their daughters and sons, grandchildren, nieces or nephews, students, scout troop members, and summer campers. Until mandatory celibacy is declared dead, however, secrecy surrounds all forms of priestly sexual acting out and the threat of blackmail hangs over the heads of those priests and bishops. In addition, the chasm between celibacy as preached and celibacy as lived—an unspoken known wrapped in eroticized secrecy—will continue to protect networks of sexual secrets like those marking the sexual abuse of minors and, even more, its cover-up.

CHAPTER 7

Homosexuality

Secreted and Scapegoated

Homosexuality* within the priesthood was until recently an even more secreted phenomenon than sexual abuse of minors or the sexual acting out of heterosexual priests with adult women. While many priests are homosexual, the Church's official position devalues homosexual orientation and outlaws homosexual activity. It is once again the paradox between homosexuality as taught and homosexuality as lived within the Catholic Church that contributed to the cover-up of the sexual abuse of minors.

The Theology of Sexual Orientation

If desire is what you *yearn* to do and sex is what you *do*, sexual orientation determines *with whom* you do what you desire to do when you decide to do it. The Church teaches that homosexuality is an intrinsic disorder, and Catholic gays and lesbians are instructed never to act on their desires for sexual intimacy with same-gendered individuals. This position is an internally logical outgrowth of the requirement that every sexual act must be open to biological procreation. Since same-gendered sexual unions cannot lead to conception, Catholic teachings, in turn, refuse to legitimate enacted homosexuality.

Thomas Fox summarizes the vicissitudes of late twentieth-century attitudes about homosexuality within the Church.[1] As in the non-Catholic contemporary culture, voices within the Church were raised suggesting that homosexuality is a God-given gift rather than a biological error or

---

*Homosexuality is no more monolithic than heterosexuality and can be defined in a number of ways (Mark D. Jordan, *Silence of Sodom Homosexuality in Modern Catholicism* [Chicago: University of Chicago Press, 2000], 108). Here, it refers to a male priest whose primary sexual attraction is to other adult men.

109

moral evil rooted in sin.[2] Jesuit John McNeill, for example, was permitted to publish a 1976 book challenging the church's theology of homosexuality. McNeill believed then that the Church was ready to acknowledge that "the new evidence coming from the fields of scriptural studies, history, psychology, sociology, and moral theology seriously challenged every premise on which the traditional teaching was based."[3] McNeill was overly optimistic, and, in 1977, the Vatican ordered him into silence on the topic of homosexuality, an order he followed for almost a decade.

Under Pope John Paul II, the institutional Church employed an increasingly strident voice in addressing homosexuality. In 1986 and again in 1992, the Vatican issued letters to bishops instructing them about "pastoral" approaches to Catholic homosexuals.[4] A 1986 Halloween letter, issued by Cardinal Ratzinger (Pope Benedict XVI), head of the Congregation for the Doctrine of the Faith, reiterated the definition of homosexuality as objectively disordered and oriented toward evil. It suggested that homosexuals seeking the same civil rights afforded to heterosexuals invited violence against themselves. When Rev. John J. McNeill broke his Vatican-imposed silence to protest the 1986 letter, he was dismissed from the priesthood.

The 1992 Vatican letter asserted that it was neither unjust nor undesirable to discriminate against homosexuals in certain employment situations like teaching, housing, adoption, and service in the military. The United States Conference of Major Superiors of Men and a few American bishops took exception to the Vatican's instructions. The CMSM wrote: "We are shocked that the statement calls for discrimination against gay men and lesbian women. . . . Moreover, we find the arguments used to justify discrimination based on stereotypes and falsehoods that are out of touch with modern psychological and sociological understandings of human sexuality."[5] Thomas Gumbleton, auxiliary bishop of Detroit, publicly responded: "This [the Vatican letter] is clearly based on an ignorance of the nature of homosexuality. . . . The church should affirm and bless the gay community for teaching what it means to love."[6] That has not yet occurred. Rather, beginning in 2003, the Vatican and many Catholic bishops led vigorous attacks on the same-sex marriages and civil unions allowed in several American states.[7] Joseph Cardinal Ratzinger (Pope Benedict XVI) stated in a 2003 letter that allowing gays to adopt children would "actually mean doing violence to these children" since they would be raised "in an environment that is not conducive to their full human development."[8] Similarly, Sean Cardinal O'Malley, archbishop of Boston, testified before the Massachusetts legislature that adoption by gays could lead to polygamy and incest and would be dangerous to society.[9] The irony of Church officials apparently unselfconsciously advising society about how best to protect children from violence is difficult for many observers to swallow, given what has been learned about the endangerment of tens of thousands of children *within* the Church.

In November 2005 the Vatican issued an instruction regarding homosexuality in which it reaffirmed the Church's teaching that homosexual acts always are immoral and contrary to natural law. It said:

> The Catechism distinguishes between homosexual acts and homosexual tendencies. . . . As regards to deep-seated homosexual tendencies, which are present in a certain number of men and women, these also are objectively disordered and are often a trial for such people. They must be accepted with respect and sensitivity; every sign of unjust discrimination in their regard should be avoided. These people are called to fulfill God's will in their lives and to unite to the sacrifice of the Lord's Cross the difficulties they may encounter.[10]

In other words, homosexuals should refrain from ever acting on their desires for sexual union and accept their concomitant suffering in unity with Jesus' suffering on the cross.

It is interesting to consider here the Church's diametrically opposed conceptualizations of celibacy, which in some ways could be considered an orientation toward sexuality, and homosexuality. Both approaches to sexuality are statistically abnormal in that they are lived out by a small percentage of the general population. The Church idealizes one and devalues the other. Perhaps instead it would be productive, humane, and spiritually sound for Catholic officials to assume relational views of *both* celibacy and homosexuality. Here, each sexual orientation could be evaluated according to the relational context in which it is expressed. Celibacy and homosexuality, along with heterosexuality, could be deemed ethical, procreative, and spiritually meaningful to the extent that the psychological and spiritual growth of individuals and those in relationship with them were enhanced by the union. Similarly, any enacted sexual orientation could be considered destructive if it impeded an individual's or couple's relationship with self, other, and God.

The Church does not take that approach. Like much of Catholic sexual theology, the Church's position on homosexuality partly represents a refusal to integrate the voluminous psychological, sociological, anthropological, and biological data generated over the past few decades indicating that homosexuality is a naturally occurring sexual orientation that is no more or less intrinsically disordered than heterosexuality.[11] In other words, it is not one's sexual orientation that connotes good or evil, health or pathology, spiritual soundness or sin, but rather the ways in which one expresses sexuality. As with the various kinds of heterosexual activities a person can enact, the grace or dis-grace of a homosexual union is embedded in the relational context in which it occurs. If homosexual love and sex are grounded in mutuality, if they promote growth and an individual's and couple's capacity for love, they are to be celebrated and supported, not damned. Instead, the Church's condemnation of homosexual activity can support the internalization of self-hatred that plagues many homosexuals, reducing their capacity to live lives of respect and love for self, other, and God.[12]

Elizabeth Johnson, in discussing women, argues against the Church's demand that all women take on the same gender roles.[13] Her project applies as well to official demands that sexual orientation and activity be homogenized into a one-size-fits-all heterosexuality based on perpetual openness to procreation. Johnson asserts: "Community then comes about not as the result of suppressing differences and homogenizing everyone into sameness, but by respecting and celebrating persons in all their differences within multiple larger narratives and actions for the common good."[14]

John McNeill specifically takes the Church to task on the theology of sexual orientation. Although McNeill is speaking to his Church about homosexuality, he could as easily be addressing the attitude of many churchmen toward sexual abuse victims:

> At this point, the ignorance and distortion of homosexuality . . . lead us who are gay Catholics to issue the Vatican a stern warning. Your ignorance can no longer be excused as inculpable; it has become of necessity a deliberate and malicious ignorance. . . . We cried out to you for bread, you gave us a scorpion instead. . . . Just as you apologized to the Jews for supporting anti-Semitism for centuries, so today you must repent and apologize for the centuries of support you have given homophobia.[15]

The Sexual Orientation of the Priesthood

While the Church's position on homosexuality eventually might have taken its place among the other aspects of Catholic sexual theology generally discounted by the laity and many priests, the hypocrisy of a Church condemning homosexuality while depending on a significantly gay priesthood to run it and to administer its sacraments is directly implicated in the Church scandal. The unspoken known that the priesthood is more homosexual than the wider culture is countered by an edict to priests not to speak openly about their sexual orientation but rather to preach about the evil of enacted homosexuality. Mixed messages, sexual secrets, and denied realities abound in a clerical Wonderland in which the institutional Church appears to play the Queen of Hearts. Secrecy about and cover-up of the sexual abuse of minors becomes an almost inevitable component of such a crazy and crazy-making realm.

Contemporary researchers suggest that between 28 percent and 56 percent of the American priesthood is homosexual.[16] Even Rev. Andrew Greeley's lower estimate of 16 percent represents a percentage of the priestly population probably exceeding that of the general public.[17] Most commentators agree that the percentage of homosexual priests has increased since the 1970s as many heterosexual priests left the priesthood to marry.[18] Mark Jordan suggests that even the obsessive attempts by researchers to pin down the number and percent of gay priests and seminarians betray the Church's anxiety about homosexuality.[19] They also give voice to the idea that homosexuality is unnatural and therefore must be carefully tracked in the priesthood so we know if there is "too much" of it going around.

Most psychologically healthy gay men are attracted to the priesthood for the same reasons that attract mature heterosexual men. They love God, desire to pursue a life of deepened spirituality, and are committed to living out gospel values within a community of faith. One gay priest I know, for example, ministers to hospice patients and their families, patiently and compassionately helping all to come to terms with temporal death. Interested in working with the elderly, he also is the chaplain for a community of nuns not just facing their own deaths and the demise of their peers, but also confronting the potential end of their religious community because of decreasing vocations. Finally, he serves as chaplain to a nursing home populated with underprivileged and often abandoned elderly men and women. His challenge is to sustain faith and hope in the midst of much despair. Decent and faithful gay priests like this man, no matter the depth of their service and spirituality, however, are also drawn into complicity with an institution that finds them inherently flawed and inclined toward sin.

It is probable that gay men always have been attracted to the priesthood in numbers disproportionate to their presence in the wider society. Until very recently, and in some cases still, Catholic boys who recognized their homosexuality faced the scorn of family, friends, and Church. Taught that acting on their sexual and love strivings is intrinsically evil and mortally sinful, the Catholic gay man faces painful conflicts between his identity and his attachment relationships. Entering the priesthood was a move that, until quite recently, evoked family pride, with the seminarian or priest being held in great esteem by his relational community. Inactive priest Steven Rosczewski, for example, says he knew he was gay before he entered the seminary but "[g]oing into the seminary seemed like the best of all possibilities. I could get an esteemed position within Catholic culture, and I had a safe place to go where people wouldn't ask why I didn't have a girlfriend."[20] Similarly, inactive Dominican friar Mark Dowd says he remembers being relieved as a young man when he could deflect questions from relatives about the absence of a girlfriend in his life by stating his intention to become a priest.[21]

Some gay men therefore sought and still seek the priesthood as a place in which to hide their sexual orientation while earning admiration and affection, rather than shaming and alienation, from those they hold dear. In these cases, Mark Jordan suggests that the priesthood offers an opportunity for gay men to exchange their "anguished identity as an outsider for a respected and powerful identity as an insider."[22]

Gay men also may be attracted by the aesthetics of the priesthood and by the ability to camp it up regularly in lace and satin, as much liturgy is conducted in the gorgeous drag of liturgical vestments. Years ago, priests also cross-dressed on a daily basis in skirted cassocks, which some priests still favor and which are becoming even more popular with younger clergy and seminarians, a population thought to be increasingly homosexual. Clerical garb allows gay priests to play with gender twisting at the same moment they drape both their sexual orientation and their sexual equipment in layers of secrecy. Thus, liturgical vestments and cassocks permit some gay priests to communicate about themselves in silence through camp, defined in Jordan as "a style of resistance and self-protection, a way of identifying with other queer people across invisibility and disgrace."[23]

Camp itself can be viewed as a play on meaning that expresses paradox. Camp and camping, from the Latin *campus* or open field, often are associated with "manly" ruggedness (think boot camp, Outward Bound, cowboys by the campfire). Camp, deriving from the French *camper* or pose, is used by the gay community to label a playful and provocative presentation of self, one that is the antithesis of the Marlboro Man's manhood and sexuality.

Camp and its association with a homosexual orientation are found up and down the hierarchical ladder. Bishops as well as priests engage in camp as a way of both expressing and hiding something about their sexuality and gender. Jordan reports, for example, that Francis Cardinal Spellman, former archbishop of New York and known colloquially as "Nellie

Spellbound," enjoyed drag and the company of young men.[24] The cardinal was said to be distraught when the pope ordered bishops to cut their trains from ten yards to two.[25] Apparently Spellman felt that if he preached in St. Patrick's Cathedral, he should have a cathedral-length train to complement his position. And, as one Catholic man quoted in Jordan said, "Mass was the ballet of my youth."[26] Here, gay priests and bishops harness the accoutrements of clerical power and refinement in campy language and rituals that both obscure and reveal their sexual orientation.

It is also logical to hypothesize that homosexual men would be attracted to the all-male environment of the priesthood. Further, when boys entered the seminary as young teens, the explosion of pubescent sexual strivings had only one direction in which to travel. Surrounded by men and boys in an environment that rendered women dangerous, except for idealized mothers and the Virgin Mary, an adolescent seminarian was left with few choices. He pretty much could lust after his mother or he could lust after those around him, many of them gay men. Once again we encounter the paradox of an organization teaching that homosexuality is disordered and then constructing an environment that maximally elicits homosexual yearnings.

Catholic gay priests are instructed not to disclose their sexual orientation.[27] In early 2006, for example, William Cardinal Levada, head of the Vatican's Congregation for the Doctrine of the Faith, asserted that a priest who discloses his homosexual orientation interferes with a Catholic's ability to see the priest as a representative of Christ.[28] Throughout the sexual abuse crisis, there were less than a handful of gay parish priests (among more than twenty-five thousand parish priests in all) who publicly came out, and those courageous men put their careers on the line to do so.[29] One such priest is Rev. Fred Daley of Utica, New York, who, in 2004, came out to his bishop, parishioners, and the wider community.[30] For thirteen years, Daley has served an impoverished neighborhood where he established housing for refugees and shelter for girls living in the street, opened a soup kitchen, and provided affordable day care.[31] Fr. Daley, who says he is celibate, became increasingly uncomfortable with Vatican pronouncements about homosexuality and decided to come forward. While some Catholics are distressed by his revelations, most have been supportive. Rev. James Martin, a Jesuit and associate editor of *America*, calls Daley a "courageous . . . poster priest" for homosexual clergy. Martin is quoted as saying, "He is a parish priest, he works with the poor, his bishop and parishioners seem to support him, and this is not his one issue."

Inactive priest Christopher Schiavone was sent for treatment at Southdown Institute, a Canadian facility for priests, after he had sex with a subordinate priest. He describes the impact on him of the secrecy about homosexuality demanded by the Church:

> Soon after I arrived at Southdown . . . one of the therapists, Richard Gilmartin, . . . said, "We don't have secrets; our secrets have us." . . . I recall them because they were such an accurate and powerful description of my own experience as a closeted gay man and celibate priest. As long as I needed to conceal the full truth of my identity from my family, my parishioners, and my superiors, everything in my life was controlled and distorted by my secret. I could not seek out healthy, functional relationships on my home turf, so I settled for the vicarious pleasure of observing free-range men in the gay bars of other cities where I took vacations. I could not experience sexual expression in mature relationships, so I'd sneak into the Glad Day Book Store on Boylston Street to buy soft-core gay porn; hoping, *praying,* that no one I knew would see me. I should have worried more that I couldn't see myself.[32]

Schivaone's regret that he did not know himself well is poignant and meaningful. Many gay men growing up in what has been until recently a pervasively homophobic society have lived in closets in which they sometimes deny who they are even to themselves. The antihomosexual theology of the Catholic Church, conveyed in homosocial seminary environments likely to stimulate forbidden and derided sexual desires, often constructed for the young gay priest a particularly suffocating closet.[33] Here, the self-hatred plaguing many gay men could be magnified for gay priests, some of whom tried to cope by strenuously denying their sexual orientations, even turning hatred outward toward other gay men. Denial and dissociation on this scale encourages the denial of other sexual secrets like the sexual abuse of children.

Nothing psychologically sound or, I suspect, spiritually enriching can emanate from such hypocrisy. Surely, the pope, cardinal, bishop, or priest who cannot look in the mirror and acknowledge his reflection as a homosexual man will have difficulty looking into the face of a sexually abusive brother and naming what he sees. Rather, he is likely to close his eyes to true evil because his own humanity has been mislabeled as inclining toward evil. He may also blame or ignore the victims of sexual abuse, unconsciously turning away from his own victimization by his Church and the wider society. Closets, then, are built within closets and lies pile up until it would be hard to find the truth, much less speak the truth, about priests who are sexually abusive and what they do, even if one were inclined to tell the truth, which the institutional Church does not appear to be.

Sexually Active Homosexuality in the Celibate Priesthood

Before discussing active homosexuality in the priesthood, it is important to note that there are many fine homosexual priests who uphold their vows or promises and who do great good within the Church. These are men who, like their straight colleagues, have integrated their sexual orientation, and perhaps even their sexual activity, with a mature sense of their responsibility to model the values of the Gospels. Certainly, New York City embraced self-identified gay priest and chaplain to the Fire Department of New York, Mychal Judge, as its own personal patron saint after his heroism and death on September 11, 2001. His sexual orientation mattered not at all that day, nor all those that preceded it, as he ministered to the needs to his beloved fire folk who, in turn, held him dear. If the "macho" and still almost all-male FDNY could claim a gay priest as one of their most beloved "guys," they may have something to model for the Catholic Church. There are many other priests like Judge in the Church, homosexual priests whose priesthoods have little to do with their sexual orientations and much to do with their capacity for loving ministry.

Like some heterosexual priests, some gay priests are sexually active. Mark Jordan captures the paradoxical role of enacted homosexuality in the Church:

> Within any society that universally persecutes same-sex desires, those desires will be kept silent. When members of that society's religious institutions feel them, they will treat them as secrets. When they act on their desires, they will do so secretly. . . . The most elaborate societies will be found in religious institutions that condemn same-sex desires fiercely while creating conditions under which they can flourish: the situation of modern Catholicism.[34]

In 1050, Peter Damian wrote about, "networks of sodomites . . . who sin together then absolve one another in the confessional."[35] Damian claimed that some bishops and their priests were involved with each other,[36] and, as with heterosexual pontiffs, homosexual popes were not exempt from indulging their same-sex desires. Popes John XII (955–964), Boniface VIII (1294–1303), Paul II (1464–1471), Sixtus IV (1471–1484), Leo X (1513–1521), and Julius III (1550–1555) all were described as active homosexuals by commentators of their times.[37] Boniface VIII, for example, allegedly termed same-sex sexual union as no more sinful than rubbing your hands together.[38]

Homosexual activity can begin in seminary, sometimes initiated by faculty members, rectors, or spiritual advisers.[39] Bishop Anthony O'Connell, formerly of Palm Beach, for example, resigned after acknowledging having sexually abused a minor seminarian when he was a seminary rector years before.[40] Jordan describes one seminary spiritual director who "massaged" students, grooming them for the ensuing copulation.[41] When he was confronted about his activities, he denied doing anything wrong, also denied being gay, and castigated effeminacy in the priesthood.[42] Paul Hendrickson, quoted by John Cornwell, tells of his five-year experience with his seminary spiritual advisor:

> I would go in, sit in a chair beside his desk, talk for a short while, await his nod, unzipper my trousers, take out my penis, rub it while I allowed impure thoughts to flow through my brain, and, at the point where I felt myself fully large and close to emission, say, "Father, I'm ready now." He would then reach over and hand me a black wooden crucifix . . . and I then would begin reciting the various reasons why I wished to conquer this temptation. . . . The power of the crucified Savior in my left hand as overpowering the evil and impurity and the world in my right.[43]

Hendrickson's ordeal incorporates sadomasochism along with sexual overstimulation. It is, however, a striking metaphor for the way in which some within the Church stimulate homosexual desire then denounce it.

When seminary officials imposed sexual activity on adolescents or when they engaged sexually with older seminarians, it was sexual abuse or harassment first and homosexual sex second. The younger the seminarian, the more confusing would sex with a father/Father figure be in terms of the boy's own sexual development. In addition, to the extent that the seminarian identified with the older man as a role model and spiritual father, it increased the possibility that, later, the seminarian—now a priest or even a seminary official himself—might act out his internal psychosexual conflicts on another young male.

It was and also continues to be in seminary that some young men have their first homosexual experience with peers, perhaps even falling in love for the first time. Years ago, seminaries attempted to forestall homosexual acting out with rituals that were likely only to increase longing, like banning special friendships between seminarians and directing them to wear bathing suits in the shower. When homosexuality was more dissociated from the consciousness of the wider society, so too homosexual affairs among seminarians may have been less visible. Mark Jordan takes to task, however, Church spokesmen who pretend that seminary homosexuality can be attributed to Vatican II liberalizations and therefore can be snuffed out with stricter selection criteria and seminary discipline.[44] Rather, Jordan claims that seminary sex is as old as the Church—as Peter Damian's writings from the eleventh century appear to confirm—and asserts that what has changed is the naming of behavior, not the behavior itself.[45]

Since the sexual abuse scandal exploded in 2002, some seminaries have been cast as "pink palaces" in which seminarians and their staffs openly tolerate gay sex while sometimes discriminating against straight seminarians by excluding them, usually subtly, from the social world of the seminary. Former seminarian Andrew Krzmarzick entered the Theological College in Northeast Washington (D.C.) in 1997 and soon grew uncomfortable with the lack of open discussion about the predominance of gay students, some of whom he claims were sexually active.[46] For Krzmarzick, the discomfort was created not by the presence of many gay students, nor even as much by the ostensible active sexuality, as by the refusal of anyone in the seminary to speak openly about something "known by everyone but never really acknowledged."[47] Similarly, Chris Higgins and Dennis Caulfield, former seminarians at Rome's prestigious English College, fell in love and began a sexual relationship when they were students.[48] They report that other seminarians had sex in parks or Roman nightclubs catering to gays.[49] For these men as well, it was the startling contrast between what was preached about homosexuality and what was lived out by homosexual priests that was most difficult to bear.[50] Caulfield, in fact, cites his perception that "[s]ome of the people who were the most anti-gay and inclined to invoke the Church's teaching to put other people down were people who I knew to be gay themselves and mixed in gay circles with other gay men."[51] Finally, Hoge and Wenger found that 41 percent of priests felt that there was or probably was a homosexual subculture in the seminary they attended.[52] The perception was correlated with age.[53] Among diocesan priests over age sixty-six, only 3 percent held this opinion, that number increased to 11 percent for those between fifty-six and sixty-five years old, 25 percent for priests between ages forty-six and fifty-five; 38 percent for men between thirty-six and forty-five yeas old; and 47 percent for clergy age thirty-five and under.[54]

It may well be that as the number of gay seminarians increased, as the wider society became more accepting of homosexuality, and as the strictures against particular friendships in the seminary relaxed, gay seminary students felt more comfortable seeking out each other's company and pursuing mutual interests. In these situations, the homosexual students may have provided support for one another. Hoge and Wenger quote thirty-two-year-old Father Charles, "Did guys who were gay socialize together? Yes, I think they did, but not to the exclusion of anybody else. And sometimes I think that socialization is probably very helpful in terms of getting the affective support that people needed for themselves."[55]

It is important to note that Hoge and Wenger are not clear about what constitutes a "gay subculture," other than gay men seeking each other's friendship and company, sometimes to the perceived exclusion of heterosexual men. There always have been affiliation networks in seminaries, however, which could be labeled "subcultures." Caricatured stereotypes include beer-guzzling, macho, jock seminarians and sherry-sipping bookworms devoted to classical music. In these cases also, one group might feel themselves marginalized by the other and might in fact be excluded in some ways. It is necessary therefore to examine more carefully the extent to which gay seminarians have been any more interpersonally cohesive and therefore potentially cordoned off from their peers than other "subcultures" within seminaries. It is at least possible that some of the complaints derive from an overreaction to *any* obvious gays in the priesthood. In other words, the preppy, jock man may simply be more generally accepted than, for instance, the artistic gay man, so the former's "culture" is not called problematic while the latter's is denigrated.

Some former seminarians report that sexually active gay seminarians sometimes can be protected, while gay students who simply speak openly about their sexual orientation are punished. Gavan Meehan, former seminarian at St. John's Seminary Brighton, Massachusetts, alleges that he was dismissed from seminary because he was open about his sexual orientation and, although celibate, was outspoken about issues regarding sexuality.[56] Meehan is quoted as saying: "I felt like I had to point out the hypocrisy. If you talk about being gay, even if you're celibate, that gets you in trouble. But if you're actually having sex and covering your bases, you don't have to worry about a thing."[57] This dynamic was repeated during the sexual abuse crisis when abusing priests were protected while priests who blew the whistle on their sexually transgressing brethren were punished. Here again, it is the silence—the insistence that the known be neither acknowledged nor spoken—that is experienced as most insidious and distressing by many witnesses to the system. It is also this silence that sets a template for meeting other sexual knowns with silence and secrecy, including the sexual abuse of minors.

For some priests, active homosexuality continues or begins after ordination. Sipe estimates that approximately 50 percent of homosexual priests act on their desires at least some of the time, a number consistent with his findings about heterosexual priests.[58] Also like heterosexual priests, gay clergy's sexual relationships range from the long-term and stable to the fleeting or promiscuous.[59] Further, like their straight counterparts, sexually active homosexual priests are found in every segment of the priesthood, including among bishops. One gay priest is quoted as saying, "I bumped into an auxiliary bishop at a gay hotel and saw the ordinary [bishop] of a diocese at a gay bar across country."[60]

When the hierarchy is involved in sexual relationships with lower clergy, sex and power conflate in ways that can heighten eroticism for the bishop while frightening the priest being seduced. Sipe tells of a young priest who was invited to an out-of-town conference by his bishop and, there, was propositioned by another bishop.[61] When the priest turned down the offer, the bishop reportedly responded, "You know, Father, if you want to progress in this organization, you are going to need friends."[62] The linkage between sex and career advancement is disturbing and represents the kind of corruption of power rife in the sexual abuse crisis.

Other homosexual priests have sex with each other or with gay men they meet in bars or through friends. Archbishop Rembert Weakland of Milwaukee was forced to resign in 2002 when it was learned he had paid $450,000 to a man with whom he had a consensual sexual affair.[63] Thomas Martin, assistant manager of a Springfield, Massachusetts gay bar, The Pub, counts a number of priests among his regular customers.[64] Another Springfield-area priest, Rev. James A. Sipitkowski, was photographed in women's clothing with other scantily clad men, according to another priest who found the pictures.[65] The obituary of another former Springfield priest disclosed a twenty-five-year relationship with another man, a period including the last three years of his priesthood.[66] One priest told me that he frequently left his job as chaplain to an order of nuns after hearing confessions on Saturday and headed for the gay bars of a nearby city where he would sometimes get picked up for one-night stands. Another priest confided that he and his longtime lover, who is also a priest, and three other sexually active gay priests were planning a vacation at a European gay resort. In 2002, New Hampshire Bishop John McCormack, former chair of the United States Conference of Catholic Bishops (US-CCB) Ad Hoc Committee on Sexual Abuse and former auxiliary bishop in Boston under Bernard Cardinal Law, directed a priest to clear out the home of another priest found dead surrounded by sex-enhancing drugs, gay pornographic videos, leather thongs, and artificial genitalia.[67]

Although the institutional Church downplays the homosexual activity of its priests, the deaths of Catholic clergy suffering from AIDS challenge that minimization. In early 2000, the *Kansas City Star* reported that priests were dying of AIDS at more than double the rate of the general adult male population in states in which death certificates were publicly accessible.[68] Richard Selik, an AIDS specialist with the Centers for Disease Control and Prevention, supported the *Star's* claim that priests were dying of AIDS at rates higher than other men over twenty-five.[69] In 1987, one in twelve seminarians at the prestigious North American College seminary in Rome tested positive for HIV.[70] Fr. Michael Peterson, former president of St. Luke's Institute, a treatment facility for troubled priests, died of the disease,[71] as did one Chicago priest who claimed to have infected eight other priests.[72] The *Kansas City Star's* investigation revealed that prior to 2000, AIDS had claimed: "a priest who had served as an AIDS consultant to the Vatican, a rector of a seminary in the Midwest, two seminary directors, three college chaplains, the spiritual director of a seminary, a Catholic prep school principal, and a former employee of the National Conference of Catholic Bishops."[73] An auxiliary bishop of New York, Eamon Moore, in 1995 became the first bishop known to have died of AIDS.[74]

Despite evidence that homosexually active priests were contracting HIV in relatively large numbers, the official Church stuck with its story that there are very few homosexually oriented priests in the priesthood and fewer still who are sexually active.[75] Donald Cozzens states, "Church officials themselves stood guard at the closet doors."[76] While the Church refused to acknowledge the realities lived out by their homosexual priests, both celibate and sexually active, some officials within the Church were eager to scapegoat these nonexistent priests as the source of the sexual abuse scandal.

Homosexuality and Sexual Abuse

Roman Catholic priests were reported to have abused mostly males.[77] One study found that 64 percent of the accused priests abused only males; 22.6 percent abused only females; 3.6 percent abused both females and males; and, in 10 percent of the cases, the gender was unknown.[78] Other research indicated that 78 percent of allegations received in 2004 were from males, while 22 percent were from females.[79]

Not only were most reported victims of Catholic priests male, they also were pubescent. Almost 60 percent of male victims were first abused between the ages of ten and fourteen.[80] These are not, however, fully developed males and would not be attractive to mature homosexual men.

Sherrel L. Hammer, M.D., of the University of Hawaii measured the onset of puberty by the nature of the boy's pubic hair and by testicular volume and length.[81] She concludes that male puberty begins, on average, at 12.2 (pubic hair) or 11.2 (testicular growth) but is not completed until 14 years of age. Similarly, Kirby Parker Jones, M.D., of the University of Utah cites 11.6 as the age of onset of male puberty and asserts that the pubertal process continues for two years.[82]

Kohansky and Cohen, experts in the field of sexual offenders, suggest that sexual abuse of a pubertal boy may have signified sexual merger with a male perceived to be a psychosexual peer of the abuser.[83] In addition, it may have represented an unconscious act of hostility toward a boy who otherwise could look forward to a sexual life closed off to the priest. In other words, the abuser, who could have entered a minor seminary at age fourteen or fifteen, may have unconsciously acted against his victim's sexuality at the same age he was when he entered the minor seminary, symbolically disempowering the victim sexually as he himself was disempowered.

The gender and age of so many victims created space for Catholic commentators to link homosexuality and sexual abuse, with some Vatican officials, bishops, and conservative Catholics scapegoating homosexual priests for causing the scandal. Jorge Arturo Cardinal Medina Estevez, now retired prefect for the Congregation for Divine Worship and Discipline of the Sacraments, declared that homosexual men, or men with homosexual tendencies, are not suitable to be ordained and that it is pastorally risky to have homosexuals in the priesthood.[84] An American official in the Vatican's Congregation for Bishops, Rev. Andrew Baker, agreed.[85]

Author David Gibson notes that Baker feels gay men cannot be priests for a variety of reasons, including what Baker says are their tendencies toward substance abuse, sexual addiction, and depression; their duplicitous or pretentious behaviors, which can infect the souls of other seminarians; their inability to control sexual impulses; and the negative impact of their effeminate ways on priests striving for a proper manhood.[86] Baker also holds that gay men are unsuited for the priesthood because, since they are attracted to men, they cannot enter into a spousal relationship with the Church as their bride.[87] Further, since homosexual men must be celibate to be in full communion with the Church, celibacy does not represent a sacrifice for gay priests.[88]

The cardinal and Rev. Baker spoke from Rome. Closer to home, conservative Deal Hudson of *Crisis Magazine* blamed the sexual abuse scandal on gay priests, saying, "I think the primary source of this crisis is homosexual activity among clergy."[89] It was later revealed by the *National Catholic Reporter* that Hudson had lost his faculty position at Fordham University years ago after having been credibly accused of sexually assaulting one of his female students.[90] Similarly, Rev. Charles Dahlby accuses American bishops of ordaining and protecting homosexual priests who then abused children.[91] Linking homosexuality and pedophilia, Dahlby claims that both are perversions that need to be eradicated in the priesthood.[92]

In November 2005, the Vatican issued directives cautioning seminary directors about accepting homosexual candidates for the priesthood. The document instructed rejection of applicants who have not lived celibately for at least three years, who are part of a "gay culture" or who support gay affirmations like Gay Pride parades, or whose homosexuality is "deep-seated."[93] The document links homosexuality with affective immaturity and suggests that only men with "homosexual tendencies that might only be a manifestation of a transitory problem, as for example, delayed adolescence" are suitable for the priesthood.[94] The introduction to the directive seems to refer obliquely to the sexual abuse crisis, and perhaps to the contemporary push for gay unions and marriages, when it says that the instruction is "made more urgent by the current situation."[95] Further, a committee of clergy, commissioned to conduct visitations at American seminaries, planned to focus intently on the place of *homo*sexuality in these training facilities.[96] The Vatican's intervention regarding gays in the priesthood drew criticism from experts on sexual offenders.

Robert Geffner, psychologist and editor of the *Journal of Child Sexual Abuse*, stated that research indicates that homosexuals are no more likely than heterosexuals to violate minors sexually.[97] Leslie Lothstein, director of psychology at Hartford Hospital's Institute of Living, treated many sexually active priests, including some who abused minors. Lothstein insisted that the sexually active gay priests he treated had sex with age-appropriate men and that even priests who abused minor males were, in fact, mostly heterosexual.[98] He asserted that priests abused minor males in part because they were the most available victims and because they were "safer" to violate than minor girls, especially adolescents, who could get pregnant.[99] Lothstein said: "As a clinician, I can tell you that the gay priests I treat are having sex with age appropriate men. They may be violating their celibacy but not with children. . . . I've seen so many heterosexual priests who have . . . sex with teenage boys because they can't get them pregnant."[100]

David Finkelhor, director of Crimes against Children Research Center at the University of New Hampshire, views sexual attraction to minors as a separate sexual attraction, an opinion also espoused by John Bancroft, physician and director of the Kinsey Institute for Research in Sex, Gender, and Reproduction.[101] Groth and Oliveri studied over three thousand sexual offenders and did not find even one homosexual man who shifted from an attraction to adult men to a desire for minors.[102] Conversely, they found that men who were nonexclusively fixated on children, or who regressed from an attraction to adults to an interest in children, all described themselves as heterosexual and, in addition, usually were homophobic.[103] Similarly, Dimock concluded that most minor boys are abused by heterosexual men, some of whom are indifferent to the gender of their victims, choosing either girls or boys based on the minor's availability and vulnerability.[104] Fred Berlin, sexual offender expert at John Hopkins University School of Medicine and long-time advisor to the United States Conference of Catholic Bishops, stated that there is no evidence linking homosexuality with child abuse.[105] Michael Kimmel, professor of sociology at Stony Brook University, agreed that homosexuality and sexual abuse of minors are not correlated and that the selection of victims often depends more on availability than gender.[106] Finally, Hindman and Peters found that when three cohorts of sexual offenders were polygraphed, 47 percent of them acknowledged having molested boys while only 17 percent of the perpetrators self-reported that information.[107] Perhaps more sexual predators abuse boys than once was thought but are reluctant to say so and to be perceived as homosexuals.

As Lothstein, Dimock, and Kimmel suggest, victim gender selection by priests partially reflected opportunity rather than sexual orientation. Consider, for example, prison sex in which heterosexual males with more power and authority within the inmate population select and rape other, less-powerful men to achieve sexual release and to impose their power on another person. Boys were much more available to priests than were girls. Parents were thrilled to have a priest single their boy out for attention and encouraged their sons to spend time with Father, even allowing them to travel with the priest. Even years ago, parents would not have felt as comfortable having their girls spend too much time with the priest, and he, in turn, would have known it would look suspicious to have girls tagging after him. Further, many priests were frightened of and misogynistic toward girls and women so would be put off from having sex with them. Seminarians, remember, were taught the doctrine of "custody of the eyes."[108] This doctrine instructed them not even to look at women but rather to lower their eyes in the presence of a female.[109] Priests, as Lothstein suggests, might also be wary of impregnating pubescent or postpubescent girls.[110] Finally, some priests defined celibacy as refraining from sexual relationships with women and thus could convince themselves that sex with minor males did not jeopardize their celibate status.

Vatican officials, in their search to blame the sexual abuse scandal on someone or something external to the failings of the Church itself, conflated sexual orientation with psychosexual maturation and with criminal behavior. Psychosexually mature, adult homosexual men have consensual sex with other adult men, much as psychosexually mature, adult heterosexual men have consensual sex with adult women. Criminal heterosexuals sexually violate adult women and children of both genders; almost surely some criminal homosexuals sexually victimize adult men and some minors. These are crimes of power, ultimately having little to do with sex or the sexual orientation of the criminal. Both in and out of the priesthood, there also may be some psychosexually immature heterosexual or homosexual men who turn to minors of either gender because, in the subjective experience of the offender, the young people are considered to be psychosexual peers. While researchers and clinicians working with sexual offenders maintain that the vast majority of perpetrators are heterosexual, we must also consider the possibility that some sexual abusers are homosexual men who deny their orientation, replacing recognition and acceptance with homophobia. Other priest abusers may have never consolidated any sexual orientation, claiming to be heterosexual in the breach of their confusion, conflict, or ignorance. All priests who abuse are criminals, although the potential for rehabilitation may differ among types of offenders. The imperative point here is that, for the sexual perpetrators in any one of these groups, their criminal behaviors stem not from their sexual orientation but rather reflect psychological immaturity, arrested development, or antisocial, criminal proclivities, a fact relentlessly presented to the Vatican and just as relentlessly ignored.[111]

The Vatican's restrictions on accepting gay men into the priesthood will be unlikely to have much impact on criminal priests or more troubled priests, other than implicitly directing them to lie about their orientation, thus remaining psychosexually immature and potentially dangerous to adult parishioners and minors. Instead, the Vatican's policy will primarily persecute gay men who have accepted their homosexuality enough to speak about it. Fr. Gerard Thomas, a gay priest writing under a pseudonym, says "The only gay men who will enter [the seminary] will be either clueless, closeted or lying. This is a disastrous way to prepare men for healthy life as a priest, and gives rise to the very environment that everyone wanted to avoid: the repressed, fearful seminary where sexuality is a forbidden topic."[112] Rev. Paul Michaels agrees that the instruction will reduce the pool of applicants to the seminary as well as inducing some seminarians and ordained priests to leave, adding to an already daunting shortage of priests in the United States.[113]

The attempts by some Catholic lay commentators, priests, bishops, and Vatican officials to blame homosexual priests for the sexual abuse scandal are, in and of themselves, another scandal. It is a morally corrupt strategy to deflect responsibility for the crisis onto the vulnerable and already marginalized. The Vatican's remarks on homosexual priests were so provocative and inconsistent with contemporary understandings of homosexuality, in fact, that the Episcopal bishops of Massachusetts went public with unusually open criticism of the Catholic Church. Bishops M. Thomas Shaw and Roy F. Cederholm warned that Vatican attempts to link homosexuality with the sexual abuse crisis were irresponsible, incorrect, and invited hate crimes against gays.[114] Similarly, Rev. Kenneth Himes, chairman of the theology department at Boston College, advised bishops who want to understand the causes of the sexual abuse crisis to begin by investigating their own offices rather than focusing on the extent of homosexuality in American seminaries.[115] Himes said, "What really created the sexual abuse crisis was not poor formation of priests in the seminaries, but poor personnel management in chanceries. . . . I wonder when the Vatican and American bishops will investigate their own chanceries."[116]

The Catholic Hierarchy

CHAPTER 8

Where Were the Pastors?

[P]astoralism focuses more on people than on rules and is . . . more understanding than judgmental, and more pragmatic than ideological. The pastoral person is guided by the wisdom of experience. He or she responds to the needs of flesh and blood individuals.

—Rev. Richard P. McBrien, Theologian[1]

Bishops have both pastoral and institutional responsibilities. As guardians of the institutional Church, they are chief executives of nonprofit corporations that deliver a myriad of educational and social service programs, pay numerous employees, manage investments, conserve art, settle legal conflicts, and oversee properties and buildings. As pastors, on the other hand, bishops must care for the Catholics in their dioceses; they are to extend the love, mercy, and compassion they believe derive from Jesus Christ and his Apostles to the priests, religious men and women, and laypeople living in their ecclesiastical domains. Even in the best of times, the pastoral and corporate demands of a diocese can clash, engendering conflicting agendas. At times of crisis, the potential incompatibility of executive and pastoral roles may challenge a bishop's ability to hold in mind simultaneously his divergent responsibilities and cares. To achieve that balance, always emphasizing pastoral duties, however, is a bishop's job. Pope Benedict XVI, in fact, emphasized a bishop's pastoral responsibilities in his first papal encyclical: "He [the bishop] promises expressly to be, in the Lord's name, welcoming and merciful to the poor and to all those in need of consolation and assistance."[2]

When it came to the sexual abuse of minors by Catholic priests, many bishops sacrificed the kind of pastoral love and concern described by Mc-

Brien and Pope Benedict in order to protect the institutional Church. With armies of lawyers, insurance company executives, and public relations strategists in tow, bishops tried to conceal rather than openly confront the burgeoning sexual abuse crisis. In the process, they acted too much like "branch managers for a multinational religious corporation," rather than pastorally attending to their brother priests, alleged victims of their priests, and stricken laity.[3]

Revictimizing the Victims

It is perhaps particularly difficult to comprehend the lack of compassion shown by many in the hierarchy toward victims, survivors, and their families.

In some cases, bishops simply refused to meet with victims. Justin Cardinal Rigali, former archbishop of St. Louis and now cardinal archbishop of Philadelphia, declined to meet with any alleged victims/survivors in his nine years in St. Louis, despite repeated requests from those alleging that they had been sexually abused.[4] Archbishop Harry Flynn of St. Paul and Minneapolis, and chair of the Ad Hoc Committee on Sexual Abuse of the United States Conference of Catholic Bishops (USCCB), refused in October 2002 to meet with an alleged female victim/survivor who expressed interest in dropping her lawsuit in exchange for a meeting with Flynn during which they would discuss policies and procedures designed to more effectively prevent sexual abuse.[5] Flynn would not receive the woman if either her lawyer or a victim's advocate accompanied her.[6] At about the same time, SNAP (Survivor Network for those Abused by Priests) requested a meeting with Flynn, who, by January 2003, had not responded because, according to his spokesperson, "The archbishop has been very busy. It just fell between the cracks."[7]

It is challenging to imagine what could be a higher priority for the chair of the hierarchy's committee on sexual abuse than meeting with as many alleged victims of sexual abuse as possible, as well as with abusing priests, rank-and-file priests, and the laity about just this issue. In fact, it would seem reasonable to expect that Archbishop Flynn would consider his primary pastoral mission to be learning everything possible about sexual abuse and its impact on the Church community directly from those affected by it. Or, as Rev. Thomas Doyle, a canon lawyer and victims' advocate, advised the bishops,

> [D]rop everything, realize that these boys and girls, men and women
> who were sexually abused as children, . . . are not the enemy. They've

been deeply, deeply, deeply hurt—devastated. They're the most important people in the Church. Drop your meetings, your social events, your guest appearances. Go to them. One by one, sit in their homes, listen to them, let them cry, let them be angry, but help take some of that pain away. Do what Christ would do. Do what a real priest would do. . . . [Christ] was out getting his hands dirty and his feet dirty with people. That's what should happen here.[8]

Some bishops suggested that they were unable to meet with victims because of legal constraints imposed by their lawyers. While attorneys may have advised diocesan leaders about the potential legal pitfalls of personally seeing victims, ultimately it was the client who decided what his policy was in these matters. Bishops abdicated their pastoral responsibilities when they hid behind their lawyers, deflecting responsibility for decisions that were hurtful to those already violated by clergy and, ultimately, deepening the crisis. Papal biographer George Weigel said,

A bishop whose lawyers advise him not to meet with a victim of sexual abuse or with the victim's family because of possible legal implications needs different lawyers—lawyers who understand what a bishop is, and who has the legal wit and skill to make sure that when the bishop exercises genuine pastoral care and responsibility, he does not end up compromising his legal position or his diocese's.[9]

Trina Cysz and Martin Bono said they sued the Diocese of Springfield, Massachusetts, only because the diocese did not respond pastorally to their complaints against two different priests.[10] Had more bishops been willing to reach out to victims personally, there may have been less need for lawyers. Many victims never wanted to become plaintiffs in the first place but only wanted their Church, through the bishop, to do the right things: to apologize for harm done and to commit to better behaviors in the future.

Frequently, when a bishop did speak directly with an alleged victim or the family, he attempted to impose silence on complainants. Eugene Kennedy says, "The victims and their families, following the prevailing cultural practice [of the Church], were to put this out of their minds, never talk of it to anyone, after all, you don't want to hurt Father, do you? Keep this to yourself, in the mantra of that hierarchically dominated culture's ultimate undoing, for the good of the Church."[11]

Psychologically reversing the roles of victim and victimizer, these bishops denied the seriousness of the crime, devalued the victim, and tried to project shame, guilt, and responsibility for protecting the Church onto the individuals alleging that harm had been done to them.

Former Phoenix Bishop Thomas J. O'Brien, for example, was noted for his efforts to keep alleged victims and their families quiet about sexual abuse.[12] When Betty Shannon's three children were abused by Fr. Mark Lehman, O'Brien called Mrs. Shannon and told her that she needed to stop talking about the abuse.[13] O'Brien's policy was to refrain from consoling or supporting victims, a strategy he attributed to advice from legal counsel.[14] In June 2003, Bishop O'Brien avoided indictment for obstruction of justice by publicly acknowledging that he covered up sexual abuse complaints for years.[15] Shortly thereafter, the bishop resigned after he was arrested for leaving the scene of a fatal hit-and-run accident.[16] O'Brien left his victim in the street, did not respond to calls from police in the days after the incident, and tried to have his car windshield, shattered by the impact of the victim's body, repaired the morning of his arrest.[17] Comparisons with O'Brien's treatment of sexual abuse victims were inevitable. SNAP's Paul Pfaffenberger reportedly commented, "He once again ignored victims and drove away."[18]

A Long Island grand jury concluded that well into the 1990s, after the bishops ostensibly were addressing sexual abuse more openly and appropriately, the Diocese of Rockville Centre consciously worked to "trick and silence victims, cover up crimes, avoid scandals, and hold down financial consequences."[19] In evaluating the response of the diocese to alleged victims, the grand jury stated, "The response of priests in the diocesan hierarchy to allegations of criminal sexual abuse was not pastoral. In fact, although there was a written policy that set a pastoral tone, it was a sham."[20] Monsignor Alan Placa, former vice chancellor of the diocese, was the chief contact for victims.[21] In April 2003, Placa resigned after being accused of sexually molesting three adolescent males twenty-five years ago.[22]

In addition to trying to silence the voices of abused Catholics and their representatives, some dioceses suggested that victims or their families were responsible for the sexual violations. In 1995, for example, Archbishop Oscar Lipscomb of Mobile, Alabama, stated in a court deposition that, in order to evaluate the emotional consequences for a fourteen-year-old boy sexually violated by a priest, he would, "want to know . . . is [the boy] totally innocent, unspoiled, pure, or is he somebody who in his own way may have invited or even initiated these kinds [of acts]."[23] In Dallas, chancery official Monsignor Robert Rehkemper suggested that the victims of Fr. Rudy Kos shared responsibility for their abuse as did their parents, asserting that anyone past the age of reason (seven years old according to the Church) knows right from wrong.[24] Jurors in the Kos case were so disturbed by the Dallas diocese's lack of pastoral concern for victims that they took the unusual step of admonishing Church officials to "admit your guilt and allow these young men to get on with their lives."[25] The Diocese of Covington, Kentucky, responded to a lawsuit, brought by a man who was thirteen years old when he allegedly was abused by a priest, by suggesting that "the plaintiff may have assumed a known and obvious risk" or "may have been comparatively negligent."[26] In its response to a lawsuit, the Diocese of Stockton claimed that an alleged victim of confessed child molester and former priest Oliver O'Grady did not take adequate "care, caution, or prudence" to avoid being molested when he was O'Grady's altar boy.[27]

As evidenced here, dioceses often played legal hardball in responding to plaintiffs suing the Church. In New Jersey, the Diocese of Camden under Bishop Nicholas DiMarzio, now bishop of Brooklyn, authorized private investigators to obtain information about plaintiffs in sexual abuse lawsuits by questioning their neighbors, ex-wives, relatives, friends, or current and former employers, in the process revealing the plaintiffs' alleged sexual abuse histories.[28] Two plaintiffs claimed that investigators hired by the diocese had suggested to neighbors or former employers that the plaintiffs might be abusing children themselves.[29] In Boston, Cardinal Law's interim successor, Bishop Richard G. Lennon, now bishop of Cleveland, allowed his legal counsel to subpoena therapists working with alleged survivors of abuse,[30] stimulating a firestorm of protests from survivors, victim advocates, and mental health professionals who perceived the deposition of therapists as an act of reabuse.[31] Finally, the Archdiocese of Seattle hired a lawyer, Jessie Dye, as their pastoral outreach coordinator for victims.[32] Victims alleged that they were not told that Dye was an attorney. Further, the survivors said that Dye actively discouraged them from hiring their own attorneys. John Shuster, an inactive Washington priest, told reporters that "the Archdiocese of Seattle uses the hot line to identify all victims who might sue and lure them in, to get as much information as possible so they can prep their own team of lawyers."

All the adversarial tactics employed by the Church were legal, and most were standard boilerplate defenses marshaled in personal injury lawsuits. Spokespeople for bishops cited the legality of their defense strategies and justified them as necessary to protect the assets of the Church in order keep dioceses running.[33] Although these litigation approaches were legally available to the bishops, there were strong arguments against the morality of employing them in sexual abuse cases.

First, in a number of cases, the guilt of the abuser already had been established in courts of law or by his own admission. Under these circumstances, it seemed indefensible for the Church to attempt to wear victims down through aggressive legal maneuvers. Second, for bishops to avail themselves of defenses that, although legal, were likely to further damage the psyche and souls of alleged victims required a splitting of moral experience that was disquieting.

The Catholic Church is adamant that Catholics may not access certain legal solutions to personal problems, even financially crippling difficulties, because the Church teaches that they are morally unacceptable. Catholics are not to engage in any sexual activity outside of marriage; may not use artificial contraception even if additional children would be emotionally or economically detrimental to the family; may not obtain abortions to terminate unwanted pregnancies even if the pregnancy would result in devastating financial, educational, or psychological consequences for the pregnant woman or couple; and may not use condoms to stop the spread of HIV/AIDS, a disease that both kills and costs society a great deal of money in direct services to sufferers. The same bishops, therefore, who would tell a couple that they cannot continue a fulfilling sexual relationship while using artificial contraception to plan the size of their family to meet their psychological and economic resources, justified attempts to discredit alleged victims of sexual abuse on economic grounds.

Donald Cozzens comments on the lack of pastoral sensitivity apparent in these legal tactics:

> [T]he church ... sometimes betrays its pastoral sentiments by employing legal strategies and deposition tactics that have upset and angered victims and parishioners alike. . . . Church officials appear to think they are justified in using hardball tactics in response to what they consider to be the hardball tactics of victims and their attorneys. The effects of such assumptions on the part of the church have compounded the pain and suffering of victims. The damage done to the church's image when such power tactics are employed is considerable.[34]

Finally, the bishops' legal strategies appeared to contradict the gospel on which their mission is founded. As reported in Matthew (5:23–26, 40–41), Jesus said:

> Come to terms quickly with your accuser while you are on the way to court with him or your accuser may hand you over to the judge, and the judge to the guard, and you will be thrown into prison. Truly I tell you, you will never get out until you have paid the last penny . . . and

if anyone wants to sue you and take your coat, give your cloak as well; and if anyone forces you to go one mile, go also the second mile.

Although many bishops lacked a pastoral attitude toward victims, there were some ecclesiastical pastors. Retired Archbishop Rembert Weakland and current Archbishop Timothy Dolan of Milwaukee apologized together to a former altar boy who had been sexually abused by a priest almost thirty years prior.[35] The victim/survivor termed the meeting with the bishops "a session in restorative justice."[36] Archbishop Dolan also publicly supported legislative changes in Wisconsin to require clergy to become mandated reporters of suspected cases of sexual abuse.[37] Archbishop Michael J. Sheehan took over the Santa Fe, New Mexico, diocese in 1993 when it was in the midst of a sexual abuse scandal and earned praise from prosecutors and victims for his cooperation with legal authorities and his pastoral outreach to victims.[38] When he temporarily assumed responsibility for the Phoenix diocese as well, Sheehan vowed to meet one-on-one with victims, saying, "[T]hey were abused one to one, and they should receive an apology one to one."[39] After the Archdiocese of Louisville settled with 243 victims of sexual abuse by its priests, Archbishop Thomas Kelly opened his doors to any victim/survivor who wanted to meet with him.[40] One victim, Mike Turner, who once had called on Kelly to resign, described the archbishop as "warm, receptive, and a pleasure to talk to" in a postsettlement meeting.[41] In San Bernadino, Bishop Gerald Barnes included an extended story of one victim's molestation in a diocesan newsletter handed out to each parishioner in the diocese's 110 parishes.[42] Barnes also talked about the consequences of sexual abuse by priests in a video shown at every Mass in the diocese one Sunday.[43]

Enabling and Abandoning Abusers

In September 2002, Pope John Paul II addressed 120 newly appointed bishops and exhorted them to consider the meaning of having priests place their hands in those of their bishop at the moment of ordination. The pope said, "The young priest chooses to entrust himself to the Bishop and, for his part, the Bishop obliges himself to look after those hands. In this way, the Bishop becomes responsible for the destiny of those hands he grasps within his hands. A priest must be able to feel, especially in moments of difficulty or loneliness, that his hands are held tightly by those of his Bishop."[44] As heinous as the crime of sexual abuse is, the priests who committed these crimes were ordained to be their bishops' spiritual sons.

Many American bishops, however, responded to abusive priests mostly in unpastoral ways.

When a bishop reassigned a sexual offender to a new location with access to children, that priest was enabled by his bishop to continue violating minors. Whatever a bishop's conscious motives were in making these reassignments, the covert communication to the priest was that he was free, if not encouraged, to find new victims. In some instances, it seemed that a bishop almost ensured the inevitability of a priest reabusing as when Bishop Gerard Frey formerly of Lafayette, Louisiana, appointed Gilbert Gauthe to be a Boy Scout chaplain after Gauthe already had come to Frey's attention for molesting a young boy.[45] Similarly, Bishop Odore Gendron formerly of Manchester, New Hampshire, assigned Rev. Paul Aube to a Rochester, New Hampshire, parish and put him in charge of a youth program even though Aube had confessed to molesting a minor and specifically asked his bishop for an assignment away from children.[46] Aube allegedly abused at least seven minors in Rochester.[47]

A reasonable person with no particular expertise in social sciences or criminal justice would not arrange for a known diamond thief, even a one-time thief, to work as an unsupervised night watchman at Harry Winston, especially without informing the famous jeweler's management about the new employee's background. In fact, as early as 1956, Bishop Matthew F. Brady of New Hampshire knew that a sexually trangressive priest should not have access to new potential victims.[48] Brady removed Fr. John T. Sullivan from ministry after a series of sexual incidents, including the impregnation of a woman who almost died after an attempted abortion. Not only did Brady keep Sullivan out of his own diocese, he wrote numerous letters to other bishops informing them of Sullivan's sexual problems and crimes and urging them not to take him into ministry in their dioceses. Yet bishops across the country kept men who had abused in ministry with access to minors and thereby failed these priests by not doing everything possible to make sure that they could not violate a child or adolescent again.

Bishops sometimes blamed poor advice from mental health professionals for sending sexually abusive priests to new locations where they would be in contact with minors. It was disingenuous, however, for bishops to hide behind their acceptance of what may have been inaccurate psychological feedback when they refused to take seriously years of social science advice about other human behaviors like birth control, divorce, or homosexuality. As they criticize "cafeteria Catholics" for choosing to adhere to some Church teachings while discarding others, the bishops have little credibility as "cafeteria advisees" who picked the psychological findings most helpful in excusing their own behaviors while discarding others.

While it is likely that unrealistically optimistic prognoses were generated by some clinicians, especially before research in the field of sexual abuse began to be published in the mid- to late 1980s, it is also true that some bishops placed priests back in ministry against professional advice.[49] Further, Leslie Lothstein of the Institute of Living, a treatment facility that worked with many priests who had abused, asserted that referring bishops often withheld pertinent facts about a priest's background, including his prior offenses.[50] Lothstein cites as an example a deposition in which a Connecticut bishop said "he withheld crucial information about a priest's long history of molesting minors from the Institute of Living (where the priest was sent for psychological evaluation and treatment) because he did want to spoil the reputation of the priest."[51]

In addition to the clinical and evaluative problems this kind of deception presented for treatment facilities, it discouraged the referred priest from being honest about his background, which, in turn, limited the potential for truly effective treatment. Rather, the priest was allowed or even covertly encouraged by his bishop to continue the lies and secrecy associated with sexual abuse and antithetical to successful psychological growth. Emerging from an evaluation or course of treatment that was founded on a sham, then placed by his bishop in another location with minors available to him, the priest in these circumstances was unlikely to experience a conversion and, in fact, having "gotten over" on a treatment facility with the help of his bishop, could construe that he had been given implicit permission by Church officials to resume his sexual victimizations.

After the scandal became national news in early 2002, and especially after the USCCB's passage of the Charter for the Protection of Children and Young People at the bishops' June 2002 meeting in Dallas, the hierarchy began to remove from ministry any priest against whom even one credible accusation of sexual abuse had been lodged, even if it were decades ago. This policy became commonly known as the bishops' "zero tolerance" position. By the end of 2004, over seven hundred priests had been removed from ministry.[52] Many of these men were moved into secular lives with which they had no lived experience. Although the Church often continued to pay a salary or retirement and provided health benefits, the priests were ripped from the only communities many of them had known since adolescence. The bishops were under enormous pressure to take this approach, and although many laypeople and even professionals, including this writer, encouraged zero tolerance at the time, the luxury of further reflection leads to the conclusion that the policy was not only unpastoral, but also potentially dangerous both for the priests and for the wider society.

Removing a priest from ministry *and* ousting him from his community of brother priests represented an assault on the man's identity. His title, attire, home, job, and clerical kinship networks were wrested from the priest through potentially traumatic processes in which little regard was shown for the unique circumstances of each individual. Traumatic loss often engenders depression, substance abuse, and/or regression to more immature and primitive modes of cognition, affective regulation, impulse control, judgment, and senses of self and others. Since 1993, for example, over two dozen clergy suicides have been linked to the sexual abuse of minors.[53]

Bill Marshall, an expert with over thirty-five years of research and clinical experience with rapists and child molesters, told Vatican officials in April 2003 that a priest removed from ministry for sexual abuse was at great risk to kill himself or to reoffend.[54] Unfortunately, we already know that reabuse occurred in some cases. Richard J. Mieliwocki was suspended from the priesthood in the Archdiocese of Newark in 2003 after he was accused of sexual misconduct going back to 1988.[55] He was arrested in 2004 and charged with molesting four adolescent males while working as a social worker in a substance abuse program.[56] Gary J. Plunkett was suspended from the priesthood in the Diocese of Peoria in May 2003 due to sexual abuse allegations and was arrested in December of that year for molesting an adolescent boy.[57] Barry Ryan, another suspended priest who had served in Brooklyn and Queens, admitted to abusing a six-year-old boy on Long Island in 2003.[58] Vincent McCaffrey, a former priest of the Archdiocese of Chicago with a long history of abusing boys, pleaded guilty in 2002 to possession of over four thousand images of child pornography.[59] At trial, McCaffrey told the court, "I cannot be cured." These priests and others who were released from ministry may have regressed enough to abuse minors again, even if they had not offended for many years. Stripped of most essential elements of their identities, including the ability to say Mass, some priests were likely to displace their fears, disempowerment, shame, and rage onto new victims over whom they could feel temporarily dominant and in control.

Priests may be even more likely to reoffend than some other sexual abusers. Researchers Hanson, Steffy, and Gauthier found that men who had never married, admitted to previous offenses, chose only male victims, and had poor relationships with their own fathers were more likely to reabuse than other men.[60] Many priests fell into this category. For their sakes and to protect society, the bishops would have been both prudent

and pastoral to try to arrange ongoing care and supervision of priest offenders who were not going to jail. Instead, bishops abandoned their spiritual sons seemingly as heartlessly as they had the victims of these priests.
Many bishops rid their dioceses of accused priests and disclaimed further
responsibility for them, as when Archbishop Harry Flynn said, "Once a
priest has been laicized [a course of action he expected most bishops to
pursue in cases of abusive priests], then it would not be the responsibility
of the bishop to follow that person, it would be the responsibility of the
civil authorities in any town or jurisdiction."[61] As Catholic commentator
Richard John Neuhaus put it, however, "The bishop is charged with the
discipline and care of his priests. Abandoning their care cannot be the
right answer to having failed in their discipline."[62]

Had bishops acted as pastors first, even after a priest was jailed, hos-
pitalized, dismissed from ministry, or laicized, his bishop would feel a
responsibility to maintain regular communication with his priest, a man
recognized by the bishop as a son in deep and ongoing need of ministry.
Archbishop John Favalora of Miami, for example, makes yearly Christmas
visits to a seminary classmate who is serving a life sentence for raping a
young boy; the bishop is adamant that "[e]veryone, no matter what the
circumstances, is entitled to experience the healing touch of Jesus."[63]

Pastoral bishops, even under enormous public pressure to *do* something about the sexual abuse crisis, might have considered ways in which
they could fulfill their paternal and pastoral covenants with their priests
and their obligations to protect children by devising residential centers in
which abusing priests not going to prison could pray, repent, say Mass privately, and engage in productive work in tightly supervised communities.
While some priests might have chosen to live in the secular world when
they were removed from active ministry, others might have accepted the
opportunity to live out their lives in residential houses of prayer, penance,
productivity, and provisioning; situations enhancing the safety of abusive
priests and society alike.

At the 2002 National Assembly of the Conference of Major Superiors
of Men—the analogue to the USCCB for members of religious orders—
held in Philadelphia a few months after the USCCB's Dallas meeting, the
leadership of the religious orders insisted that sexually abusive priests and
brothers would be removed from ministry but remain members of their
religious communities.[64] The orders committed to supervise and restrict
their members who had abused but also to offer them a home and a life of
prayer and repentance. Insisting that even abusers were brothers in Christ
and members of a family, the orders refused to follow the bishops' lead
in ridding their communities of sexually abusive religious men. It was, of

course, easier for religious communities to continue in relationship with their abusive members since there were abbeys, monasteries, or other specific community residences in which these men could be assigned and supervised; dioceses did not have existing community residences in place.

In addition to fulfilling the orders' understanding of the gospel message, the decision to keep abusive priests within the community of religious men made psychological sense. Healing for any human being takes place in relationship. With the secrets of their abusive brothers exposed and with reflection on the community mores that perpetuated silence about sexual crimes, religious communities could become more transparent and honest "families." Under the best circumstances, nonabusing priests and brothers, living in community with identified perpetrators, might identify their own potential for violence and exploitation of others. Accepting, naming, and developing a relationship with our own often-dissociated capacity for evil reduces the likelihood that we will enact evil or tolerate its enactment within the "family." At the same time, the abuser who receives love and acceptance from his community, balanced with clarity and enforcement of necessary limitations, is the one most likely to change if change is at all possible. If an abuser has any capacity for empathy, it will grow only if he receives empathy from others. Empathy here is not mindless sympathy but rather recognition received from another who sees the abuser clearly, refuses to be deluded by him, and also tenaciously remains in relationship with him.

Neglecting Good Priests

In addition to victims and abusing priests, bishops had a pastoral responsibility to care for their decent priests who were reeling from the sexual abuse scandal. A pastoral bishop concerned about these men would have met personally with every priest in his diocese to process exactly how the new sexual abuse norms would be implemented in their diocese and to anticipate with them what the short- and longer-term effects might be on the ministries of these priests. During these meetings, the bishop would have listened to concerns, answered questions, and taken seriously suggestions made by his troops in the field about protecting children while upholding the due process rights of priests. Also at these meetings, a pastoral bishop, perhaps assisted by appropriate civil and canon law consultants, would have mapped out strategies for priests to respond to false allegations so that good priests inaccurately accused would not feel abandoned or forced into an isolated corner. A pastoral bishop would have met personally with, and arranged group meetings for, seminary classmates and friends of priests credibly accused and removed from ministry so that these clergy could mourn and express the full range of their reactions. Further, a pastoral bishop would have encouraged all his priests to meet regularly with each other for support and reflection and would have been open to comments and criticisms growing out of those meetings.

At the same time that he supported his priests, a pastoral bishop would have made clear his intolerance for the sexual violation of minors. He would have made explicit his determination to protect children and would have encouraged priests to come to him with any concerns about relationships fellow priests had with minors. Priests leaving these meetings would feel reassured that their spiritual father could combine love, compassion, and tough-mindedness in protecting the innocent and meting out justice to the predatory.

Such pastoral sensitivity rarely was shown toward a bishop's demoralized and frightened community of priests. Rather, the country's priests were devastated both by the depth and breadth of the sexual abuse scandal and by their bishops' apparent lack of empathy for them. For the most part, priests who asked questions about their bishops' actions were ignored,[65] urged to return to unquestioning obedience,[66] or ordered to be silent.[67]

A late 2002 nationwide poll found that two-thirds of American priests disapproved of the way in which their bishops were handling the crisis.[68] Scores of these priests experienced themselves as abandoned by their bishops. Texas-ordained Long Island, New York, pastor Rev. Malcolm Burns reportedly acknowledged to parishioners that he no longer was sure that priests could or should obey their bishops at all times.[69] Rev. Walter H. Cuenin of Boston reportedly stated, "The general feeling among priests around the country is we were hung out to dry."[70] Another Southern California priest reportedly expressed his desire to see a bishop or cardinal go to jail.[71] For priests to speak openly of their disappointment in their bishops and to question publicly their promises of obedience suggested that the bishops' lack of pastoral attention toward these priests deeply hurt and angered them.

There were, of course, bishops who tried to minister to their rank-and-file priests at the same time that they juggled lawsuits, removed priests from ministry, responded to media clamor, and were confronted by demands from victims' groups. Archbishop Timothy M. Dolan of Milwaukee, for instance, showed temperance toward and tolerance for 163 Wisconsin priests who sent letters to him and then USCCB President Wilton Gregory urging that mandatory celibacy be opened for discussion among the bishops, particularly in view of the ever-increasing priest shortage.[72]

While Dolan disagreed with his priests, he did so respectfully and without any apparent rancor.[73] The process in which he engaged was one of a father remonstrating with but not retaliating against rebellious but maturely adult sons. Whatever one's feelings are about the subject matter, Dolan's response to his priests was a reassuring reminder that bishops can take seriously their role as pastors to their priests.

Affronting the Laity

It is clear that bishops ignored the spiritual needs of their laity as they moved abusive priests to new locations without telling the parents of potential victims about the background of a new priest in their midst. Dismissing priests accused of sexual abuse without arranging for their ongoing supervision also offended Catholic laity and other individuals into whose communities potentially dangerous priests moved. To that extent, bishops robbed parents of their right to exercise informed supervision of their children and to protect them from unnecessary danger. Once the scandal became public in 2002, most bishops made little effort to be present to the laity in order to address their concerns and pain directly. Rather, many bishops communicated with the laity by letters read at Mass by their already demoralized priests.

That pastoral sensitivity still could be an elusive diocesan quality well into the scandal was demonstrated in the summer of 2003 when the Archdiocese of Boston quietly changed important clauses in the sexual abuse policies drafted by two lay advisory groups and published with much fanfare by the diocese in May 2003.[74] The changes reportedly were made without the knowledge of the members of either lay group commissioned to help the archdiocese craft its sexual abuse policies. They represented substantive modifications that limited a victim's access to records of church proceedings in cases of accused priests. Maureen Scannell Bateman, chairwoman of one of the lay panels, reportedly complained that the policy changes came with "no notice from the archdiocese that they were going to change the policy. We labored and labored over our report. Why would they then change [it] without telling anyone? That's a very valid question." A noted sexual abuse expert and past member of one of Boston's lay commissions, Dr. David Finkelhor, reportedly expressed concern that "the church has reverted to making decisions about the child protection policy without any outside input" and thus was backsliding into the kind of maneuvering that brought about the crisis in the first place. Terrence Carroll, former chair of the Seattle Archdiocese's case-review board on sexual abuse of minors, complained that the diocese, under Archbishop

Alex Brunett, had not responded to the board's report on sexual abuse in the diocese but rather had dismissed the board.[75]

While many bishops failed to provide pastoral leadership to the laity of their dioceses, some did, especially after the crisis burgeoned in 2002. Syracuse Bishop James Moynihan, for example, conducted a "Time of Healing" prayer service during which he got down on his knees and apologized to his laity, reportedly saying, "People of this region have been harmed and their faith has been sorely tested by the sins of priests and bishops. I stand before you tonight to tell you I repent for the sins that have been committed and I repent for the harm that has been done."[76] More trusting of their bishop than most bishops had been of their laities, the parishioners of Syracuse were comforted by Moynihan's actions and expressed hope that healing could begin in that diocese.[77] Similarly, Archbishop Michael J. Sheehan of Santa Fe reportedly exhorted the laypeople of his diocese not to put their faith in priests or bishops but, rather, to put it in the Lord where it could not be hurt.[78] In a letter mailed to 180,000 Catholic homes in the Archdiocese of Baltimore, William Cardinal Keeler released details about all priests credibly accused of abuse in his diocese and also revealed financial data related to sexual abuse.[79] Keeler apologized to the laity personally saying,

> My fellow bishops and I must respond to the violence already visited on our children by saying we are sorry. At times, we have let our fears of scandal override the need for the kind of openness that helps prevent abuse. In the past, we sometimes have responded to victims and families as adversaries, not as suffering members of the Church. . . . I humbly ask forgiveness for my mistakes. Please pray for me so that I may better serve.[80]

Short on Priests, Short on Pastoral Promise

Perhaps influencing the bishops' pastoral lapses was the pressure they felt from an increasing priest shortage. Since the 1960s, there has been a growing priest shortage in the United States.[81] In 2004, there were about 43,000 priests in America, down from over 58,600 in 1965.[82] Only 533 new priests were ordained in 2004, down to about half of 1965 levels.[83] At the same time, the number of registered Catholics is increasing, thereby forcing fewer priests to minister to more Catholics.[84] In 2003, over 16 percent of American parishes had no resident priest and 60 percent of active priests served alone in a parish or rode a circuit covering several communities.[85] For every 100 priests dying or retiring, only 35 new priests are being ordained,[86] and, of these, studies project that from 3 to 7 of them will leave the priesthood within five years of being ordained.[87]

Compounding the problem of a declining number of priests is the aging of the priesthood. In 2000, the average age of diocesan priests was fifty-nine, and for vowed religious priests, it was sixty-three.[88] In 2003, there were more American priests older than ninety than there were priests younger than thirty.[89]

There are many reasons for the priest shortage in this country. Catholics have been an upwardly mobile population, especially in the postwar period.[90] The priesthood is no longer considered a royal road to education, power, and respectability, especially by Catholic mothers who can take as much pride in their sons who become doctors, lawyers, teachers, and captains of industry as they once did in their sons who became priests. Many Catholic parents today sense the loneliness and difficulty of a priest's life, seeing it as far from an idealized life's calling, and actually discourage their sons from pursuing the priesthood. Rev. Donald Cozzens relates a story in which a young man expresses interest in the priesthood to a priest after Sunday Mass. As the priest hands the boy vocation materials, they are snatched away by the young man's mother, who says, "No son of mine is going to be a damn priest. . . . Nothing against you, Father. It's just that no son of mine is going to be a priest."[91] Cozzens also cites a USCCB study indicating that one in five Catholic parents would strongly discourage their child from becoming a priest, and two-thirds would withhold encouragement from a son expressing interest in the priesthood.[92]

While it is too early to discern the impact of the sexual abuse crisis on seminary applicants, it is reasonable to assume that it will have at least a short-term negative effect. Further, the Vatican's linkage of homosexuality with the sexual abuse crisis and the 2005 instruction against the ordination of homosexuals may decrease the number of homosexual men willing to pursue the priesthood as well as leading other ordained homosexuals to resign. One gay Franciscan seminary student was quoted as saying, "I do think about leaving. It's hard to live a duplicitous life."[93] One priest, Rev. Leonard Walker of Mesa, Arizona, resigned as a pastor and took a leave of absence from his Salvatorian religious order after the Vatican instruction was announced. Walker said, "It's like a Jew wearing a Nazi uniform. I could no longer stay in that institution with any amount of integrity."[94] Finally, the single greatest documented cause of decreased applications to seminaries and increased resignations among the ordained is mandatory celibacy.[95] Yet, Pope John Paul II stood by the centrality of celibacy for the priesthood and Pope Benedict XVI continues to do so.

As in the sexual abuse crisis, the reasons for the priest shortage were externalized and blamed on a materialistic and decadent culture rather than on internal obstacles to the recruitment of excellent priests. In 2003, the Vatican rejected arguments that opening the priesthood to married men would resolve the priest crisis, instead advising current priests to dedicate themselves to attracting new candidates by educating young people and their families about the priesthood and encouraging them to consider religious vocations.[96] The instruction begged the possibility that Catholic families already have some accurate perceptions of the priesthood and would prefer that their children look elsewhere for a fulfilling life.

Bishops who, over the years, developed a realistic appraisal of the priest shortage were caught in a conflict. Under John Paul II, there was the papal version of the problem, which considered it terminable and remedial through prayer and increased recruitment efforts, there were the facts of the worsening shortage unfolding before the bishops' eyes, and there was the fear that only the papal narrative could be verbalized without risking loss of papal favor and affection. In addition, because the pope declared that increased devotion and energetic recruitment could add to the priestly supply, a bishop whose seminaries stayed sparsely populated and/or whose ordained priests kept resigning might feel ashamed and threatened with the loss of the love of his spiritual father. It would be reasonable to think that, perhaps unintentionally, some bishops kept problematic priests in ministry in order to maintain their numbers. Monsignor Lawrence Breslin, former rector of Mount St. Mary's Seminary, for example, believes that Fr. Daniel C. Clark, accused of abusing nineteen children ages five to seventeen, was ordained against the advice of the seminary because the diocese was "desperate for bodies."[97]

Bishops Need Pastoring Too

In order to nurture well, we need to have been nurtured well early on in our lives and must continue to feel succored as an adult. Therefore, for American bishops to function first as pastors it was essential that they feel recognized, supported, and pastored by the pope and other Vatican officials. Under John Paul II, however, the American bishops were deprived of that. Rather, they were caught in a double bind in which one reality, verbally validated by a system, was contradicted by other realities, apparent at least to some members of system, but which there was a covert edict not to notice or speak about. Double binds work because there is a threat, usually implicit, to a potential "whistleblower" that they will lose the love of and attachment bond with the individual(s) in power if they speak openly about that which contradicts the system's allowable version of truth.

Rev. Thomas Reese describes the double binding at work in the Vatican when he quotes one priest with years of curial contact and another former curial worker:

> You know what you're expected to say [about anything], even though deep down you may think otherwise. When an encyclical comes out, you're expected to get behind it and say this is a very much needed statement and it just shows how close the church is to things, close to people. You say, well, the Holy Father is always right. . . .

> Loyalty means never criticizing a papal decision. You might thoroughly disagree but you do not criticize this in public. . . . It would be disloyal if I did that. When these things happen on a very high level, I said, well I accept every decision that the Holy Father is going to make and I accept it in silence.[98]

The stakes are thus high in this double binding Vatican system; most Vatican clergy and religious toe the line most of the time. Rather than reaching out pastorally to his American bishops, John Paul and his Vatican court double bound the U.S. prelates. First, despite ample evidence to the contrary, the Vatican insisted for a long time that sexual abuse was a peculiarly American, or at least a peculiarly Western, problem.[99] This paradigm was suited to the pope's contention that much of Western society had succumbed to a culture of death in which freedom, coupled with responsibility, had been degraded into license and moral relativism to the detriment of souls.[100]

In the pope's remarks to the American cardinals, summoned to Rome in April 2002 to discuss the sexual abuse scandal, John Paul subtly linked the crisis with the laxity of American sexual morals. Further, he implied that U.S. bishops failed to protect children, at least in part, by tolerating equivocation on Catholic moral teachings. Most commentators focused on the pope's declaration that there is no place in the priesthood and religious life for those who would harm the young.[101] His next sentence, however, read, "[People] must know that bishops and priests are totally committed to the fullness of Catholic truth on matter of sexual morality."[102] In the summary statement of the meeting, the same tone was taken: "[T]he pastors of the Church need clearly to promote the correct moral teaching of the Church and publicly to reprimand individuals who spread dissent and groups which advance ambiguous approaches to pastoral care."[103] Far from looking inward at teachings, traditions, and structures of the Church that may support sexual acting out and secrecy, John Paul reinforced the rightness of the Church and implied that enhanced fidelity to sexual teachings would solve the problem.

It may have rankled some cardinals that in a different room of the Vatican, Joseph Cardinal Ratzinger (Pope Benedict XVI), then powerful leader of the Congregation for the Doctrine of the Faith, was under some pressure from the media to confront longstanding sexual abuse charges against Legion of Christ founder and papal favorite Fr. Macial Maciel.[104] Nine former Legionaries, including a retired Spanish priest, a New York psychology professor, a professor at the U.S. Defense Languages School, a Harvard-trained scholar of Latin American studies, a lawyer, a rancher, an engineer, a schoolteacher, and a now-deceased priest and former university president, all accused Maciel of sexually abusing them when they were seminarians.[105] They all signed sworn affidavits, which were submitted to the Vatican, and also filed a lawsuit with the Vatican against Maciel.[106] As of November 2003, they had received no response.[107] When ABC reporter Brian Ross questioned Ratzinger about the case in April 2002, the cardinal reportedly slapped Ross's hand and appeared visibly upset.[108] Fr. Maciel consistently denied all the charges but the lack of thorough investigation was troublesome, especially in the context of other complaints about the Legion's recruitment and formation programs, which some former members liken to cultish brainwashing.[109] In May 2006, Pope Benedict XVI implicitly acknowledged the validity of allegations against Maciel by restricting the eighty-six-year-old priest's ministry and assigning him to a life of private prayer and penitence.[110]

Caught in a double bind in which the pope was lecturing one thing to his American cardinals while practicing something quite contradictory down the hall about which no one could openly speak, the cardinals returned to the United States with a mandate to fix the problem of sexual abuse, identified as their problem, on their own. Further, the pope and other Vatican officials implicitly conveyed that the bishops must address the scandal without capitulating to the demands of the media, civil authorities, or a decadently sexualized modern public.[111] As Eugene Kennedy beautifully described it, the American bishops found themselves jammed between the rock of Peter and a hard place, caught between incompatible demands of their own hierarchy and the various voices of America.[112]

In Dallas 2002, the U.S. bishops attempted to resolve the scandal by developing the *Charter for the Protection of Children and Young People* and their "zero tolerance" norms. Once again, however, they were undermined by the Vatican. Not only did a Vatican review lead to several substantive changes in the norms, it also was later disclosed that the pope had already developed, in April 2001, norms for handling of sexual abuse complaints.[113] These were secret norms shared with some bishops on a case-by-case basis.[114] If in his April 2002 meeting with the American cardinals John Paul had a good idea of what he would and would not accept as a sexual abuse policy, and, further, if he knew he had drafted a sexual abuse response plan a year before the meeting, why not put all the papal cards out on the table ahead of time? It is difficult to understand why he would put his spiritual sons in such a potentially humiliating position. They were sent back to the United States to do something that their "father" had already done and about which he would, in any case, have the final say.

CHAPTER 9

Clerical Narcissism

> Clericalism is the conscious or unconscious concern to promote
> the particular interests of the clergy and to protect the privilege and
> power that traditionally has been conceded to those in the clerical
> state. . . . Among its chief manifestations are an authoritarian style of
> ministerial leadership, a rigidly hierarchical worldview, and a virtual
> identification of the holiness and grace of the church with the clerical
> state and thereby with the cleric himself.[1]
>
> —Conference of Major Superiors of Men

Cardinals and bishops are considered princes of the Roman Catholic Church and frequently are addressed as "Your Excellency" or "Your Eminence." Despite the overtones of royalty, however, the office of bishop is not intended to be a promotion nor a symbol of elevated status and prestige; it is supposed to be a ministry of service.[2] George Weigel puts it this way: "The episcopal ring is not a medieval hangover suggesting a liege lord; the episcopal ring is a wedding ring, a sign of the bishop's marriage to his people, for better or worse, for richer or poorer, in sickness and in health."[3] The notion of bishop-as-servant, unfortunately, can be difficult to discern in some chanceries where velvet-draped rooms, fine food and wine, and chauffeured limousines are more apparent than humble servitude. Many commentators, in fact, cited clericalism as a major factor in the bishops' cover-up of sexual abuse by priests.[4] Russell Shaw, for example, former spokesman for the United States Conference of Catholic Bishops (USCCB), asserts that clericalism results in a culture of secrecy and elitism that is conducive to covering up a scandal like the sexual abuse of minors by priests.[5]

Clericalism justifies rigidly hierarchical power arrangements by declaring that, by virtue of his papal or ecclesiastical caste, the individual is *entitled* to the power he wields and the deference he demands. It is a phenomenon that divides people into categories, emphasizing status differences rather than the commonalities of the human condition. Clericalism is likely to correlate with a diminished capacity for empathy, for mindfully and with full heart finding the "me in thee," especially in those seemingly most unlike the clericalist. Clericalism therefore is a close relative of pathological narcissism. Psychoanalyst Lawrence Josephs presents a paradigm of narcissism that is particularly helpful in describing the influence of clericalism on bishops confronted with sexual abuse by priests.[6]

The Center of Attention

Josephs finds that the pathological narcissist has an overwhelming need to always be the center of attention.[7] Ecclesiastical narcissists grab center stage through their personal acquisitions, titles, and ability to command an audience at will. Cardinal Law, for example, insisted on being addressed as "Your Eminence" at all times,[8] and it is not uncommon for bishops to expect to be called "Bishop" even by priests with whom they have served for a long time. Perhaps the prelate cited most often as a self-imaged prince among princes, however, is Edward Cardinal Egan, former bishop of Bridgeport and currently cardinal archbishop of New York.

As bishop of Bridgeport, Egan allegedly refused to meet with a mother who wanted to tell him about a priest who attempted to molest her son, and he also allegedly failed to notify law enforcement authorities when a priest impregnated a fifteen-year-old girl.[9] In New York, he had not met with victims of priest abuse as of September 2003, was unavailable to celebrate Mass for members of the USCCB's National Review Board when they visited New York, forbade National Review Board members from attending a Knights of Malta dinner unless they were Knights themselves, prevented Kathleen McChesney, then executive director of the USCCB's Office for Child and Youth Protection, from speaking at a New York parish, and declined to meet with National Review Board members other than at their Washington, D.C., office.[10] During a press interview in August 2002, just after the Dallas USCCB meeting, Egan demonstrated an apparent love for center stage. In the midst of a lengthy reminiscence about his years as a priest in Rome, he recounted that before a piano concert began one night, he influenced the musicians to change their scheduled performance to include a Schubert piece played the way he loved it to be.[11] When Pope John Paul II called the American cardinals to Rome to discuss the abuse scandal, most of the prelates were housed at the North American College; Cardinal Egan stayed at a five-star hotel.[12]

Appearances Count

According to Josephs' paradigm of disordered narcissism, the narcissist is deeply concerned with appearances and the accoutrements of status.[13] For some bishops, their gold crosses, bishops' rings, and personal furnishings perhaps become overvalued as symbols of ecclesiastical rank. Along the way, their pastoral hearts may harden and they can lose their moral and ethical compasses. They seem to forget the need to earn and to keep earning the reverence of their priests and laity as they become focused on the trappings of a position about which they feel entitled rather than custodial. Bishop William Murphy of Rockville Centre, New York, seems to provide an example of excessive concern with the material symbols of prestige.

Murphy, a former assistant to Boston's Bernard Cardinal Law, supervised at least one third of the sexual abuse cases that came to light in that archdiocese.[14] Attorney General Thomas F. Reilly of Massachusetts said of Bishop Murphy: "[E]ven with undeniable information available to him on the risk of recidivism, Bishop Murphy continued to place a higher priority on preventing scandal and providing support to alleged abusers than on protecting children from sexual abuse."[15]

In 2001, Murphy was assigned to lead his own diocese on Long Island. Shortly after his arrival, he decided to convert a convent, originally built for fifty-six nuns, into his new residence and asked the six religious women still living there to find another home.[16] The five-thousand-square-foot structure was renovated to include a large bedroom, marble bath, sitting room, and study for Murphy, a new dining-room table seating twelve, and a kitchen equipped with a Sub-Zero refrigerator, Viking professional range, and wine cellar for fifty bottles of wine with different temperature settings for white and red wines.[17]

When the press raised questions about the bishop's new home, he explained that the convent "was close to the cathedral, which of course is my cathedral, and it makes sense that if I could be close to my cathedral, I should be."[18] He added that it was important for the Rockville Centre bishop to have a fitting home in which to welcome "influential prelates."[19] The cathedral, of course, is not the personal property of Bishop Murphy but rather is the edifice in which every bishop of Rockville Centre serves the Catholics who worship there. Shortly after the renovation story became public, the diocese's Catholic Charities announced that a $140,000 deficit, about the cost of Murphy's new Oriental rugs and kitchen appliances, was forcing them to end a home care program for indigent and mentally ill people.[20]

Josephs points out that while the narcissist privileges the tangible symbols of his status, he holds as irrelevant less concrete attributes like moral sensibility, relational attachments, honesty, and maturity.[21] Bishop Murphy conveyed an apparent attachment to things rather than people, including sexually victimized children, and he seemed lacking in empathic connections with other less fortunate than he.

Similarly, Roger Cardinal Mahony of Los Angeles was accused of failing to attune to the subjective experience of sexual abuse survivors when he consecrated a side chapel to them in his new cathedral, nicknamed the "Taj Mahony."[22] Mahony invited the media to the dedication of the chapel but neglected to invite the abuse survivors to whom he said he was paying tribute, nor had he consulted any of them before deciding to "honor" them with a chapel.[23] Seemingly unperturbed by the survivors outside the cathedral protesting the ceremony, Mahony defended his decision to consecrate the chapel by asserting, "We need to get this [the sexual abuse issue] resolved."[24] Mahony's confidence in his own approach and his indifference to the reactions of the very individuals with whom resolution needed to be negotiated illustrates Josephs's contention that narcissists operate from egocentric organizations of thought.[25] The narcissist, and I posit the clericalist as well, does not feel the need to consult others because he knows his own view is the correct one, and, therefore, any view diverging from his is, by definition, incorrect.

Clericalist Defenses

Because the narcissist is convinced of his superiority over other people and is certain, therefore, that his opinions, decisions, and behaviors are correct, reproach is intolerable. His internal world remains at a prereflective level of awareness, rarely subject to introspective contemplation and articulation.[26] When the clericalist's worldview or actions are questioned, he defends his self-image through what psychoanalyst Otto Kernberg describes as primitive defense mechanisms consistent with early, immature stages of development.[27] As the sexual abuse crisis within the Catholic Church unfolded, many bishops resorted to these defensive strategies to deflect attention from their own responsibility for the scandal. Denial, projection, circling the wagons, and devaluing the integrity of critics were particularly in evidence.

Denial

Denial was used by some bishops to minimize the scope and meaning of the sexual abuse of young people by priests, and to shed personal accountability for the abuse. It is clear that some bishops, like Bernard Cardinal Law, simply lied outright about what they knew about sexual abuse by their diocesan priests and when they knew it.[28] "Truth" is as the clerical narcissist declares it to be; it is not necessarily a narrative tied in some way to history or factual reality. In this case, lying somehow does not count as immoral to the dissembler because protecting power and prestige while avoiding scandal are higher priorities than is telling the truth.

While some bishops lied, others minimized the scope and meaning of the problem by claiming that priests sexually violate minors no more often, and perhaps less frequently, than other men in society.[29] Although there is little reliable epidemiological data on the percentage of men who sexually violate young people, some bishops and Vatican officials talked about no more than 2 percent of priests abusing minors and equated that with the prevalence of sexual abusers in the wider society. Data derived by the media, which indicated that in some dioceses well over 5 percent of priests were known to have abused minors,[30] simply were ignored by these speakers until research conducted for the USCCB confirmed the higher percentages.

At the November 2005 meeting of the USCCB, Bishop William Skylstad, the group's president, asserted that a "handful" of abusive priests had forced the rest of the priesthood to "endure an avalanche of negative public attention."[31] Three years into the scandal, Skylstad, whose Spokane diocese was in bankruptcy over sex abuse claims there, seemed to continue to deny both the dimensions of the sexual abuse problem and the part the bishops played in creating it.

Projection

Projection was employed to shift the blame for the scandal onto other individuals and groups. W. W. Meissner asserts that projective defenses and paranoid thinking are common in groups, like the Catholic Church, that he says are organized by a cultic process, "a group process by which the group establishes and defines itself over [and] against other competing and oppositional groups."[32] He maintains that projection defines the boundaries of the in-group, especially when a threat to its integrity is perceived, by attributing to outside individuals and groups qualities inherent in the in-group but unacknowledged by its members. The projective mantra of the defensive in-group, according to Meissner, is, "Outsiders are dishonest, deceitful, and dangerous, not us—even when these undesirable characteristics are as generously distributed within the ingroup as outside it."[33]

Two projective statements were repeatedly used in the sexual abuse scandal. Both suggest the possible operation of paranoid cognitive processes and projective defenses that also are cited as common to the narcissistically disordered character described by Josephs.[34] One projection blamed the media for distorting the scope of the sexual abuse crisis; the other attributed interest in the scandal to anti-Catholic bias.

At the 2002 USCCB meeting in Dallas, history professor Scott Appleby of Notre Dame turned projection on its head by properly crediting the press for services rendered to the Church:

> [T]he media did not create this scandal. . . . Indeed, the mainstream media has done the Church a service by exposing that which was shrouded in darkness . . . that the media has focused with such intensity on the scandal is a kind of testimony, odd though it may be, to the fact that American society rightly expects more of the Church.[35]

Bishop Wilton Gregory, then president of the USCCB, was one prelate who, in 2002, struggled against the projective mechanism of press blaming when he told the bishops gathered in Dallas that the scandal was the Church's self-inflicted wound and that criticism of the press was misplaced.[36] A year later, however, his tune had changed. Addressing the Religion Newswriters Association in September 2003, Gregory criticized the media for the intensity with which they covered the scandal, saying: "I think the media last year did help the church to take some steps that will wring this terrible stain out of her life. . . . However, the way the story was so obsessively covered resulted in unnecessary damage to the bishops and the entire Catholic community."[37] Gregory accused the media of failing to emphasize that most incidents of sexual abuse by priests took place decades ago. While the media indeed followed the Church scandal closely, it follows many scandals obsessively as Monica Lewinsky, former U.S. Representative Gary Condit, sports star and accused sexual assaulter Kobe Bryant, Martha Stewart, and O. J. Simpson all learned. Moreover, Gregory's comments missed the essential point. No matter when the sexual abuse of minors by priests occurred, had most bishops acted responsibly, there never would have been a scandal. The key aspect to the scandal was the bishops' unwillingness to respond with pastoral hearts to sexual abuse, and that lack of pastoral sensitivity unfortunately is not even minutes into the past in some chanceries. Rev. Andrew Greeley, in fact, suggests that bishops still fail to grasp the true nature of their role in the sexual abuse scandal:

> [B]ishops . . . may express verbal apologies. They certainly are sorry that they have attracted unfavorable media attention. . . . However, they do not seem to have any sense of the suffering of victims nor any real guilt that they were personally responsible for this suffering. . . . How can one be guilty of so many objective mortal sins and not break down in pain? Why don't they rush off to monasteries to expiate?[38]

A partial answer to Greeley's questions seems to be that bishops embedded in a clerical culture are not looking inward to the source of the scandal; they are issuing projective accusations to those around them.

Another frequently repeated projective remark was that public interest in the sexual abuse scandal was fueled by anti-Catholics inside and outside the Church. This argument held that the bishops may have made mistakes over the years or shown errors in judgment, but hateful anti-Catholics were hitting good men when they were down in order to promote agendas that contradict the teachings of the Church. Once again, Bishop Wilton Gregory followed his pastoral and passionate address to his ecclesiastical colleagues in Dallas with a speech six months later that raised the possibility that he too had succumbed to clericalist projections:

> As bishops, we should have no illusions about the intent of some people who have shown more than a casual interest in the discord we have experienced within the church this year. There are those outside the church who are hostile to the very principles and teachings that the church espouses, and have chosen this moment to advance the acceptance of practices and ways of life that the church cannot and will never condone. Sadly, even among the baptized, there are those at extremes within the church who have chosen to exploit the vulnerability of the bishops at this moment to advance their own agendas.[39]

There are many Catholics who disagree with and choose in good conscience not to follow some Church teachings, especially those related to birth control, premarital sex, divorce and remarriage, and homosexuality. There also undoubtedly are anti-Catholic forces outside the Church who would like to see the Church founder. The anti-Catholicism charge was applied promiscuously, however, to Catholic and non-Catholic writers and speakers justifiably outraged by the facts of the sexual abuse crisis and by the hypocrisy of bishops who for years preached a stringent sexual morality while tolerating sexual depravity among their priests.

Clerically narcissistic bishops, unwilling to submit to well-founded criticism of their past and present behaviors regarding sexual abuse of minors, appeared to play the anti-Catholicism card to silence their accusers. It can be fairly argued, however, that it was from *within* the ranks of the hierarchy that anti-Catholicism, if it played a part in this scandal at all, was most forcefully enacted. Bishops like Bernard Law, John McCormack of New Hampshire and his predecessor Odore Gendron, Thomas Daily formerly of Brooklyn, Thomas O'Brien formerly of Phoenix, William Murphy of Rockville Centre and his predecessor John McGann, Alfred Hughes of New Orleans, Anthony Bevilacqua formerly of Philadelphia and his predecessor John Krol, Daniel Pilarzcyk of Cincinnati, and Robert Banks formerly of Green Bay, all of whom were found by grand juries or prosecutors to have endangered minors by placing them in the paths of known sexual abusers in order to prevent scandal, conducted themselves in what might qualify as an anti-Catholic manner. Specifically, these men and other bishops seemed to lose track of Jesus' admonition, reported in Matthew (16:6): "If any of you puts a stumbling block before one of these little ones who believe in me, it would be better if a great millstone were fastened around your neck and you were drowned in the depth of the sea." We have not yet witnessed a bishop jumping into the sea with a rock tied around his neck. Rather, most who appeared forgetful of Jesus' charge remain in their chanceries, many feeling unfairly chastised by the press, survivors' groups, some priests, and members of the laity.

Instead of facilitating heartfelt reflection on and repentance for the wrongs committed by bishops, the Church and its prelates were portrayed as the real victims who were being unfairly persecuted. When that defensiveness sparked even more outrage among commentators, some bishops appeared perplexed and self-justifying. For example, Thomas Daily, bishop of Brooklyn until August 2003, likened the criticism he received for his role as an advisor to Cardinal Law in Boston and his protection of sexually abusive priests to a cross he carried in imitation of Christ.[40] He also said that he had read the writings of Edith Stein (a Jewish woman who converted to Catholicism and became a vowed religious woman, died in Auschwitz because of her Jewishness, and was canonized as a saint by John Paul II) and identified with her.[41]

Bishop Daily seemed to be missing an important point in these self-evaluations: Both Jesus and Edith Stein were innocents sacrificed for political reasons. Daily, on the other hand, was found by the attorney general of Massachusetts to have "had a clear preference for keeping priests who sexually abused children in pastoral ministry and generally followed a practice of transferring those priests without supervision or notification to new parishes."[42] Instead of communicating guilt, shame, or remorse about his endangerment of children, Bishop Daily portrayed himself as a humble man fully prepared to shoulder a cross of unearned rebuke. Under the circumstances, that self-image depicted the narcissistic sense of moral superiority and false humility endemic to clericalism.

Circling the Wagons

In order to prevent direct challenges to their clerical culture, some bishops tended to surround themselves with groups and individuals unlikely to threaten their worldview. In selecting experts to advise them about sexual abuse, for example, these bishops took an insular approach. They usually chose from among their own, like Rev. Stephen Rosetti of Church-affiliated St. Luke's Institute, or from those with whom they had worked before, like Fred Berlin, M.D., of Johns Hopkins' Sexual Disorders Clinic, a facility for sexual perpetrators.

At the same time that bishops chose certain advisers, they ignored others who offered to help them and had the qualifications to do so. Prior to the mid-1980s, there were few acknowledged experts on sexual abuse. By the early 1990s, however, there was a cadre of credentialed experts who could have been useful to prelates interested in responding pastorally and effectively to both abusing priests and victim/survivors. In early 1993, for example, four health professionals—Drs. Carol and Theodore Nadelson and Drs. Carolyn and Eli Newberger—with over one hundred years of combined experience in sexual abuse and child protection, were invited to lunch with Bernard Cardinal Law; William F. Murphy, now bishop of Rockville Centre, New York; and John McCormack, now bishop of Manchester, New Hampshire.[43] The four luncheon guests advised their hosts that most men who sexually abuse could not be cured and suggested reporting abusive priests to civil authorities, an idea that Cardinal Law reportedly dismissed. Carol Nadelson offered to help the diocese review screening procedures for seminarians; the Newbergers volunteered to develop a reporting process. None of these experts ever heard from the Archdiocese of Boston again.

Similarly, officials from the diocese of Erie, Pennsylvania, met with pedophilia expert Justine Schober, M.D., who also offered a pessimistic assessment of recovery prospects for abusing priests.[44] She was never contacted by the Erie diocese again. A nationally acknowledged pioneer in sexual abuse research, Dr. David Finkelhor of the University of New Hampshire, served as a member of the Law Commission that developed recommendations for the sexual abuse policy publicly accepted and secretly revised by the archdiocese.[45] Although Finkelhor credited the archdiocese with making progress in its efforts to respond more effectivey to sexual abuse by clergy, he expressed concern about its unwillingness to access other experts who could provide valuable assistance but who might be out of step with some Church teachings or who might not even be Catholic.[46] The apparent shortsightedness depicted in these vignettes had a long history in the Catholic Church and stemmed in part from the Church's uneasy relationship with science, modernity, and postmodernity.

Until 1967, and thus during most of the training and priesthood of virtually all bishops presiding over the sexual abuse crisis, the Catholic Church was at war with modernity, especially modern approaches to history and the hard and social sciences. In 1907, Pope Pius X (1903–1914) issued the encyclical *Pascendi Domenici Gregis*, which defined the Church's relationship with modernity until Vatican II.[47] Strongly criticizing modernity, Pius said: "Were one to attempt the task of collecting together in one place all the errors that have been broached against the faith and to concentrate the sap and substance of them all into one, he could not better succeed than the Modernists have done."[48]

Pascendi directed the bishops to ban modernist works from seminaries, to forbid the faithful—on pain of excommunication—from reading modernist thinkers, and to prohibit clergy from meeting in groups lest modernist ideas infect their discussions. Every priest was required to swear an oath against modernism; the oath was not discontinued until 1967.[49] Although Vatican II and encyclicals like *Pacem in Terris* and *Gaudium et Spes* threw the Church into dialogue with science, social science, and technology, almost all the bishops in power during the sexual abuse scandal and the decades leading up to it had been trained to mistrust science and modern thinking.[50]

Pope John Paul II welcomed many modernist ideas and, in fact, convened an international research conference at the Vatican Observatory in 1987 in order to stimulate deeper dialogue between theology and science, especially physics.[51] During his papacy, however, much of Western intellectual thought had moved on to postmodern notions that focused especially on deconstructing and reformulating paradigms of gender, sexuality, power, and authority—all aspects of relational life implicated in the sexual abuse scandal. John Paul was strongly opposed to the relativism expressed in postmodern ideas. Relativism by its nature challenged the inflexibility and supposed timelessness of Church teachings, especially those regarding sex, gender, and power. Bishops—who had achieved success in a patriar-chal, homosocial society; who, for most of their lives, had been taught to distrust soft and hard science; and whose pope instructed them to work against acceptance of postmodern ideas—may have been uncomfortable with sexual abuse experts, many of whom embraced ideas the bishops perhaps did not fully understand or considered threatening.

Contrasting the bishops' approach to sexual abuse and their engage-ment with other social issues is instructive. When the USCCB decided to issue a pastoral letter on nuclear war in 1983, they consulted with a wide range of foreign policy experts, ethicists, and other authorities on war and peace.[52] Similarly, prior to their publication of a 1986 pastoral letter on economic justice, the bishops invited the opinions of over two hundred experts in fields related to the economy.[53] Faced with the need to develop policies regarding the sexual abuse of minors by priests, however, the bishops did not seek out the best available minds of their day. When I addressed the USCCB Dallas 2002 conference, for example, it was grati-fying but also shocking that so many bishops personally thanked me for helping them appreciate sexual trauma from the experience of the victims *for the first time.* Given the amount of time most bishops had been devot-ing to the sexual abuse scandal, it was disquieting to sense their naivete about its impact on victims.

The Dallas USCCB meeting was an aberration in that laypeople, in-cluding survivors of sexual abuse, were invited to address the bishops and had some hard words for them. It may have inflicted on many bishops what Meissner terms a narcissistic defeat and degradation.[54] He says that such narcissistic wounds to the identity of members of an in-group like the bishops stimulate countermeasures to restore and enhance the depleted ego of the group.[55] Subsequent USCCB meetings were only for bishops and their staffs, except for reports from the National Review Board, and these meetings can be viewed, in part, as attempts to return the group ego to its pre-Dallas state of narcissistic cohesion.

As early as the June 2003 USCCB meeting, it appeared that efforts to restore the bishops' sense of themselves were underway. In his report to the bishops, Archbishop Harry J. Flynn, chair of the Ad Hoc Com-mittee on Sexual Abuse, acknowledged that there was a long road ahead in fully addressing the sexual abuse of minors by priests.[56] He credited the bishops with having made great strides, however, and, to applause from his colleagues, expressed his confidence that the bishops would suc-ceed in resolving the scandal and would protect children in the future.[57] Survivors affiliated with SNAP (Survivor Network for those Abused by Priests) requested some kind of dialogue with the bishops at that meeting but were rebuffed.[58] Flynn explained that the national conference already had heard the pain of victims and needed to hear no more except at the diocesan level as individual bishops saw fit.[59] Further, bishops like Francis Cardinal George of Chicago, Donald Wuerl of Pittsburgh, and Daniel Buechlin of Indianapolis once again complained that the media, the public, and people with "agendas" to dismantle the teachings of the Church were exploiting and exaggerating the scope of the crisis and the efficacy of the bishops' implementation of sexual abuse norms adopted the previous year.[60]

While few would argue that most dioceses across the nation had taken concrete steps to protect children more effectively, the crisis was far from over in June 2003. Given the magnitude of the bishops' failures to confront sexual abuse effectively in the past and, in some places, in the present, one would hope that the bishops would realize that they needed to hear repeatedly from survivors, their advocates, professionals who have researched sexual abuse and who work with survivors, rank-and-file priests demoralized by the crisis, and laypeople wondering whether they can trust their Church to do right. Instead, only one year after Dallas, the bishops internally articulated the status of the scandal, applauded their self-defined successes, and chose not to hear from anyone who might have had a different take on things.

Devaluing Critics

Finally, attempts by clerical narcissists to devalue others, such as survivor groups, the press, and lay critics, may also stem from unconscious envy. Josephs states that, for the pathological narcissist, moral goodness is assigned from without rather than being achieved from within.[61] For some bishops, this may translate into a prideful sense that their moral goodness has been recognized and externally proclaimed by the pope when they are chosen as bishops. Indeed, these bishops may have had a history of experiencing goodness and a perfectly calibrated moral compass as things they acquired through ordination rather than qualities they needed to develop throughout the life cycle as internal resources through which to live their priesthoods.

When a clericalist bishop unconsciously perceives genuineness, integrity, true goodness, and generosity coming from the inside of another, envy can be stimulated that, in turn, evokes a determination to unmask the other as a phony. In this case, the clericalist may search to find and to expose another's Achilles' heel in order to restore his own narcissistic equilibrium and sense of moral superiority. Vague and unsubstantiated allegations that critics of the hierarchy were using the crisis deceitfully to achieve selfish ends resembled a defense against unconscious envy. Here, there was no room for others who had profound concerns about a beloved Church and who genuinely wanted a more open dialogue about the implications of the sexual abuse scandal. From the perspective of clerical culture, such people only could be enemies of the in-group, in this case, the hierarchy.

One of the most disquieting examples of a clericalist attack apparently designed to discredit a prominent critic of the Church involved former Governor Frank Keating of Oklahoma, who served for a year as chair of the National Review Board. Keating resigned in June 2003 after making a controversial remark comparing some bishops' attempts to maintain secrecy about sexual abuse in their dioceses with the Cosa Nostra's demands for secrecy among its membership.[62] In October 2003, Keating alleged that Rev. Edward Weisenburger, vicar general of the Oklahoma City diocese, had attempted to smear him by e-mailing to Rev. William Woestman, a member of the Archdiocese of Chicago's tribunal, remarks focusing on Keating's disagreement with Church teachings on capital punishment but also asserting that Keating did not attend Sunday Mass regularly and had a mistress, who Weisenburger mentioned by name.[63] Fr. Woestman confirmed that he received the e-mail, which he passed on to Francis Cardinal George of Chicago, who then sent it to Anne Burke, another member of the National Review Board. It also reached Bishop Wilton Gregory of the USCCB, who is reported to have apologized for the letter. Keating strongly and publicly denied missing Mass or having a girlfriend. If a number of members of the hierarchy indeed were involved in spreading potentially damaging untruths about Keating because they were threatened by his criticism and insistence on ecclesiastical compliance with sexual abuse norms, it represented clericalism at its worst.

Career Clericalism

Identification with clerical narcissism began early for some future bishops. Priests and former priests describe seminary classmates who from the beginning of their formations sought the power and prestige associated with ecclesiastical life.[64] Fr. Richard John Neuhaus describes this kind of careerism: "Recently, a priest who had served for years as an official in the chancery office was ordained an auxiliary bishop. 'At last,' he declared, 'I am fully a priest.' . . . There may be a shortage of priests but there is no shortage of priests who would like to be bishops."[65] Perhaps insecure, immature, or predisposed to a narcissistic character style, these men sought identities through their priestly state rather than bringing into their priest-hood well-developed psychological systems of self. Too many of these men may have remained boys, entering seminaries looking for a new family who would care for them as minors rather than relate to them as men. Cozzens puts it this way:

> The seminary . . . is a kind of antechamber to the home he will find in the church as a priest. If he follows the rules, pleases his ecclesial "parents," he will be taken care of. He will be clothed in special robes, given an identity, enhanced with status, provided with leisure for prayers, study and recreation, and exposed to the arts. . . . And if he is docile and shrewd, he may find himself in a special place of honor in this second home.[66]

To be awarded that seat of honor—the bishop's throne—however, often required that the upwardly moving priest relinquish his own intellect and will, along with a range of human capacities, among them sexual and af-fective passion, compassion, and respect for the subjectivity of another. Accepting objectification and a faux self-less-ness as the price of career advancement, the clerical narcissist perhaps traded genuine individuality for reassurance about his membership and eventual leadership in an ex-clusive club of men considered by each other to be morally and spiritually superior to those outside the in-group.

Josephs posits that, during developmental years, the future narcissist frequently feels it necessary to conform to the role expectations demanded by parents so that the parents could feel good about themselves.[67] Here, we see an analogy to the Catholic clericalist-to-be. During his formation and as an advancing cleric, the priest netted in clericalism may have felt compelled to meet or exceed the exacting yet flattering role demands placed on him by superiors. Inactive priest Paul Dinter says that these priests "learn how to mirror the needs of those in authority, bringing all their learned skills as compliant sons to the challenging task of pleasing the omnipotent spiritual father."[68] As time went on, these priests perhaps increasingly identified with the ecclesiastical fathers they served, and their own sense of entitlement expanded accordingly.

Clericalism Starts at the Top

Clericalism needs fertile relational soil in which to root, and the Vatican is home to many narcissistic family elders who export clericalism through-out the Catholic diaspora. At the Vatican, covert but intense ambition and careerism are common attributes of clergy. Competition and jealous protection of one's turf can infect priests trying to move up in a system within which promotions often depend much more on loyalty to the Holy See than on job competence.[69] Paul Dinter, who worked in Rome for some time, says, "Roman ecclesiastics participate in a self-confirmatory culture that censures outside influences and contrary opinions as those 'of the world' against which they are defending the Church."[70] These very real limitations, combined with substantial power, can result in an organizational system whose members simply reflect each other's smug and unchallenged certainty that their "truths" are unassailably correct. In that case, clericalism becomes a euphemism for a potentially destructive arrogance overlaying ignorance.

Throughout the sexual abuse crisis, statements from a number of Vatican officials seemed to convey an arrogant dismissal of the scope and meaning for many faithful Catholics of the sexual abuse of minors by priests and, even more, of the hierarchy's attempts to cover it up. Both Archbishop Tarcisio Bertone, secretary of the Congregation for the Doctrine of the Faith, and Archbishop Julian Herranz, head of the Pontifical Council for the Interpretation of Legislative Texts, for example, agreed that bishops should not be required to report sexual abuse by priests to civil authorities.[71] Bertone was quoted as saying that clergymen should not have to fear legal consequences when they confided in their bishops and that society "must also respect the 'professional secrecy' of priests."[72] Neither of these men seemed to think that protecting children and adolescents from sexually predatory priests was as vital as maintaining the special status of priests who apparently were to be held above the law.

Early on in the scandal, Vatican spokesmen denied the scope of the sexual abuse problem by defining it first as a uniquely American problem and then as a limited, Anglo-Saxon phemonenon.[73] That attempt to circumscribe the problem fit Pope John Paul II's perception that Westerners are obsessed with sex in cultures dominated by moral relativism. Since 2002, however, reports of sexual abuse by priests, enshrouded in secrecy imposed by their bishops, have been publicized worldwide.[74] It is now clear that the American hierarchy's approach to sexual abuse of minors by its priests was patterned similarly around the globe. Further, between 1990 and mid-2003, twenty-one bishops from ten countries resigned because of sexual misconduct with adults or minors or because of their mishandling of the sexual misconduct of other priests.[75]

Denial seemed to be reflected in claims by Vatican officials that the incidence of sexual abuse by priests was very small. Dario Cardinal Castrillon Hoyos, once considered to be a *papabile*, or candidate for pope, and Joseph Cardinal Ratzinger (Pope Benedict XVI) both asserted that the percentage of abusive priests was as low as or lower than that found in other segments of society.[76] As Rev. Stephen Rossetti pointed out, however, reliable epidemiological studies on child abusers simply do not exist, making it impossible for anyone to compare accurately sexual abuse inside the Church with that occurring in the wider society.[77] In any case, these Vatican officials, like their counterparts in the American hierarchy, skirted the essential point that it was the covering up of abuse that created a scandal, not the abuse itself.

Like many American bishops, Vatican officials also appeared to employ projection to externalize blame for the crisis onto forces outside the Church, particularly the media.[78] The intensity of their language exceeded even that of U.S. bishops. Archbishop Julian Herranz, for example, suggested that some media outlets intended to "sully the image of the church and the Catholic priesthood, and to weaken the moral credibility of the magisterium."[79] It is difficult to imagine what could detract more effectively from the moral credibility of the Catholic Church than its hierarchy's complicity in the sexual abuse of thousands of minors. Oscar Andres Cardinal Rodriguez Maradiaga of Honduras, once thought to be another papal contender, accused the American press of persecuting the Catholic Church in ways similar to Nero, Diocletian, Hitler, and Stalin.[80] Further, he blamed the Jews for the scandal, a disturbingly anti-Semitic charge for which there is no evidence.[81]

Church Teachings Relevant to Clericalism

Catholic teachings regarding the ontological change occurring in a priest at the moment of ordination, and the apostolic succession of bishops, can be harnessed by the narcissistic priest or bishop to fuel the grandiosity and entitlement associated with clericalism.

Ordination and Ontology

The Church holds that when a man receives the sacrament of Holy Orders and is ordained a priest, an ontological change occurs. He literally no longer is the man he was prior to ordination. Rather, the essence of his being is changed so that he becomes an *alter Christus*, another Christ.[82] Theologians and Church historians have argued about the literalness of the ontological change associated with ordination. Some commentators on the priesthood assert that Vatican II recast the role of the priest, deemphasizing claims of an inherent difference from other baptized Catholics.[83]

In this view, priests have roles to play in the Church that are different from but not superior to those of the laity. Monsignor Philip Murnion, for example, says,

> There is renewed interest in discussing the "ontological change" brought about by ordination. . . . The person ordained to be priest is meant to be really different. If this is not to mean reverting to differences of status and privileges, to claims of prestige and acts of domination, it will be because we will foster a priesthood whose . . . sense of shared priesthood with the people, and shared ministry with men and women in parish ministry, enable him to help people be aware of the presence of Jesus in sacrament and their community, in family and work.[84]

For the priest who is vulnerable to clericalist narcissism, and to the bishop embedded in it, the interpretation of ontological change that posits an actual merger with the being of Jesus Christ at the moment of ordination can support a belief that clergy are called by God to be inherently superior to other human beings.[85] In fact, in a reversal of intended roles, the clericalist bishop may come to expect that he will be served *by* his priests and the faithful of a diocese rather than living out *with* them mutually constructed service to the whole faith community. Murnion comments on that possibility when he says that some contemporary "priests are concerned that such claims (like those related to ontological change) not encourage the distortion of charism (a divinely conferred gift or power) into the entitlements of clericalism."[86]

Apostolic Succession

Apostolic succession is another concept that can be used by narcissistic clerics to justify their sense of entitlement to privilege, deference, and unquestioned authority. At the most literal level of interpretation, apostolic succession connotes a belief that bishops are direct successors of the original Apostles, who in turn are viewed as Christ's choices to lead a Church; it depicts bishops who are ordained in an unbroken line by the laying on of hands, bishop to bishop, from the Apostles until today.[87] Some modern biblical scholars find no credible evidence for the notion of apostolic succession as a historically accurate paradigm.[88] Rather, it seems more suitable as a metaphor applied to the bishop as a disciple of Christ who carries particular pastoral and educational duties deriving from Christ's ministry and the propagation of that ministry through the Apostles and other early disciples. Walter Cardinal Kasper, president of the Pontifical Council for

Promoting Christian Unity, for example, is quoted by Fr. Richard John Neuhaus as saying of apostolic succession: "This is not a succession in the linear sense, where one office-bearer follows another; rather, new members are co-opted and integrated into the apostolic college with its mission that is carried on from age to age." Neuhaus himself believes in apostolic succession but thinks the bishops have distorted their roles through clericalism: "And so in the bishops we are to see the apostles, whose successors they are, in distressing disguise . . . reinforced by a culture of clericalism in which bishops and priests, and especially priests who would be bishops, tacitly assume that they are the Church which it is the purpose of the laity to keep in business."[89]

Clericalism is not unique to the Catholic priesthood and brotherhood of bishops. In the secular world, it manifests as an elite professionalism that demands deference and certain entitlements based on status or rank rather than performance. Medicine, the military, academia, and my own field of psychoanalysis all have been characterized as vocations infected with the rot of secular clericalism. It is interesting to note, in fact, that the substantive democratization of psychoanalysis that occurred over the past two decades was in part influenced by the resuscitation of trauma as an acknowledged factor in adult psychopathology and by the infusion of women into the halls of psychoanalytic power. Concomitantly, psychoanalytic writing about treating traumatized patients, especially adult survivors of childhood sexual abuse, emphasized the negative impact on those treatments of perceived arrogance and assumed power on the part of the analyst.

All Bishops Are Not Clericalists

At the same time that clericalism exists in other fields, all bishops are not clericalists. A good number of them have lived out recognition that deference and true authority cannot be demanded from anyone but rather must be authorized and constantly reauthorized by the faith community served by any bishop. Bishop Paul Bootkoski of the Diocese of Metuchen, New Jersey, exemplifies a prelate seemingly immune from clericalism.

I interviewed Bootkoski, who is called Bishop Paul, in 2002. His chancery is in a closed Catholic high school and is modestly appointed. He is on a first-name basis with his staff and eats lunch in the cafeteria with other employees. When I asked him why he was made a bishop, Bishop Paul responded that it was because his name ended in "ski," suggesting that Pope John Paul II liked appointing a Polish bishop. The bishop's capacity to poke fun at himself implied a confidence and warmth that made him approachable. Aware that a vulnerability to clericalism accompanies elevation to the bishop's chair, Bootkoski dines regularly with old friends who "knew him when," call him Paul, and can tease him about any signs of budding elitism.

Bishop Paul has met with numerous survivors, recognizes their suffering, and apologizes to them for the abuse. He urges them "not to let what happened to them get between them and their God." Unlike many other bishops, Bootkoski has victims and members of survivors groups on the diocesan advisory board that examines sex abuse claims.[90] Also, unlike many bishops appointed by John Paul II who came to their chanceries from other administrative positions and who had little, if any, pastoral background, Bishop Paul spent most of his career as a pastor. As a university chaplain, he developed an appreciation of the issues young people confront and, as a suburban pastor, he was close to the joys, sorrows, and tensions families encountered over time. Perhaps because of these pastoral experiences, Bootkoski hesitates to exclude individuals from the Church. Rather, he tries to reach out to people, especially those who may feel alienated from Catholicism.[91]

Bootkoski seems to have a sense of proportion about himself and his position. He does not always wear clerical dress in his spare time and chuckled about his civilian outfit attracting Cardinal Law's attention at one USCCB meeting. Coming into the hotel in "civvies," Bishop Paul was at the bottom of an escalator Cardinal Law was riding. When Law saw him, he said in a somewhat scolding tone, "Bishop Bootkoski, you're not in uniform."

Bootkoski's comfort with himself apart from the accoutrements of his ecclesiastical position suggests that he may continue to avoid the pitfalls of clericalism while serving his diocese, most of all, as a pastor. Other bishops, more caught up in clericalism than Bootkoski, might review Jesus' admonition to the Pharisees (Luke 11:42–44), the hierarchy of that day:

> But woe to you, Pharisees! For you tithe mint and rue and herbs of all kinds, and neglect justice and the love of God; it is these you ought to have practiced, without neglecting the others. Woe to you Pharisees! For you love to have the seat of Honor in the synagogues and to be greeted with respect in the marketplaces. Woe to you! For you are like unmarked graves, and people walk over them without realizing it.

Priests, Laypeople, and Culture

CHAPTER 10

Perpetrators, Priests, People in the Pews

Perpetrators: Who Were They?

A discussion of abusive priests is burdened with the same handicap inherent in any attempt to generalize about sexual offenders. In truth, none of us knows very much about sexual predators because the majority of them never are identified. What we do know is based on research with offenders who have come to the attention of either the mental health or the criminal justice systems. This is a biased sample—a grouping of individuals who may or may not represent the wider universe of the population being considered. In referring to studies of these biased samples, therefore, we must be cautious in assuming that they validly inform us about sexually transgressive priests. Richard Sipe, for example, feels that priests represent men who live in a culture different than the general population and cannot be compared with other sexual offenders.[1] On the other hand, Karen Terry, primary researcher for a study of abusive priests and expert in the area of sexual offenders, feels that there is no reason to conclude that abusive priests differ significantly from other men who abuse.[2] With these considerations in mind, we turn to available data to discuss abusive priests.

Empirical Data on Abusive Priests

Since discussions about offending priests take place amid murky scientific data, it is helpful to begin with the most solid empirical information available. In this section, I use the findings of *The Nature and Scope of the Problem of Sexual Abuse of Minors by Catholic Priests and Deacons in the United States: A Research Study Conducted by the John Jay College of Criminal Justice* (hereafter called the John Jay Study), commissioned by the United States Conference of Catholic Bishops to capture descriptive data on the sexual abuse of children by Catholic priests between 1950 and 2002.[3] Some of these findings are augmented by the *Report on the Implementation of the Charter for the Protection of Children and Young People* (hereafter called the 2004 Study), which included information about sexual abuse reported in the calendar year 2004.[4] Because the John Jay Study encompasses data only through the end of 2002 and the 2004 Study covers only calendar year 2004, there are no data for calendar year 2003.

NUMBER OF ABUSING PRIESTS

John Jay researchers concluded that 4,392 priests were credibly accused of sexual abuse of minors between 1950 and 2002.[5] During 2004, another 411 priests were newly credibly accused of abuse.[6] If we assume that a similar number of offenders were newly identified in 2003, the year with no reported data, it suggests that between 1950 and 2004, at least 5,214 Roman Catholic priests were credibly accused of sexually abusing a minor. This accounts for approximately 4.75 percent of the priesthood.

These numbers are probably low for a variety of reasons. Two percent of diocesan priests and 20 percent of religious priests were not included in the John Jay Study.[7] In the 2004 Study, 7 percent of dioceses and eparchies (Eastern rite equivalents of dioceses) and 29 percent of religious communities failed to provide data.[8] Therefore, there is some undercounting of abusive priests in both studies. In addition, data collection in each depended on the willingness and ability of bishops and provincial superiors to self-report all pertinent information. Given the historical reluctance of many bishops to face squarely sexual abuse within their dioceses, it is possible that some bishops withheld relevant information. Further, some bishops over the years had successfully intimidated victims or their families from following through on sexual abuse complaints, so no records would exist in these cases. Moreover, record keeping was sloppy in some chanceries and provincial offices, raising the probability that some allegations were not available to be counted. Finally, it is almost certain that some victims have not yet, and may never, report their victimizations. The John Jay Study determined, in fact, that less than 13 percent of allegations were made in the years they occurred and more than 25 percent were lodged more than thirty years after the reported abuse began.[9]

GEOGRAPHIC DISTRIBUTION OF ABUSERS

Sexual abuse of minors by priests occurred at similar rates nationwide, suggesting that sexual abuse was not confined to urban areas or to areas of the country considered to be particularly sexually liberal or especially sexually conservative.[10]

In 2005, a controversy over the geographical distribution of clergy abuse erupted between conservative Pennsylvania Senator Rick Santorum and other politicians over remarks made by Santorum in 2002. Santorum, a staunch Roman Catholic, had suggested that the Archdiocese of Boston had a particularly egregious sexual abuse problem because of Boston's liberal culture. He was quoted as saying, "When the culture is sick, every element of it becomes infected. While it is no excuse for this scandal, it is no surprise that Boston, a seat of academic, political and cultural liberalism in America, lies at the center of the storm."[11] Alan Cooperman, reporter for the *Washington Post,* pointed out that although Boston was among the top ten dioceses in terms of percentage of abusive priests, the Diocese of Covington, Kentucky, had the highest percentage of alleged abusers while in San Francisco, surely a city known for liberal attitudes toward sexuality, only 1.6 percent of the priesthood had been reported as abusive between 1950 and 2002.[12]

PERPETRATORS BY YEAR OF ORDINATION

The percentage of priests who allegedly abused minors varied by year of ordination. According to the John Jay Study, the approximate percentage of all priests ordained in a given year that were credibly accused of abuse were:

Ordination Year	Accused[1]	Ordination Year	Accused[1]
1960[2]-1962	6.0	1982	6.0
1963	8.0	1983	5.0
1964	7.5	1984	3.0
1965, 1966	8.0	1985, 1986	4.0
1967	7.5	1987	3.0
1968	8.0	1988, 1989	4.0
1969	7.0	1990	3.0
1970	8.0	1991	2.0
1971, 1972	6.0	1992	1.0
1973	9.0	1993	2.0
1974	8.0	1994	1.0
1975	9.0	1995, 1996	2.0
1976, 1977, 1978, 1979	6.0	1997	1.0
1980	7.0	1998	2.0
1981	5.0	1999, 2000	1.0

1. The John Jay study included a graph of ordination but exact percentages were not reported. Approximates based on the graph are used here.

2. Data were not available prior to 1960.

The percentages from 1984 to the present are likely to be understated given the age at which priests first begin to abuse (see below) and considering the length of time it often takes for victims to come forward to report their abuse. On the other hand, seminaries began psychological evaluations of candidates in the 1980s, perhaps screening out at least some potential abusers.[13] There also are data on sexual abuse in the wider society suggesting that there has been some decline in the incidence of abuse since 1990, perhaps due to increased cultural awareness of and thus vigilance about childhood sexual abuse, as well as due to the concomitant early detection and incarceration of more offenders.[14]

It is startling to see that from 1963 through 1980 the percentage of abusing priests per ordination class never fell below close to 6.0 and, in some years, rose to 9.0. Eleven percent of the 1983 ordination class working in the Diocese of Los Angeles were alleged to have abused minors.[15] Therefore, we would expect to see increases in the percentage of abusive priests in ordination classes after 1980, even if they do not reach previous heights.

DATES OF BIRTH

In the John Jay Study, almost two-thirds of abusive priests were born before 1940; almost 90 percent before 1950.[16] They grew up in a time of sexual repression in the wider society and, especially, in Catholic communities. In Catholic families and schools, children learned that sex was dangerous and sinful unless it occurred in marriage. Normal developmental sexual activities, like masturbation and sexual fantasy, were deemed sinful, and so the Catholic child and adolescent had no help processing and learning adaptive expressions of their emerging sexuality. In addition, priests born prior to 1950 often entered minor seminaries at fourteen or fifteen years of age, preparing for a celibate life as they had just moved through puberty and before they had grown into a mature psychosexuality. When some priests from these age cohorts acted out sexually, they may have chosen minors who were experienced as psychosexual equals.

AGE OF PRIEST AT FIRST INCIDENT OF OFFENSE

In the John Jay Study, the average age of a priest at his first reported incidence of sexual abuse was thirty-nine.[17] That age rose from thirty-eight in the 1950s to forty-eight in 2002.[18] Prior to the study, conventional wisdom held that priests tended to abuse shortly after ordination when they left the protected environment of the seminary and were out in parishes running youth activities.

The John Jay results need further analysis but they suggest that priests may have begun to abuse only after a decade or more of ordained priesthood. Perhaps priests at that point in their careers more fully realized what they had sacrificed in choosing a celibate life. Many male relatives and parishioners of similar age would have established careers and family lives that perhaps stimulated the priest's envy and disillusionment with his own situation. Psychosexually immature and sexually inexperienced, some priests may have sexually appropriated young people in an enactment of anger, envy, and sense of inadequacy as a man in society, and in order to achieve a subjective sense of empowerment.

HISTORY OF PERSONAL VICTIMIZATION

Only 6.8 percent of accused priests in the John Jay Study reported histories of childhood abuse, with just over 4 percent claiming to have been sexually abused as a minor.[19] Researchers note that these numbers reflect only what was available in diocesan or provincial files and may understate the number of priests with abusive backgrounds. Certainly, these statistics defy clinical lore that the majority of sexual offenders were sexually violated earlier in life.[20] Sexual offender researchers Hindman and Peters, however, studied three cohorts of sexual perpetrators in Oregon and found that only about 30 percent of the men divulged sexual abuse histories under polygraph.[21] During nonpolygraphed self-reports, approximately two-thirds of the offenders reported having been sexually violated as children, numbers more in keeping with clinical reports.[22]

While the John Jay numbers may understate the incidence of childhood sexual abuse among abusing priests, clinical reports may overstate that phenomenon. Many sexual predators are adept at eliciting sympathy from others and may realize that they will receive more consideration from law enforcement, juries, or mental health practitioners if they are viewed as sexual victims as well as victimizers.

NUMBERS OF VICTIMS PER PRIEST

According to the John Jay Study, 55.7 percent of credibly accused priests had only one victim; 26.9 percent had two or three; 13.9 percent had four to nine; and 3.5 percent had ten or more.[23] These are probably the least credible findings of the study. First, these statistics convey only the number of victims who came forward to accuse a priest and whose allegations were recorded and turned over to researchers. We know that many victims never disclose their abuse, or at least never report it to the Church, and we can be skeptical that all accusations indeed were recorded and submitted to John Jay. For example, one of my patients was abused by her grandfather beginning at age four. When she was eight years old, she told her parish pastor about the victimizations during a weekly Confession. The priest suggested that they talk about it more extensively in his rectory office and he then sexually abused her weekly from ages eight to twelve. Six years later, he officiated at her wedding. This woman never reported the priest to anyone and spoke of her violations only in treatment.

In the 2004 Study, half of the new allegations were lodged against priests who already had been accused of sexual abuse in prior years.[24] Just those new results would change the John Jay data, increasing the number of victims for up to 350 priests included in that research.

Next, sexual predators rarely are honest about their histories as offenders. Hindman and Peters, for example, found in three studies that sexual victimizers self-reported 1.5, 2.5, and 2.9 victims each on average.[25] Under polygraph, however, the same offenders disclosed an average of 9.0, 13.6, and 11.6 victims respectively, four to six times the number of victims self-reported by the perpetrators.[26] The actual number of victims of priest abuse in the United States between 1950 and 2004 is probably more accurately estimated at forty thousand to sixty thousand minors, not just over eleven thousand as reported in the John Jay and 2004 studies.

AGE OF VICTIMS

Both the John Jay Study and the 2004 Study found that the majority of victims were abused between the ages of ten and fourteen.[27] The John Jay Study, however, suggests that, over the decades, there was a shift toward male victims reporting having been abused for the first time between fifteen and seventeen years of age.[28] The percentage of teens violated for the first time in that age group rose from 26 in the 1970s to 55 in the 1990s.[29] Interestingly, however, because the average age of the priest when he began to abuse also increased over time, the average age difference between perpetrator and male victim seems to have remained fairly constant, at over twenty years. The age difference heightens the picture of sexual abuse as a crime of power. In most cases, it represented imposition of sex on a much younger male in relationship with an authority figure.

There are a number of other perspectives to take on the apparent aging of victims at first incidence of abuse. First of all, it is possible that the age of victims appears to increase because older boys more quickly reach the developmental milestones that trigger recognition that something is wrong in their lives. In other words, the more recent the year of abuse, the more likely it is that victims who were older in that year come forward first because they see that their lives are developing differently from, and not as well as, the lives of their agemates. In this case, we would expect to see the average age of first victimization decrease among 1980s and 1990s victims as victims who were younger in those years reach those same stages of life and come forward.

It is also possible that younger boys were not as available to priests in later years as fewer children attended Catholic elementary schools or were involved in Catholic youth activities than in earlier years. Too, by the 1980s, parents who had troubled children—the most vulnerable to abuse—were relying less on Catholic priests to counsel their children and more on guidance counselors and psychotherapists in and out of the public school systems. One family I worked with in the mid-1980s, for example, said that, years ago, they would have taken their two boys to the priest to straighten them out, but now they all were in psychotherapy.

Finally, as priests entered seminary later, their own psychosexual development may have moved toward late adolescence rather than puberty. When they crossed the line with a minor, they may have felt more comfortable with older boys who seemed like psychological peers. I think that, as time goes on, the victims who were younger when they were abused in the 1980s and 1990s will begin to come forward as they recognize problems in their lives, realigning the findings of the John Jay Study.

It is important to note that girls were abused most frequently at ages eleven to fourteen, with almost 40 percent of female victims in that age group.[30] As with male victims, the age of abuse onset appeared to increase over the years, probably also because the younger female victims have not yet come forward.

ABUSIVE ACTS

In the John Jay Study, most abusing priests committed acts more serious than "just" touching under a victim's clothes.[31] About one third of abusing priests sexually penetrated their victims or engaged them in oral sex, both representing very serious abuse.[32] Only 2.9 percent of abusing priests engaged solely in sex talk or pornography use; just 9 percent only touched over the victim's clothes or had the victim's touch over the cleric's clothes; and only 15.8 percent stopped at touching under the clothing.[33] In the majority of cases, therefore, the victimizing priest imposed serious sexual violations on his victim.

In addition, few priests sexually assaulted their victims only one time. Over half of reporting victims claimed to have been abused by their violator "numerous times," while only 29 percent claim to have been abused just once.[34] This finding argues against constructing sexual abuse by a priest as a momentary lapse of judgment but rather presses for viewing the perpetrator as dangerously likely to reabuse a young person many times.

Conventional wisdom has held that alcohol abuse by the perpetrator is often implicated in sexual victimization of a minor. In fact, however, the John Jay Study concluded that the abusing priest used alcohol and/or drugs only 21.6 percent of the time.[35] Again, this militates against an assumption that a priest will not abuse if he is clean and sober.

POSITION OF PRIEST AT TIME OF ABUSE

John Jay results indicate that nearly 67 percent of abusive priests were pastors or associate pastors; another 10 percent were resident priests.[36] Although all sexual abuse is terrible, sexual violation by a parish priest, who by virtue of his position is emplaced as "über-Father" of the members of his congregation, is especially egregious.

Pornography

Since the sexual abuse scandal broke open, there has been increasing media coverage of priests engaging in Internet pornography, often kiddie porn.[37] Rev. Gary Michael Hotley of Point Loma, California, for example, admitted looking at Internet child porn for years and had a collection of child erotica and gay porn in his bedroom and in his office.[38] Authorities found that Rev. Timothy Szott of Utica, New York, had thousands of child porn images on his laptop and church computers.[39] Rev. Matthew J. Kornacki, former assistant director of continuing formation for priests in the Archdiocese of Philadelphia and former director of Spiritual Year Programs at St. Charles Borromeo Seminary, pleaded guilty to possessing child pornography on his laptop computer.[40] Rev. Matthew Bagert of Grand Prairie, Texas, had pornographic images of boys, aged four to fourteen, on his church computer and was charged with felonious possession of child porn.[41] In Austria, over ten thousand Catholics formally withdrew from the Church after the publicized discovery of over forty thousand pornographic images on computers at St. Poelten Seminary.[42] The 2004 Study indicated that nine cases or 1 percent of 2004 allegations were related solely to child pornography.[43]

A priest's use of pornography can carry various meanings. Sipe suggests that, for some priests, pornography is a passing interest that may be a source of sexual education.[44] Priests, if organized psychosexually at an adolescent level, may use pornography in an adolescent way—to learn about what they are not doing in "real" life and to provide masturbatory fantasy material. Other priests may use pornography more regularly as a substitute for sexual activity with others. Yet others may enter into active sexuality through pornography, following that with contact with men, women, or children. While some of the priests recently arrested for child pornography possession apparently had no histories of sexually abusing children, others both viewed kiddie porn and molested children. Rev. Vincent McCaffrey of Chicago, for example, admitted to serial molestations of minors and was arrested for having over four thousand images of child pornography.[45]

In recent years, federal agencies have implemented national programs to detect and arrest Internet users of kiddie porn. It is likely that Catholic priests will continue to be identified and taken into custody in these sting operations.

The John Jay Study and the 2004 Study provide descriptive data on abusive priests, giving us a perspective on the aggregate characteristics of Catholic clergy who abused minors. They were not intended to generate insights into the psychology of perpetrating priests. Experts in the field of sexual offenders offer a few theories about the personality dynamics and motivations of these men.

Perpetrator Dynamics

One established classification of abusers divides them into "fixated" and "regressed." Fixated perpetrators are primarily drawn to children or adolescents and rarely have sexual relationships with peers of either gender.[46] Regressed abusers, on the other hand, are usually heterosexual men who are primarily drawn to adult women as sexual partners but who, under sufficient external or psychological stress, regress to an earlier stage of psychosexual development and seek children or adolescents as sexual partners.[47] Many priest abusers seem to represent a hybrid of these categories. Men who perhaps never grew beyond an adolescent stage of psychosexual development themselves, they did not "regress" but rather may have chosen victims that were experienced as psychological peers. In some cases, they then became fixated on achieving a sense of power, esteem, and masculinity through sexual merger with and domination of these victims.

Another typical classification divides perpetrators into pedophiles and ephebophiles; either can be fixated or regressed. Pedophiles are sexually attracted to prepubescent children with whom they are emotionally identified.[48] Rarely do they appreciate the impact of abuse on their victims and can seem quite childlike themselves. Ephebophiles tend to be organized at an adolescent level of psychosexual development and thus seek pubescent young people to abuse.[49] Ephebophiles who choose girls may be excited by purity and virginity; those who choose boys are seeking genital sex with a psychological agemate.[50] As we have seen, many clerical ephebophiles probably would be deterred from having sex with a virgin, even if they were themselves heterosexual. The Church's idealization of virginity and female purity, coupled with the devaluation of women as potential seductresses, likely would render girls taboo as sexual objects for many priests. Sex with a girl therefore may have been literally unimaginable in a way sex with a boy was not, no matter the sexual orientation of the priest.

Researchers and clinicians familiar with sexual offenders offer a spectrum of diagnostic characteristics,[51] personality types,[52] family patterns,[53] developmental experiences,[54] and attachment capabilities[55] found among abusive priests. Unfortunately, many priests who do not abuse anyone have similar profiles, making predictive diagnoses difficult.

Central to abuse, however, is the perpetrator's inability or unwillingness to forge an empathic connection to his victim, to imagine what it is like to be in the victim's shoes. Psychoanalyst Daniel Gensler cites grandiosity and a sense of entitlement as important factors in the abuser's failures of empathy.[56] These qualities are synchronous with the kind of clerical narcissism discussed in the last chapter.

Throughout their formation and priestly life, many abusive priests simultaneously were deprived and instilled with a sense of grandiose entitlement. On the one hand, they were deprived of relational intimacy and sexual succor. At the same time, they were trained to believe that they were called to a more spiritually meaningful vocation than other men and women and, thus, were entitled to deference. Often, they were allowed to operate beyond the law as when they were given a pass for speeding or even drunk driving. Within the Church, they were the law, and the laity, including young people, were expected to obey them. Some priests, perhaps predisposed to pathological narcissism, may have felt entitled to use young people to soothe themselves. These men attended to their needs and insecurities by using children and adolescents without any empathic understanding of their impact on the young people or on their families.

It is frustrating but true that sexual offenders are a heterogeneous group who often seem to resemble nonabusers more than they do each other. No matter how well seminaries and religious orders screen their applicants, there will be child abusers in the future. It requires the entire community of bishops, priests, and laity to identify and intervene in the sexual violation of the Church's young. In the past, that wider community has been part of the problem much more than part of the solution.

"Omertà" in the Priesthood

It is not unusual for fellow seminarians or brother priests to sense something amiss in a colleague before anyone else does. Especially in the past, priests lived in communities—vowed religious men still do—and had some sense of the personalities, habits, and relationships of other priests. Historically, clergy have been silent about their brethren's suspicious behaviors. Like the unspoken vow of secrecy at work among the thin blue line of police, centuries of priests engaged in an unspoken but powerful "omertà" through which they maintained each other's secrets, even if those involved criminal activities. Inactive priest Francis McGillicuddy puts it this way: "You would never even breathe that a priest would commit sexual abuse. It would never be verbalized. It was unthinkable. . . . A priest's loyalty to his brothers was expected, and it was sometimes enforced by church hierarchy. Secrets were kept. Sometimes people even kept secrets from themselves."[57] McGillicuddy was in seminary with Rev. Paul Shanley, one of Boston's more notorius molesters, and he spent free time with Rev. Antonio Girardin and Rev. Thomas Lee, both of whom were accused of sexual abuse of minors.[58] He said he never suspected any of them of sexual abuse until the Church scandal erupted in 2002.

Author David Gibson describes a conversation with Rev. Robert Bullock, a Boston priest who eventually signed the petition asking Cardinal Law to step down. In reflecting upon the abuse scandal in Boston, Bullock is quoted as saying: "We didn't protect the children. They were our brothers who did these things. We heard the rumors. We heard the suspicions. Only two or three of us spoke up at great risk to themselves. What is it that made us, the Boston presbyterate, to be so supine, so inert, so passive, so unwilling to react, to take risks, and to speak out?"[59] One answer to Fr. Bullock's question is that when priests did speak up about their abusive brothers, too often they suffered greater consequences than the perpetrators.

Examples of this kind of response to complaints about an abusive priest abound. In one controversial case, Fr. James Haley of Virginia provided Bishop Paul Loverde of the Arlington diocese with evidence that Haley's pastor, Jim Verrechia, was involved in a sexual affair with a married female parishioner and also regularly visited gay pornography sites on the Internet.[60] While nothing untoward happened to Fr. Verrechia, Fr. Haley was transferred to a new parish. Here, he met Fr. William Erbacher who showed Haley his collection of homosexual pornography featuring young boys. Again, Fr. Haley went to Bishop Loverde and again he was transferred. Although the activities of both Fr. Verrechia and Fr. Erbacher eventually were made public by sources other than Fr. Haley, Bishop Loverde permanently suspended Haley from the Arlington diocese in 2003 after Haley testified in a legal deposition about sexual acting out by fellow priests.

In 1997, Fr. John Conley of San Francisco reported to the diocese his suspicions about a "wrestling match" between a priest and a teenager and, with the knowledge of the diocese, described his concerns to the district attorney.[61] Although the diocese later acknowledged that Fr. Conley was rightly worried about the priest's behavior, Conley was placed on adminis-trative leave for what were termed "unrelated behavioral problems." It was only after suing the diocese for what he claimed was retaliation for report-ing suspected child abuse that Fr. Conley was returned to his diocese as a priest in good standing. He received a financial settlement as well.

A lay brother told the chancellor of the Tucson diocese in 1977 that he suspected that Monsignor Robert Trupia was molesting altar boys.[62] The brother, a former policeman and now a California priest, provided the chancery with statements from alleged victims. He was rebuked by the chancellor and told that such statements could get a priest into trouble. Trupia was suspended from the priesthood in 1991 and was arrested in 2002 on charges that he had abused altar boys in Yuma, Arizona, in the 1970s.

In the early 1980s, Rev. James Gigliotti told officials in the Archdio-cese of Philadelphia that a fellow priest, Rev. James J. Brzyski, was molest-ing children.[63] He reports that Rev. John W. Graf, then assistant chancel-lor to John Cardinal Krol, told him to keep his mouth shut about the allegations, suggesting the directive came from the highest authority in the diocese. Although Brzyski was removed from his parish, the police were not informed, parishioners were not told the reason for the removal, and Brzyski remained a visitor in the homes of his former parishioners where he continued to molest children. Eventually, Brzyski left the priesthood and moved to Virginia where he was accused of molesting a seventeen-year-old boy.

Rev. Thomas P. Doyle was a priest on the fast track in the early 1980s. He worked with Archbishop Pio Laghi, then papal nuncio (the Vatican's ambassador) to the United States. Doyle's habitat was Embassy Row in Washington, D.C., where he hobnobbed with politicians and diplo-mats from all over the world. During the Gauthe case, Doyle, Rev. Mi-chael Peterson, president of St. Luke's Institute where Gauthe and many other priests were treated after their sexual misconduct was exposed, and Gauthe's lawyer, Ray Mouton, collaborated on what became known as the Peterson-Mouton-Doyle Report. That report was uncannily prescient in depicting the scope and likely consequences of the sexual abuse of young people by priests in the United States.

By the end of 1985, every American bishop leading a diocese had been sent a copy of the report. While the bishops ignored the content of the report, Doyle was duly noted for his role in writing it. He lost his job in the nuncio's office and moved to the Air Force as a chaplain. Since then, Doyle has worked tirelessly on behalf of victims here and abroad—offering plaintiffs' attorneys invaluable insights into the inner workings of the Church, testifying for victims, encouraging laypeople to challenge the failures of the Church to protect the young.

Several months before he was to retire from the military, Doyle was severed from his position and therefore from a higher military pension by Archbishop Edwin F. O'Brien of the Archdiocese for the Military Services.[64] The dismissal followed Doyle's disagreement with several policies advocated by O'Brien. O'Brien did not meet with Doyle before or after terminating his chaplaincy nor was Fr. Doyle given the opportunity to explain himself.[65] Many believed Doyle was being punished for his outspoken criticism of the hierarchy's response to the sexual abuse crisis.

After leaving the armed forces, Doyle settled in the D.C. area. Theodore Cardinal McCarrick refused to extend faculties to Fr. Doyle, depriving him of the right to function as a priest in the Archdiocese of Washington. Neither Doyle nor his Dominican provincial superior feels that any other American bishop would extend faculties to him either.

Tom Doyle is warm; he is generous and generative; he is very funny; he is smart. It is clear that he is courageous. His immersion in trauma also is etched in his face and reflects in his eyes. In short, Tom Doyle is a priest. Many crossing his path recognize him as a "friend of God and prophet."[66] Elizabeth Johnson defines a friend of God as someone who enters "into a mutual relationship with God, freely, with trust and affection; . . . caring passionately about what God cares about."[67] Being a prophet, according to Johnson, "is to raise your voice in criticism against injustice. . . . In the worst moments, being a prophet also means to comfort others with words of hope. . . . [B]eing a prophet means, as Jesus said, being without honor in your own country and among your own people."[68] Tom Doyle, friend of God and prophet, broke "omertà" and has been cast out by the bishops who seem terrified that the truths he tells threaten their power. He is an exemplar of the consequences historically visited upon priests who spoke out about a brother priest's misbehavior, even when the activity in question was the sexual violation of a minor child.

People in the Pews

While many Catholic laypeople truly never suspected that their priest was sexually victimizing minors, and others spoke up forcefully long ago, still others enabled the abuse. Some Catholic men and women must have turned a blind eye to signs that a priest's behavior with a minor was odd or inappropriate. For example, it is difficult to believe that a housekeeper who saw Father regularly take a boy upstairs to his room in the rectory would not have a tinge of discomfort or doubt about that behavior. Similarly, lay teachers or nuns whose students were taken from their classrooms by priests at irregular times and returned in somewhat different emotional or cognitive states must have had a passing sense of something being awry. Other laity, sometimes even the parents of victims, refused to believe reports of sexual abuse and supported the priest at the expense of the victim. The laity's collusion with their domination by the clergy, even when that involved sexual violation of a minor, bespoke both cultural and spiritual dynamics.

The parents of most of the victims of priestly sexual abuse taking place in the 1960s, 1970s, and early 1980s were raised at the tail end of what Eugene Kennedy calls the "Brick and Mortar" stage of the American Catholic Church.[69] From the time of the great immigration of the mid- and late nineteenth century until just past the middle of the twentieth century, the Catholic Church flourished in America. In many cities, a Catholic's social status was identified as much by parish affiliation as by street address, and there was reasonably friendly rivalry between parishes about being "best." There was real anti-Catholicism in the country leading Catholics to be both protective of and defensive about their Church.

The parish priests were the center of Catholic life and were held in awe by their flocks, especially the women. Not infrequently there was a cadre of parish women who covertly but intensely competed with each other over which one of them had Father to dinner or about whose apple pie he raved most. The priest often was also a source of advice and comfort about alcoholic husbands who drank their paychecks or hit the kids, or about kids who were heading in the wrong direction. Because there were so many priests, they were able to function as pastors to their flocks, playing the roles of therapist, social welfare representative, and shepherd to the living, the troubled, the sick, the dying, and the dead.

In addition to the loyalty and affection he earned through performance of pastoral functions, the priest on the altar was revered as Christ's delegate on earth. Through the spiritual gifts received at ordination, the priest brought the living presence of Jesus into the lives of his parishioners every week in ways only he could. He also delivered the Word of God to the minds and hearts of a community of faithful taught to be passively receptive and obedient to his teachings.

To question the integrity of a priest was unthinkable to most Catholics of the "Brick and Mortar" Church. Rather, the obvious failings of a priest, such as a tendency to drink too much or to snap at children running across the freshly cut lawn of the rectory, were excused or denied by many members of the congregation. If Catholic parents or other parishioners had an uncomfortable feeling about a priest's relationship with a minor, they were likely to feel badly about themselves for allowing such suspicions to enter their minds. In this way, they were not much different from most people in society confronted with the possibility that someone they knew was sexually abusing a child. For Catholics, however, society's typical denial of the sexual victimization of children was enhanced by the deeply felt need to think only the best about Father and by the demands for loyalty placed on laity by a clericalist caste.

Sadly, when and if parents or parishioners did complain about a priest, they could expect to be scolded by priests and shunned by fellow parishioners. For example, when the Gastal family of Louisiana went public with Fr. Gilbert Gauthe's abuse of their son, Scott, in the sexual abuse case that ushered in the current crisis, so many members of the small community stopped buying from Glenn Gastal's feed store that he was forced to close it down.[70] When Elizabeth Evarts and the Hanson family of Phoenix went to court over Fr. Mark Lehman's molestations of their daughters, both families had their tires slashed and received death threats.[71] They also were confronted in court by their fellow parishioners and pastor, who openly supported the offending priest. One parishioner called Patty Hanson, mother of two victims, a "blasphemous bitch" when they met on the street.[72] After Fr. Lehman was sentenced to ten years of prison in a plea-bargain arrangement, a number of parishioners threw a farewell party for him.[73]

While it may be understandable in some intellectually abstract way that Catholics maintained blind faith in their clergy until 2002 when the sexual abuse crisis blew open, it is seemingly less comprehensible that, even now, sizable numbers of Catholics defend sexually abusive priests.

When William Cardinal Keeler of Baltimore published the names of fifty-six priests accused of sexual abuse in his archdiocese, parishioners at St. Mark's Church in Catonsville learned that six of them had served in their parish.[74] Some parishioners appreciated Keeler's openness but others like Cindy Keenan equivocated, saying, "Everybody seems like they're jumping on the bandwagon. And you know what? I don't think we should judge."[75] Another St. Mark parishioner, Marion Rupertus, said of one of the priests, "He was a good pastor. We all commit sins, and we all hope God will forgive us."[76] In these cases, lay Catholics may value forgiveness at the expense of accountability. While a criminal can be forgiven spiritually for his offenses, society must at the same time hold him and his abettors accountable for the crime(s) committed.

In 2004, Rev. Michael Benham was removed from ministry because of credible sexual abuse allegations that he had abused a minor in the 1970s when he was a priest at St. John Neponk Church in Racine, Wisconsin.[77] John Moe, a parishioner at one of Fr. Benham's later assignments, responded, "I was stunned and saddened. . . . But I don't expect to block him out of my life. I believe in forgiveness and I have no reason to suspect that he did any of that activity here."[78] Marie, a parishioner from St. Lucy's in the Archdiocese of Philadelphia, commented that you cannot know if all the accusers were telling the truth, "People lie, and papers lie, and who even knows?"[79] Even more startling was the response of a Polish parish in New Britain, Connecticut, when a visiting Polish priest, Rev. Roman Kramek, was arrested and confessed to having intercourse with a seventeen-year-old girl he had been asked to counsel after she was raped by someone else.[80] Not only did parishioners at Sacred Heart Church in New Britain raise bail money for Fr. Kramek, a number of laypeople and their pastor cast aspersions on the rape victim.[81] Sacred Heart's pastor, Rev. Paul Wysocki, called the victim a tramp and suggested that her accusations were fueled by a desire for money.[82] Although Wysocki's comments were condemned by then Hartford Archbishop Daniel Cronin, parishioners like Grazyna Pominanowska were not convinced that Kramek's confession meant he actually committed the crime.[83] Pominanowska said, "We don't know in what to believe. . . . The press writes a lot about this case, but they may be passing on the wrong information. They make us believe what they want, but we simply want to know the truth."[84]

One sees the power of denial at work in these statements. Denial walks hand in hand with sexual abuse, wherever that abuse occurs. The perpetrator almost always denies what he has done and certainly denies the consequences for the victim. Victims too often deny their victimizations for long periods of time and tend to deny the meaning sexual abuse has in their lives. Mothers in incestuous families and people who just hear or read about a child being abused often respond first with denial or minimization.

In part, denial is related to our unwillingness to think that we, or those we love, could be vulnerable to abuse. We all would prefer to think that it could never happen to us or to our children because we would not let it happen. So, if we hear about sexual abuse, the first temptation is to say that it could not have happened—especially if we know and like the accused perpetrator. When Olan Horne of Lowell, Massachusetts, came forward about being sexual abused by Rev. Joseph Birmingham, later recognized as a serial abuser, one fellow parishioner spit at him and said, "I knew Birmingham. This didn't happen."[85] The second temptation is to rationalize that if it happened, the young person or his or her caretakers must have allowed it to happen. When Phil Saviano and other alleged victims of Rev. David Holley filed suit against the Diocese of Worcester, Massachusetts, Saviano received a fax from a parishioner saying, "You fucking pussies ought to let go of the past and the blow jobs you all enjoyed."[86] Finally, we can insist that even if it happened, it does not mean something essential about the perpetrator and will not really have a detrimental impact on the victim. We may also deny the occurrence or meaning of sexual abuse because we feel powerless to do anything about it and would like to avoid that uncomfortable feeling of powerlessness.

I think we also deny the reality of sexual abuse because it is a heinous crime that raises questions about the evil that "everyperson" is capable of enacting. Perpetrators are one of us; they live in our midst, they father our children; they teach or coach our students; they are neighbors who walk their dogs with us; they sell us our green groceries or fix our cars or dry clean our clothes; they sit next to us in Church; sometimes they even preach to us in church and administer sacraments to us in God's name. To stand in the reality of the occurrence and meaning of sexual abuse challenges all of us to examine our own potential for evil. That is a tall order and most of us prefer to turn away, denying that we, or anyone we know, ever could assault a child. History recalls that the residents of Oswiecim smelled the smoke of burning human bodies for years and claimed that they knew nothing.

Lay denial of sexual abuse by a priest suggests yet other dynamics at play. Rev. Dr. Laurie Ferguson, a Presbyterian minister, and Rev. Anne Richards, an Episcopalian priest, both have served on clergy misconduct committees for their denominations. Both have been startled at the denial they encountered from congregations whose pastors were credibly accused of misconduct—of criminally abusing a child or abrogating their fiduciary responsibility for adult parishioners by entering into a sexual relationship with them.[87] Richards says that, in her experience, denial was most intransigent at the parish level: "Without exception, and even in the most dramatic cases of prolonged, egregious misconduct, the parishioners refused to believe that their priest had transgressed; they reacted with great rage and steadfastly tried to find alibis or excuses for him."[88]

Ferguson suggests that the laity's denial of credible abuse supports their idealization of a pastor's position as a perfect conduit for their own spiritual functioning and ultimate salvation.[89] To that extent, they relinquish responsibility for their own spiritual growth and relationship with God, turning it over to the idealized cleric. Ferguson says it so well, she is worth quoting at length:

> In an unconscious bargain, they [the laity] traded their internal and independent spiritual power for a dependent relationship on a pastor's faith and charisma. They idealized him as the one who really knew and spoke for God and, in consequence, they lived out an immature faith that refused to recognize any wrong doing. . . . Their reliance on the idea of his perfection was more compelling than the suffering of any one individual, particularly someone viewed as powerless, a minor, or a woman.[90]

In Roman Catholicism, the laity's predilection to put a priest in charge of their soul and salvation intersected with the Church's demand that they do so. Trained to, "pray, pay, and obey," the Catholic laity was ill equipped to assess their priests through a mature and critical process of discernment. Rather, abuse went on and, when it was exposed, too many laypeople still refused to know.

CHAPTER 11

The Secret Is Revealed

External Factors

Sexual Abuse Acknowledged as a Social Problem

Prior to the 1980s, the sexual abuse of children and adolescents was a well-kept secret throughout society. It was the women's movement of the 1970s that dragged incest and sexual abuse into the public eye, along with other forms of domestic violence and crimes against women and children. Throughout the 1980s and 1990s, methodologically sound empirical studies were published indicating that approximately one third of all women and one fourth of all men are sexually abused prior to the age of eighteen.[1] These studies found that young people were most often abused by someone they knew and trusted—a family member or someone who had authority over them like a camp counselor, teacher, scout leader, or religious leader. Researchers and clinicians developed an increasingly comprehensive literature elaborating short-term and long-term consequences of sexual abuse and outlining various treatment approaches.[2] Victims of childhood sexual abuse began to speak about their experiences publicly, knowing for the first time in their lives that they were not alone.[3] Talk-show host Oprah Winfrey, a sexual abuse survivor herself, worked tirelessly and responsibly to publicize the after-effects of early sexual trauma and to support programs that protect children and help recovering adults. Television programs and movies like *Something about Amelia, Law and Order: Special Victims Unit, Nuts, The Prince of Tides, Mystic River, Sleepers,* and *The Boys of St. Vincent's,* the latter based on the clergy abuse of orphans at Mt. Cashel in Newfoundland, portrayed the impact of early sexual trauma.

By the mid-1990s, too much data about sexual abuse had been generated for all but the most skeptical, the most naive, or the most ill intended to deny that the sexual exploitation of minors has been a social problem of substantial magnitude. The social milieu was ripe to take seriously a sexual abuse scandal like the one unfolding within the Catholic Church.

Therapists Replace Confessors

Psychiatrists and psychoanalysts have seen patients since the late 1800s, but psychotherapy for a long time was limited to a relatively small segment of the population who could afford the time and money it required and who believed in its efficacy. It was not until after World War II that psychologists, clinical social workers, and other mental health professionals were able to obtain state licenses enabling them to make therapy available to more people. Concurrently, state and local community mental health centers and substance abuse treatment clinics sprung up offering low-cost mental health services to even more individuals.

At the same time that psychotherapy resources were expanding, priests were in shorter supply and were aging as a group. In increasing numbers of parishes, priests simply were not available to give ongoing advice or counseling to parishioners; other clerics, years older than many of their flock, were not perceived to be acceptable helping professionals. As one acquaintance in her forties told me, "My mother would rather die than see a therapist; she brought all her problems to our priest—when she brought them anywhere at all. I would rather die than talk about my life with a priest but never miss an appointment with my shrink." This move from priests to therapists was rapid, taking less than one generation and markedly dividing postwar Catholic parents from their children. A corollary of the shift was a weakening of the power of priests in the internal lives of enough parishioners such that, when the sexual abuse scandal broke in 2002, a critical mass of Catholics paid attention to it.

Changing Views of Authority

"Brick and Mortar" Catholics for the most part bowed to both secular and religious authorities, generally trusting leaders in both realms to conduct themselves with integrity. The World War II generation had given their youths to a war believed to be just and necessary. When they came home, many joined companies or unions that promised lifelong job security and a pension later in life. The government offered them GI loans for college and low interest rates on home mortgages. Within their faith, we have seen that Catholics of this era (and older) were prepared to "pray, pay, and obey," trusting that their bishops, cardinals, and pastors were decent and honest. Of course there were Catholics who were cynical about the clergy even then, but the majority of the laity lived their lives according to the teachings of Church authorities.

The children and grandchildren of that generation forged a very different relationship with authority. Living through the deceptions of the military during Vietnam, Watergate, Ford's pardon of Richard Nixon, the Iran-Contra scandal, Whitewatergate, and 9/11, Americans in their fifties and younger had less faith than their elders in the trustworthiness of national leaders. Similarly, as technology changed the needs of the workforce, job security became a memory. Finally, scandals at companies like Archer Daniels Midland, Enron, and WorldCom convinced many citizens that business leaders were no more reputable than politicians. And Catholics, as we have seen, experienced a watershed moment in their faith when Pope Paul VI issued *Humanae Vitae*. The laity de facto deprived the institutional Church of its authority to instruct them in matters of morality, and, by the turn of the new century, most Catholics formed their moral choices based more on personal belief and experience than on Church instructions.[4] By 2005, fewer than 20 percent of Catholics felt that the Church should have the final say on the use of artificial contraception and fewer than one third thought the Church was the final authority on abortion.[5]

The sexual abuse crisis further challenged the Church's hierarchical power structure. Paul Dokecki quotes Eugene Kennedy and Sarah Charles's treatment of authority and authoritarianism:

> The [sexual abuse crisis] derives in a major way from the fact that hierarchies don't work anymore, if they ever really did. . . . This is because we are in an age of space exploration, technology, and instant worldwide communication that guarantees the failure of hierarchical authoritarianism's attempts to constrain and control knowledge and information and to deny mature people a role in organizational decisionmaking.[6]

American Catholics influenced by new views of power relationships were less likely to submit to the prelates' explanations for the crisis or glib reassurances that Church officials would take care of everything: "Don't worry, you can trust us." Rather, they looked with skepticism at public remarks made by Church officials and were ready to hear more about the scandal in order to draw their own conclusions.

The Media Is the Medium

Print and TV handling of the crisis from 2002 forward diverged greatly from the kid-gloves approach the Church had relied on for decades. During the "Brick and Mortar" days of the Church, the press rarely reported on any misbehavior by Catholic priests, much less that by bishops. In part, this was in keeping with the deferential media standards applied in those days to other professionals and public figures. One need only compare the media's devotion to the Bill Clinton/Monica Lewinksy affair with their silence about John F. Kennedy's dalliances with Judith Exner and others to note the change in journalistic standards and values. Like politicians, priests who drove drunk, lifted funds from the collection plate, or sexually acted out profited from the media's past discretion about publicizing high crimes and misdemeanors committed by community figures.

The media's hands-off approach to the Church also stemmed from their fear of retaliation if they published articles critical of the Catholic Church. Historian and religious studies professor Philip Jenkins points out that diocesan officials usually were successful in prevailing upon newspaper editors or local radio or TV media to refrain from commenting on a priest's behavior, no matter how criminal it was.[7] If a media outlet was foolish enough to defy the Church, a boycott of the publication often ensued. In the 1940s, a Washington, D.C., newspaper printing an article about an adolescent girl's alleged abuse by nuns in a Catholic home for delinquents lost 40 percent of its circulation in two weeks.[8] Finally, newspaper editors were concerned that they would be labeled anti-Catholic if they published the crimes of priests or were critical of the Church in print.[9]

In the early days of the Catholic sexual abuse scandal, newspapers still took risks in publishing articles exposing priests or criticizing bishops. When the Louisiana *Times of Acadiana* published a series of stories on the Gauthe case in the early 1980s, an advertising boycott was organized in part by Monsignor Alexander Sigur, pastor of a nearby parish. In 1985 in Pittsburgh, Elinor Bergholz of the Pittsburgh *Post-Gazette* received hate calls and mail, and even lost friends among Catholic colleagues, when she reported on a sexually abusive priest in western Pennsylvania.[10] Bernard Cardinal Law, furious when the *Boston Globe* aggressively pursued the case of serial abuser Rev. James Porter in 1992, initially accused the secular media of anti-Catholic bias in blowing the case out of proportion. Law's incensed response to the *Globe*'s coverage of the Porter story has become legendary: "By all means, we call down God's power on the media, particularly the *Globe*."[11] By 1992, however, things had changed. God apparently decided to send his power down instead on Cardinal Law; the paper continued to publish and prosper, while by 2002, the cardinal was a recluse in his chancery, with celebrated appearances as a deponent in sexual abuse cases. By the end of 2002, he had resigned as cardinal archbishop of Boston, in part due to the unrelenting media coverage of the scandal in Boston.

An important factor in liberating newspapers and television reporters to pursue the Church's sex abuse scandal was the early and continuous coverage of the story by the *National Catholic Reporter (NCR).*[12] Tom Fox, publisher of *NCR*, began reporting on sexual abuse cases in 1983 and, positioning himself as a "loving critic of the Church," insisted that the unfolding crisis be reported with both tenacity and a sense of responsibility.[13] Jenkins states that *NCR* was the first media outlet to label correctly the sexual abuse of minors by priests as a problem that was nationwide, systemic to the Catholic Church, and a crisis in its proportions.[14] Here was exposure of the abuse scandal and criticism of the Church, including the hierarchy, relentlessly pursued with integrity by the Church's own. The secular media was therefore freer to report, and they did.

Media coverage of the sexual abuse crisis gradually increased and spread across the United States throughout the 1990s, but it was not until the John Geoghan case was reported in early 2002 that newspaper, television, and Internet attention to the scandal exploded. As the Boston papers, led by the *Boston Globe*, uncovered not just the extent of Geoghan's abuse but, more importantly, the protection of abusive priests over decades by the archdiocese, papers nationwide began to investigate more closely instances of sexual abuse by priests in their own communities. In 2002, the Religion Newswriters Association voted the Catholic Church's sexual abuse crisis the top story of the year.[15] The association also awarded its "Into the Darkness Award" to the American Catholic hierarchy, naming it the group who that year had done the most to hide information from the media and the public.[16] In 2002, the *Globe* was honored with the Associated Press Managing Editor's Freedom of Information Award and the Worth Bingham Prize honoring the best investigative reporting in American newspapers and newsmagazines.[17] In 2003, the paper received the Selden Ring Award for Investigative Reporting and the Pulitzer Prize for their coverage of the Church crisis.[18] In 2005, the *Dallas Morning News* received the Dallas Bar Association's award for excellence in legal reporting for its series on Catholic priests around the world who were accused of sexual abuse but not punished by the Church.[19] Far from shutting papers down, tough reporting on sexual abuse by priests and cover-ups by bishops garnered respect and awards for the media.

Until well into the 1960s, the church could influence the sales of books and movie tickets as well as the circulation of newspapers. Catholic groups like the Legion of Decency rated every film released in the United States, advising Catholics which movies were suitable for viewing by the faithful. Attending a film banned for Catholics was a sin. Many Catholics of that era checked movie ratings in their diocesan newspapers or local parish bulletins before setting out to the movies, so filmmakers were cautious about the ways in which they portrayed Catholics and Catholic clergy. Similarly, the National Office for Decent Literature advised Catholics about books that were acceptable reading material and those that were banned for Catholics. The Church thus influenced the way in which it was depicted in fact and fiction, and clergy relied on that protective climate.

By 2002, those days were long gone and books, movies, and legitimate theater productions about the scandal came out and helped spread the word about the crisis. Television movies like *Our Fathers,* based on David France's book by the same name, and the documentary *Twist of Faith* brought the scandal into American homes in living color. Movie theaters offered *The Magdalene Sisters,* a gut-wrenching depiction of Ireland's residential laundries; *Holy Water-Gate: Abuse Cover-Up in the Catholic Church,* a documentary of survivor stories; and *Deliver Us from Evil,* another documentary about the crisis. *Doubt, a Parable,* an off Broadway production about a young priest who may have abused a black boy in a New York Catholic school won rave reviews, moved to Broadway, and won a Pulitzer, while Martin Moran's moving, Obie-award-winning, one-man show, *The Tricky Part,* toured the country telling of his recovery from childhood sexual abuse by a seminarian.

Finally, the Internet facilitated nationwide tracking of the Catholic scandal. Religious communication professor Stephen O'Leary asserts, in fact, that the "Internet has fundamentally altered the balance that governed the relationship between media institutions and more traditional powers such as the Church."[20] In 2002, Bill Mitchell, online editor and marketing director for the Poynter Institute, a school for journalism, established the *Clergy Abuse Tracker.*[21] Every day, articles from media outlets across the country were compiled and posted for anyone following the crisis to read. In 2004, the *National Catholic Reporter* took over the *Abuse Tracker* at www.ncrnews.org/abuse. The *Abuse Tracker* makes clear the national and even international scope of the sexual abuse of minors by priests, rendering it more difficult for Church officials to claim that just a few bad apples here or there abused young people. Besides the *Abuse Tracker,* websites were set up by many groups involved in the crisis and covered a spectrum of viewpoints. Catholics became inveterate bloggers, even referring to their many sites as St. Blog's parish.[22]

Beginning in 2002, the Catholic Church learned the hard way that the media was no longer malleable and that, in the age of cybercommunication and instant messaging, the Church never again could control to its satisfaction the flow of information about its operations.

Law and Order

Paralleling the impact of the media on the scandal, the legal system began to battle with the Church in ways that were beyond anyone's imagination just a few decades earlier.

In many places and for many decades, police, judges, and prosecutors helped the Church to keep its secrets about clergy misconduct. In the late 1950s, for example, Manchester, New Hampshire, police were informed by the parents of two eighth graders that Rev. Donald M. Osgood had molested their children.[23] The police referred the matter to then Bishop Matthew F. Brady and noted in their report, "Parents and the boys stated they would keep this in deep secrecy."[24] In Toledo, Anthony Bosch, police chief from 1956 to 1970, reportedly enforced an unwritten policy that no Catholic priests could be arrested.[25] Former Toledo police officer Gene Fodor states that a cop would be fired if he arrested a priest, even if the charge involved sexual violation of a minor.[26] Retired Toledo detective John Connors acknowledges that when he was informed by officials at a local Catholic high school that Rev. Dennis Gray, eventually accused of abusing over a dozen boys, might be molesting children at Gray's cottage, he told the school administrators to keep Fr. Gray away from children but did not file a police report.[27] Fr. Gray later left the priesthood with no record and became a probation officer and a public school administrator.[28] In a 2002 deposition, former Archdiocese of Boston official and former Brooklyn Bishop Thomas V. Daily testified that the Archdiocese of Boston had an understanding with local police that the Church, rather than law enforcement authorities, would handle priests accused of sexual abuse.[29] As recently as 2000, a West Texas prosecutor agreed to let the Church send a seminarian home to Spain after he admitted pulling down a boy's pants and touching his buttocks.[30]

By the 1980s, lawyers were representing plaintiffs in lawsuits against allegedly abusive priests and the dioceses that shielded them. Like the media, these attorneys initially were blasted by Church authorities and laypeople for coming after accused priests or the bishops who abetted them. For example, when attorney Bruce Pasternack of New Mexico began to represent plaintiffs in lawsuits involving abusive priests, he was called a "money-grubbing Jew, priest-hater, and Catholic-basher."[31] One investigator for the Archdiocese of Santa Fe reportedly called Pasternack "a Jew bastard."[32] Always a disgusting slur, the anti-Semitic smearing of Pasternack was particularly ironic since the cathedral in Santa Fe honors the Jewish merchants of the area who helped pay to finish building the edifice when the Catholics ran out of money.[33] Pasternack did not convince his critics when he stated quite reasonably, "I'd sue a Buddhist monk, a Protestant minister or a rabbi. I don't have any animosity toward the Catholic Church. I just have animosity for people who rape children."[34] Jeff Anderson, a Minnesota attorney who has been involved in over five hundred lawsuits against the Church, has received bags of hate mail.[35] One writer called him "the scum maggot of this country," while another insisted that "[w]hen the Catholic Church needs advice from a WASP, Swede, bigoted shyster lawyer, we'll ask for it."[36] Outside Boston, plaintiffs' attorney Eric MacLeish received bomb threats at his office, someone threatened to kidnap his daughter from daycare if he continued representing sexual abuse victims suing the Church, and a weapon was fired outside his home while he and his wife watched television.[37]

Tenacious plaintiffs' attorneys were instrumental in generating settlements in many dioceses. By August 2005, the Church had paid out more than $1 billion in claims and there was no immediate end in sight.[38] Lawyers can receive up to 30 to 40 percent of the proceeds from these cases. It is important to note, however, that especially in the 1980s, 1990s, and into 2002, there was no guarantee that these cases would generate any money at all. All the investment is up front for the lawyers who may or may not recoup their expenses, and not until years later when cases settle or receive jury awards. In Rhode Island, for example, Carl P. DeLuca, a plaintiffs' attorney representing alleged survivors against the Diocese of Providence, borrowed and then fell behind on a $50,000 loan to keep his business open, bought his own home back in a tax sale, and let go of his BMW, office staff, and downtown Providence office.[39] His colleague in the cases, Timothy J. Conlon, had his car repossessed and a foreclosure notice issued on a summer cabin in New Hampshire.[40] Eventually, the Providence diocese settled thirty-six claims for a total of $13.5 million.[41]

Many plaintiffs' attorneys involved in the sexual abuse scandal are or were Catholics whose relationships with their faith were forever changed by their involvement with the scandal. Richard Cappalli, another Providence attorney, was so disillusioned with the Church that he and his wife stopped practicing their religion.[42] John Manly, a California attorney representing victims up and down the West Coast, wears a Miraculous Cross medal he received in second grade, and he continued to attend Mass during his first case against the Church.[43] He will always consider himself a Catholic but can no longer bear to attend Mass. He says:

> But how do I explain to my children what I know and still sit in the pews? It's a feeling of loss. I'm in a spiritual desert. I have two young ones who aren't baptized. . . . I don't know what to do. I have memories of great priests who were my teachers, my mentors. Now, I look back and think, "What do I do with those memories as an adult?"[44]

Prosecutors, once reluctant to take on the Catholic Church, began grand jury investigations or other special investigations of the Church's role in the sexual abuse of minors in Maine; Massachusetts; Westchester County, New York; Philadelphia, Pennsylvania; New Hampshire; Suffolk County, New York; Phoenix, Arizona; Toledo, Ohio; Ventura, California; and Los Angeles, California. Grand jurors and attorneys general were dismayed by what they learned, and they shared their findings with the public. In Massachusetts, Attorney General Thomas P. Reilly wrote,

> The widespread abuse of children in the Archdiocese of Boston was due to institutional acceptance of abuse and a massive and pervasive failure of leadership. For at least six decades, three successive Archbishops, Bishops and others in positions of authority within the Archdiocese operated with tragically misguided priorities. They chose to protect the image and reputation of their institution rather than the safety and well being of the children entrusted to their care. They acted with a misguided devotion to secrecy. And they failed to break their code of silence even when the magnitude of what had occurred would have alerted any reasonable, responsible manager that help was needed. Still, the failure of the Archdiocese leadership has been too massive and too prolonged, and the Archdiocese has yet to demonstrate a commitment to reform proportional to the tragedy it perpetrated.[45]

Grand jurors in Suffolk County, New York, said about the Diocese of Rockville Centre:

> Priests assigned to and working in the Diocese of Rockville Centre committed criminal acts in violation of New York State Penal Law Article 130, Sex Offenses, and other statutes designed to protect the health, safety and welfare of children. These criminal acts included, but

were not limited to, Rape, Sodomy, Sexual Abuse, Endangering the Welfare of a Child and Use of a Child in a Sexual Performance. Not one priest in the Diocese who knew about these criminal acts reported them to any law enforcement agency. The Grand Jury concludes that the conduct of certain Diocesan officials would have warranted criminal prosecution but for the fact that the existing statutes are inadequate.[46]

In late 2005, a particularly scathing grand jury report was issued in Philadelphia. It began:

> This report contains the findings of the Grand Jury: how dozens of priests sexually abused hundreds of children; how Philadelphia Archdiocese officials—including Cardinal Bevilacqua and Cardinal Krol—excused and enabled the abuse. . . . Some may be tempted to describe these events as tragic. Tragedies such as tidal waves, however, are outside human control. What we found were not acts of God, but of men who acted in His name and defiled it. . . . When we say abuse, we don't just mean "inappropriate touching" (as the Archdiocese often chose to refer to it). We mean rape. Boys who were raped orally, boys who were raped anally, girls who were raped vaginally. . . . [I]n its callous, calculating manner, the Archdiocese's "handling" of the abuse scandal was at least as immoral as the abuse itself.[47]

Anthony Cardinal Bevilacqua, retired cardinal archbishop of Philadelphia, was not just a canon lawyer but also held an American civil law degree, so he had to know the criminality of his abusive priests' behavior and of his own in covering up the abuse. The grand jury lamented that statutes of limitation prevented them from indicting the abusers or Cardinal Bevilacqua.[48]

Attorney General Peter W. Heed of New Hampshire concluded:

> Based on this evidence, the AGO (Attorney General's Office) was prepared to present indictments to the Hillsborough County Grand Jury on December 13, 2002, charging the Diocese of Manchester with multiple counts of endangering the welfare of a minor in violation of RSA 639:3. On December 10, 2002, the Diocese entered into an agreement with the State that ended the criminal proceedings. With an understanding of the evidence obtained by the State and the elements required to prove a criminal violation of the New Hampshire child endangerment statute, RSA 639:3, I, the Diocese acknowledged that

the State had evidence likely to sustain a conviction against the diocese for child endangerment.[49]

In order to avoid prosecution, the Diocese of Manchester had to sign an agreement with the attorney general's office in which the diocese promised to implement certain policies regarding sexual abuse and to submit to regular audits by the state.

As in New Hampshire, former Bishop Thomas J. O'Brien of the Diocese of Phoenix avoided criminal indictment only by acknowledging that he had covered up sexual abuse by priests for decades.[50] In 2003, Archbishop Daniel Pilarczyk of Cincinnati pleaded nolo contendere on behalf of the archdiocese to five misdemeanor counts of failing to report a felony.[51] The archdiocese thus was the first U.S. diocese to be convicted of criminal charges in the sexual abuse crisis.[52] The plea deal was reached after the archdiocese struggled for two years against Hamilton County prosecutor Michael K. Allen's demands for documents related to sexual abuse by priests and occurred only as a new grand jury was to be impaneled to consider whether diocesan officials had covered up sexual abuse crimes committed by priests.[53]

Bristol County, Massachusetts, District Attorney Paul F. Walsh published the names of twenty-one priests from the Diocese of Fall River who had been accused of sexual abuse taking place throughout the past fifty years, saying that he would no longer enshroud those names in secrecy.[54] He also took former Fall River Bishop Sean O'Malley, now cardinal archbishop of Boston, to task for failing to submit those names to the district attorney years ago, before the statute of limitations ran out on potential criminal prosecutions.[55]

In Ventura County, California, and in Los Angeles, district attorneys have relentlessly pursued the release of documents related to sexually abusive priests in the Archdiocese of Los Angeles while Roger Cardinal Mahony has fought just as tenaciously to keep the documents out of the hands of the authorities.[56] That battle was still wending its way through the courts in early 2006.

Like prosecutors, judges who once might have been inclined to go easy on the Church often, although not always, ruled in favor of plaintiffs demanding the release of once-secret diocesan documents and making other arguments that, in turn, pushed dioceses toward settling lawsuits.[57] The Diocese of Spokane, Washington, and its bishop, William Skylstad, president of the United States Conference of Catholic Bishops (USCCB), were unpleasantly surprised when federal bankruptcy judge Patricia Williams ruled that Catholic schools, churches, and parish properties, including churches, are owned by the diocese and therefore can be liquidated to settle sex abuse lawsuits.[58] Skylstad had argued that the property belonged to the individual entities rather than the diocese, and he successfully appealed the ruling.[59] In February 2006, Spokane agreed to settle with seventy-five victims for $46 million. Important nonfinancial concessions included Bishop William Skylstad's concession that plaintiffs would be called "victims" rather than "alleged victims"; that these victims could return to the parishes in which they were abused, speak about their experiences, and possibly confront their molesters; and that a full page of the diocesan newspaper would be devoted to written submissions by victims every month for the next three years.[60] Parishes in Spokane blocked the settlement until each parish can calculate its share of the financial burden. Late in 2005, Judge Elizabeth Perris also ruled that the bankrupt Archdiocese of Portland, Oregon, rather than individual entities, owns its Catholic parishes and schools, a decision that may be affected by Spokane's successful appeal of a similar judicial ruling.[61]

The Catholic Church's sexual abuse scandal and the litigation associated with it set in relief two issues that state legislatures in many states began to reexamine. First, states began reconsidering statutes of limitation for sexual abuse as they heard testimony regarding the length of time it takes for victims to come forward and as grand juries around the country expressed their frustration at being hampered from indicting abusers and their abettors.[62] Similarly, legislators in a number of states introduced bills adding clergy to their state's list of professionals mandated to report known or suspected sexual abuse to civil authorities, although most legislatures exempted information divulged in the confessional.[63] These bills did not always pass the first time around, but the debate lifted consciousness about the long-term impact of sexual abuse and the issue is likely to be of continuing legislative concern.[64]

Victim/Survivor and Advocacy Groups

Victim/survivor groups and groups that advocate for survivors play an important role in keeping the sexual abuse of minors by Catholic priests in the public eye and provide a powerful forum for the voices of survivors to be heard.

The two major groups for victims/survivors are the Healing Alliance (formerly The Linkup) and SNAP (Survivor Network for those Abused by Priests). As they evolved from their beginnings in Chicago, the Linkup increasingly focused on creating healing opportunities for victims/survivors while SNAP was more visible as a political force. SNAP comments in the press on developments in the crisis, organizes grassroots efforts to change state laws regarding sexual abuse statutes of limitation and child abuse reporting responsibilities, and works with plaintiffs' attorneys to support litigation against the church.

The Linkup (www.healingall.org), claiming more than three thousand members, was founded in Chicago by Jeanne Miller in 1991.[65] During most of the contemporary crisis, the group was directed by Susan Archibald, a survivor of priest abuse.[66] Achibald resigned in 2006 and was replaced by Jonia Mariechild. In 2004, The Linkup opened The Farm, a thirteen-hundred-acre center offering retreats and health and wellness experiences that combine a number of therapeutic modalities. In 2005, The Linkup morphed into the Healing Alliance to connect with other organizations and individuals providing healing resources for survivors.[67]

The philosophy of The Farm suggests that healing "means reframing our experience and reforming our story so that our lives are not defined by the past, so that we are not continually recycling our pain, and the shadow which has blocked our inner light gently lifts away."[68] The Farm's mission statement captures a vital aspect of recovery from abuse—the individual's transformation from a survivor of abuse who happens to be a person, to a person who happens to be a survivor of abuse. If survivors cannot eventually transcend their abuse in this way, they continue in bondage to those experiences, losing the fullness of their present and future as well as of their past. Yale theologian David Kelsey captures the notion well:

> A problem with defining personal identity [as the subject of horrific events] is that it distorts one's identity by binding it to the horrific situations in the past. The problem lies not so much with the horror as with the pastness. If what justifies one's life and shows that it is indeed worth living is surviving a set of horrendous events, then everything that happens later and everything one does later must be interpreted and shaped by reference to those past events. One's future is defined by, and so is in bondage to, an event in the past.[69]

The Healing Alliance works in the present to offer to victims/survivors opportunities to take physical, psychological, and spiritual steps away from their abusive pasts into more integrated and hopeful futures.

SNAP (www.snapnetwork.org) was founded in Chicago in 1989 by Barbara Blaine, also a survivor of priest abuse.[70] Since then, it has grown into a national network with over seven thousand members. Today, Barbara Blaine continues as president of SNAP while David Clohessy, another priest abuse survivor, serves as national director. Their mission statement, printed on their website, states that they want to end the cycle of abuse (1) "by supporting one another in personal healing" and (2) "by pursuing justice and institutional change by holding individual perpetrators responsible and the church accountable."[71]

SNAP's strength is the sophisticated public relations and political strategies it has developed to keep the Catholic sexual abuse crisis in the public eye, to keep the pressure on bishops to respond appropriately to sexual abuse by priests, and to lobby for legislative changes in state reporting laws and statute of limitation parameters. In addition to listing their press releases and official statements on their website, Blaine, Clohessy, and a few other figures in SNAP are routinely quoted in the media as they respond to news related to the Catholic scandal.[72] SNAP members at times picket and leaflet churches and secular locales in order to reach out to survivors who still may suffer in silence, educate local church and secular communities about developments in their area, focus media attention on specific news concerning the sexual abuse crisis in a given area, and warn communities about predators living in their midst.[73] They also draw attention to bishops and priests who they feel are particularly supportive of sexual abuse victims and of reforms, within the church and in the secular world, needed to protect children.[74] In the legislative arena, SNAP has worked toward abolishing or at least lengthening the statutes of limitations that apply to child abuse.[75] Without SNAP's relentless and highly successful publicizing of developments in the Catholic sexual abuse scandal as well as their support for thousands of survivors who without SNAP may never have come forward, it is unlikely that the crisis would have remained as prominent in the public square as it has since 2002.

My own concerns about SNAP relate to their outreach to victims. While they run support groups for survivors all over the country, their approach to healing is not clear. Beyond giving survivors a place to tell their stories, SNAP does not seem to offer an integrated, professionally supported program survivors can use to begin to move *through* their abuse issues. Not only is there nothing as integrated and professionally assisted as the Healing Alliance, their support groups do not incorporate tried-and-true self-help techniques like AA's sponsorship tradition that provides new members with specific mentors and a stepped approach to healing. Repeated airing of abuse stories and current struggles, without concomitant processes to integrate and detoxify abuse-related memories and emotions, unfortunately can be retraumatizing to many survivors, potentially miring them in disruptive affects. While hundreds of victims feel that SNAP has given them a new lease on life, others perceive themselves as used in the organization's sociopolitical efforts or deem the group too focused on anger rather than healing.[76] Paul Schwartz of Kansas, for example, is quoted as saying, "Every conversation I've ever had with SNAP is, 'Oh, we're going to bring [the church] down.' How's that going to help me? The Catholic Church did not cause my anger and rage, the abuse did."[77]

It is difficult for any organization successfully to combine healing efforts with energetic and aggressive political confrontation and advocacy. SNAP might want to consider dividing itself into a recovery division and a reform division, each run by different leaders. In that way, each division could consult with advisors and devise the programs best suited for what are, in fact, quite different and sometimes contradictory agendas.

Both SNAP and the Healing Alliance have been criticized for accepting money from plaintiffs' attorneys. The Healing Alliance also has taken donations from Catholic dioceses and religious orders.[78] Mitchell Garabedian, a Boston plaintiffs' attorney, told *Forbes* that such a "symbiotic alliance [between victims groups and lawyers] made [him] squeamish."[79] Some survivors feel that such donations enhance public perceptions that victims are just out to get money from the Church.[80] SNAP insists that it does not refer survivors to specific lawyers, but because of the amount of money potentially available to lawyers representing sexual abuse survivors, the appearance of impropriety or of excessive coziness between victim groups and attorneys is problematic.[81] One way to address these issues is for the groups to be transparent about their finances, publishing yearly, audited financial statements on their websites. Both the sources of funding and the expenditures of the organizations should be detailed, and relevant policy statements—like attorney referral directives—should be highlighted. Since the victims/survivors groups have led the way in rightly demanding transparency from the Church in dealing with sexual abuse of minors by priests, they have a heightened responsibility to put, quite literally, their own money where their mouths are.

In addition to groups *of* victims and survivors, the Catholic scandal gave birth to groups established to advocate *for* victims, to organize and disseminate information about the crisis, to support healing, and to present the debate on suggested Church and state reforms. Among the best known and most effective of these are SurvivorsFirst (www.Survivorsfirst.org) and Bishop-Accountability (www.bishop-accountability.org), both of which were founded in Boston and now are led by Paul Baier, Terence McKiernan, and Anne Barrett Doyle.[82] SurvivorsFirst is a survivor support organization that facilitates communication in the survivor/advocate community through e-mail lists and bulletin boards.[83] Bishop-Accountability is a Web archive and research organization that posts numerous documents informing the public about the depth and breadth of the Catholic sexual abuse scandal, including grand jury reports issued in jurisdictions across the country, lists of priests accused or removed for child sexual abuse, archival data from various dioceses, news reports on the crisis, and information about legal settlements throughout the nation.[84]

Both SurvivorsFirst and Bishop-Accountability depend on donations, and both state clear donation policies on their websites. SurvivorsFirst, for example, does not accept donations from plaintiffs' attorneys, and Bishop-Accountability will not accept donations from anyone who wants to influence what is posted on the site for financial or business advantage.[85]

The victims/survivors groups, combined with other advocacy organizations, ensured that the Catholic sexual abuse scandal did not disappear from the public scene. Their efforts also intervened in the secrecy on which the Church had depended for centuries to hide their problems and scandals.

Internal Factors

Within the Catholic Church there also were forces at work that kept the sexual abuse scandal front and center in Catholic discourse.

Conservatives and Liberals Hijack the Crisis

Although Catholics and non-Catholics alike tend to think of the Church as monolithic, that is not true. Conservative Catholic thinking differs from liberal or progressive Catholic thinking on a number of key issues, and representatives from each would imagine very different churches. The sexual abuse crisis was harnessed by each camp to "prove" that the opposition's Catholicism contributed to the scandal.

While there also are some disagreements within groups, conservative Catholics generally feel that many Vatican II "reforms" were misinterpreted, carried to excess, and should be rolled back.[86] Conservative political commentator and Roman Catholic Pat Buchanan, in fact, termed Vatican II "an unrelieved disaster for Roman Catholicism."[87] Conservatives found in the sexual abuse scandal evidence that theological dissent,[88] disobedience of Church teachings (especially regarding sexuality),[89] tolerance for homosexuality,[90] and rampant materialism and secularism[91] created space for the abuse of minors by priests and for the bishops' timidity in squarely facing the problem. Catholic conservative George Weigel said,

[The crisis] . . . is the result of a Catholic "ecology" damaged by a culture of dissent that has persistently promoted "Catholic Lite" views of core beliefs and institutions. . . . This culture of dissent . . . has contempt for the church's sexual ethic; indeed, widespread dissent among theologians and priests from the church's settled teachings about the nobility of sexual love within marriage helped create a situation in which some priests gave themselves passes on sexual misbehavior and some bishops failed to recognize sin for what it was.[92]

There are several problems with the conservative critique. For one thing, conservatives seemed to cast the sexual abuse crisis in terms of failings of faith instead of commission of crimes. No matter what combination of factors led to the scandal, it primarily reflected criminal behavior and the criminal cover-up of crimes by the hierarchy. Conservatives also failed to recognize that most of the priests identified as having abused minors over the past fifty years were squarely situated in pre–Vatican II childhoods and seminary training. In other words, they were products of preconciliar values and traditions, even if their crimes were committed after the Second Vatican Council. The same was true for almost every bishop presiding over the crisis. The conservative groups likewise did not confront indications that sexual abuse of minors by Catholic priests has been a problem for centuries and apparently has been robust in the face of shifting secular and theological trends.

For liberal Catholics, the sexual abuse scandal bespoke the truncating of Vatican II's progressive ideas by the authoritarian papacy of John Paul II,[93] the fundamental flaws of mandated celibacy,[94] the lack of power and voice for the laity within the Church,[95] misogynistic exclusion of women from the priesthood,[96] and an archaic theology of sexuality.[97] Liberal Catholic commentator James Carroll writes that "the recent priest abuse scandal, tied to questions of sexuality and gender, became a scandal tied expressly to power when bishops put the clerical state ahead of children. . . . The patriarchal misogyny of the clerical culture is broadly discredited . . . the Church needs democracy."[98] Liberals also accused conservatives of their own brand of doctrinal selectivity, saying that while the conservatives upheld official Catholic sexual teachings, they were likely to ignore teachings on economic rights, Third World debt, and world poverty.[99]

Like some conservatives, some liberals focused more on the cultural and church history elements of the sexual abuse scandal than on its criminality. They also glossed over the fact that religions with ordained female clergy and married priests also are confronted with sexual abuse, albeit more often of adult parishioners than minors. What liberals did get right, however, was the role of secrecy and clerical elitism in the sexual abuse crisis.[100]

Priests Raise Their Voices

A 2002 *Los Angeles Times* poll of 1,854 American priests indicated that two thirds of them disapproved of the way bishops were responding to the sexual abuse crisis.[101] As the scandal wore on, some priests took the highly unusual step of publicly lifting their voices to comment on the sexual abuse crisis and on other concerns about the institutional Church and their place in it. One bishop even broke ranks with his brethren.

Early in 2006, Detroit Auxiliary Bishop Gumbleton, long known for his commitment to social justice, publicly disclosed that as a teenager he had been sexually abused by a priest.[102] He then called for state legislatures to temporarily remove statutes of limitation that prevented victims of priest abuse from suing the church, a position vigorously opposed by bishops around the country.[103] Gumbleton was criticized by some victims for waiting so long to come forward and for refusing to name his deceased perpetrator.[104] At the same time, he was taken to task by the Archdiocese of Detroit and by the general counsel of the United States Conference of Catholic Bishops, Mark Chopko, who argued that Gumbleton's position jeopardized the patrimony of the Church.[105] Gumbleton responded, "I figure whatever the price, you have to speak the truth. . . . If it costs us lots in material goods, the spiritual purification will be worth it."[106]

In 2002, a group of priests formed the Boston Priests Forum. They hoped to create a group within which priests could study contemporary issues facing the priesthood and the wider Church and together reflect on them from theological and moral perspectives.[107] Later that year, in a previously unthinkable move, fifty-eight priests of the Archdiocese of Boston signed a letter to Bernard Cardinal Law asking him to resign for the good of the archdiocese:

> It is with a heavy heart that we write to request your resignation as Archbishop of Boston. We have valued the good work you have done here in Boston including, but not limited to: your advocacy for the homeless, your outreach to the Jewish community, your opposition to capital punishment, and your leadership welcoming immigrant people. However, the events of recent months and, in particular, of these last days, make it clear to us that your position as our bishop is so compromised that it is no longer possible for you to exercise the spiritual leadership required for the church of Boston.

As leaders of many of the parishes that make up this Archdiocese we hear from the people their call for a change in leadership. The revelations that have come to light a few days ago challenge the credibility of your public statements. The people of this Archdiocese are angry, hurt and in need of authentic spiritual leadership. We believe that despite your good work in the past you are no longer able to provide that leadership.

While this is obviously a difficult request, we believe in our hearts that this is a necessary step that must be taken if healing is to come to the Archdiocese. The priests and the people of Boston have lost confidence in you as their spiritual leader.[108]

Although some priests were even angrier with Law than the letter suggests, most were acutely stressed and pained by openly challenging a bishop they had promised to obey.[109]

In 2002 in New York, similarly dispirited priests from three dioceses formed Voice of the Ordained to "draw strength from one another; have opportunities for prayer and discussion; educate ourselves about the issues; and have a vehicle through which to give voice to our concerns."[110] Like the members of the Boston Priest Forum, the New York priests were particularly concerned about the way the sexual abuse crisis was being handled by then Brooklyn Bishop Thomas Daily, Rockville Center Bishop William Murphy, and New York City's Edward Cardinal Egan, but they also wanted a venue to discuss church reforms they thought were needed. Fifty-two of Murphy's four hundred priests wrote to him saying, "We have perceived a general malaise and even an abiding anger within our beloved diocese. . . . We perceive a fairly widespread dissatisfaction with the way you have related to some clergy and laity, and we sense a certain lack of confidence in your pastoral leadership."[111]

In Wisconsin, priests of the Archdiocese of Milwaukee established the Milwaukee Archdiocese Priest Alliance. Shortly after forming in 2003, 163 members, representing over one third of the priests of the archdiocese, signed a letter to the United States Conference of Catholic Bishops asking that the priesthood be opened to married men.[112] Inspired by the Milwaukee group, Priests' Forum for the Eucharist, representing one thousand priests from many areas of the country, joined in 2004 to organize a nationwide effort by clergy to push for the end of mandatory celibacy.[113] Priests organizing to plead for married clergy stated that they were mostly responding to the priest shortage and the decreasing availability of priests to meet the needs of Catholic laity. Still another group of twenty-three

Chicago priests wrote a letter to the Vatican in April 2004 protesting what they viewed as increasingly demeaning language toward homosexuals.[114]

In addition to organized groups of priests, individual priests took substantial risks in speaking up about the crisis and other issues of debate in contemporary Catholicism. Close to half the witnesses cooperating with the Suffolk County, New York, grand jury investigation of sexual abuse in the Rockville Centre Diocese were Catholic clergy.[115] Rev. Walter Cuenin of Massachusetts, an advocate for acceptance of homosexuality, the ordination of women, reconciliation with divorced Catholics, and increased lay power in the Church, cited the scandal as indicative of the need for change in the institutional Church.[116] Speaking from the pulpit one day, Cuenin said, "When you think of the pain that has been suffered by children and their families, a renewal of our Church is the only redemption. Otherwise, their pain has been in vain."[117] Testifying before New York state legislators at a forum on child abuse, New Jersey priest Rev. Bob Hoatson told lawmakers, "My church has disgraced itself by covering up [sexual abuse]. . . . The leaders of my church, frankly, have selected evil over good, denial over admission, lying over truth-telling."[118] Rev. James J. Scahill, a pastor in western Massachusetts, withheld the bishop's portion of the weekly collection plate in order to protest the Diocese of Springfield's continued support for a priest who was a convicted child molester and leading suspect in the murder of a child.[119] When the diocese finally suspended support for the former priest, Richard R. Lavigne, Scahill sent the bishop the $60,000 his parish had held back from the diocese.[120] In addition to his financial protest, Fr. Scahill became an outspoken critic of his diocese's response to the sexual abuse crisis, saying at one point, "The bishops are spending more time with their lawyers than with their consciences."[121] At St. Dominic's Church in Oyster Bay, New York, Rev. Malcolm Burns knelt before the crucifix one Sunday saying, "I want to pray with you on my knees as the leper from the Gospel begged Jesus. A leprosy is among us, and priests need to be cleansed. . . . I am not even sure I believe in my own life as a priest right now."[122] Two New Jersey priests joined with another two from Illinois and North Carolina to release a statement calling on the USCCB to "investigate claims against bishops who were complicit in the abuse scandal, at least after 1985 when it became clear that priest predators should not be in active ministry."[123] Revs. Kenneth Lasch, Robert Hoatson, Tom Doyle, and Patrick Collins labeled their efforts "Project Millstone," a reference to the Gospel of Matthew (16:6).[124] After the Philadelphia Grand Jury report was released castigating the Archdiocese of Philadelphia for years of enabling the sexual abuse of children, three hundred priests met with Justin Cardinal Rigali and some shared with the press the anger and criticism turned toward the cardinal by some of his priests.[125] One moral theologian, for example, reportedly chastised Rigali for defending his predecessors' "good intentions" and pointed out that the sexual victimization of children was so horrific that, from a Catholic moral perspective, it rendered meaningless whatever intentions diocesan officials may have had when they enabled the ongoing violation of children.[126]

All this may seem unremarkable to Americans accustomed to free speech and a constitutional right to assemble. Within the Catholic Church, however, it had been simply unthinkable that so many priests, albeit still a minority of all active priests, would openly criticize their bishops or publicly call into question Church teachings. It was emblematic of the disturbance created within the priesthood by the sexual abuse crisis that those priests felt both called by conscience and empowered to take the Church, especially the hierarchy, to task. The activism of these priests also symbolized their alienation from bishops they once would never have considered disobeying. As New York canon lawyer Msgr. William A. Vavaro put it at the first meeting of Voice of the Ordained, "The father-son sense of trust [between bishop and priest] has been destroyed and it will take a generation to restore that."[127] Rather than relying on the bishop-priest bond for emotional sustenance, many of the vocal priests strengthened their bonds with each other and with lay Catholics who also were disillusioned with their Church.

It is unclear how effective the efforts by some priests to assume a more powerful voice in the Church can be. At this point, the activist priests represent a minority of Catholic clergy, many of whom shun priests who speak against the hierarchy or publicly question Church teachings. Some priests feel that their organized approaches to bishops have improved communication on the local level, but they do not see any wider institutional response to their concerns.[128] In addition, they do not find bishops willing to represent the views of priests outside the diocese. For example, while Bishop William Murphy of Rockville Centre met with disgruntled priests in his diocese, he told at least one of them that "my home is Rome," suggesting that his essential alliance is with Vatican officials, not with the priests and laity of his diocese.[129]

Other bishops took stronger steps to indicate their displeasure with outspoken priests. Rev. James A. "Seamus" MacCormack, a New Hampshire priest who openly criticized Bishop John McCormack's handling of the sexual abuse crisis and who also spoke publicly about a priest found dead amid a large collection of pornography and sexual paraphernalia, was removed from his parish. He eventually sued the diocese for silencing him, receiving a settlement that required secrecy about its terms.[130] In Phoenix, Bishop Thomas Olmstead ordered nine priests and a religious brother "under obedience to him" to remove their names from a document supporting the moral integrity of homosexuality.[131] Diocese of Altoona-Johnstown, Pennsylvania, Bishop James Adamec issued a gag order to all priests in his diocese, forbidding them, on pain of excommunication or suspension, from publicly disagreeing with diocesan policies.[132]

Many priests and laity in Boston believe that Sean Cardinal O'Malley implemented systematic punishment of priests who spoke publicly against Church teachings or who were activists in the sexual abuse crisis.[133] The archdiocese denied that the removal of certain parish pastors and other relocations of clergy were at all connected to their activities during the sexual abuse crisis, but, in fact, O'Malley instituted the "largest dislocation of priests in archdiocesan history and . . . is subjecting priests to an unprecedented level of scrutiny, accompanied by explicit and implicit threats of discipline."[134] Coincidentally or not, Boston pastors most willing to speak openly with parishioners and sometimes with the press about their disagreements with Church policies and diocesan officials were among the sixty-six priests whom O'Malley removed from their positions.[135] Rev. Thomas A. Mahoney, chairman of the board of the Boston Priests Forum, told the *Boston Globe*: "I do think there are people being targeted: those who haven't capitulated to the desires of the diocese. . . . It's whether you're willing to play along or not. Basically, there's an atmosphere that's one of intimidation: It's expected that you will be loyal, and, if you're not, you're a dissident and you're a target."[136]

The hierarchy of the Catholic Church perhaps experience themselves as threatened by priests who think and speak for themselves, and therefore they try to silence or punish those priests. The sexual abuse crisis, however, is a neon sign advertising the need for courageous priests to continue to lift their voices in challenge to the institutional teachings, policies, and paradigms of power that facilitated the sexual victimization of so many thousands of young Catholics. The *National Catholic Reporter* exhorted these priests in a 2004 editorial:

> To the priests, we say it is impossible to know where your initiatives will lead. Who can say if you'll find someone to talk to, an honest dialogue that doesn't begin with all the questions answered? We can only encourage you not to abandon your questions—about ordination, about leadership and accountability, about the church's approach to homosexuals. Know that your concern for the welfare of the Eucharistic

community—the entire community—is deeply appreciated. Keep leading. Keep listening to your people.[137]

The Laity Speak Out

Catholic laypeople, disillusioned by the narrative of sexual abuse by priests and disgusted by the hierarchy's role in the scandal, or moved to defend their Church's teachings and personnel, raised their voices in unprecedented numbers.

A number of polls conducted after the scandal broke open in 2002 tracked perceptions Catholics had about their Church. The surveys made it clear that Catholic laity held the bishops primarily responsible for the abuse of children. In 2001, Zogby found that 85 percent of American Catholics believed their bishops were doing a good job; by April 2002, only 59 percent continued to think so.[138] Ninety-six percent thought the pope should discipline bishops who allowed abusers to stay in ministry.[139] Another 2002 survey by ABC/*Washington Post* concluded that 70 percent of American Catholics disapproved of the Church's handling of the sexual abuse crisis.[140] Time did not improve things. Zogby found in 2003 that 69 percent of Catholics felt that the Church hierarchy was more concerned with its image than with pastoring its people.[141] In 2004, a Catholic University of America/Purdue University poll established that almost 80 percent of Catholics were ashamed and embarrassed for their Church and nearly three-quarters thought that the failures of bishops in responding to sexual abuse were a bigger problem than the abuse itself.[142] In 2005, a research team reported on Gallup Poll results indicating that 58 percent of registered Catholic parishioners and 76 percent of Catholics not registered in a parish perceived the hierarchy to be out of touch with lay concerns.[143] While Catholics had been privately disagreeing with the institutional Church for decades, the sexual abuse scandal transformed private deliberation into public discourse for many Catholics.

It began at the top with members of the National Review Board. The first leader of the NRB, former Oklahoma Governor Frank Keating, expressed his disagreement with the hierarchy from the moment he started his job with them. He urged the bishops to welcome lay reform groups into their midst, saying, "I just do not understand what is to be feared from conversation, what is threatened by dialogue and discussion."[144] Keating openly stated that bishops who had transferred abusive priests from one parish to another should resign, and he urged laypeople to attend Mass in other dioceses or withhold donations to the Church if they were unhappy with their own bishop.[145] He made it clear that he saw "episcopal neglect" as central to the abuse crisis and pledged to investigate the role of the bishops in facilitating the scandal.[146] About a year after his appointment, Keating became so frustrated by what he perceived to be some bishops' continued willingness to cover up wrongdoing, he likened them to "La Cosa Nostra."[147]

When Governor Keating resigned his position with the NRB shortly after making the La Cosa Nostra remark, his successor, Judge Anne M. Burke of Illinois, expressed disappointment with what she termed his "unfortunate words."[148] Within two years, however, Burke was so disillusioned with the hierarchy that she too began to speak out, urging lay Catholics to "[r]aise some hell. . . . Be vigilant. Be outspoken. And demand transparency. . . . No more passive Catholics. That's my mantra now."[149] Familiarity with the hierarchy had apparently bred contempt as Burke identified the "downright vengeance" she had experienced with bishops during the NRB's investigation of their response to sexual abuse in their dioceses.[150] Further, she lamented that even after the "cataclysmic failure" of the hierarchy to protect children, there were still many bishops who wanted to return to the old ways of handling abuse.[151] On the lecture circuit, Burke said that the Catholic Church needed to be "reborn" and that heroic laity were needed to take responsibility for demanding a renewed Church.[152] Similarly, Nicholas Cafardi—another former National Review Board member, canon lawyer, and dean emeritus of Duquesne University Law School—was disappointed that some bishops resisted the efforts of the board: "To have some bishops fighting us every step of the way was disillusioning. . . . To just have them disdain our work or question our motives was very difficult."[153]

Answering the clarion call, laity across the country asserted their authority as adult members of a religious faith and demanded more voice in the operations of their Church. Even recognizing the Catholic Church as belonging as much to the laity as to the clergy and hierarchy, including the pope, represented a maturational step for many lay Catholics. Through their activism, many authorized themselves to claim their Church as their own and to define their role within it. Like children following healthy psychological development within a dysfunctional nuclear family, Catholic laity grew up and began to take responsibility for their own spirituality. They insisted that they could continue to love and respect their faith while strenuously disagreeing with clerical "parents" who had neglected and abused them and who they perceived to be more concerned with preserving their own power than with nourishing their families. Turning away from what they construed to be the spiritual corruption of their leaders,

Catholics turned to each other and to supportive priests for sustenance and shared power. Like Americans have done so often when they have been disappointed in their leadership, Catholic laypeople organized.

In cities across the country, the laity came together to picket churches and cathedrals to protest the actions of American bishops and cardinals. In Scranton, Pennsylvania;[154] Rockville Centre, Long Island;[155] Louisville, Kentucky;[156] Cincinnati, Ohio;[157] Manchester, New Hampshire;[158] Dallas, Texas;[159] and, of course, in Boston,[160] groups of laity protested at diocesan cathedrals and demanded that their bishops resign for mishandling the sexual abuse of minors by priests. Parishioners from S. S. Philip and James Parish in Grand Mound, Iowa, accused Davenport Bishop William Franklin of incomplete compliance with the diocese's sexual misconduct policies and informed him that they could "no longer maintain our silence, as silence constitutes consent to sexual abuse of our children."[161] Protesters in Los Angeles picketed the opening of Roger Cardinal Mahony's new cathedral to push for the release of documents related to the sexual abuse of children in that diocese.[162] Catholics in Naples, Florida, sent donation checks to the Diocese of Venice with "VOID" written across them to protest that diocese's response to the sexual abuse of minors by priests.[163] After release of the grand jury report in Philadelphia, Catholics confronted Justin Cardinal Rigali after a speech he delivered at Villanova University.[164] One woman asked the cardinal how he could square the emphasis on human dignity in his address that night with his support of "criminal cardinals who have protected oral and anal rape," while another woman informed Rigali that he was, in her opinion, a phony.[165] At parish meetings throughout the Philadelphia archdiocese, Catholic laypeople expressed their rage and despair that their priests and clerical leaders had allowed so many minors to be abused by priests, and they called on some enabling clergy cited by the grand jury to resign.[166]

Boston's Sean Cardinal O'Malley removed Rev. Walter Cuenin, a popular pastor, from Our Lady Help of Christians parish in Newton, Massachusetts, for reasons considered specious by the laity there. In addition, O'Malley replaced Cuenin with Rev. Christopher Coyne, who had once been a spokesman for Cardinal Law. Parishioners protested Cuenin's removal and successfully ousted Fr. Coyne as their pastor by withholding contributions and staying away from Mass.[167] A lay group's ability to force a pastor out of his position is remarkable and very rare.

The best known organization of laypeople developed after the scandal broke is Voice of the Faithful (www.votf.org), claiming over thirty thousand members and dedicated to supporting victims of sexual abuse, encouraging good priests, and working to change the Church into a "four sided table" at which laity, abuse survivors, priests, and bishops share power.[168]

Lay voices also were raised in support of the Church. When Texans organized to demand the resignation of Bishop Charles Grahmann of Dallas, other Catholics started a website (www.pleasebishop.com) to counter calls for Grahmann's resignation.[169] Opus Bono Sacerdotii (Work for the Good of the Priesthood) was founded by financial systems analyst Joe Maher to provide spiritual and financial support for priests accused of sexual misconduct.[170] In Louisville, www.ThankYouFather.com was established simply to provide a venue for thanking priests appreciated by their laity.[171] Faithful Voice (www.Faithfulvoice.com) was founded to counter Voice of the Faithful, and the Catholic League (www.catholicleague.org) could be counted on to defend the Church and the handling of the abuse crisis.

It is not clear how effective lay groups can be in obtaining real power within the Church. Many bishops banned VOTF from meeting on Church property and seem to feel that the Church can wait out the latest wave of demands for enhancing the position of the laity.[172] In addition, new priests being ordained are said to be more conservative than their elders who are now retiring. The newer priests often see themselves as spiritually elevated above the laity and are unlikely to welcome power sharing with their laypeople.[173] Perhaps most important is that groups like VOTF are populated with senior Catholics and are not attracting substantial numbers of younger Catholics. Rather, the younger the Catholic, the less invested he or she is in the institutional Catholic Church.[174] While younger Catholics hold creedal beliefs similar to their elders—belief in Jesus' resurrection and the importance of the Eucharist—they differ greatly from the VOTF generation in other ways. As a group, they do not feel that attending Mass regularly is crucial to their faith; they are less certain than their elders that the Catholic Church has more access to spiritual truth than other religions do; and they are essentially uninfluenced by the Church's moral teachings.[175] In other words, they are not Catholic activists.

Whatever the future may be of Catholic lay movements in the United States, it is certain that the raising of lay voices during the sexual abuse scandal was yet another factor ensuring that it did not recede from public view.

Is Everything Old New Again?

In 1988, a student at Niles College in Illinois allegedly awoke to find his pants pulled down and Daniel McCormack, a fellow student bound for the Roman Catholic seminary at Mundelein, standing over his bed.[1] He was advised by another student to inform the Archdiocese of Chicago.[2] Church officials say he did not; he will not say what he did.[3]

Daniel McCormack became a Chicago priest. One morning in 2000, the mother of a fourth-grade boy reportedly told a nun that Fr. McCormack had asked her son (alleged victim 1) to take his pants down in the sacristy of Holy Family Church.[4] The nun states that after meeting with McCormack alone, the mother did not want her to pursue the case. Still concerned, however, the nun related the incident to an official at Chicago Catholic Schools who told her to let the matter go if the parent was not pushing it. Instead, she hand delivered a written account of the incident to the school administrator. Later, Chicago Catholic Schools denied any record of the nun's complaint, a claim she calls "outrageous."[5]

In August 2005, Chicago police investigated an allegation that McCormack had sexually molested an eight-year-old boy (alleged victim 2) twice in December 2003 at St. Agatha's parish where he served as pastor.[6] Later that month, the police told the Illinois Department of Children and Family Services (DCFS) about the accusation.[7] DCFS proceeded with its own investigation and, in November 2005, found the charges to be credible. Archdiocesan officials say they were never alerted to the DCFS findings.

Chicago prosecutors reportedly told archdiocesan officials in September 2005 that accusations had been made against Rev. McCormack but that there was insufficient evidence to file charges.[8] Police say that the archdiocese requested access to the police notes on the accusation but was told it would have to obtain a subpoena to get those records; the archdiocese apparently did not take that step.[9] Sometime after that, DCFS asserts that it was informed by McCormack's attorney that the priest had been sent to Maryland to be evaluated, probably at St. Luke's Institute, a treatment facility for troubled priests.[10] Three months before McCormack was arrested, an archdiocesan review board reportedly recommended that he be removed from ministry.[11] Cardinal George acknowledged the recommendation but said it was "informal," as if that should make a difference.[12]

Fr. McCormack was returned to his position at St. Agatha's. A colleague, Rev. Tom Walsh, was asked to "monitor" McCormack, who was instructed not to have unsupervised contact with children.[13] He continued to coach the boys' basketball team at St. Agatha's school, however, and the principal says he was not alerted to any allegations against McCormack.[14] McCormack allegedly abused a child in January 2006.[15]

In January 2006, a second boy from St. Agatha's (alleged victim 3) reported to police that Fr. McCormack had molested him two to three times a month from ages nine to thirteen.[16] These allegations apparently supported the earlier allegations (alleged victim 2), and McCormack was charged with aggravated criminal sexual abuse of two young boys.[17] Since then, up to a dozen other alleged victims have come forward with reports of sexual abuse by Fr. McCormack.[18] Attorney Jeffrey Anderson, one of the best-known lawyers for victims suing the Catholic Church, is representing one of McCormack's alleged victims and was quoted as saying, "They still haven't got the message. The archdiocese has been operating in secrecy, not candor."[19]

Francis Cardinal George's initial response to the publicity about McCormack was to defend his decision to keep the priest at St. Agatha's. He claimed that there were no procedures allowing him to remove a priest from ministry when sexual abuse complaints were lodged by someone other than the victim or the victim's parents;[20] asserted that prosecutors were not helpful to the archdiocese; criticized DCFS for not providing more timely information about their investigation of McCormack;[21] and suggested that victim groups were partly responsible for the problem because they discourage victims from reporting abuse to dioceses.[22] Jimmy Lago, the archdiocesan chancellor, blamed the nun who reported McCormack to the Chicago Catholic School authorities for not also reporting him to DCFS.[23] As the weeks went on, however, Cardinal George appeared to take more and more personal responsibility for keeping McCormack in ministry after allegations of sexual abuse were made against him. George met several times with reporters,[24] sent letters to the priests and people of the archdiocese,[25] and met with more than two hundred parishioners at St. Agatha's to express his remorse.[26]

Illinois Appellate Court Judge Anne Burke, former chair of the US-CCB's National Review Board, expressed disgust with George's decisions and his initial defenses and said that "this situation, if it's true, [is] worse than Boston, because it's four year later."[27] She suggested that the National Review Board investigate the Chicago archdiocese's compliance with the bishops' sexual abuse policies, but the *Chicago Tribune* reported that US-CCB spokesman Monsignor Frank Maniscalco replied that such oversight is not the purview of the National Review Board.[28] When asked how dioceses *are* held accountable for following the mandates of the Charter for the Protection of Children and Young People, he reportedly refused to respond.[29]

By the end of February 2006, SNAP (Survivor Network for those Abused by Priests) was calling on George to resign; archdiocesan spokespeople responded that the cardinal would not step down.[30] The archdiocese did, however, take the unusual step of hiring an outside consulting firm to evaluate procedures for responding to sexual abuse allegations.[31] Defenbaugh & Associates criticized the archdiocese for egregious failures in the McCormack case, ranging from "shoddy record-keeping and a profound lack of communication to inadequate monitoring policies that put children in danger."[32] Apparently, the archdiocese had allegations against McCormack dating back to his seminary days in 1968, yet had kept him in ministry with access to children until he was arrested.[33] The report also concluded that the archdiocese failed to adequately monitor accused priests.[34] Operating under an "honor system," these priests reported their activities to monitors who were not well trained or well informed about their charges. In addition, there were no concsequences for priests who did not cooperate with what was essentially self-monitoring. McCormack, for example, had taken three minors on a 2005 Labor Day trip to Minnesota while the priest assigned to "monitor" him was away from the rectory.[35]

The McCormack story is all too familiar. The name of the allegedly abusive priest could be Geoghan and the cardinal could be Law. Cardinal George's failure to respond appropriately and pastorally to sexual abuse allegations against a priest is stunning. It is very unlikely, however, that George's mismanagement of a priest's sexual abuse of minors is unique among the bishops.

Perhaps more bishops than before "get it," but some like Cardinal George clearly do not, or at least do not get it enough of the time. Priests of integrity, laypeople, survivors, and their advocates must continue to watch their church leaders carefully and must go on raising their voices to demand that children in the Church be kept safe. Bishops and other Church officials must be held accountable to keep in the forefront of their ministry the words of Jesus recorded by Matthew:

> At that time the disciples came to Jesus and asked: Who is the greatest in the kingdom of heaven? He called a child, whom he put among them and said, "Truly I tell you, unless you change and become like children, you will never enter the kingdom of heaven. Whoever becomes humble like this child is the greatest in the kingdom of heaven. Whoever welcomes one such child in my name welcomes me." (Matt. 18:1–5)

Notes

Personal Preface

1. David France, *Our Fathers: The Secret Life of the Catholic Church in an Age of Scandal* (New York: Broadway Books, 2004), 335–37, 340–52.

2. Thomas P. Reilly, *To the People of the Commonwealth of Massachusetts,* 23 July 2002, www.bishop-accountability.org (accessed 20 December 2005), 38–39.

3. Peter Steinfels, "Inquiry in Chicago Breaks Silence on Sex Abuse by Catholic Priests," *News York Times,* 24 February 1992.

CHAPTER 1 From the Bayou to Boston

1. Jason Berry, *Lead Us Not into Temptation: Catholic Priests and the Sexual Abuse of Children* (Urbana: University of Illinois Press, 2000); Frank Bruni and Elinor Burkett, *A Gospel of Shame: Children, Sexual Abuse, and the Catholic Church* (New York: Perennial, 2002), 30–31; Investigative Staff of *The Boston Globe, Betrayal: The Crisis in the Catholic Church* (Boston: Little, Brown and Company, 2002), 37–39; Philip Jenkins, *Pedophiles and Priests: Anatomy of a Contemporary Crisis* (Oxford: Oxford University Press, 1996), 3; Garry Wills, *Papal Sin: Structures of Deceit* (New York: Doubleday, 2000), 182.

2. The narrative of the Gauthe case presented here is based on Berry, *Lead Us Not into Temptation.*

3. Berry uses pseudonyms for a number of Gauthe's victims and their families. The Sagreras are the "Robichauxs" in Berry. Their real names were published in Michael Paulson, "Lessons Unlearned: Church Struggle Pains LA Region Stung by Abuse in the 80s," *Boston Globe,* 12 June 2002.

4. Paulson, "Lessons Unlearned."

5. Berry, *Lead Us Not into Temptation.*

6. Pat Grossmith, "Allegations Revealed in Manchester Diocese Settlement," *Union Leader,* 13 October 2002.

7. Nancy Phillips, "A Past of Hurt, a Mission to Help," *Philadelphia Inquirer,* 6 October 2002.

8. Ellen Goodman, "A New Chapter in Church Tale," *Boston Globe,* 8 December 2002.

9. Elizabeth Hamilton and Eric Roth, "A Predator Blessed with Charm," *Hartford Courant,* 15 September 2002.

10. Donald Cozzens, *Sacred Silence: Denial and the Crisis in the Church* (Collegeville, MN: Liturgical Press, 2002), 62; Eugene Kennedy, *The Unhealed Wound: The Church, the Priesthood, and the Question of Sexuality* (New York: St. Martin's Press, 2002), xxvii; A. W. Richard Sipe, *Sex, Priests, and Power: The Anatomy of a Crisis* (New York: Brunner/Mazel, 1995), 12, 29; Wills, *Papal Sin,* 300.

11. Bruni and Burkett, *Gospel of Shame*, 111–30.

12. Michael Rezendes, "Church Allowed Abuse by Priest for Years," *Boston Globe,* 6 January 2002.

13. John Jay College of Criminal Justice, *The Nature and Scope of the Problem of Sexual Abuse of Minors by Catholic Priests and Deacons in the United States* (Washington, DC: U.S. Conference of Catholic Bishops, 2004), 6, 7.

14. Mary L. Paine, and David J. Hansen, "Factors Influencing Children to Self-Disclose Sexual Abuse," *Clinical Psychology Review* 22 (2002): 271–95; Daniel W. Smith, et al., "Delay in Disclosure of Childhood Rape: Results from a National Survey," *Child Abuse & Neglect* 24 (2000): 273–87.

15. Associated Press, "Some Major Settlements in Catholic Clergy Sexual Abuse Cases," *Salt Lake City National Wire,* 6 August 2005.

16. David Finkelhor, *Child Sexual Abuse: New Theory and Research* (New York: Free Press, 1984), 1–3; Diana E. H. Russell, *The Secret Trauma: Incest in the Lives of Girls and Women* (New York: Basic Books, 1986), 59–74; A. Urquiza and L. M. Keating, "The Prevalence of Sexual Victimization in Males," in *The Sexually Abused Male,* vol. 1, ed. Mic Hunter (Boston: Lexington Books, 1990); Gail E. Wyatt, "The Sexual Abuse of Afro-American and White Women in Childhood," *Child Abuse & Neglect* 9 (1985): 507–19.

17. Associated Press, "Abuse is No. 1 Reason Teachers Lose Licenses in W. Va.," *Herald-Mail,* 17 October 2005.

18. Ibid.

19. "Damning Anglican Sex Abuse Report Revealed," *Australian Broadcasting Company,* 31 May 2004.

20. Laurie J. Ferguson, "A Protestant Response to Clergy Sexual Abuse"; Anne Richards, "Clergy Sexual Misconduct in the Episcopal Church"; and L. Murdock Smith, "Women Priests and Clergy Sexual Misconduct." All of these chapters can be found in Mary Gail Frawley-O'Dea and Virginia Goldner, eds. *Predatory Priests, Silenced Victims* (Hillsdale, NJ: Analytic Press, 2007).

21. G. Rosenblatt, "A Rabbi Accused of Sexual Abuse Seeks to Reinvent Himself," *Jewish Journal of Greater Los Angeles,* 1 October 2004; Charlotte R.

Schwab, *Sex, Lies, and Rabbis* (Bloomington, IN: AuthorHouse, 2002); J. Wiener, "An End to Denial," *Jewish Journal of Greater Los Angeles,* 7 September 2001.

22. Associated Press, "Islamic Schools under Scrutiny," *CNN,* 18 September 2005; Charles P. Freund, "Madrassas Molesters," *Reason,* April 2005.

23. "Child-Abuser Monk Commits Suicide," *BBC News,* 17 May 2005.

24. "Hardly Krishna," *The Age,* 2 June 2003.

25. *Catholic Educators Announce School and Enrollment Statistics,* National Catholic Education Association, 16 March 2005.

26. *The Catholic Church in America,* U.S. Conference of Catholic Bishops, December 2003.

27. Ibid.

28. "The Catholic Charities Network at a Glance," *Catholic Charities Information,* www.catholiccharitiesinfo.org/news/statistics.htm (accessed 16 December 2005).

29. Associated Press, "Some Major Settlements."

30. John Rivera, "Keeler Letter Reveals Abuse: Cardinal Says 83 Priests Accused over 7 Decades; 'Spiritual Equivalent of Murder'; $4.1 Million in Settlements Go to 8 Victims in 20 Years," *Baltimore Sun,* 25 September 2002.

31. William Cardinal Keeler, *A Public Accounting,* Archdiocese of Baltimore, September 2002.

32. Andrew Delbanco, *The Death of Satan: How Americans Have Lost the Sense of Evil* (New York: Farrar, Straus and Giroux, 1995), 54.

33. Ibid.

34. Ibid.

35. Sue Grand, *The Reproduction of Evil: A Clinical and Cultural Perspective* (Hillsdale, NJ: Analytic Press, 2000), 11.

36. Brooks Egerton and Reese Dunklin, "Catholic Bishops and Sexual Abuse," *Dallas Morning News,* 13 June 2002.

37. Joe Ruff, Associated Press, "Nebraska Bishop Skips Some Abuse-Prevention Measures," *Corvallis Gazette-Times,* 2 February 2004.

38. Richard N. Ostling, "Catholic Bishops' President Defends American Priests after a Negative 'Avalanche' over Abuse," *Boston Globe,* 14 November 2005.

39. Michael Paulson, "Resignation Has Not Ended Law's Role in Church," *Boston Globe,* 21 June 2003.

40. Tom Fox, "Cardinal Law's New Appointment," *National Catholic Reporter,* 29 May 2004.

41. "Editorial," *National Catholic Reporter,* 1 August 2003.

42. Michel Foucault, *The History of Sexuality: An Introduction. Volume 1* (New York: Knopf, 1990), 1–13.

43. Maureen Dezell, "A Story of Sisters Who Showed No Mercy," *Boston Globe,* 10 August 2003.

44. Gertrude Himmelfarb, *The De-Moralization of Society* (New York: Knopf, 1996), 23.

45. Investigative Staff, *Betrayal, 145.*

46. Monica McGoldrick and John K. Pearce, "Family Therapy with Irish Americans," *Family Process* 20 (1981): 223–44.

47. Ibid., 232.

48. Thomas Keneally, "Cold Sanctuary: How the Church Lost Its Mission." *New Yorker,* 17 June 2002.

49. Ibid.

50. McGoldrick and Pearce, "Family Therapy," 226.

51. Ibid.

52. Ibid.

53. Mary Gordon, "How Ireland Hid Its Own Dirty Laundry," *New York Times,* 3 August 2003.

CHAPTER 2   Surviving Soul Murder

1. This man has gone public with his story. Still, in the interest of privacy, I have changed certain biographical details to obscure his identity.

2. Michael D. Sallah and David Yonke, "Believers Betrayed," *Toledo Blade,* 2 December 2002.

3. Philip Jenkins, *Pedophiles and Priests: Anatomy of a Contemporary Crisis* (Oxford: Oxford University Press, 1996), 38, 40–41.

4. Investigative Staff of *The Boston Globe, Betrayal: The Crisis in the Catholic Church* (Boston: Little, Brown and Company, 2002), 6, 17 18.

5. Robert Brodsky, "Tragic End for Ridgewood Man Who Claimed Abuse by Priest," *Queens Chronicle,* 2 October 2003; Stan Finger, "Group Helps Victims of Clergy Abuse Discuss Past," *Wichita Eagle,* 2 February 2003; Lisa Lisanti, "Memories Haunt Victims of Abuse," *Express-Times,* 26 January 2003, www.pennlive.com (accessed 26 January 2003); Pam Louwagi, "A Family's Faith Is Shaken after Their Sons Were Abused," *Star-Tribune,* 24 September 2002; Doug Mandelaro, "Lawyer Advocates for the Abused," *Democrat and Chronicle,* 18 February 2003; Michael Paulson, "Lessons Unlearned," *Boston Globe,* 12 June 2002; Nancy Phillips, "A Past of Hurt, a Mission to Help," *Philadelphia Inquirer,* 6 October 2002; Sallah and Yonke, "Believers Betrayed."

6. The Vogel story is taken from Louwagie, "A Family's Faith Is Shaken."

7. Phillips, "A Past of Hurt."

8. Rosemary Radford Ruether, *Women and Redemption: A Theological History* (Minneapolis: Fortress Press, 1998), 59.

9. Ronald D. Fairbairn, "The Repression and Return of Bad Objects," In *Psychoanalytic Studies of the Personality* (London: Routledge and Kegan Paul, 1952), 66.

10. Elizabeth Hamilton and Eric Rich, "A Predator Blessed with Charm," *Hartford Courant,* 15 September 2002.

11. Louwagie, "A Family's Faith Is Shaken."

12. Paulson, "Lessons Unlearned."

13. Sallah and Yonke, "Believers Betrayed."

14. Ibid.

15. Lisanti, "Memories Haunt Victims."

16. Mandelaro, "Lawyer Advocates."

17. Ibid.

18. Fairbairn, "Repression and Return of Bad Objects."

19. Richard B. Gartner, "Predatory Priests: Sexually Abusing Fathers," *Studies in Gender & Sexuality* 5 (2004): 31–56.

20. Ibid., 46.

21. Jody Messler Davies and Mary Gail Frawley, *Treating the Adult Survivor of Childhood Sexual Abuse: A Psychoanalytic Perspective* (New York: Basic Books, 1994), 75.

22. Eric Convey, "Abuse Victims Learn Settlement Amounts," *Boston Herald,* 21 December 2003.

23. Paul A. Long, "Diocese to Abuse Victims: Tell Church," *Kentucky Post,* 23 April 2003.

24. "The Church on Trial: Part 1," *CBS News,* 12 June 2002.

25. William Lobdell, "Orange County: He Got Justice, Now Wants to Give It," *Los Angeles Times,* 5 June 2003.

26. Louise Armstrong, *Kiss Daddy Goodnight: A Speak-Out on Incest* (New York: Pocket Books, 1978), 260.

27. Gartner, "Predatory Priests."

28. Ibid.

29. Bessel van der Kolk, "The Complexity of Adaptation to Trauma: Self-Regulation, Stimulus, Discrimination, and Characterological Development," in *Traumatic Stress: The Effects of Overwhelming Experience on Mind, Body, and Society,* ed. Bessel van der Kolk, Alexander C. McFarlane, and Lars Weisaeth (New York: Guilford Press, 1996), 182–213.

30. Allan N. Schore, *Affect Regulation and the Origin of the Self: The Neurobiology of Emotional Development* (Hillsdale, NJ: Lawrence Erlbaum Associates, 1994).

31. Jonathan R. T. Davidson and Bessel van der Kolk, "The Psychopharmacological Treatment of Post-Traumatic Stress Disorder," in *Traumatic Stress,* 510–24.

32. Material on Kevin McDonough is taken from Bella English, "He Was So Angry, Upset, and Ashamed, I Know It Affected His Whole Life," *Boston Globe,* 18 September 2002.

33. Ibid.

34. Philips, "A Past of Hurt."

35. Daniel Wakin, "Praise for a Priest in Abuse Inquiry Angers His Victim," *New York Times,* 2 March 2003.

36. Sallah and Yonke, "Believers Betrayed."

37. Studies correlating sexual abuse and prostitution are cited in John Briere, *Therapy for Adults Molested as Children: Beyond Survival* (New York: Springer Publishing, 1989), 23; Richard B. Gartner, *Betrayed as Boys: Psychodynamic*

Treatment of Sexually Abused Men (New York: Buildford Press, 1999), 80–81; Diana E. H. Russell, *The Secret Trauma: Incest in the Lives of Girls and Women* (New York: Basic Books, 1986), 167.

38. John Briere and Marsha Runtz, "Suicidal Thoughts and Behaviors in Former Sexual Abuse Victims," *Canadian Journal of Behavioral Sciences* 18 (1986): 413–23

39. van der Kolk, "Complexity of Adaptation to Trauma."

40. Gartner, *Betrayed as Boys*, 80–81.

41. Hamilton and Rich, "A Predator Blessed with Charm."

42. Ibid.

43. Gregory A. Hall, Peter Smith, Andrew Wolfson, and Deborah Yetter, "Church in Crisis," *Courier-Journal,* 29 September 2002.

44. Gartner, "Predatory Priests."

45. Ibid.

CHAPTER 3 Suffering, Submission, and Sadomasochism

1. Elisabeth Schüssler Fiorenza, *In Memory of Her: A Feminist Theological Reconstruction of Christian Origins* (New York: Crossroad, 2000), 123, 119.

2. James Carroll, *Toward a New Catholic Church: The Promise of Reform* (Boston: Houghton Mifflin, 2002), 77.

3. Rev. Michael Papesh, personal communication, February 2006.

4. Ibid.

5. Ibid.

6. Carroll, *Toward a New Catholic Church,* 80.

7. Richard P. McBrien, *Catholicism: New Study Edition,* rev. and updated (San Francisco: HarperSanFrancisco, 1994), 441–46.

8. Ibid.

9. Elizabeth A. Johnson, *She Who Is: The Mystery of God in Feminist Theological Discourse* (New York: Crossroad, 2001), 158, notes, 296.

10. Ibid, 158.

11. Ibid.

12. W. W. Meissner, *The Cultic Origins of Christianity: The Dynamics of Religious Development* (Collegeville, MN: Liturgical Press, 2000), 96, 98–99, 104, 107–9.

13. Ibid., 106–9.

14. "Saints and Angels," *Catholic Online,* www.catholic.org/saints.

15. Ibid.

16. Ibid.

17. Ibid.

18. Ibid.

19. Ibid.

20. Robert Hanley, "Paterson's Bishop Arrives, Preaching and Politicking." *New York Times,* 2 July 2004.

21. Ibid.

22. Ibid.

23. Karol Jackowski, *The Silence We Keep: A Nun's View of the Catholic Priest Scandal* (New York: Harmony Books, 2004), 50.

24. Garry Wills, *Why I Am a Catholic* (Boston: Houghton Mifflin, 2002), 22.

25. Ibid.

26. Ibid.

27. Ibid.

28. Jason Berry and Gerald Renner, *Vows of Silence: The Abuse of Power in the Papacy of John Paul II* (New York: Free Press, 2004), 172.

29. Erica Johnson, "Priest Pleads Guilty in 5 Sex Cases," *Las Vegas Sun,* 2 January 2003.

30. Christopher West, *Theology of the Body Explained: A Commentary on John Paul II's "Gospel of the Body"* (Boston: Pauline Books and Media, 2003), 289, 322, 323, 336.

31. Christopher Dickey and Rod Nordland, "Precious Suffering," *Newsweek,* 28 February 2005, 26.

32. Jackowski, *Silence We Keep,* 50.

33. Thomas J. Reese, *Inside the Vatican: The Politics and Organization of the Catholic Church* (Cambridge: Harvard University Press, 1996), 166.

34. Ibid., 164.

35. Jay P. Dolan, *In Search of American Catholicism: A History of Religion and Culture in Tension* (Oxford: Oxford University Press, 2002), 210; Eugene Cullen Kennedy, "Dallas: The Last Remake of Frankenstein," *National Catholic Reporter,* 16 August 2002.

36. Garry Wills, *Papal Sin: Structures of Deceit* (New York: Doubleday, 2000), 3.

37. Paul Collins, *The Modern Inquisition: Seven Prominent Catholics and Their Struggles with the Vatican* (Woodstock: Overlook Press, 2001); Donald Cozzens, *Sacred Silence: Denial and the Crisis in the Church* (Collegeville, MN: Liturgical Press, 2002), 13.

38. John Cornwell, *Breaking Faith: Can the Catholic Church Save Itself?* (New York: Penguin Compass, 2001), 210–14.

39. Ibid., 210.

40. Ibid.

41. Ibid., 198–201.

42. Alan Cooperman, "Catholic Bishops Look for Leadership," *Washington Post,* 19 June 2003; Reese, *Inside the Vatican,* 33.

43. Reese, *Inside the Vatican,* 42–65.

44. Cornwell, *Breaking Faith,* 259.

45. Jessica Benjamin, *The Bonds of Love: Psychoanalysis, Feminism, and the Problem of Domination* (New York: Pantheon Books, 1988), 51–84; Emmanuel Ghent, "Masochism, Submission, and Surrender," *Contemporary Psychoanalysis* 26 (1990): 108–36.

46. Ghent, "Masochism, Submission, and Surrender," 110–13.

47. Ibid., 111.

48. Ibid.

49. Ibid., 113.

50. Ibid., 115.

51. Ibid., 111.

52. Ibid.

53. Ibid.

54. Ibid., 115–16.

55. Benjamin, *Bonds of Love*, 56.

56. Ibid.

57. Ghent, "Masochism, Submissoin, and Surrender," 125.

58. Benjamin, *Bonds of Love,* 65.

59. Johnson, *She Who Is,* 209.

60. Eugene Kennedy, *The Unhealed Wound: The Church, the Priesthood, and the Question of Sexuality* (New York: St. Martin's Press, 2002), 40–41.

61. Ibid., 65.

62. Bill Rams, Fermin Leal, and Greg Hardesty. "Ex-Priest Reportedly Left Note," *Orange County Register,* 28 May 2003.

63. Associated Press, "Parishioners Pack Church for Funeral of Priest who Apparently Committed Suicide," *Boston Globe,* 3 January 2003.

64. Felix Doligosa Jr., "Ex-Priest Kills Self with Gun," *Rocky Mountain News,* 23 September 2005.

65. Kevin Harter, "Judge: Priest Was Funeral Home Killer," *Pioneer Press,* 4 October 2005.

66. Ibid.

67. Meg Jones, "Details Paint Disturbing Portrait of Priest," *Milwaukee Journal Sentinel,* 5 October 2002.

68. Teresa Malcolm, "Family Assists Other in Memory of Eric," *National Catholic Reporter,* 4 June 2002.

69. Ibid.

70. Ibid.

71. Stephanie Saul, "Alleged Sex Victim Dies," *New York Newsday,* 25 September 2003.

72. Mike Kelly, "Abuse Victim Suffered to the End," *Record,* 16 October 2003.

73. Steve Woodward, "Lawyer Asks for Church Counseling Aid after Third Suicide by Sex-Abuse Claimant," *Oregonian,* 17 August 2005.

74. Bella English, "He Was So Angry, Upset, and Ashamed. I Know It Affected His Whole Life," *Boston Globe,* 18 September 2002. Brian MacQuarrie, "McSorley's Death Recalls a Life Long Lost," *Boston Globe*, 13 June 2004.

75. Sarah Lyall, "Irish Recall Sad Homes for 'Fallen' Women," *New York Times,* 28 November 2002.

76. Mary Gordon, "How Ireland Hid Its Own Dirty Laundry," *New York Times,* 3 August 2003.

77. Hilary Brown and Matt McGarry, "Ireland's Dirty Laundry," *ABCNews.com,* 26 January 2003.

78. Ibid.

79. Lyall, "Irish Recall Sad Homes."

80. Ibid.

81. Ibid.

CHAPTER 4 Embodied and Gendered Souls

1. Gillian Walker, "Eunuchs for the Kingdom: Constructing the Celibate Priest," *Studies in Gender & Sexuality* 5 (2004): 233–57.

2. Mark D. Jordan, *Telling Truths in Church: Scandal, Flesh, and Christian Spech* (Boston: Beacon Press, 2003), 87.

3. Ibid.

4. Ibid, 83.

5. Christopher West, *Theology of the Body Explained: A Commentary on John Paul II's "Gospel of the Body"* (Boston: Pauline Books and Media, 2003), 230.

6. Ibid.

7. Rev. William Reynolds, personal communication, December 2002.

8. Ibid.

9. West, *Theology of the Body*, 5. West's book in its entirety is an exegesis of John Paul II's theology of the body.

10. Ibid., 284.

11. Ibid. 10; Muriel Dimen, *Sexuality, Intimacy, Power* (Hillsdale, NJ: Analytic Press, 2003), 124, 134.

12. Dimen, *Sexuality, Intimacy, Power,* 135–49.

13. For a concise review of contemporary gender theories and a solid bibliography, see Virginia Goldner, "Toward A Critical Relational Theory of Gender," *Psychoanalytic Dialogues* 1 (1991): 249–72.

14. Dimen, *Sexuality, Intimacy, Power,* 178.

15. Ibid., 179.

16. Elisabeth Schüssler Fiorenza, *In Memory of Her: A Feminist Theological Reconstruction of Christian Origins* (New York: Crossroad, 2000). Schüssler Fiorenza's book addresses the issue of women in ministry in the early Church and cites numerous other scholars in this field.

17. Donald B. Cozzens, *The Changing Face of the Priesthood* (Collegeville, MN: Liturgical Press 2000), 72–80; John McDargh, "Reveling in Complexity: Dittes' Male Metaphors and Their Bearing on the Crisis of Clergy Sexual Abuse," *Pastoral Psychology* 52, nos. 1–2 (2003): 147–61.

18. Ruth Stein, "Vertical Mystical Homoeros: An Altered Form of Desire in Fundamentalism," *Studies in Gender & Sexuality* 4, no. 1 (2003): 53.

19. Ibid.

20. McDargh, "Reveling in Complexity," 155.

21. Andrea Celenza, "Sexual Misconduct in the Clergy: The Search for the Father," *Studies in Gender & Sexuality* 5 (2004): 213–32.

22. Stein, "Vertical Mystical Homoeros," 55.

23. Ibid., 55.

24. Ibid., 41.

25. Celenza, "Sexual Misconduct in the Clergy," 225.

26. Cozzens, *Changing Face of the Priesthood*, 57.

27. Ibid., 58.

28. Ibid., 59.

29. Ibid.

30. Ibid., 76.

31. McDargh,"Reveling in Complexity."

32. Cozzens, *Changing Face of the Priesthood*, 76–77.

33. Ibid., 56.

34. Gillian Walker, "Reflections on Celibacy and the Role of Women in the Church," *Studies in Gender & Sexuality* 5 (2004): 81–102.

35. Ibid., 91.

36. Schüssler Fiorenza, *In Memory of Her*, 33.

37. Ibid., xxi.

38. A. W. Richard Sipe, *Sex, Priests, and Power: Anatomy of a Crisis* (New York: Brunner/Mazel, 1995), 106, citing W. A. Jurgens, *The Priesthood: A Translation of the Peri Hierosynes of St. John Chrysostom* (New York: Macmillan, 1955), 49.

39. Ibid.

40. Ibid., 106–7, citing Heinrich Kramer and James Sprenger, *Malleus Maleficarum* (New York: Dover, 1971), 43, 45, 46.

41. Andrew M. Greeley, *Priests: A Calling in Crisis* (Chicago: University of Chicago Press, 2004), 90.

42. Elizabeth A. Johnson, *Truly Our Sister: A Theology of Mary in the Communion of Saints (New York: Continuum, 2003),* 11.

43. Ibid., 7.

44. Giacomo Biffi, "La Presenza Della Virgine," *L'Osservatore Romano,* 23 December 1989, and *Washington Post,* 23 December 1989 in Sipe, *Sex, Priests, and Power,* 107, references, 195.

45. Daniel Williams and Alan Cooperman, "Vatican Letter Denounces 'Lethal Effects' of Feminism," *Washington Post,* 1 August 2004.

46. Matt Kelly, "Mixed Blessings," *Boston Magazine,* July 2004.

47. Ibid.

48. Angela Bonavoglia, *Good Catholic Girls: How Women Are Leading the Fight to Change the Church* (New York: 10 Regan Books, 2005), 36.

49. Ibid.

50. Steve Arney, "Judge: Church's Response to Report Disappointing," *Pantagraph,* 24 April 2004.

51. West, *Theology of the Body.* West discusses the pope's gender theory throughout his exegesis of the theology of the body.

52. Ibid., 75.

53. Ibid., 344.

54. Ibid., 423.

55. Johnson, *Truly Our Sister,* 62.

56. Ibid., 63.

57. Emily Anthes, "More Join Abuse Suit against Nuns," *Boston Globe,* 18 August 2004; Associated Press, "Focus of Catholic Sexual Abuse Suits Now Includes Nun," *WAVE 3 News,* 2 August 2004; Jon Frank, "Former Nun Sentenced for Molestation 35 Years Ago," *Virginian-Pilot,* 22 September 2004; Walter Robinson and Sacha Pfeiffer, "Nun Placed on Leave after Abuse Allegation," *Boston Globe,* 11 November 2002; Louis Rom, "Devotion and Deceit," *Times* (Lafayette, LA), 28 August 2002.

CHAPTER 5 Degraded Sexual Desire and Theologized Sex

1. Definition of desire and first entry for lust from the Merriam-Webster Online Dictionary, www.m-w.com; second entry for lust from Muriel Dimen, *Sexuality, Intimacy, Power* (Hillsdale, NJ: Analytic Press, 2003), 163, 170.

2. Thomas C. Fox, *Sexuality and Catholicism* (New York: George Braziller, 1995), 14.

3. Gillian Walker, "Eunuchs for the Kingdom of Heaven: Constructing the Celibate Priest," *Studies in Gender & Sexuality* 5 (2004): 248.

4. Ibid., 249.

5. Ibid.

6. Ibid., 250.

7. Ibid.

8. Fox, *Sexuality and Catholicism,* 24.

9. Ibid.

10. Ibid.

11. Ibid., 25.

12. Ibid., 27.

13. Ibid.

14. Ibid.

15. Walker, "Eunuchs for the Kingdom," 252–53.

16. Ibid., 250.

17. Christopher West, *The Theology of the Body Explained: A Commentary on John Paul II's "Gospel of the Body"* (Boston: Pauline Books and Media, 2003), xv.

18. Ibid., 206.

19. Ibid., 171.

20. Ibid., 86.

21. Ibid.,131.

22. Marina Warner, *Alone of All Her Sex: The Myth and Cult of the Virgin Mary* (New York: Vintage Books, 1983), 51.

23. As West notes in *Theology of the Body,* 171.

24. Karol Jackowski, *The Silence We Keep: A Nun's View of the Catholic Priest Scandal* (New York: Harmony Books, 2004), 90, 91, 146.

25. Ibid., 88–91.

26. Ibid., 140.

27. Ibid., 145.

28. Dimen, *Sexuality, Intimacy, Power,* 163.

29. Ibid., 9.

30. Jody M. Davies, "Between the Disclosure and Foreclosure of Erotic Transference-Countertransference: Can Psychoanalysis Find a Place for Adult Sexuality?" *Psychoanalytic Dialogues* 8 (1998): 76, in Dimen, *Sexuality, Intimacy, Power,* 172.

31. A. W. Richard Sipe, *Sex Priests and Power: Anatomy of a Crisis* (New York: Brunner/Mazel, 1995), 7.

32. West, *Theology of the Body,* 375, 419, 430.

33. Dimen, *Sexuality, Intimacy, Power,* 290.

34. Garry Wills, *Papal Sin: Structures of Deceit* (New York: Doubleday, 2000), 100.

35. Ibid., 94.

36. Ibid. .

37. Ibid., 89.

38. John Heaps, *A Love That Dares to Question: A Bishop Challenges His Church* (Grand Rapids, MI: Eerdmans, 1998), 89.

39. Ibid.,74.

40. Andrew M. Greeley, *Priests: A Calling in Crisis* (Chicago: University of Chicago Press, 2004), 75–76.

41. Peter Steinfels, *A People Adrift: The Crisis of the Roman Catholic Church in America* (New York: Simon and Schuster, 2003), 257.

42. Ibid., 255–56.

43. Daniel Wakin, "Bishops Open New Drive Opposing Contraception," *New York Times,* 13 November 2003.

44. Paul R. Dokecki, *The Clergy Sexual Abuse Crisis: Reform and Renewal in the Catholic Community* (Washington, DC: Georgetown University Press, 2004).

45. Ibid., 98.

46. Ibid.

47. Ibid.

48. Ibid.

49. Ibid., 99

50. Ibid.

51. Ibid., 100

52. Ibid.

53. Angela Bonavoglia, *Good Catholic Girls: How Women Are leading the Fight to Change the Church* (New York: 10 Regan Books, 2005), 129.

54. Ibid.

55. Ibid.

56. Thomas C. Fox, "A Wondrous Dance of Sex and Spirit," *National Catholic Reporter,* 13 December 2002, 6.

CHAPTER 6 Celibate Sexuality and Sexually Active "Celibates"

1. James Carroll, *Toward a New Catholic Church: The Promise of Reform* (Boston: Houghton Mifflin, 2002), 9; William Cleary, "Researcher Studies Why Priests Quit," *National Catholic Reporter,* 23 May 2003.

2. George Weigel, *The Courage to be Catholic: Crisis, Reform, and the Future of the Church* (New York: Basic Books, 2002), 155–60.

3. "Retired Bishop Is Seeking Rome's Permission to Marry," *Total Catholic,* 1 January 2003; John Cornwell, *Breaking Faith: Can the Catholic Church Save Itself?* (New York: Penguin Compass, 2001); Paul E. Dinter, *The Other Side of the Altar: One Man's Life in the Catholic Priesthood* (New York: Farrar, Straus and Giroux, 2003), xii, 103; Karol Jackowski, *The Silence We Keep: A Nun's View of the Catholic Priest Scandal* (New York: Harmony Books, 2004), 14–15, 60–62, 103; Michael Rezendes, "Church to Disclose Records of Clergy Accused by Adults," *Boston Globe,* 29 January 2003; A. W. Richard Sipe, *Celibacy in Crisis: The Secret World Revisited* (New York: Brunner-Routledge, 2003), 27.

4. Thomas P. Doyle, "Canon Law and the Clergy Sex Abuse Crisis: Failure from Above," in *Sin against the Innocents: Sexual Abuse by Priests and the Role of the Catholic Church*, ed. Thomas G. Plante (Westport, CT: Praeger, 2004), 26.

5. Thomas P. Doyle, A. W. R. Sipe, and Patrick J. Wall, eds., *Sex, Priests, and Secret Codes: The Catholic Church's 2,000-Year Paper Trail of Sexual Abuse* (Los Angeles: Volt Press, 2006).

6. Garry Wills, *Papal Sin: Structures of Deceit* (New York: Doubleday, 2000), 125.

7. Thomas C. Fox, *Sexuality and Catholicism* (New York: George Braziller, 1995), 179.

8. Sipe, *Celibacy in Crisis,* 273.

9. Wills, *Papal Sin,* 136.

10. Gillian Walker, "Reflections on Celibacy and the Role of Women in the Church," *Studies in Gender & Sexuality* 5 (2004): 91.

11. Wills, *Papal Sin.*

12. Fox, *Sexuality and Catholicism,* 178.

13. Ibid.*,* 179.

14. Richard P. McBrien, "Obligatory Celibacy," *Essays in Theology,* 22 April 2002.

15. Fox, *Sexuality and Catholicism,* 180.

16. Sipe, *Celibacy in Crisis,* 90.

17. Ibid., 181.

18. Eugene Kennedy, *The Unhealed Wound: The Church, the Priesthood, and the Question of Sexuality* (New York: St. Martin's Press, 2002), 147–48.

19. Ibid., 151.

20. Christopher West, *Theology of the Body Explained: A Commentary on John Paul II's "Gospel of the Body"* (Boston: Pauline Books and Media, 2003), 286.

21. Dinter, *Other Side of the Altar,* 71.

22. Wills, *Papal Sin,* 186.

23. Dinter, *Other Side of the Altar,* xii.

24. Rev. James Lex, with Ann M. Ennis, *Fifty Years in a Jealous Marriage: Seeking a Healthy Sexuality in a World of Power and Control* (Lima, OH: CSS Publishing 2002), 61.

25. "Argentine Priest Reveals Sex Life," *BBC* News, 10 June 2004; Uki Goni, "Sex Priest Stuns Argentina with Love Memoirs," www.guardian.co.uk, 20 June 2004.

26. Tom Heneghan, "Popular French Priest Confesses Sin, Backs Reform," *Reuters,* 27 October 2005.

27. Ibid.

28. Sipe, *Celibacy in Crisis,* p. 89

29. Ibid., 50.

30. Ibid., 50–51.

31. Andrew M. Greeley, *Priests: A Calling in Crisis* (Chicago: University of Chicago Press, 2004), 34–40.

32. Dean R. Hoge and Jacqueline E. Wenger, *Evolving Visions of the Priesthood: Changes from Vatican II to the Turn of the New Century* (Collegeville, MN: Liturgical Press, 2003).

33. Dean R. Hoge, *The First Five Years of the Priesthood: A Study of Newly Ordained Catholic Priests* (Collegeville, MN: Liturgical Press, 2002).

34. Dinter, *Other Side of the Altar,* 106.

35. Ibid.

36. Jason Berry and Gerald Renner, *Vows of Silence: The Abuse of Power in the Papacy of John Paul II* (New York: Free Press, 2004), 71.

37. Sipe, *Celibacy in Crisis,* 50–53.

38. Donald B. Cozzens, *The Changing Face of the Priesthood* (Collegeville, MN: Liturgical Press, 2000), 40–41.

39. Ibid.

40. Ibid., 41.

41. A. W. Richard Sipe, *Sex, Priests, and Power: Anatomy of a Crisis* (New York: Brunner/Mazel, 1995), 121.

42. Ibid.

43. Michael Rezendes, "Church to Disclose Records of Clergy Abused by Adults," *Boston Globe,* 29 January 2003.

44. Information regarding Samide's case is taken from Stephanie Saul, "Judge to Church: Reinstate Principal," *New York Newsday,* 9 April 2003.

45. The data about Ms. Phelps and Fr. Kenny is taken from J. Michael Parker, "New: Archdiocese Says It Settled Sex Suit to Protect Plaintiff," *San Antonio Express-News,* 21 February 2003.

46. Rev. Ann F. C. Richards, "Sexual Misconduct by Clergy in the Episcopal Church," *Studies in Gender & Sexuality* 5 (2004): 139–66.

47. "In News: Nuns Were Victims Too," *St. Louis Post-Dispatch,* 7 January 2003; Jerry Filteau, "Study Says Two-Fifths of U.S. Nuns Suffered Some Form of Sexual

Abuse," *Catholic News Service,* 8 January 2003; Bill Smith, "Nuns as Sexual Victims Get Little Notice," *St. Louis Post-Dispatch,* 4 January 2003.

48. David France, *Our Fathers: The Secret Life of the Catholic Church in an Age of Scandal* (New York: Broadway Books, 2004), 391.

49. David Gibson, *The Coming Catholic Church: How the Faithful Are Shaping a New American Catholicism* (San Francisco: HarperSanFrancisco, 2003), 257.

50. Ibid.

51. Ibid.

52. Smith, "Nuns as Sexual Victims Get Little Notice.."

53. Filteau, "Study Says Two-Fifths of U.S. Nuns Suffered Some Form of Sexual Abuse.."

54. Gibson, *Coming Catholic Church,* 202.

55. Kennedy, *Unhealed Wound,* 16.

56. Sigmund Freud, *Moses and Monotheism,* in *The Standard Edition of the Complete Psychological Works of Sigmund Freud* (London: Hogarth Press and the Institute of Psychoanalysis, 1953–1974), 23:7–137.

57. Calvin A. Colarusso, "Traversing Young Adulthood: The Male Journey from 20–40," *Psychoanalytic Inquiry* 15 (1995): 75–91.

58. Michael J. Diamond, "Boys to Men: The Maturity of Masculine Gender Identity through Paternal Watchful Protectiveness," *Gender & Psychoanalysis* 2(1997): 447.

59. Ibid., 447.

60. Cozzens, *Changing Face of the Priesthood,* 73.

61. "The Church on Trial: Part 1," *CBS News,* 12 June 2002.

62. Ibid.

63. Janine Chasseguet-Smirgel, *The Ego Ideal: A Psychoanalytic Essay on the Malady of the Ideal* (London: Free Association Books, 2003).

64. Damon Linker, "Fatherhood, 2002," *First Things,* November 2002, 8.

65. Andrea Celenza, "Sexual Misconduct in the Clergy: The Search for a Father," *Studies in Gender & Sexuality* 5 (2004): 220; Dinter, *Other Side of the Altar,* 35; Hoge, *First Five Years,* 83–85.

66. Hoge, *First Five Years,* 83–85.

67. Celenza, "Sexual Misconduct in the Clergy," 219–20.

68. Dinter, *Other Side of the Altar,* 35.

69. Sipe, *Celibacy in Crisis,* 17.

70. Maureen Call, "Tests Confirm Priest Fathered 2," *Enterprise,* 28 October 2003; Brooks Egerton, "Bishop Letting Priest Work: He Has Admitted to Fathering Child; Diocese Cites Lawsuit Dismissal," *Dallas Morning News,* 14 May 2003; Zaheera Wahid, "Ex-Priest Faces Sex Charges: He Is Alleged to Have Fathered Child with a Teenager while He Was at St. Edward Catholic Church in Dana Point," *Orange County Register,* 25 September 2002.

71. Call,"Tests Confirm Priest Fathered 2."

72. Ibid.

73. Stephen Kurkjian and Walter F. Robinson, "A 'Classic Misuse of Power':

Children of Woman Who Died in Affair with Priest Speak out," *Boston Globe,* 29 December 2002.

74. Ibid.

75. Ibid.

76. Ibid.

77. Ibid.

78. Call, "Tests Confirm Priest Fathered 2."

79. Carol McGraw, "Charge against Plesetz Echoed: A Woman in Irvine Says She, Too, Had a Child by Former Catholic Priest Assigned to Dana Point Church." *Orange County Register,* 27 September 2003.

80. Steve Myers, "Woman Says Counseling Halted in Retaliation," *Mobile Register,* 5 November 2003.

81. Berry and Renner, *Vows of Silence,* 92–93.

82. Ibid., p. 94.

83. Ibid.

84. Sipe, *Celibacy in Crisis,* 125.

85. Ferdinand Patinio and AFP, "In Rulebook for Priests: Two Kids and You're out," *Manila Times,* 20 November 2003; Linette C. Ramos, " 'Strict Rules' for Papa Priests," *Philippines Sun Star,* 21 November 2003.

86. Material regarding Pius IX and Edgardo Mortara relies on Wills, *Papal Sin,* 40–45.

87. Ibid., 43.

88. John Cornwell, *The Pontiff in Winter: Triumph and Conflict in the Reign of John Paul II* (New York: Doubleday, 2004), 156.

89. Michelle Nicolosi and Claudia Rowe, "The 11 Abuse Cases the P-I Examined," *Seattle Post-Intelligencer,* 19 August 2004; Michelle Nicolosi, "Man Says Sex with Priest Began at 11: The Cleric, Convicted of Taking Indecent Liberties, Calls Accuser a Liar," *Seattle Post-Intelligencer,* 20 August 2004; Claudia Rowe, "Colombian's 'Adoption' by Priest Too Good to Be True: An Unwanted Name, A Life Not of his Choosing," *Seattle Post-Intelligencer,* 20 August 2004; Claudia Rowe and Michelle Nicolosi, "Accused Priests Took in Minors: When Fathers Acted as Fathers, Complaints Often Followed," *Seattle Post-Intelligencer,* 19 August 2004.

90. All data about Albert Green/Ed Olszewski derive from Nicolosi, "Man Says Sex with Priest Began at 11."

91. Ibid.

92. Ibid.

93. Sipe, *Celibacy in Crisis,* 9.

94. Hoge and Wenger, *Evolving Visions of the Priesthood,* 50.

95. "A Survey of Roman Catholic Priests in the United States and Puerto Rico: June 27–October 11, 2002," *Los Angeles Times,* 20 October 2002.

96. Gibson, *Coming Catholic Church,* 261.

97. Ibid., 256.

98. Ibid., 253–55.

CHAPTER 7 Homosexuality: Secreted and Scapegoated

1. Thomas C. Fox, *Sexuality and Catholicism* (New York: George Braziller, 1995), 129–61; John J. McNeill, *The Church and the Homosexual,* 4th ed. (Boston: Beacon Press, 1993), xi–xxii.

2. Fox, *Sexuality and Catholicism,* 154.

3. John Cornwell, *Breaking Faith: Can the Catholic Church Save Itself?* (New York: Penguin Compass, 2001), 129.

4. Fox, *Sexuality and Catholicism,* 148–57.

5. McNeill, *Church and the Homosexual,* xix.

6. Fox, *Sexuality and Catholicism,* 155.

7. Dan Kennedy, "Rome Casts Its Ballot (continued)," *Boston Phoenix,* 8–14 August 2003; Michael Paulson, "Vatican Warns on Same-Sex Marriage," *Boston Globe,* 1 August 2003.

8. Manny B. Marinay, "Venomous Ratzi Rattles Gay Flock," *Manila Times,* 22 June 2005; Paulson, "Vatican Warns on Same-Sex Marriage."

9. Kennedy, "Rome Casts Its Ballot."

10. Zenon Cardinal Grocholewski, *Instruction: Concerning the Criteria of Vocational Discernment Regarding Persons with Homosexual Tendencies in View of Their Admission to Seminaries and Holy Orders* (Vatican, 4 November 2005).

11. Interested readers can refer to Henry Abelove, Michele Aina Baracle, and David M. Halperin, eds., *The Lesbian and Gay Studies Reader* (London: Routledge, 1993); Bertram Cohler and Robert Galatzer-Levy, *The Course of Gay and Lesbian Lives: Social and Psychoanalytic Perspectives* (Chicago: University of Chicago Press, 1999); Richard Isay, *Being Homosexual: Gay Men and Their Development* (New York: Farrar, Straus and Giroux, 2001); Vittorio Lingiarde and Jack Drescher, eds., *Mental Health Professions and Homosexuality* (Northvale, NJ: Haworth Press, 2003); A. W. Richard Sipe, *Celibacy in Crisis: The Secret World Revisited* (New York: Brunner-Routledge, 2003), 131–70.

12. McNeill, *Church and the Homosexual,* xv.

13. Elizabeth A. Johnson, *Truly Our Sister: A Theology of Mary in the Communion of Saints* (New York: Continuum, 2003), 107.

14. Ibid.

15. McNeill, *Church and the Homosexual,* xix.

16. Donald B. Cozzens, *The Changing Face of the Priesthood* (Collegeville, MN: Liturgical Press 2000), 99; Mark D. Jordan, *The Silence of Sodom: Homosexuality in Modern Catholicism* (Chicago: University of Chicago Press, 2000), 99–110; Sipe, *Celibacy in Crisis,* 51, 136–38, 148, 155, 164, 322.

17. Andrew M. Greeley, *Priests: A Calling in Crisis* (Chicago: University of Chicago Press, 2004), 39.

18. Cozzens, *Changing Face of the Priesthood,* 97; Sipe, *Celibacy in Crisis,* 137.

19. Jordan, *Silence of Sodom,* 109–10.

20. Michelle Bearden, "Pride in a Pulpit," *Tampa Tribune,* 6 October 2002.

21. Mark Dowd, "Gays in the Priesthood," *Tablet,* 15 May 2001.

22. Jordan, *Silence of Sodom,* 159.

23. Ibid.,182.

24. Ibid., 198–99.

25. Ibid., 198.

26. Ibid., 187.

27. Rev. James Martin, S.J., personal communication.

28. "Levada Urges Gay Priests to Remain in Closet," *Catholic News,* 28 February 2006.

29. Jordan, *Silence of Sodom,* 184.

30. Rachel Zoll, Associated Press, "Gay Priests Conflicted as Church Leaders Set to Discuss Restrictions," *Day,* 13 November 2005.

31. Charles Radin, "A Gay Priest Receives the Sacrament of Acceptance," *Boston Globe,* 6 November 2005. The rest of the material on Fr. Daley is taken from this article.

32. Christopher Schiavone, with Janice Page, "Broken Vows," *Boston Globe,* 8 December 2002.

33. David France, personal communication, February 2006.

34. Jordan, *Silence of Sodom,* 7.

35. Ibid., 85.

36. Ibid.

37. David France, *Our Fathers: The Secret Life of the Catholic Church in an Age of Scandal* (New York: Broadway Books, 2004), 92; Jordan, *Silence of Sodom,* 117–18.

38. Jordan, *Silence of Sodom,* 117–18.

39. Sipe, *Celibacy in Crisis,* 141.

40. Associated Press, "Bishops Who Quit amid Sex Scandals," *New York Times,* 12 December 2002.

41. Jordan, *Silence of Sodom,* 177.

42. Ibid.

43. Cornwell, *Breaking Faith,* 164.

44. Jordan, *Silence of Sodom,* 143.

45. Ibid.

46. Hanna Rosin, "Conflict—and then some . . . ." *Washington Post,* 21 July 2002.

47. Ibid.

48. Dowd, "Gays in the Priesthood."

49. Ibid.

50. Ibid.

51. Ibid.

52. Dean R. Hoge and Jacqueline E. Wenger, *Evolving Visions of the Priesthood: Changes from Vatican II to the Turn of the New Century* (Collegeville, MN: Liturgical Press 2003), 102.

53. Ibid.

54. Ibid.

55. Ibid., 104–5.

56. Sacha Pfeiffer, "Seminary Ouster of Outspoken Gay Points up Issues: Focus Put on Orientation," *Boston Globe,* 25 November 2002.

57. Ibid.

58. Sipe, *Celibacy in Crsis,* 51.

59. Ibid.

60. Jordan, *Silence of Sodom,* 103–4.

61. A. W. Richard Sipe, *Sex, Priests, and Power: Anatomy of a Crisis* (New York: Brunner/Mazel, 1995), 173.

62. Ibid.

63. Tom Heinen and Mary Zahn, "Weakland Begs for Forgiveness: Says Earnings Didn't Cover Settlement," *Milwaukee Journal-Sentinel,* 1 June 2002; Marie Rohde, "Weakland Denied He Abused Man Archdiocese Paid $450,000: Archbishop Asks Vatican to Hasten Retirement," *Milwaukee Journal Sentinel,* 24 May 2002.

64. Bill Zajac, "Gay Priests in a Barely Closed Closet," *Mass Live,* 29 February 2004; Thomas Martin, personal communication.

65. Zajac, "Gay Priests in a Barely Closed Closet."

66. Ibid.

67. Sam Dillon, "New Hampshire Bishop Embroiled in Abuse Disputes," *New York Times,* 22 October 2002.

68. Donald B. Cozzens, *Sacred Silence: Denial and the Crisis in the Church* (Collegeville, MN: Liturgical Press, 2002), 130–31; David Gibson, *The Coming Catholic Church: How the Faithful Are Shaping a New American Catholicism* (San Francisco: HarperSanFrancisco, 2003), 176–77; Sipe, *Celibacy in Crisis,* 133.

69. Cozzens, *Sacred Silence,* 131.

70. France, *Our Fathers,* 189.

71. Jason Berry, *Lead Us Not into Temptation: Catholic Priests and the Sexual Abuse of Children* (Urbana: University of Illinois Press, 2000), 233–34.

72. Jason Berry and Gerald Renner, *Vows of Silence: The Abuse of Power in the Papacy of John Paul II* (New York: Free Press, 2004), 37.

73. Cornwell, *Silence of Sodom,* 158.

74. Ibid., 159.

75. Cozzens, *Sacred Silence,* 131.

76. Ibid.

77. John Jay College of Criminal Justice, *The Nature and Scope of the Problem of Sexual Abuse of Minors by Catholic Priests and Deacons in the United States* (Washington, DC: United States Conference of Catholic Bishops, 2004); United States Conference of Catholic Bishops (USCCB), *Report on the Implementation of the Charter for the Protection of Children and Young People* (February 2005).

78. John Jay College, *Nature and Scope of the Problem,* 6.

79. USCCB, *Report on the Implementation of the Charter,* 7, 8.

80. Ibid., 9.

81. Sherrel L. Hammer, "Chapter XX.I. Puberty," *Case Based Pediatrics for*

Medical Students and Residents, Department of Pediatrics, University of Hawaii, March 2002.

82. Kirby Parker Jones, "The Beginning and End of Reproductive Life: Pubertal and Midlife Changes," University of Utah Medical School, 1997.

83. Gerald E. Kohansky and Murray Cohen, "Priests Who Sexualize Male Minors: Psychodynamic, Characterological, and Clerical Cultural Considerations," in *Predatory Priests, Silenced Victims,* ed. Mary Gail Frawley-O'Dea and Virginia Goldner (Hillsdale, NJ: Analytic Press, 2007).

84. Nicole Winfield, Associated Press, "Cardinal Says Gays Shouldn't Be Priests," *Boston Globe,* 6 December 2002.

85. Gibson, *Coming Catholic Church,* 176–77; Winfield, "Cardinal Says Gays Shouldn't Be Priests."

86. Gibson, *Coming Catholic Church,* 176–77.

87. Ibid., 177.

88. Ibid.

89. Michael Paulson, "Gay Seminarian Ban Weighed: Vatican Drafting a Ruling Expected in the Next Year," *Boston Globe,* 6 November 2002.

90. Joe Feuerhard, "The Real Deal," *National Catholic Reporter,* 19 August 2004.

91. Fr. Charles Dahlby, "Scandal in the Roman Catholic Church," *Catholic Citizens of Illinois,* 28 October 2003.

92. Ibid.

93. Zenon Cardinal Grocholewski. *Instruction: Concerning the Criteria of Vocational Discernment.*

94. Ibid.

95. Ibid.

96. Peter Steinfels, "Analysis: Crucial Issue for Catholics," *New York Times* and *Salt Lake Tribune,* 30 September 2005.

97. Marilyn Elias, "Is Homosexuality to Blame for Church Scandal?" *USA Today,* 15 July 2002.

98. Katherine DiGiulio, "Interview of Dr. Leslie Lothstein," *National Catholic Reporter,* 16 August 2002.

99. Ibid.

100. Ibid.

101. Elias, "Is Homosexuality to Blame for Church Scandal?"

102. Richard B. Gartner, *Betrayed as Boys: Psychodynamic Treatment of Sexually Abused Men* (New York: Guilford Press, 1999), 98–100.

103. Ibid., 99.

104. Ibid.

105. Associated Press, "Researchers Study Gays in Catholic Priesthood," *Boston Channel,* 20 September 2005; Michael Paulson, "Outrage at Vatican's US Hunt for Gay Seminarians," *Sydney Morning Herald,* 17 September 2005.

106. Michael Kimmel, "Focus on Pedophiles, Not Gays," *New York Newsday,* 14 October 2005.

107. Jan Hindman and James M. Peters, "Polygraph Testing Leads to Better

Understanding of Adult and Juvenile Sexual Offenders," *Federal Probation* 65 (2001): 8–14.

108. Jordan, *Silence of Sodom,* 162.

109. Ibid.

110. DiGiulio,"Interview of Dr. Leslie Lothstein."

111. Associated Press, "Researchers Study Gays in Catholic Priesthood," *Boston Channel,* 20 September 2005.

112. Fr. Gerard Thomas, "A Source of Scandal," *Beliefnet,* accessed 2 January 2006.

113. Paul Michaels, "Don't Dare to Speak Its Name," *Tablet,* 24 September 2005.

114. Michael Paulson, "Gay Comments Concern Bishops," *Boston Globe,* 10 December 2002.

115. Paulson,"Outrage at Vatican's US Hunt for Gay Seminarians."

116. Ibid.

CHAPTER 8 Where Were the Pastors?

1. Richard P. McBrien, "On Being a Pastoral Bishop," *Essays on Theology,* 18 May 1998.

2. Pope Benedict XVI. *Deus Caritas Est: Encyclical Letter of the Supreme Pontiff to the Bishops, Priests and Deacons, Men and Women Religious, and All the Lay Faithful,* Vatican, 25 December 2005, 31.

3. Fran Ferder and John Heagle, "Time for Bishops to Listen, Take Ordinary Catholics Seriously," *National Catholic Reporter,* 19 July 2002.

4. Laurie Goodstein, "St. Louis Archbishop to Take over Philadelphia Archdiocese," *New York Times,* 16 July 2003.

5. Warren Wolfe, "Archbishop Flynn to Meet with Sex-Abuse Victims Group," *Star Tribune,* 14 January 2003.

6. Ibid.

7. Ibid.

8. "Interview with Rev. Thomas Doyle," *Religion and Ethics Newsweekly,* 27 January 2003.

9. George Weigel, *The Courage to be Catholic: Crisis, Reform, and the Future of the Church* (New York: Basic Books, 2002), 113.

10. Bill Zajac, "Sex Abuse Suits Last Resort, 2 Say," *Mass Live,* 24 September 2003.

11. Eugene Kennedy, *The Unhealed Wound: The Church, the Priesthood, and the Question of Sexuality* (New York: St. Martin's Press, 2002), xxvii.

12. "Diocese Downplays Abuse Scope: Cases Show Patterns of Suppression by Bishop," *Arizona Republic,* 10 November 2002; Laurie Roberts, "Bishop's Heart Grows Heavy under Weight of Evidence," *Arizona Republic,* 7 December 2002.

13. Roberts, "Bishop's Heart Grows Heavy. "

14. "Diocese Downplays Abuse Scope."

15. Rachel Zoll, Associated Press, "Expert: Prosecutor's Deal with Phoenix Bishop Minimizes Damage to Church," *Times-Picayune,* 6 June 2003.

16. Rachel Zoll, Associated Press, "O'Brien Resignation Another Blow for Fractured Catholic Church," *San Diego Union-Tribune,* 18 June 2003.

17. Dennis Wagner, "Romley: Bishop Will Be Treated Like Any Criminal Suspect," *Arizona Republic,* 17 June 2003.

18. Zoll, "Expert: Prosecutor's Deal."

19. Robert D. McFadden, "L.I. Diocese Tricked Victims of Sexual Abuse, Panel Says," *New York Times,* 11 February 2003.

20. Ibid.

21. Carol Eisenberg, "A Protector or Predator?" *New York Newsday,* 11 February 2002.

22. Ibid.

23. "Sex Abuse Victim Wants Archbishop to Step Down," *NBC 15,* 13 May 2003.

24. Donald B. Cozzens, *Sacred Silence: Denial and the Crisis in the Church* (Collegeville, MN: Liturgical Press, 2002), 93–94.

25. Investigative Staff of *The Boston Globe. Betrayal: The Crisis in the Catholic Church* (Boston: Little, Brown and Company, 2002), 43.

26. Paul A. Long, "Church: We're Not Blaming Victims," *Kentucky Post,* 28 February 2003.

27. Associated Press, "Stockton Diocese: Man Didn't Do Enough to Avoid Alleged Molest," *Mercury News,* 15 August 2003.

28. Peter McAleer, "Victims: Church Violates Privacy," *Press of Atlantic City,* 20 October 2002.

29. Ibid.

30. Pam Belluck, "Church Seeks Therapy Records," *New York Times,* 17 January 2003; Denise Lavoie, Associated Press, "Lawyers for Boston Archdiocese Question Therapists Who Worked with Alleged Victims," *Boston Globe,* 17 January 2003; Michael Rezendes and Walter V. Robinson, "Church Lawyers to Question Therapists," *Boston Globe,* 17 January 2003.

31. Paul La Camera, "The Immorality of Subpoenaing the Therapists of Victims of Clergy Abuse," *Boston Channel,* 1 February 2003; Eileen McNamara, "Opinion: A Matter of Choice," *Boston Globe,* 26 January 2003; Michael Paulson, "Abuse Specialists Challenge Church Defense Tactic: Assert Depositions Will Betray Victims," *Boston Globe,* 22 January 2003; Robin Washington, Eric Convey, and Tom Mashberg, "Victims' Advocates Rip Church over Deposition of Therapist," *Boston Herald,* 17 January 2003.

32. Material on Seattle is taken from Claudia Rowe, "Archdiocese Hired Lawyer to Reach out to Accusers in Sex Scandal," *Seattle Post-Intelligencer,* 27 September 2004.

33. Rezendes and Robinson, "Church Lawyers to Question Therapists"; Bill Zajac, "Diocese: Church Alleges Conflict: The Plaintiff's Lawyers Filed a Motion

to have Superior Court Judge Constance M. Sweeney Rule on First Amendment Issues," *Mass Live,* 12 February 2003.

34. Cozzens, *Sacred Silence,* 141.

35. Meg Kissinger and Tom Heinen, "Weakland, Dolan Meet with Victim: Extraordinary Session Focuses on 'Road to Healing' in Abuse," *Milwaukee Journal-Sentinel,* 10 July 2003.

36. Ibid.

37. Dennis A. Shook, "Archdiocese Supports Bill on Mandatory Reporting: Priests Expected to Reveal Instances of Sexual Abuse," *Waukesha Freeman,* 17 June 2003.

38. Joseph A. Reaves and Fred Bayles, "O'Brien's Policies Reversed," *Arizona Republic,* 21 June 2003.

39. Michael Clancy, "Archbishop Promises to Meet Abuse Victims," *Arizona Republic,* 24 June 2003.

40. David McArthur, "Abuse Victims Meet with Archbishop," *World Now News,* 31 October 2003.

41. Ibid.

42. Jeff Gottlieb, "Molestation Victim Gets Story Told in Churches," *Los Angeles Times,* 27 January 2003.

43. Ibid.

44. John Paul II, "Address of John Paul II to a Group of 120 Newly Appointed Bishops from 33 Countries," *Speeches of John Paul II,* 23 September 2002.

45. Jason Berry, *Lead Us Not into Temptation: Catholic Priests and the Sexual Abuse of Children* (Urbana: University of Illinois Press, 2000), 82.

46. Jonathan Van Fleet, "Church Officials Asked Police Not to Charge Priest after Sex Incident with Teen," *Telegraph,* 3 March 2003.

47. Ibid.

48. Information regarding Bishop Brady and Father Sullivan is taken from Alan Cooperman, "One Diocese's Early Warning on Sex Abuse: '50s Records Reflect Bishops Taking Risks," *Washington Post,* 22 April 2003; Kathryn Marchocki, "Files: Church Understood Priest Abuse in 1950s," *Union Leader/Sunday News,* 6 March 2003.

49. Walter V. Robinson, "Judge Finds Records, Law at Odds: Lack of Care Seen in Assigning Priests," *Boston Globe,* 26 November 2002.

50. Leslie M. Lothstein, "Men of the Flesh: The Evaluation and Treatment of Sexually Abusing Priests," *Studies in Gender & Sexuality* 5 (2004): 167–96; A. W. Richard Sipe, *Celibacy in Crisis: The Secret World Revisited* (New York: Brunner-Routledge, 2003), 208.

51. Lothstein, "Men of the Flesh."

52. Bret Schulte, "Struggling to Keep the Faith," *US News & World Report,* 27 December 2004.

53. Sipe, *Celibacy in Crisis,* 193.

54. Sarah Crosbie, "Kicking out Sex-Molester Priests Called a 'Recipe for Disaster,'" *Kingston Whig-Standard,* 26 April 2003.

55. Maria Vogel-Short, "Swift Action Restores Trust at Daytop," *Observer-Tribune,* 6 January 2005.

56. Ibid.

57. "Police, Fire and Courts," *Peoria Journal Star,* 19 December 2003.

58. Jennifer Sinco Kelleher, "Priest Pleads Guilty," *New York Newsday,* 1 October 2004.

59. Allison Hantschel, "Priest: I Can't Stop Molesting Children," *Daily Southtown,* 10 December 2002.

60. P. Karl Hanson, Richard A. Steffy, and Rene Gauthier, "Long-Term Follow-up of Child Molesters," *Public Safety and Emergency Preparedness,* No. 1992–02, February 1992.

61. Ann Rodgers-Melnick, "Bishops Lauded for Progress as Conference Ends," *Pittsburgh Post-Gazette,* 22 June 2003.

62. Richard John Neuhaus, "Seeking a Better Way," *First Things,* October 2002, 84.

63. Naoki Schwartz, "Miami Archbishop Criticized for Friendship with Child Abuser," *Miami Sun-Sentinel,* 4 September 2002.

64. Conference of Major Superiors of Men, *Improving Pastoral Care and Accountability in Response to the Tragedy of Sexual Abuse,* 10 August 2002.

65. Amy Pagnozzi, "Priest Still Waiting for Cronin's Answer," *Hartford Courant,* 6 September 2002; "Priest Says People, Not Clergy, Will Prevail," *Hartford Courant,* 19 November 2002.

66. Michael Paulson, "Lennon Appeals to Archdiocese for Greater Unity," *Boston Globe,* 16 April 2003.

67. Gil Donovan, "Priests Say Bishop Issues Gag Order," *National Catholic Reporter,* 14 March 2003; Bishop Joseph Adamec, "Decree," Altoona-Johnson Diocese, 2 September 1999.

68. Larry B. Stammer, "Most Priests Say Bishops Mishandled Abuse Issue: Many Believe that the U.S. Church's Charter, though Protective of Children, Is Unfair to Clerics, and Many Are Angry at Prelates," *Los Angeles Times,* 20 October 2002.

69. Rita Ciolli, "A Priest Repents for His Brethren: Oyster Bay Congregants Moved by Gesture," *New York Newsday,* 17 February 2003.

70. Matt Carroll, "Bishops' Policy Flawed, Priests Say," *Boston Globe,* 19 October 2002.

71. Stammer, "Most Priests Say Bishops Mishandled Abuse Issue."

72. Tom Heinen, "Dolan Meets with Petition Organizers: No Discipline Imposed over Letter on Celibacy," *Milwaukee Journal-Sentinel,* 3 September 2003.

73. Ibid.

74. Material about changes to the child protection policies of the Archdiocese of Boston are taken from Ralph Ranalli, "Church Limits Access to Records on Abuse," *Boston Globe,* 17 September 2003.

75. Terrence Carroll, "Transparency Still Lacking in Catholic Sex-Abuse Scandal," *Seattle Times,* 3 August 2005.

76. Renee K. Gadoua, "Moynihan Apologizes for Abusive Priests," *Post-Standard*, 31 October 2003.

77. Ibid.

78. Laurie Goodstein, "For the U.S. Catholic Church, a Mobile Unit of Superhealers," *New York Times*, 22 June 2003.

79. John Rivera, "Keeler Letter Reveals Abuse," *Baltimore Sun*, 25 September 2002.

80. Ibid.

81. Joe Feuerherd, "Just How Bad Is It?: Priest Shortage Worse than Experts Predicted; Laity, Foreign Priests, Filling in Gap," *National Catholic Reporter*, 17 October 2003, 3–5; Dean R. Hoge and Jacqueline E. Wenger, *Evolving Visions of the Priesthood: Changes from Vatican II to the Turn of the New Century* (Collegeville, MN: Liturgical Press, 2003), 14; Richard A. Schoenherr, *Goodbye Father: The Celibate Male Priesthood and the Future of the Catholic Church* (Oxford: Oxford University Press, 2002), xii, xiv–xxiv, xxvii, xxviii, xxx, 5–13, 15–28, 67, 93, 125, 180, 187, 214–16.

82. Schulte, "Struggling to Keep the Faith.."

83. Ibid.

84. Schoenherr, *Goodbye Father*, 17–18.

85. Jane Lampman, "A Married Priesthood? A Shortage of Roman Catholic Priests Has Led Some Clergy to Call for Celibacy to Be Optional. Though Controversial, 'Rent-A-Priest' Helps Fill the Gap for Some Catholics," *Christian Science Monitor*, 4 September 2003; Peter Steinfels, *A People Adrift: The Crisis of the Roman Catholic Church in America* (New York: Simon and Schuster, 2003), 317.

86. Dean R. Hoge, *The First Five Years of the Priesthood: A Study of Newly Ordained Catholic Priests* (Collegeville, MN: Liturgical Press, 2002), 2.

87. Ibid., 3.

88. Ibid., 2.

89. Feuerherd, "Just How Bad Is It?"

90. Donald B. Cozzens, *The Changing Face of the Priesthood* (Collegeville, MN: Liturgical Press, 2000), 132–33.

91. Ibid.,134.

92. Ibid., 142.

93. Laurie Goodstein, "Gay Men Ponder Impact of Proposal by Vatican," *New York Times*, 23 September 2005.

94. Michael Clancy, "Anti-Gay Edict Stirs Priest to Step Down," *Arizona Republic*, 29 November 2005.

95. Schoenherr, *Goodbye Father*, 19.

96. Nicole Winfield, "Vatican Reaffirms Celibacy for Priests: Church Emphasizes Religious Vocations," *Boston Globe*, 29 April 2003.

97. Andrew Wolfson, "Priest's Abuse of Children Was Known for Years: Records Paint a Disturbing Portrait of Daniel C. Clark's Addiction to Child Sex and the Church's Response to It," *Courier-Journal*, 4 May 2003.

98. Thomas J. Reese, *Inside the Vatican: The Politics and Organization of the Catholic Church* (Cambridge: Harvard University Press, 1996), 165.

99. Investigative Staff of *The Boston Globe, Betrayal,* 5; Stephen J. Rossetti, *A Tragic Grace: The Catholic Church and Child Sexual Abuse* (Collegeville, MN: Liturgical Press, 1996), 16–18.

100. John Cornwell, *Breaking Faith: Can the Catholic Church Save Itself?* (New York: Penguin Compass, 2001), 122; John Paul II, *Evangelium Vitae,* 25 March 1995.

101. Phillip Lawler, "Moral Leadership of American Hierarchy under Scrutiny at Rome Meeting," *AD 2000,* June 2002, 9.

102. Ibid.

103. Ibid.

104. Brian Ross, "Priestly Sin, Cover-Up: Powerful Cardinal in Vatican Accused of Sexual Abuse Cover-Up," *ABC News,* 26 April 2002.

105. "Maciel Case Belies Church Promises to Combat Abuse," *National Catholic Reporter,* 21 November 2003.

106. Ross, "Priestly Sin, Cover-Up."

107. Lawler, "Moral Leadership of American Hierarchy under Scrutiny."

108. Ross, "Priestly Sin, Cover-Up."

109. Jose Barba-Martin, "Ladies and Gentlemen of This Committee on Human Rights: Text to Be Read at the Hearing Session of the Human Rights of Children and Youth Committee of the United Nations in Geneva, on October 9th, 2002," *Chiesa Newsletter,* 4 April 2003; Gary Stern, "Legionaries Not without Its Critics," *Journal News,* 4 June 2003.

110. Ian Fisher and Laurie Goodstein, "Vatican Punishes a Leader after Abuse Charges," *New York Times,* 19 May 2006.

111. Jason Berry and Gerald Renner, *Vows of Silence: The Abuse of Power in the Papacy of John Paul II* (New York: Free Press, 2004), 139–45.

112. Eugene Cullen Kennedy, "Dallas: The Last Remake of Frankenstein," *National Catholic Reporter,* 16 August 2002.

113. John Paul II, *Sacramentrium Sanctitatis Tutela,* 30 April 2002.

114. John L. Allen Jr., "Secret Vatican Norms on Abuse Show Conflicts with U.S. Policy," *National Catholic Reporter,* 29 November 2002.

CHAPTER 9 Clerical Narcissism

1. Conference of Major Superiors of Men, "In Solidarity and Service: Reflections on the Problem of Clericalism in the Church," quoted in *The Changing Face of the Priesthood,* by Donald B. Cozzens (Collegeville, MN: Liturgical Press, 2000), 118, 187.

2. Richard P. McBrien, "The Office of Bishop," *Tidings,* 2 August 2002; George Weigel, *The Courage to Be Catholic: Crisis, Reform, and the Future of the Church* (New York: Basic Books, 2002), 94.

3. Weigel, *Courage to Be Catholic.*

4. Scott Appleby, "The Church at Risk," paper presented at the United States Conference of Catholic Bishops Spring Meeting, Dallas, 13 June 2002; Donald B. Cozzens, *Sacred Silence: Denial and the Crisis in the Church* (Collegeville, MN: Liturical Press, 2002), 112–13; David Gibson, *The Coming Catholic Church: How the Faithful Are Shaping a New American Catholicism* (San Francisco: HarperSanFrancisco, 2003), 197–219; Eugene Kennedy, *The Unhealed Wound: The Church, the Priesthood, and the Question of Sexuality* (New York: St. Martin's Press, 2002), 64–70; Jane Lampman, "A Church Culture Draws Scrutiny," *Christian Science Monitor,* 10 December 2002.

5. Lampman, "Church Culture Draws Scrutiny."

6. Lawrence Josephs, *Character Structure and the Organization of the Self* (New York: Columbia University Press, 1992), 194–216.

7. Ibid., 197.

8. Investigative Staff of the *The Boston Globe, Betrayal: The Crisis in the Catholic Church* (Boston: Little, Brown and Company, 2002), 146.

9. "A Cardinal without Credibility," *Hartford Courant,* 16 June 2003.

10. "New York Cardinal Accused of Snubbing Bishops' Lay Review Board," *Catholic News,* 17 January 2003; Laurie Goodstein, "Cardinal Egan Spurns Members of Review Board Studying Abuse," *New York Times,* 15 January 2003.

11. Daniel J. Wakin, "Cardinal Egan Defends Record in Abuse Cases," *New York Times,* 16 August 2002.

12. Investigative Staff of *The Boston Globe, Betrayal,* 161.

13. Josephs, *Character Structure,* 199, 203.

14. Thomas P. Reilly, *To the People of the Commonwealth of Massachusetts,* www. bishop-accountability.org, 23 July 2002, 38–39.

15. Ibid., 39.

16. Dick Ryan, "One Bishop's High Cost of Living," *National Catholic Reporter,* 25 October 2002, 6.

17. Jimmy Breslin, "LI Bishop's Mansion: Biggest Waster of Money, Bar Nun," *New York Newsday,* 8 October 2002; Rita Ciolli, "The Bishop's New Digs," *New York Newsday,* 6 October 2002.

18. Ciolli, "Bishop's New Digs."

19. Ibid.

20. Gibson, *Coming Catholic Church,* 307.

21. Josephs, *Character Structure,* 200.

22. Gibson, *Coming Catholic Church,* 299.

23. George Neumayr, "Cardinal Stonewaller," *Spectator,* 27 May 2003.

24. Ibid.

25. Josephs, *Character Structure,* 199.

26. Ibid., 202.

27. Otto Kernberg, *Severe Personality Disorders* (New Haven: Yale University Press, 1984), 15–19.

28. Reilly, *To the People of the Commonwealth,* 25.

29. Cozzens, *Sacred Silence,* 92.

30. Laurie Goodstein, "Decades of Damage; Trail of Pain in Church Crisis Leads to Nearly Every Diocese," *New York Times,* 12 January 2003.

31. Richard N. Ostling, "Catholic Bishops' President Defends American Priests after a Negative 'Avalanche' over Abuse," *Boston Globe,* 14 November 2005.

32. W. W. Meissner, *The Cultic Origins of Christianity: The Dynamics of Religious Development* (Collegeville, MN: Liturgical Press, 2000), 3.

33. Ibid.

34. Josephs, *Character Structure,* 205.

35. Appleby,"Church at Risk."

36. Wilton D. Gregory, "A Catholic Response to Sexual Abuse: Confession, Contrition, Resolve," paper presented at the United States Conference of Catholic Bishops Spring Meeting, Dallas, 13 June 2002.

37. Ann Rodgers-Melnick, "Bishop Finds Favor and Faults in Sex Abuse Scandal Coverage," *Post-Gazette,* 6 September 2003; Peter Smith, "Stories Obscured Facts in Sex Scandal," *Courier-Journal,* 6 September 2003.

38. Andrew Greeley, "Are Bishops Sorry at All?" *Chicago Sun Times,* 3 August 2003.

39. Associated Press, "Text of Bishop Gregory's Remarks," *New York Newsday,* 11 November 2002.

40. Andy Newman, "In a Troubled Twilight, a Bishop Speaks," *New York Times,* 3 November 2002.

41. Ibid.

42. Reilly, *To the People of the Commonwealth,* 32–33.

43. Material about the lunch is taken from Rita Ciolli, "Experts Lament Unheeded Advice," *New York Newsday,* 10 February 2003.

44. Scott Westcott, "Rebuilding Trust 2: What Becomes of Abusive Priests?" *Times-News,* 1 July 2003.

45. Brad Morin, "UNH Expert Unveils Report on Sexually Abusive Priests," *Foster's Democrat,* 9 October 2002.

46. Ibid.

47. Pope Pius X, *Pascendi Domenici Gregis: Encyclical of Pope Pius X on the Doctrines of the Modernities,* 9 August 1907.

48. Ibid., 39.

49. Garry Wills, *Why I Am a Catholic* (Boston: Houghton Mifflin, 2002), 214–15.

50. Pope John XXIII, *Pacem in Terris: Encyclical of Pope John XXIII on Establishing Universal Peace in Truth, Justice, Charity, and Liberty,* 11 April 1963; Pope Paul VI, *Gaudium et Spes: Pastoral Constitution on the Church in the Modern World,* 7 December 1965.

51. George Weigel, *Witness to Hope: The Biography of Pope John Paul II* (New York: Cliff Street Books, 2001), 551–52.

52. Jay P. Dolan, *In Search of an American Catholicism: A History of Religion and Culture in Tension* (Oxford: Oxford University Press, 2002), 200.

53. Ibid., 202.

54. Meissner, *Cultic Origins of Christianity,* 99.

55. Ibid.

56. Ann Rodgers-Melnick, "Bishops Lauded for Progress as Conference Ends," *Post-Gazette,* 22 June 2003.

57. David O'Reilly, "Bishops Vow to Rid Church of Clergy Sex Abuse," *Philadelphia Inquirer,* 21 June 2003.

58. Kevin Murphy, "Bishops End Conference without Hearing from Victims," *Philadelphia Inquirer,* 21 June 2003.

59. Ibid.

60. Michael Paulson, "Abuse Crisis Exploited, Prelates Say," *Boston Globe,* 20 June 2003.

61. Josephs, *Character Structure,* 208.

62. Rachel Zoll, Associated Press, "Keating Says He Was Smeared," *Boston Globe,* 1 October 2003.

63. Jerry Filteau, "Former Sex Abuse Panel Head Says He Was Subject of Smear Campaign," *Catholic News Service,* 2 October 2003; Frank Keating, "The Last Straw: Quitting the Bishops' Review Board," *Crisis Magazine,* 1 October 2003.

64. Tom Hogan, "My Turn: Is It Too Late to Save the Catholic Church?" *Newsweek,* 30 June 2003; Investigative Staff of *The Boston Globe, Betrayal,* 143.

65. Richard John Neuhaus, "The Meaning of Apostolic," *First Things,* November 2003, 77.

66. Cozzens, *Changing Face of the Priesthood,* 77.

67. Josephs, *Character Structure,* 197, 198.

68. Paul E. Dinter, *The Other Side of the Altar: One Man's Life in the Catholic Priesthood* (New York: Farrar, Straus and Giroux, 2003), 199.

69. Thomas J. Reese, *Inside the Vatican: The Politics and Organization of the Catholic Church* (Cambridge: Harvard University Press, 1996), 163, 165.

70. Dinter, *Other Side of the Altar,* 185.

71. Reese Dunklin and Brooks Egerton. "Vatican Panelists Names Examined: Two Have Advised Bishops Not to Report Abusers; Some Fear a Stacked Deck," *Dallas Morning News,* 24 October 2002.

72. Ibid.

73. Dunklin and Egerton, "Vatican Panelists Names Examined"; Investigative Staff of *The Boston Globe, Betrayed,* 5; Robert Pigott, "Vatican to Reinforce Catholic Orthodoxy," *BBC News,* 8 January 2003.

74. *Argentina:* Kevin Hall, Knight Ridder, "Claim about Charity Leader Rivets Public in Argentina," *Boston Globe,* 2 December 2002; Leslie Moore, "Sex Abuse Allegations Rock Bastion of Catholicism," *Boston Globe,* 15 September 2002. *Australia:* Associated Press, "Former Catholic Priest Sentenced to More Than 10 Years' Prison for Child Sex Offenses," *Boston Globe,* 13 September 2002; "80-Year-Old Marist Brother Jailed," *Herald and Weekly Times,* 29 November 2002; Gary Hughes, "Church Abuse: The Full Picture," *The Age,* 25 May 2003. *Austria:* "St. Poelten Scandal Sees Hundreds Leaving the Catholic Church," *Die Presse,* 20 August 2004; William J. Kole, "Austrians Leave Catholic Church in Droves after Summer

of Scandal," *CBC News,* 24 September 2004. *Brazil:* John L. Allen Jr., "Sex Abuse in Brazil: Abuser Priest Provides Checklist for Selecting Victims," *National Catholic Reporter,* 21 November 2005; Raymond Collit, Reuters, "Brazil Priest Sentence Fuels Pedophilia Scandal," *San Diego Union-Tribune,* 23 November 2005. *Canada:* "Woman Sues Priest," *CBC News,* 18 February 2003; R. G. Dunlop, "Abuse by Clergy in Canada is Described: Victims Say That Country Trails U.S. in Dealing with Issues," *Courier-Journal,* 23 February 2003. *Chile:* "Catholic Priest Sentenced in Chile for Sexual Abuse," *Voice of America,* 24 June 2003. *Czechoslovakia:* "Whistleblower Wants Apology from Church," *Prague Post,* 2 April 2003. *England:* "British Cardinal Calls for Church Honesty," *Catholic News,* 24 October 2002; "Sex Shame of Priests," *Yorkshire Post Today,* 21 November 2005; Elena Curti, "High Price of Broken Trust," *Tablet,* 9 July 2005; Ruth Gledhill, "Church Pays Hush Money to Sex Abuse Victims," *Times,* 20 November 2002; Reuters, "Cardinal Makes Apology in British Priest Case," *Boston Globe,* 21 November 21, 2002; Helen Studd, Ruth Gledhill, and Claire McDonald, "Child Abuse 'Hotspots' Uncovered in Five Catholic Dioceses," *Times,* 21 November 2002. *France:* "Church in Europe Getting Ready to Fight Clergy Sex Abuse," *Catholic News,* 30 August 2002. *Germany:* Associated Press, "German Bishops OK Sex-Abuse Plan," *Dallas Morning News,* 28 September 2002; Globe Staff and Wire Services, "The World Today: Germany: Catholic Church Offers Apology for Sex Abuse," *Boston Globe,* 28 September 2002. *Hong Kong:* Helen Luk, "Former Priest in Hong Kong Convicted in Sex Abuse Case," *Boston Globe,* 28 January 2003. *Ireland:* Ireland's scandal · rivals that of the United States. Interested readers can access the archives of the *Irish Independent* from 2002 on, available at www.unison.ie/irish_independent. com. Other articles include "Priest Addresses Sex Crimes from Pulpit," *Donegal News,* 8 November 2002; Brian Lavery, "New Irish Police Squad to Investigate All Clerical Abuse Cases," *New York Times,* 22 October 2002; Charles Sennott, "Clerical Abuse Roils Ireland's Church: Allegations against Priests, Cardinal Mirror Boston Case," *Boston Globe,* 11 November 2002. *Italy:* "Italian Priest Arrested for Prostitution, Pornography," *A (Australian) BC News,* 7 May 2003; Richard Owen, "Priests and Teachers on Trial in Italy over 'Paedophile' Ring," *Times,* 19 October 2004. *Jamaica:* Barbara Gloudon, "Children's Bodies on the Auction Block," *Jamaica Observer,* 23 January 2004. *Malawi:* Brian Ligomeka, "Monsignor Tamani Supports Sexual Abuse," *Malawi Standard,* 2 January 2003. *Malta:* Karl Schembri, "Police Investigate Priests for Alleged Paedophilia in Church Institution," *Malta Independent,* 28 September 2003. *Mexico:* Associated Press, "Bishops Not to Sanction Priest Shown Having Sex in Video," *San Francisco Chronicle,* 6 January 2003; Marion Lloyd, "Priest's Accusers Pose Test for a Powerful Institution," *Boston Globe,* 22 December 2002; *Philippines:* "Church's Moral Clout Eroding," *Manila Times,* 4 June 2002; Isagani Cruz, "Culprits in the Cloister," *Inq 7 News,* 27 September 2003; Ferdinand G. Patinio, "34 Catholic Priests Suspended," *Manila Times,* 29 September 2003; *Poland:* "Priest Arrested for Child Abuse," *News 24,* 31 May 2003; Associated Press, "Faithful in Pope's Homeland Press Church to Act on Sex Abuse," *Star Tribune,* 28 September 2003; *Scotland:* Stephen Fraser, "Catholic

Church Appoints Child Protection Director," *Scotland on Sunday,* 27 April 2003. *South Africa:* "Fear in the House of God," *All Africa News,* 24 May 2003; "Church Seeks Database on Abusers," *Sunday Times,* 5 June 2003; Jonathan Ancer, "Church in Moral Crisis, Says New Archbishop," *Mercury,* 30 June 2003.

75. Associated Press, "Worldwide, 21 Roman Catholic Bishops Have Resigned amid Church Sex Scandal since 1990," *Times-Picayune,* 18 June 2003.

76. Dunklin and Egerton, "Vatican Panelists Names Examined"; Gil Donovan, "Psychologists Dispute Ratzinger's Figures," *National Catholic Reporter,* 10 January 2003.

77. Donovan, "Psychologists Dispute Ratzinger's Figures."

78. John L. Allen Jr., "Mexican Cardinal Sees Media Persecution in U.S. Scandal," *National Catholic Reporter,* 12 August 2002; Kristin Lombardi, "Law's Disgrace," *Boston Phoenix,* 20 December 2002.

79. Allen, "Mexican Cardinal Sees Media Persecution."

80. Ibid.

81. James Carroll, "One Cardinal's Old Impulse to Blame Jews," *Boston Globe,* 12 August 2003.

82. Scott Hahn, "The Paternal Order of Priests," *Lay Witness,* May/June 2003.

83. John Cornwell, *Breaking Faith: Can the Catholic Church Save Itself?* (New York: Penguin Compass, 2001), 152–54; Cozzens, *Changing Face of the Priesthood,* 12–13; Paul Lakeland, *The Liberation of the Laity: In Search of an Accountable Church* (New York: Continuum, 2003), 80–81.

84. Philip J. Murnion, "Priest: Beyond Employee, to Minister of the Sacred," *National Catholic Reporter,* 27 September 2002.

85. Ibid.

86. Ibid.

87. Richard P. McBrien, *Catholicism: New Study Edition*, rev. and updated (San Francisco: HarperSanFrancisco, 1994), 658, 744.

88. Ibid., 868.

89. Richard John Neuhaus, "The Public Square: Scandal Time III," *First Things,* August/September 2002, 93.

90. Stefanie Matteson, "Bishop Says Outreach is Key to Church's Future," *Courier News,* 7 November 2005.

91. Ibid.

CHAPTER 10   **Perpetrators, Priests, People in the Pews**

1. A. W. Richard Sipe, personal communication, October 2004.

2. Karen Terry, personal communication, January 2005.

3. John Jay College of Criminal Justice, *The Nature and Scope of the Problem of Sexual Abuse of Minors by Catholic Priests and Deacons in the United States* (Washington, DC: U.S. Conference of Catholic Bishops, 2004).

4. United States Conference of Catholic Bishops (USCCB), *Report on the Implementation of the Charter for the Protection of Children and Young People,* February 2005.

5. John Jay College, *Nature and Scope of the Problem* , 6, 7.

6. USCCB, *Report on the Implementation of the Charter,* 2.

7. John Jay College, *Nature and Scope of the Problem* , 6.

8. USCCB, *Report on the Implementation of the Charter,* 6.

9. John Jay College, *Nature and Scope of the Problem* , 72–75.

10. Ibid., 27, 30.

11. Alan Cooperman, "Kennedy Rebukes Santorum for Comments: Republican Repeats Remark Linking Scandal to Boston 'Liberalism,'" *Washington Post,* 14 July 2005.

12. Ibid.

13. Rev. James Martin, S.J., "How Could It Happen: Analysis of the Catholic Sexual Abuse Scandal," in *Predatory Priests, Silenced Victims,* ed. Mary Gail Frawley-O'Dea and Virginia Goldner (Hillsdale, NJ: Analytic Press, 2007).

14. John Jay College. *Nature and Scope of the Problem* , 24–25.

15. Jean Guccione and Doug Smith, "Study Reveals Vast Scope of Priest Abuse," *Los Angeles Times*, 13 October 2005.

16. John Jay College. *Nature and Scope of the Problem* , 40.

17. Ibid., 43.

18. Ibid.

19. Ibid., 46.

20. Stephen J. Rossetti, *A Tragic Grace: The Catholic Church and Child Sexual Abuse* (Collegeville, MN: Liturgical Press, 1996), 74; A. W. Richard Sipe, *Sex, Priests, and Power: Anatomy of a Crisis* (New York: Brunner/Mazel, 1995), 12.

21. Jan Hindman and James M. Peters, "Polygraph Testing Leads to Better Understanding of Adult and Juvenile Sexual Offenders," *Federal Probation* 65 (2001): 8–14.

22. Ibid.

23. John Jay College. *Nature and Scope of the Problem* , 51.

24. USCCB, *Report on the Implementation of the Charter*, 7.

25. Hindman and Peters, "Polygraph Testing Leads to Better Understanding."

26. Ibid.

27. USCCB, *Report on the Implementation of the Charter*, 9.

28. John Jay College, *Nature and Scope of the Problem*, 58.

29. Ibid.

30. Ibid.; USCCB, *Report on the Implementation of the Charter*, 9.

31. John Jay College, *Nature and Scope of the Problem*, 61.

32. Ibid.

33. Ibid.

34. Ibid., 62.

35. Ibid., 47.

36. Ibid., 67.

37. "Utica Priest Formally Charged with Child Porn," *Click on Detroit,* 11 June 2003; "Priest Admits Child Porn Charges," *BBC News,* 17 December 2004; "Priest Pleads Guilty to Charges of Child Porn Possession," *San Diego News,* 10 February

2005; "Priest Sentenced," *2 News*, 11 March 2005; Matthew Barakat, Associated Press, "Priest Indicted on Child Porn Charges," *WTOP Radio Network*, 15 February 2005; Gary Craig, "Priest Nabbed in Porn Inquiry: FBI Says Cleric Had Hundreds of Pictures of Children on Computer," *Democrat and Chronicle*, 11 March 2005; Brooks Egerton, "Top Catholics Subpoenaed: Lawyer Says Figures Summoned to Grand Jury in Child-Porn Case," *Dallas Morning News*, 15 March 2005; Daniel Fowler, "Jury Indicts Priest," *New Bedford Herald News*, 18 December 2004; Ron Goldwyn, "Priest Pleads Guilty to Kiddie-Porn Charges," *Philadelphia Daily News*, 24 August 2004; Allison Hantschel, "Priest: I Can't Stop Molesting Children," *Daily Southtown*, 10 December 2002; J. Harry Jones, "Ex-Pt. Loma Pastor in Child Porn Case Is Given Probation," *San Diego Union Tribune*, 11 March 2005; William J. Kole, Associated Press, "Child Porn Found at Austrian Seminary," *CNN Netscape News*, 12 July 2004; Joe Mandak, Associated Press, "Catholic Pastor Resigns over Internet Pornography Charges," *Penn Live*, 9 October 2003; Chalonda Roberts, "Priest in Court on Child Pornography Case," *WHAM News*, 14 March 2005.

38. "Priest Pleads Guilty to Charges of Child Porn Possession."

39. "Utica Priest Formally Charged with Child Porn."

40. Goldwyn, "Priest Pleads Guilty to Kiddie-Porn Charges."

41. Stephanie Sandoval, "Priest's Tip Led to Pastor's Arrest in Porn Case: He Reported Seeing Images of Nude Boys on GP Cleric's Computer," *Dallas Morning News*, 3 February 2005.

42. Kole, "Child Porn Found at Austrian Seminary"; William J. Kole, Associated Press, "Austrians Leaving Catholic Church in Droves after Summer of Scandal," *Canadian Broadcasting News*, 24 September 2004.

43. USCCB, *Report on the Implementation of the Charter*, 22.

44. A. W. Richard Sipe, *Celibacy in Crisis: The Secret World Revisited* (New York: Bunner-Routledge, 2003), 177.

45. Hantschel, "Priest: I Can't Stop Molesting Children."

46. Leslie M. Lothstein, "Psychological Theories of Pedophilia and Ephebophilia," in *Slayer of the Soul: Child Sexual Abuse and the Catholic Church,* ed. Stephen J. Rosseti (Mystic, CT: Twenty-Third Publications, 1994), 21.

47. Ibid.

48. Ibid., 33.

49. Ibid., 35.

50. Ibid.

51. Gerald E. Kohansky and Murray Cohen, "Priests Who Sexualize Male Minors: Psychodynamic, Characterological, and Clerical Cultural Situations," in *Predatory Priests, Silenced Victims,* ed. Mary Gail Frawley-O'Dea and Virginia Goldner (Hillsdale, NJ: Analytic Press, 2007); Leslie M. Lothstein, "Men of the Flesh: The Evaluation and Treatment of Sexually Abusing Priests," *Studies in Gender & Sexuality* 5 (2004): 167–95; Lothstein, "Psychological Theories of Pedophilia and Ephebophilia."

52. Ibid.

53. Kohansky and Cohen, "Priests Who Sexualize Male Minors."

54. Rossetti, *Tragic Grace*, 74–75; Sipe, *Sex, Priests, and Power*, 12.

55. Donna J. Markham and Samuel F. Mikail, "Perpetrators of Clergy Abuse: Insights from Attachment Theory," *Studies in Gender & Sexuality* 5 (2004): 197–212.

56. Daniel Gensler, "Entitlement, Temptation and Betrayal from a Psychoanalytic Perspective," paper presented at Sexual Betrayal and Scandal in the Catholic Church: Psychoanalytic, Religious, and Social Perspectives, New York, New York, 13 November 2004.

57. Gregory Kesich, "Ex-Priest Breaks Code of Silence," *Portland Press Herald/Maine Sunday Telegram,* 31 July 2005.

58. Ibid.

59. David Gibson, *The Coming Catholic Church: How the Faithful Are Shaping a New American Catholicism* (San Francisco: HarperSanFrancisco, 2003), 212.

60. Julia Duin, "Silenced Priest Warns of Gay Crisis," *Washington Times*, 15 November 2004.

61. Bob Egelko, "Court: Whistle-Blower Priest Can Sue San Francisco Arhcdiocese," *San Francisco Chronicle*, 3 January 2003.

62. "Diocese Downplays Abuse Scope: Cases Show Patterns of Suppression by Bishop," *Arizona Republic*, 10 November 2002.

63. Nancy Phillips, Mark Fazlollah, and Craig R. McCoy, "Priest: Silence Ordered on Abuse," *Philadelphia Inquirer*, 7 August 2005.

64. Bill Wineke, "Arrogance of Bishops Is Appalling," *Wisconsin State Journal*, 20 April 2004.

65. Arthur Jones, "Chaplain's Military Career Ends in Dispute," *National Catholic Reporter,* 29 April 2004.

66. Elizabeth A. Johnson, *Truly Our Sister: A Theology of Mary in the Communion of Saints* (New York: Continuum, 2003), 307.

67. Ibid.

68. Ibid.

69. Eugene Kennedy, *The Unhealed Wound: The Church, the Priesthood, and the Question of Sexuality* (New York: St. Martin's Press, 2002), 16.

70. Ibid., 125.

71. Ibid., 112–23.

72. Ibid., 118.

73. Ibid., 122

74. Gail Gibson and Laura Vozzella, "In Catonsville, a Parish Copes with Disclosures from Its Past: Archdiocese List Named 56 Accused of Sex Abuse; 6 Had Served at St. Mark," *Baltimore Sun*, 13 October 2002.

75. Ibid.

76. Ibid.

77. Megan Twohey, "Two Parishes, Two Responses to Sexual Abuse by Priest: One Church Searches for Other Possible Victims," *Milwaukee Journal-Sentinel*, 5 February 2004.

78. Ibid.

79. Mike Newell, "Thy Kingdom Come, Thy Will Be Done," *Philadelphia Weekly*, 19 October 2003.

80. Associated Press, "Polish Community Raising Money for Accused Priest," *Advocate*, 6 January 2003; Ken Byron and Bill Leukhardt, "Priest Held in Sex Assault," *Hartford Courant*, 27 December 2002; Joann Klimkiewicz and Bill Leukhardt, "Priest Released after Group Raises Bail," *Hartford Courant*, 18 January 2003.

81. Ibid.

82. Associated Press, "Polish Community Raising Money."

83. Ibid.

84. Ibid.

85. David France, *Our Fathers: The Secret Life of the Catholic Church in an Age of Scandal* (New York: Broadway Books, 2004), 332.

86. Ibid., 229.

87. Laurie J. Ferguson, "A Protestant Response to Sexual Abuse," in *Predatory Priests, Silenced Victims,* ed. Mary Gail Frawley-O'Dea and Virginia Goldner (Hillsdale, NJ: Analytic Press, 2007); Anne F. C. Richards, "Sexual Misconduct by Clergy in the Episcopal Church," *Studies in Gender & Sexuality* 5 (2004): 139–66.

88. Richards, "Sexual Misconduct by Clergy," 147.

89. Ferguson, "Protestant Response to Sexual Abuse."

90. Ibid.

CHAPTER 11 The Secret Is Revealed

1. David Finkelhor, *Child Sexual Abuse: New Theory and Research* (New York: Free Press, 1984), 1–3; Diana E. H. Russell, *The Secret Trauma: Incest in the Lives of Girls and Women* (New York: Basic Books, 1986), 59–74; A. Urquiza and L. M. Keating, "The Prevalence of Sexual Victimization in Males," in *The Sexually Abused Male*, vol. 1, ed. Mic Hunter (Boston: Lexington Books, 1990), 89–104; Gail E. Wyatt, "The Sexual Abuse of Afro-American and White Women in Childhood," *Child Abuse & Neglect* 9 (1985): 507–19.

2. Judith L. Alpert, ed., *Sexual Abuse Recalled: Treating Trauma in the Era of the Recovered Memory Debate* (Northvale, NJ: Aronson, 1995); John Briere, *Therapy for Adults Molested as Children: Beyond Survival* (New York: Springer Publishing, 1989); Daniel Brown, Alan W. Scheflin, and D. Corydon Hammond, *Memory, Trauma, Treatment, and the Law: An Essential Reference on Memory for Clinicians, Researchers, Attorneys, and Judges* (New York: Norton, 1998); Christine A. Courtois, *Healing the Incest Wound* (New York: Norton, 1988); Jody Messler Davies and Mary Gail Frawley, *Treating the Adult Survivor of Childhood Sexual Abuse: A Psychoanalytic Perspective* (New York: Basic Books, 1994); Ramon C. Ganzarin and Bonnie J. Buchele, *Fugitives of Incest: A Perspective from Psychoanalysis and Groups* (Guilford, CT: International Universities Press, 1988); Richard B. Gartner, *Betrayed as Boys: Psychodynamic Treatment of Sexually Abused Men* (New York: Guilford Press, 1999);

Denise Gelinas, "The Persisting Negative Effect of Incest," *Psychiatry* 46 (1983): 312–32; Judith L. Herman, *Trauma and Recovery* (New York: Basic Books, 1992); Derek Jehu, *Beyond Sexual Abuse* (New York: Wiley, 1988); Richard P. Kluft, ed., *Incest Related Syndromes of Adult Psychopathology* (Washington, DC: American Psychiatric Press, 1990); Ruth S. Kempe and C. Henry Kempe, *The Common Secret: Sexual Abuse of Children and Adolescents* (New York: Freeman, 1984); Selma Kramer and Salman Akhtar, eds., *The Trauma of Transgression* (Northvale, NJ: Aronson, 1991); Henry Krystal, *Integration and Self-Healing: Affect, Trauma, Alexithymia* (Hillsdale, NJ: Analytic Press, 1988); Haroold B. Levine, ed., *Adult Analysis and Childhood Sexual Abuse* (Hillsdale, NJ: Analytic Press, 1990); Mike Lew, *Victims No Longer: Men Recovering from Incest and Other Sexual Abuse* (New York: Nevraumont, 1988); Wendy Maltz and Beverly Holman, *Incest and Sexuality: A Guide to Understdanding and Healing* (Lexington, MA: Lexington, 1987); Laurie Ann Pearlman and Karen W. Saakvitne, *Trauma and the Therapist: Countertransference and Vicarious Traumatization in Psychotherapy with Incest Survivors* (New York: Norton, 1995); Frank Putnam, *The Diagnosis and Treatment of Multiple Personality Disorder* (New York: Guilford Press, 1989); Susan Roth and Ronald Batson, *Naming the Shadows: A New Approach to Individual and Group Psychotherapy for Adult Survivors of Childhood Sexual Abuse* (New York: Free Press, 1997); Leonard Shengold, *Soul Murder* (New Haven: Yale University Press, 1989); Alan Sugarman, ed., *Victims of Abuse: The Emotional Impact of Child and Adult Trauma* (Guilford, CT: International Universities Press, 1994); Bessel van der Kolk, *Psychological Trauma* (Washington, DC: American Psychiatric Press, 1987); Bessel van der Kolk, Alexander C. McFarlane, and Lars Weisaeth, eds., *Traumatic Stress: The Effects of Overwhelming Experience on Mind, Body, and Society* (New York: Guilford Press, 1996); Elizabeth A. Waites, *Trauma and Survival: Post-Traumatic and Dissociative Disorders in Women* (New York: Norton, 1993).

3. Louise Armstrong, *Kiss Daddy Goodnight: A Speak-Out on Incest* (New York: Bocket Books, 1978); Elly Danica, *Beyond Don't: Dreaming Past the Dark* (Charlottetown, P.E.I.: Gynergy Press, 1996); Sister Vera Gallagher with William F. Dodds, *Speaking Out, Fighting Back: Personal Experiences of Women who Survived Childhood Sexual Abuse in the Home* (Seattle: Madrona, 1985); Anne Heche, *Call Me Crazy* (New York: Scribner, 2001); Lew, *Victims No Longer*; Toni A. McNaronand Yarrow Morgan, eds., *Voices in the Night: Women Speaking about Incest* (Pittsburgh: Cleis Press, 1982); Elizabeth Ward, *Father-Daughter Rape* (New York: Grove Press, 1995).

4. John Cornwell, *Breaking Faith: Can the Catholic Church Save Itself?* (New York: Penguin Compass, 2001), 107, 112.

5. William V. Antiono, "American Catholics from John Paul II to Benedict XVI," *National Catholic Reporter*, 30 September 2005.

6. Paul Dokecki, *The Clergy Sexual Abuse Crisis: Reform and Renewal in the Catholic Community* (Washington, DC: Georgetown University Press, 2004), 145.

7. Philip Jenkins, *Pedophiles and Priests: Anatomy of a Contemporary Crisis* (Oxford: Oxford University Press, 1996), 59.

8. Ibid., 61.

9. Jim Clarke, "Speak out on the Catholic Church Scandal," *Canton Journal*, 5 June 2003; Mike Nichols, "Media Shared Shame over Silence," *Milwaukee Journal-Sentinel*, 7 June 2003.

10. Jason Berry, *Lead Us Not into Temptationl: Catholic Priests and the Sexual Abuse of Children* (Urbana: University of Illinois Press, 2000),190.

11. Investigative Staff of *The Boston Globe. Betrayal: The Crisis in the Catholic Church* (Boston: Little, Brown and Company, 2002), 7.

12. Jenkins, *Pedophiles and Priests*, 15.

13. Berry, *Lead Us Not into Temptation*, 33.

14. Jenkins, *Pedophiles and Priests*, 106–7.

15. Terry Mattingly, Scripps Howard News Service, "Top 10 Religion Stories for 2002," *Florida's Treasure Coast and Palm Beach News*, 28 December 2002.

16. Ibid.

17. Associated Press, "Globe Wins for Work on Abuse by Clergy," *Boston Globe*, 26 October 2002; *Globe* Staff, "Globe Wins Award for Reporting," *Boston Globe*, 4 February 2003.

18. *Globe* Staff, "Globe Receives Selden Ring Award," *Boston Globe*, 25 February 2003; Associated Press, "Pultizer Honors Globe's Priest Reporting," *New York Newsday*, 7 April 2003.

19. "DMN Journalists Honored for Legal Reporting," *Dallas Morning News*, 11 October 2005.

20. Stephen O'Leary, "A Tangled Web: New Media and the Catholic Scandals," *USC Annenberg Journalism Review*, 6 August 2002.

21. Thomas C. Fox, "Web Site Sheds Light on Media Fascination with Abuse Crisis," *National Catholic Reporter*, 12 August 2002.

22. Tim Drake, "Catholics Are 'Blogging' on the Internet . . . to Evangelize," *Catholic.net*, 12 June 2002.

23. Jack Kenny, "Jack Kenny: Did Police Aid the Church's 'Abettors'?" *Union Leader/New Hampshire Sunday News*, 9 March 2003.

24. Ibid.

25. Associated Press, "Paper: Police Helped Hide Abuse Claims," *Wired News*, 31 July 2005; Joe Mahr and Mitch Weiss, "Authorities Abetted Diocese in Hiding Sexual-Abuse Cases," *Toledo Blade*, 31 July 2005; Michael D. Sallah D. and David Yonke, "Shame, Sin and Secrets," *Toledo Blade*, 1 December 2002.

26. Mahr and Weiss, "Authorities Abetted Diocese."

27. Ibid.

28. Ibid.

29. Tom Mashberg, "Hub Ex-Vicar: Police Gave Church Leeway on Abuse," *Boston Herald*, 29 October 2002.

30. Reese Dunklin and Brooks Egerton, "Runaway Priests," *Dallas Morning News*, 5 December 2004.

31. Frank Bruni and Elinor Burkett, *A Gospel of Shame: Children, Sexual Abuse, and the Catholic Church* (New York: Perennial, 2002), 126.

32. Ibid., 128.

33. Ibid., 127.

34. Ibid.

35. David Schimke, "True Believer," *City Pages*, 16 August 2003.

36. Ember Reichgott Junge, "Jeffrey R. Anderson," *Minnesota Lawyer*, 27 January 2003.

37. Dvaid France, *Our Fathers: The Secret Life of the Catholic Church in an Age of Scandal* (New York: Broadway Books, 2004), 216.

38. Associated Press, "Some Major Settlements in Catholic Clergy Sexual Abuse Cases," *Salt Lake City National Wire*, 6 August 2005.

39. Jennifer Levitz, "Holy War," *Providence Journal*, 29 December 2002.

40. Ibid.

41. Associated Press, "Some Major Settlements."

42. Levitz, "Holy War."

43. Gustavo Arrelano, "The Army of God," *Orange County Weekly*, 13–19 August 2004.

44. Ibid.

45. Thomas P. Reilly, *The Sexual Abuse of Children in the Roman Catholic Archdiocese of Boston: Executive Summary and Scope of Investigation*, 5.

46. Rosanne Bonventre, *Grand Jury Report, CP2 § 190.85 (1) (c)*, 172.

47. Lynne Abraham, *Report of the Grand Jury in the Court of Common Pleas, First Judicial District of Pennsylvania, Criminal Trial Division*, 15 September 2005, 1–4.

48. Ibid., 1.

49. Peter Heed, N. William Delker, and James D. Rosenberg, *Report on the Investigation of the Diocese of Manchester*, 3 March 2003, Office of the Attorney General, Concord, MA, 1.

50. Joseph A. Reaves, "Bishop O'Brien Admits Cover-up in Sexual Abuse Cases," *Arizona Republic*, 2 June 2003; "Text of the Agreement (between Maricopa County Attorney Rick Romley, Bishop Thomas O'Brien, and the Roman Catholic Diocese of Phoenix)," *Arizona Republic*, 2 June 2003.

51. "Archdiocese of Cincinnati Guilty of Failing to Report Child Sexual Abuse by Priests," *Dayton Daily News*, 20 November 2003; Laurie Goodstein, "Archdiocese of Cincinnati Fined in Sexual Abuse Scandal," *New York Times*, 21 November 2003; Dan Horn, "Archdiocese Found Guilty of Failing to Report Abuse: No-Contest Plea Ends 2-Year Church Investigation," *Cincinnati Enquirer*, 21 November 2003.

52. Ibid.

53. "Archdiocese's Plea Deal: A Cleansing Act," *Cincinnati Enquirer*, 21 November 2003.

54. Daniel Barbarisi, "Mass. Prosecutor Lists Names of 21 Alleged Abusive Priests," *Providence Journal*, 27 September 2002.

55. Gregg M. Milote, "Accounts Conflict over Diocese's Cooperation," *Herald News*, 27 September 2002.

56. Grace Lee, "L.A. Cardinal under Fire," *Los Angeles Daily News*, 2 November

2002; Arthur Jones, "L.A. District Attorney Seeks Access to All Abuse Files," *National Catholic Reporter*, 7 March 2003.

57. Associated Press, "L.A. Church Abuse Testimony to Go Public," *1010 WINS*, 31 August 2005; Robin Erb, "Secret Archives at Heart of Abuse; Group Says Files Hold Key to Abuse," *Toledo Blade*, 6 March 2003; Joseph A. Reaves, "Unsung Judges Lead Way in Priest Investigations," *Arizona Republic*, 23 February 2003; David Weber, "Judge at Center of Sad Saga," *Boston Herald*, 15 December 2002.

58. Janet I. Tu and Jonathan Martin, "Spokane Churches Can Be Sold to Pay Debt, Judge Rules," *Seattle Times*, 27 August 2005.

59. Ibid.

60. Sarah Kershaw, "Rare Kind of Scandal Accord in Spokane Diocese," *New York Times*, 2 February 2006.

61. Steve Woodward, "Archdiocese of Portland Parishes Will Join Dispute," *Oregonian*, 1 July 2005; Ashbel S. Green and Steve Woodward, "Judge Says Archdiocese Owns Parishes, Schools," *Oregonian*, 30 December 2005.

62. Daniel Barrick, "State Aims for Tougher Abuse Laws," *Concord Monitor*, 5 March 2003; Rudolph Bush, "End Urged for State's Abuse-Case Time Limits," *Chicago Tribune*, 11 March 2003; "Tweaking Abuse Legislation," *Milwaukee Journal Sentinel*, 26 January 2003; Howard Fischer, "Bill Adds to Scrutiny for Sexual Offenders," *Arizona Daily Star*, 27 February 2003; Marci Hamilton, "Will State Legislatures Stand up to the Catholic Church and Pass Strong Anti-Child Abuse Laws?" *Find Law*, 24 February 2003; Jennifer Kingsley, "Schuyler Attorney to Testify about Sex Abuse," *Ithaca Journal*, 20 May 2003; Patricia Montemurri, "Church in Jeopardy of More Suits: Bill Would Provide No Time Limit for Alleged Abuse Victims to Act," *Detroit Free Press*, 12 August 2003; Ruben Rosario, "Childhood Sex-Abuse Liability," *Pioneer Press*, 14 May 2003; Kathleen A. Shaw, "Push Is on for Sex Crimes Bill," *Worcester Telegram & Gazette*, 19 November 2002; Jim Siegel, "State Aim: Curb Priest Sex Abuse," *Marion Star*, 17 June 2003; Peter Smith and Debbie Yetter, "Bill Eases Path for Child Sex-Abuse Suits," *Courier-Journal*, 15 January 2003; Janet I. Tu, "Victims' Advocated Argue Bill Must be Retroactive," *Seattle Times*, 22 January 2003.

63. Darren M. Allen, "Clergy Added to List of Mandatory Reporters," *Times Argus*, 30 April 2003; Associated Press, "Clergy May Be Required to Report Child Abuse Claims," *Olympian*, 9 March 2003; Daniel Barrick, "Lawmakers: Clergy Are Not Exempt," *Concord Monitor*, 12 February 2003; Bill Barrow, "Bill: Clergy Must Report Abuse," *Everything Alabama*, 9 April 2003; Howard Fischer, "Bill Adds to Scrutiny for Sexual Offenders," *Arizona Daily Star*, 27 February 2003; Steve Schultze and Marie Rhode, "State May Require Clergy to Report Abuse," *Milwaukee Journal-Sentinel*, 10 January 2003; Jim Siegel, "State May Try to Curb Sex Abuse Secrecy," *Telegraph-Forum*, 14 June 2003; Janet I. Tu, "Legislation to Protect Minors Introduced," *Seattle Times*, 17 January 2003; Charles Wolfe, Associated Press, "Ky. Bill to Repeal Clergy 'Silent Right,'" *New York Newsday*, 10 January 2003.

64. Brendan Farrington, Associated Press, "Bill Alllowing Lawsuits for Long-Age Child Abuse All but Dead," *Sun Sentinel*, 10 April 2003; Rachel Zoll, Associated Press, "Bills on Child Sex Abuse Languish Despite Public Anger over Crisis in Catholic Church," *San Francisco Chronicle*, 4 March 2003.

65. Lois Burling, Associated Press, "Leading Voice for Abuse Victims Says She Was Molested while at the Air Force Academy," *Star Tribune*, 15 July 2003; Bruni and Burkett, *A Gospel of Shame*, 247.

66. Burling, "Leading Voice for Abuse Victims."

67. "The Healing Alliance: Discovering Life beyond Abuse," *Linkup Website*, www.thelinkup.org.

68. "Philosophy of the Farm," *Linkup Website*, www.thelinkup.org.

69. David H. Kelsey, "Redeeming Sam," *Christian Century*, 28 June 2005, 24.

70. Bill Frogameni, "Victims' Advocate," *Toledo City Paper*, 24 April–5 May 2004.

71. "SNAP Mission Statement," *Survivor Network for those Abused by Priests Website*, www.snapnetwork.org.

72. The following are just a few examples: Associated Press, "Groups Say Bishop Ignoring Abuse Policy," *Hartford Courant*, 19 December 2003; L. Briscoe, "Victim Group Asks Church to Reward Tipsters," *Los Angeles Times*, 6 July 2003; Julia Duin, "Victims' Group Hits Church Audit," *Washington Times*, 6 January 2004; Carol Eisenberg, "Victims: Abuse Report Not a Fair Picture," *New York Newsday*, 6 January 2004; Katie Nelson, "Victims Network Asks Diocese for 'Concrete Steps,'" *Arizona Republic*, 4 July 2003; Bonnie Miller Rubin, "Resignation 'A Great Day for Survivors,'" *Chicago Tribune*, 14 December 2002; David Yonke, "Toledo Diocese Orders Limit on Victim Therapy," *Toledo Blade*, 4 September 2004.

73. Theresa Monsour, "Priest Abuse Victims Ask Area Faithful to Help Push for Talk," *Pionneer Press*, 12 January 2003; Michelle Munz, "Group Takes Its Message on Clergy Abuse to Ballpark," *St. Louis Post-Dispatch*, 22 June 2003.

74. Maya Kemen, "Rodimer Draws Critic's Praise," *North Jersey News*, 13 November 2002; Tod Sweeney, "Six Courageous Priests Praised by Abuse Victims," *Religious News*, 25 November 2003.

75. Wendy Davis, "End to Time Limits in Abuse Cases Urged," *Boston Globe*, 11 April 2003; Krystal Knapp, "Priest Sex Victims Want No Statute of Limitations," *Everything Jersey*, 5 December 2002; Stephen Scott, "Minnesota: Victims: Extend Time to File Suit," *Pioneer Press*, 1 February 2003; Warren Wolfe, "Angered by 'Disrepectful' Agenda, Flynn Cancels Meeting with SNAP," *Star Tribune*, 5 April 2003.

76. Associated Press, "Clergy-Abuse Support Group Ignites Debate," *MSNBC*, 18 December 2004.

77. Ibid.

78. Amy Green, "Clergy Abuse Victims Seek out Some Peace at the Farm in Ky," *Boston Globe*, 19 July 2004.

79. Daniel Lyons, "Paid to Picket," *Forbes Mazagine*, 15 September 2003.

80. Associated Press, "Clergy-Abuse Support Group Ignites Debate."

81. Ibid.

82. Anne Rodgers-Melnick, "Bishops Doing Little on Abuse, Group Charges," *Post-Gazette*, 19 June 2003; Maureen Turner, "Calling Church Leaders to Task," *Valley Advocate*, 1 January 2004.

83. Ibid.

84. www.bishop-accountability.org; Turner, "Calling Church Leaders to Task."

85. www.survivorsfirst.org; www.bishop-accountability.org.

86. Patrick J. Buchanan, "An Index of Catholicism's Decline," *World Net Daily Commentary*, 11 December 2002; Jenkins, *Pedophiles and Priests*, 102, 104; Richard P. McBrien, "Reformers and Restorationists," *Essays in Theology*, 1 May 2000.

87. Buchanan, "Index of Catholicism's Decline"; David Kocieniewski, "In New Jersey, an Archbishop Conservative and Controversial," *New York Times*, 30 May 2004.

88. Carol Eisenberg, "Suit Charges Seminary with Pro-Gay Teachings," *New York Newsday*, 21 January 2003; Peter Steinfels, "Excerpt: A Church at Risk," *Sojourners Magazine*, July-August 2003; George Weigel, "Catholic Church Must Lose the Psychobabble," *Los Angeles Times*, 17 December 2002.

89. Jenkins, *Pedophiles and Priests*, 102; Steinfels, "Excerpt: A Church at Risk"; Weigel, "Catholic Church Must Lose the Psychobabble."

90. Gil Donovan, "Some See Big Reforms on the Horizon," *National Catholic Reporter*, 19 July 2002; Steinfels, "Excerpt: A Church at Risk."

91. Karl Maurer, "Rev. Joseph Fession, S.J.: Bishops' Dereliction Made This Spiritual Crisis Possible," *Catholic Citizens of Illinois*, 18 September 2002.

92. Weigel, "Catholic Church Must Lose the Psychobabble."

93. Cornwell, *Breaking Faith*.

94. Donovan, "Some See Big Reforms on the Horizon"; Jenkins, *Pedophiles and Priests*, 105; Mark Silk, "Catholic Controversy II: Handling Pedophilia," *Religion in the News*, Fall 1998; Steinfels, "Excerpt: A Church at Risk."

95. Donovan, "Some See Big Reforms on the Horizon"; Jenkins, *Pedophiles and Priests*; Steinfels, "Excerpt: A Church at Risk."

96. Donovan, "Some See Big Reforms on the Horizon"; Steinfels, "Excerpt: A Church at Risk."

97. Jenkins, *Pedophiles and Priests*, 105; Steinfels, "Excerpt: A Church at Risk."

98. James Carroll, *Toward a New Catholic Church: The Promise of Reform* (Boston: Houghton Mifflin, 2002), 64, 65, 103.

99. Richard P. McBrien, "The Popes and Wal-Mart on Labor Union," *Tidings*, 13 December 2002.

100. Donovan, "Some See Big Reforms on the Horizon."

101. E. J. Dionne Jr., "Rebuked by Rome," *Washington Post*, 22 October 2002.

102. Alan Cooperman, "Bishop Says Priest Abused Him as Teenager," *Washington Post*, 11 January 2006.

103. Ibid.

104. Greg Bullough, "Gumbleton's Disclosure Underscores Differences between Survivors, Bishops," *National Catholic Reporter*, 27 January 2006.

105. Patricia Montemurri, "Bishop, Diocese Dispute Efforts," *Detroit Free Press*, 16 January 2006; Cooperman, "Bishop Says Priest Abused Him as Teenager."

106. Montemurri, "Bishop, Diocese Dispute Efforts."

107. Revs. Robert Bullock, Walter Cuenin, Paul Kilroy, John McGinty, Gerry Osterman, Thomas Powers, Daniel Riley, and Dennis Sheehan, "A Forum for Reflection and Study for Priests," *Boston Globe*, 11 April 2002.

108. *Herald* Staff, "Protest Letter Seeks Resignation," *Boston Herald*, 8 December 2002.

109. Tom Mashberg, "Priests Eye Call for Law to Quit," *Boston Herald*, 7 December 2002.

110. Dick Ryan, "Priests Voice Range of Concerns in Effort to Organize in New York," *National Catholic Reporter*, 25 October 2002, 6.

111. Bruce Lambert, "L.I. Bishop Meets Priests Critical of His Leadership," *New York Times*, 20 January 2004.

112. Monica Davey, "Milwaukee Priests Seek End to Celibacy Rule," *New York Times*, 20 August 2003.

113. Daniel J. Wakin, "Catholic Group Asks for Married Priests," *New York Times*, 28 April 2004.

114. "Priests' Tough Questions Are a Service to Their People," (editorial), *National Catholic Reporter*, 9 January 2004.

115. "Tracking Wayward Shepherds," *New York Times*, 15 February 2003.

116. Benjamin Gedan, "Outspoken Newton Priest Gets Ovation," *Boston Globe*, 9 December 2002; Bill Zajac, "Priest Sees Redemption in Change," *Mass Live*, 23 October 2002.

117. Zajac, "Priest Sees Redemption in Change."

118. Jeff Diamant, "Victims Group Denounces Firing of Priest," *Star Ledger*, 28 May 2003.

119. Bill Zajac, "Scahill Chosen 'Priest of Integrity,'" *Mass Live*, 4 June 2004.

120. Ibid.

121. Associated Press, "Pastor Criticizes Springfield Diocese Handling of Sex Abuse," *Mass Live*, 17 February 2003.

122. Rita Ciolli, "A Priest Repents for His Bretheren," *New York Newsday*, 17 February 2003.

123. Michael Miller, "Priests Seek Probe of Bishops," *Peoria Journal Star*, 6 June 2004.

124. Tom Roberts, "Healing a Betrayed Community," *National Catholic Reporter*, 4 June 2002. The passage from Matthew is as follows: "If any of you puts a stumbling block before one of these little ones who believe in me, it would be better if a great millstone were fastened around your neck and you were drowned in the depth of the sea."

125. David O'Reilly and Jim Remsen, "Priests Reportedly Chastise Cardinal," *Philadelphia Inquirer*, 28 September 2005.

126. Ibid.

127. Ryan, "Priests Voice Range of Concerns."

128. Rev. Mike Erwin, Archdiocese of Milwaukee, personal communication, October 2005; Msgr. Pflomm, Diocese of Rockville Center, personal communication, October 2005.

129. Msgr. Pflomm, Diocese of Rockville Center, personal communication, October 2005.

130. Scott Brooks, "NH Priest Praised by Church Victims Group," *Union Leader/New Hampshire Sunday News*, 13 November 2003.

131. "New Phoenix Bishop Orders Priests to Disassociate from Gay Document," *Life Site Daily News,* 28 April 2004.

132. Gil Donovan, "Priests Say Bishop Issues Gag Order," *National Catholic Reporter*, 14 March 2003.

133. Matt Viser, "Priest Was Eyed for Ouster Prior to Audit," *Boston Globe*, 20 October 2005.

134. Michael Paulson, "Dislocation, Scrutiny of Priests Raise Fears," *Boston Globe*, 2 October 2005.

135. Ibid.

136. Ibid.

137. "Priests' Tough Questions Are a Service to Their People," *National Catholic Reporter*, 9 January 2004, 2.

138. Tim O'Neill, "Scandal Rocks the Church, but Faith Remains," *St. Louis Post Dispatch*, 21 June 2003.

139. Ibid.

140. Dalia Sussman, "Church Losing Confidence," *ABC News*, 18 December 2002.

141. Ann McFeatters, "Church Reforms Needed, Poll of Catholics Shows," *Pittsburgh Post-Gazette*, 14 November 2003.

142. David Briggs, "Mistrust Lingers after Sex Abuse Scandal," *Charlotte Observer*, 4 December 2004.

143. Mary L. Gautier, "Lay Catholics Firmly Committed to Parish Life, Table 8," *National Catholic Reporter*, 30 September 2005.

144. Theo Emery, "Keating Says Church Should Embrace Reform Groups," *Boston Globe*, 4 October 2002.

145. Sam Dillon, "Church's Accounting of Abuse Is Criticized," *New York Times*, 8 December 2002; Pam Belluck, "Official Tells Catholics: Fight Abuse with Purse and Feet," *New York Times*, 5 October 2002.

146. Belluck, "Official Tells Catholics."

147. Laurie Goodstein, "Chief of Panel on Priest Abuse Will Step Down," *New York Times*, 16 June 2003.

148. Ibid.

149. David Briggs, "Catholics Urged to Stay Vigilant in Battle against Child Sex Abuse," *Cleveland Plain Dealer*, 3 March 2003.

150. Sara Toth, "Catholic Investigator Says Lay People Are Key to Recovery," *South Bend Tribune*, 21 January 2005.

151. Briggs, "Catholics Urged to Stay Vigilant."

152. Ibid.

153. Ann Rodgers, "Dean Shocked by How Other Dioceses Failed to Discipline Abusing Priests," *Post-Gazette*, 19 June 2005.

154. Charu Gupta and Christopher J. Kelly, "Demonstrators Picket Timlin," *Scranton Times-Tribune*, 3 February 2003.

155. Rita Ciolli, Bart Jones, and Erin Texeira, "Parishioners Lambaste Murphy in Sex Cases," *Newsday*, 28 April 2004; Frank Eltman, Associated Press, "Lay Group Leaders Call for LI Bishop's Resignation," *Boston Globe*, 25 July 2003.

156. Peter Smith, "Members Protest at Cathedral: Catholic Critics Want Bishops Accountable for Priest's Actions," *Courier-Journal*, 24 February 2003; Peter Smith, "Petitions Call for Archbishop to Resign: Organizers Fault Kelly's Handling of Abuse Cases," *Courier-Journal*, 14 May 2003.

157. Tom Beyerlein and Jim DeBrosse, "Catholic Leader Urged to Resign," *Dayton Daily News*, 26 November 2003.

158. Associated Press, "Group Asks Vatican to Oust N.H. Bishop," *Boston Globe*, 9 November 2003; Douglas Belkin, "Protesters Aim to Force N.H. Bishop to Step Down," *Boston Globe*, 27 January 2003; Kathryn Marchocki, "Group's Petition Seeks Resignation of Bishop," *Union Leader/New Hampshire Sunday News*, 25 July 2003.

159. Brooks Egerton, "Laymen Say Bishop Cut Deal in '97 to Go," *Dallas Morning News*, 26 January 2003; Brooks Egerton and R. Dunklin, "Lay Group Says Grahmann Should Go," *Dallas Morning News*, 20 June 2003.

160. Michael S. Rosenwald, "Cathedral Demonstration: Protesters Vow to Keep it Up," *Boston Globe*, 16 December 2002.

161. Barb Ickes, "Parish Writes Bishop about Abuse Concerns," *Quad-City Times*, 2 January 2002.

162. David Hernandez, "Sex Abuse Protesters Bring Cross, Photos to Cathedral," *Los Angeles Times*, 2 June 2003; Arthur Jones, "Abuse Victim in Holy Week Fast outside Los Angeles Cathedral," *National Catholic Reporter*, 17 April 2003.

163. Ala Scher Zagier, "Priest Scandal Depresses Dioceses Budget Already Hurting from Feeble Economy," *Naples Daily News*, 20 July 2003.

164. Frederick Cusick, "Crowd Members Lash out at Cardinal at Villanova," *Philadelphia Inquirer*, 27 September 2005.

165. Ibid.

166. Emily Lounsberry and J. Remsen, "Parishioners Vent Anger at Clergy over Abuse," *Philadelphia Inquirer*, 27 October 2005; Karin Williams, "Priest Abuse Discussed," *Phoenixville News*, 30 September 2005.

167. Matt Viser and Michael Paulson, "New Pastor Will Leave Embattled Newton Parish," *Boston Globe*, 1 February 2006.

168. Kevin Cullen, "Lay Group Requests to Engage O'Malley," *Boston Globe*, 29 July 2003.

169. Susan Hogan/Albach, "Web Site Supports Embattled Bishop," *Dallas Morning News*, 2 July 2003.

170. Alexa Capeloto and P. Montemurri, "Group Raises Funds to Help Some Priests Accused in Sex Cases," *Detroit Free Press*, 23 September 2002.

171. Peter Smith, "Online Praise Piles up for Priests," *Courier-Journal*, 24 November 2002.

172. John Chadwick, "Members Say Lay Group Not Anti-Catholic," *North Jersey.com*, 12 October 2002; Karen Kennedy-Hall, "Local Group Banned from Meeting at Churches," *Courier-Post*, 18 October 2002; Michael Paulson, "Push Is on to Quell Voice of Faithful," *Boston Globe*, 7 August 2002.

173. Laurie Goodstein, "At Seminary, New Ways for a New Generation," *New York Times*, 25 March 2002; Andrew Greeley, "Young Fogeys," *Atlantic Monthly*, January/February 2002.

174. James D. Davidson, "Belief in Church as Mediator Slips," *National Catholic Reporter*, 30 September 2005.

175. Dean R. Hoge, "Center of Catholic Identity," *National Catholic Reporter*, 30 September 2005.

Epilogue

1. Jay Levine, "Archdiocese May Have Been Warned about Priest," *CBS Chicago*, 28 January 2006.

2. Ibid.

3. Jay Levine, CBS 2 reporter, personal communication, February 2006.

4. Material about Daniel McCormack at Holy Family parish is taken from Cathleen Falsani and Frank Main, "Nun: I Reported Priest in 2000," *Chicago-Sun Times*, 26 January 2006.

5. Ibid.

6. Ibid.

7. Information about DCFS and the archdiocese relies on Ofelia Casillas and Manya A. Brachear, "DCFS Vows New Policy for Priest Abuse Cases," *Chicago-Tribune*, 23 February 2006.

8. Cathleen Falsani, "Contrite Cardinal Offers Answers," *Chicago Sun-Times*, 29 January 2006.

9. Ibid.

10. Casillas and Brachear, "DCFS Vows New Policy."

11. Gretchen Ruethling, "Board Urged Archdiocese to Pull Priest, Official Says," *New York Times*, 25 February 2006.

12. Ibid.

13. Manya A. Brachear, "Cardinal: Process 'Failed' in Abuse Case," *Chicago Tribune*, 29 January 2006.

14. Ibid.

15. "Report: Cardinal Warned of McCormack's Abuses," *NBC 5*, 24 February 2006.

16. Casillas and Brachear, "DCFS Vows New Policy."

17. Levine, "Archdiocese May Have Been Warned."

18. "Investigation of Accused Priest Widening," *CBS 2*, 22 February 2006.

19. Manya A. Brachear, "Cardinal Faces Angry Parishioners," *Chicago Tribune*, 30 January 2006.

20. Carla K. Johnson, Associated Press, "Cardinal: Mistakes Were Made," *Chicago Sun-Times*, 28 January 2006.

21. Jay Levine, "Church Places Some Blame on DCFS in Sex Scandal," *CBS 2*, 22 February 2006.

22. Brachear, "Cardinal: Process 'Failed' in Abuse Case."

23. David Heinzmann and Manya A. Brachear, "George Takes the Defensive," *Chicago Tribune*, 27 January 2006.

24. Falsani,; Cathleen Falsani, "George 'Troubled' He Didn't Act Sooner," *Chicago Sun-Times*, 3 February 2006.

25. Jamie Francisco and Jon Yates, "Cardinal's Supporters Speak up," *Chicago Tribune*, 13 February 2006.

26. Brachear, "Cardinal Faces Angry Parishioners."

27. Ruethling, "Board Urged Archdiocese to Pull Priest."

28. Heinzmann and Brachear, "George Takes the Defensive."

29. Ibid.

30. Carla K. Johnson, "Advocacy Group Calls on Cardinal George to Resign," *Chicago Tribune*, 25 February 2006.

31. Marya A. Brachear, "Outsider to Examine Abuse Cases," *Chicago Tribune*, 16 February 2006.

32. "Report Blasts Church," *Chicago Tribune,* 21 March 2006.

33. Ibid.

34. Ibid.

35. Ibid.

Bibliography

Books, Book Chapters, Journal Articles

Abelove, Henry, Michele Aina Baracle, and David Halperin, eds. *The Lesbian and Gay Studies Reader*. London: Routledge, 1993.

Allen, Charlotte V. *Daddy's Girl*. New York: Berkly Books, 1980.

Allen, John L., Jr. *All the Pope's Men: The Inside Story of How the Vatican Really Thinks*. New York: Doubleday, 2004.

———. *Conclave: The Politics, Personalities, and Process of the Next Papal Election*. New York: Image, 2002.

Alpert, Judith L., ed. *Sexual Abuse Recalled: Treating Trauma in the Era of the Recovered Memory Debate*. Northvale, NJ: Aronson, 1995.

Armstrong, Louise. *Kiss Daddy Goodnight: A Speak-Out on Incest*. New York: Pocket Books, 1978.

Benjamin, Jessica. *The Bonds of Love: Psychoanalysis, Feminism, and the Problem of Domination*. New York: Pantheon Books, 1988.

Benyei, Candace R. *Understanding Clergy Misconduct in Religious Systems: Scapegoating, Family Secrets, and the Abuse of Power*. New York: Haworth Pastoral Press, 1998.

Berry, Jason. *Lead Us Not into Temptation: Catholic Priests and the Sexual Abuse of Children*. Urbana: University of Illinois Press, 1992, 2000.

Berry, Jason, and Gerald Renner. *Vows of Silence: The Abuse of Power in the Papacy of John Paul II*. New York: Free Press, 2004.

Bleichner, Howard P. *View from the Altar: Reflections on the Rapidly Changing Catholic Priesthood*. New York: Crossroad Publishing, 2004.

Bonovoglia, Angela. *Good Catholic Girls: How Women Are Leading the Fight to Change the Church*. New York: 10 Regan Books, 2005.

Briere, John. *Therapy for Adults Molested as Children: Beyond Survival*. New York: Springer Publishing, 1989.

Briere, John, and Marsha Runtz. "Suicidal Thoughts and Behaviors in Former

Sexual Abuse Victims." *Canadian Journal of Behavioral Sciences* 18 (1986): 413–23.

Brown, Daniel, Alan W. Scheflin, and D. Corydon Hammond. *Memory, Trauma, Treatment, and the Law: An Essential Reference on Memory for Clinicians, Researchers, Attorneys, and Judges.* New York: Norton, 1998.

Bruni, Frank, and Elinor Burkett. *A Gospel of Shame: Children, Sexual Abuse, and the Catholic Church.* New York: Perennial, 2002, 1993.

Carroll, James. *Toward a New Catholic Church: The Promise of Reform.* Boston: Hougton Mifflin, 2002.

Celenza, Andrea. "Sexual Misconduct in the Clergy: The Search for the Father." *Studies in Gender & Sexuality* 5 (2004): 213–32.

Chasseguet-Smirgel, Janine. *The Ego Ideal: A Psychoanalytic Essay on the Malady of the Ideal.* London: Free Association Books, 2003.

Cohler, Bertram, and Robert Galatzer-Levy. *The Course of Gay and Lesbian Lives: Social and Psychoanalytic Perspectives.* Chicago: University of Chicago Press, 1999.

Colarusso, Calvin. "Traversing Young Adulthood: The Male Journey from 20–40." *Psychoanalytic Inquiry* 15 (1995): 75–91.

Collins, Paul. *The Modern Inquisition: Seven Prominent Catholics and Their Struggles with the Vatican.* Woodstock: Overlook Press, 2001.

Cornwell, John. *Breaking Faith: Can the Catholic Church Save Itself?* New York: Penguin Compass, 2001.

———. *Hitler's Pope: The Secret History of Pius XII.* New York: Penguin Books, 1999.

———. *The Pontiff in Winter: Triumph and Conflict in the Reign of John Paul II.* New York: Doubelday, 2004.

———. *A Thief in the Night: Life and Death in the Vatican.* New York: Penguin Books, 1989.

Courtois, Christine A. *Healing the Incest Wound.* New York, Norton, 1988.

Cozzens, Donald B. *The Changing Face of the Priesthood.* Collegeville, MN: Liturgical Press, 2000.

———. *Sacred Silence: Denial and the Crisis in the Church.* Collegeville, MN: Liturgical Press, 2002.

———. *Faith That Dares to Speak.* Collegeville, MN: Liturgical Press, 2004.

Curran, Charles E. *The Moral Theology of Pope John Paul II.* Washington, DC: Georgetown University Press, 2005.

Crosson, John Dominic. *Jesus: A Revolutionary Biography.* San Francisco: HarperSan Francisco, 1994.

Cunneen, Sally. *In Search of Mary: the Woman and the Symbol.* New York: Ballantine Books, 1996.

Danica, Elly. *Beyond Don't: Dreaming Past the Dark.* Charlottetown, P.E.I.: Gynergy Press, 1996.

Davidson, Jonathan R. T., and Bessel A. van der Kolk. "The Psychopharmacological Treatment of Post-Traumatic Stress Disorder." In *Traumatic Stress: The Effects of Overwhelming Experience on Mind, Body and Society*, ed. Bessel van der Kolk,

Alexander C. McFarlane, and Lars Weisaeth, 510–24. New York: Guilford Press, 1996.

Davies, Jody M., and Mary Gail Frawley. *Treating the Adult Survivor of Childhood Sexual Abuse: A Psychoanalytic Perspective.* New York: Basic Books, 1994.

Delbanco, Andrew. *The Death of Satan: How Americans Have Lost the Sense of Evil.* New York: Farrar, Straus and Giroux, 1995.

Diamond, Michael J. "Boys to Men: The Maturity of Masculine Gender Identity Through Paternal Watchful Protectiveness." *Gender & Psychoanalysis* 2 (1997): 443–68.

Dimen, Muriel. *Sexuality, Intimacy, Power.* Hillsdale, NJ: Analytic Press, 2003.

Dinter, Paul E. *The Other Side of the Altar: One Man's Life in the Catholic Priesthood.* New York: Farrar, Straus and Giroux, 2003.

Dokecki, Paul R. *The Clergy Sexual Abuse Crisis: Reform and Renewal in the Catholic Community.* Washington, DC: Georgetown University Press, 2004.

Dolan, Jay P. *In Search of an American Catholicism: A History of Religion and Culture in Tension.* Oxford: Oxford University Press, 2002.

Doyle, Thomas P. "Canon Law and the Clergy Sex Abuse Crisis: Failure from Above." In *Sin against the Innocents: Sexual Abuse by Priests and the Role of the Catholic Church*, ed. Thomas G. Plante, 25–38. Westport, CT: Praeger, 2004.

Doyle, Thomas P., A. W. R. Sipe, and Patrick J. Wall, eds. *Sex, Priests, and Secret Codes: The Catholic Church's 2,000-Year Paper Trail of Sexual Abuse.* Los Angeles: Volt Press, 2006.

Duff, Eamon. *Saints and Sinners: A History of the Popes.* New Haven: Yale Nota Bene, 1997, 2001.

Fairbairn, W. Ronald D. "The Repression and Return of Bad Objects." In *Psychoanalytic Studies of the Personality*, 59–81. London: Routledge and Kegan Paul, 1952.

Ferder, Fran, and John Heagle. *Tender Fires: The Spiritual Promise of Sexuality.* New York: Crossroad Publishing, 2002.

Ferguson, Laurie J. "A Protestant Response to Clergy Sexual Abuse." In *Predatory Priests, Silenced Victims: Sexual Abuse and the Catholic Church*, ed. Mary Gail Frawley-O'Dea and Virginia Goldner. Hillsdale, NJ: Analytic Press, 2007.

Foucault, Michel. *The History of Sexuality: An Introduction, Volume 1.* New York: Knopf, 1990.

Finkelhor, David. *Child Sexual Abuse: New Theory and Research.* New York: Free Press, 1984.

Flynn, Eileen P. *Catholics at a Crossroads: Coverup, Crisis, and Cure.* New York: Paraview Press, 2003.

Fox, Thomas C. *Sexuality and Catholicism.* New York: George Braziller, 1995.

France, David. *Our Fathers: The Secret Life of the Catholic Church in an Age of Scandal.* New York: Broadway Books, 2004.

Frawley-O'Dea, Mary Gail, and Virginia Goldner, eds. *Predatory Priests, Silenced Victims: Sexual Abuse and the Catholic Church.* Hillsdale, NJ: Analytic Press, 2007.

Frawley-O'Dea, Mary Gail, and Joan Sarnat. *The Supervisory Relationship: A Contemporary Psychodynamic Approach.* New York: Guilford Press, 2001.

Freud, Sigmund. *Moses and Monotheism.* In *The Standard Edition of the Complete Psychological Works of Sigmund Freud.* Vol. 23. London: Hogarth Press and the Institute of Psychoanalysis, 1953–1974.

Gabbard, Glen O., and Eva P. Lester. *Boundaries and Boundary Violations in Psychoanalysis.* New York: Basic Books, 1995.

Gallagher, Sister Vera, with William F. Dodds. *Speaking Out, Fighting Back: Personal Experiences of Women who Survived Childhood Sexual Abuse in the Home.* Seattle: Madrona, 1985.

Ganzarin, Ramon C., and Bonnie J. Buchele. *Fugitives of Incest: A Perspective from Psychoanalysis and Groups.* Guilford, CT: International Universities Press, 1988.

Gartner, Richard B. *Betrayed as Boys: Psychodynamic Treatment of Sexually Abused Men.* New York: Guilford Press, 1999.

———. "Predatory Priests: Sexually Abusing Fathers." *Studies in Gender & Sexuality* 5 (2004): 31–56.

Gelinas, Denise. "The Persisting Negative Effect of Incest." *Psychiatry* 46 (1983): 312–32.

Ghent, Emmanuel. "Masochism , Submission, and Surrender." *Contemporary Psychoanalysis* 26 (1990): 108–36.

Gibson, David. *The Coming Catholic Church: How the Faithful Are Shaping a New American Catholicism.* San Francisco: HarperSanFrancisco, 2003.

Goldncr, Virginia. "Toward a Critical Relational Theory of Gender." *Psychoanalytic Dialogues* 1 (1991): 249–72.

Grand, Sue. *The Reproduction of Evil: A Clinical and Cultural Perspective.* Hillsdale, NJ: Analytic Press, 2000.

Grassi, Domenic. *Still Called by Name: Why I Love Being a Priest.* Chicago: Loyola Press, 2003.

Greeley, Andrew M. *Priests: A Calling in Crisis.* Chicago: University of Chicago Press, 2004.

Hamilton, Marci A. *God vs. the Gavel: Religion and the Rule of Law.* Cambridge: Cambridge University Press, 2005.

Hanson, P. Karl, Richard A. Steffy, and Rene Gauthier. "Long-Term Follow-Up of Child Molesters." *Public Safety and Emergency Preparedness, No. 1992–02,* February 2002. www.pspec-sppcc.gc.ca (accessed 25 September 2004).

Heaps, John. *A Love that Dares to Question: A Bishop Challenges His Church.* Grand Rapids, MI: William B. Eerdmans, 1998.

Heche, Anne. *Call Me Crazy.* New York: Scribner, 2001.

Hendra, Tony. *Father Joe: The Man who Saved My Soul.* New York: Random House, 2004.

Herman, Judith Lewis. *Trauma and Recovery.* New York: Basic Books, 1992.

Himmelfarb, Gertrude. *The De-Moralization of Society.* New York: Knopf, 1996.

Hindman, Jan, and James M. Peters. "Polygraph Testing Leads to Better

Understanding of Adult and Juvenile Sexual Offenders." *Federal Probation* 65 (2001): 8–14.

Hoge, Dean R. *The First Five Years of the Priesthood: A Study of Newly Ordained Catholic Priests.* Collegeville, MN: Liturgical Press, 2002.

Hoge, Dean R., and Jacqueline E. Wenger. *Evolving Visions of the Priesthood: Changes from Vatican II to the Turn of the New Century.* Collegeville, MN: Liturgical Press, 2003.

Holy Bible: New Revised Standard Version with Apocrypha. New York: Oxford Press, 1989.

Investigative Staff of *The Boston Globe. Betrayal: The Crisis in the Catholic Church.* Boston: Little, Brown and Company, 2002.

Isay, Richard. *Being Homosexual: Gay Men and Their Development.* New York: Farrar, Straus and Giroux, 2001.

Jackowski, Karol. *The Silence We Keep: A Nun's View of the Catholic Priest Scandal.* New York: Harmony Books, 2004.

Jehu, Derek. *Beyond Sexual Abuse.* New York: Wiley, 1988.

Jenkins, Philip. *Pedophiles and Priests: Anatomy of a Contemporary Crisis.* Oxford: Oxford University Press, 1996.

Johnson, Elizabeth A. *She Who Is: The Mystery of God in Feminist Theological Discourse.* New York: Crossroad, 2001.

———. *Truly Our Sister: A Theology of Mary in the Communion of Saints.* New York: Continuum, 2003.

Jordan, Mark D. *The Invention of Sodomy in Christian Theology.* Chicago: University of Chicago Press, 1997.

———. *The Silence of Sodom: Homosexuality in Modern Catholicism.* Chicago: University of Chicago Press, 2000.

———. *Telling Truths in Church: Scandal, Flesh, and Christian Speech.* Boston: Beacon Press, 2003.

Josephs, Lawrence. *Character Structure and the Organization of the Self.* New York: Columbia University Press, 1992.

Kempe, Ruth S., and C. Henry Kempe. *The Common Secret: Sexual Abuse of Children and Adolescents.* New York: Freeman, 1984.

Kennedy, Eugene. *The Unhealed Wound: The Church, the Priesthood, and the Question of Sexuality.* New York: St. Martin's Press, 2002.

Kernberg, Otto. *Severe Personality Disorders.* New Haven: Yale University Press, 1984.

Kluft, Richard P., ed. *Incest Related Syndromes of Adult Psychopathology.* Washington, DC: American Psychiatric Press, 1990.

Kohansky, Gerald E., and Murray Cohen. "Priests Who Sexualize Male Minors: Psychodynamic, Characterological, and Clerical Cultural Situations." In *Predatory Priests, Silenced Victims: Sexual Abuse and the Catholic Church,* ed. Mary Gail Frawley-O'Dea and Virginia Goldner. Hillsdale, NJ: Analytic Press, 2007.

Kramer, Selma, and Salman Akhtar. *The Trauma of Transgression.* Northvale, NJ: Aronson, 1991.

Krystal, Henry. *Integration and Self-Healing: Affect, Trauma, Alexithymia.* Hillsdale, NJ: Analytic Press, 1988.

Lakeland, Paul. *The Liberation of the Laity: In Search of an Accountable Church.* New York: Continuum, 2003.

Lawler, Phillip. "Moral Leadership of American Hierarchy under Scrutiny at Rome Meeting." *AD 2000,* 15 June 2002, 9.

Levering, Matthew, ed. *On the Priesthood: Classic and Contemporary Texts.* Lanham, MD: Rowman and Littlefield, 2003.

Levine, Harold B., ed. *Adult Analysis and Childhood Sexual Abuse.* Hillsdale, NJ: Analytic Press, 1990.

Lew, Mike. *Victims No Longer: Men Recovering from Incest and Other Sexual Abuse.* New York: Nevraumont, 1988.

Lex, Rev. James, with Ann M. Ennis. *Fifty Years in a Jealous Marriage: Seeking a Healthy Sexuality in a World of Power and Control.* Lima, OH: CSS Publishing, 2002.

Linigiarde, Vittorio, and Jack Drescher, eds. *Mental Health Professions and Homosexuality.* Northvale, NJ: Haworth Press, 2003.

Lothstein, Leslie M. "Psychological Theories of Pedophilia and Ephebophilia." In *Slayer of the Soul: Child Sexual Abuse and the Catholic Church*, ed. Stephen J. Rossetti, 19–44. Mystic, CT: Twenty-Third Publications, 1994.

———. "Men of the Flesh: The Evaluation and Treatment of Sexually Abusing Priests." *Studies in Gender & Sexuality* 5 (2004): 167–96.

McBrien, Richard P. *Catholicism: New Study Edition.* Rev. and updated. San Francisco: HarperSanFrancisco, 1994.

McDargh, John. "Reveling in Complexity: Dittes' Male Metaphors and Their Bearing on the Crisis of Clergy Sexual Abuse." *Pastoral Psychology* 52 (2003): 147–61.

McGoldrick, Monica, and John K. Pearce. "Family Therapy with Irish Americans." *Family Process* 20 (1981): 223–44.

McNamee, John P. *Diary of a City Priest.* Franklin, WI: Sheed & Ward, 2001.

McNaron, Toni A., and Yarrow Morgan, eds. *Voices in the Night: Women Speaking about Incest.* Pittsburgh: Cleis Press, 1982.

McNeill, John J. *The Church and the Homosexual.* 4th ed. Boston: Beacon Press, 1993.

Maltz, Wendy, and Beverly Holman. *Incest and Sexuality: A Guide to Understanding and Healing.* Lexington, MA: Lexington, 1987.

Markham, Donna, and Samuel F. Mikail. "Perpetrators of Clergy Abuse: Insights from Attachment Theory." *Studies in Gender & Sexuality* 5 (2004): 197–222.

Martin, Rev. James, S.J. "How Could It Happen?: Analysis of the Catholic Sexual Abuse Scandal." In *Predatory Priests, Silenced Victims: Sexual Abuse and the Catholic Church*, ed. Mary Gail Frawley-O'Dea and Virginia Goldner. Hillsdale, NJ: Analytic Press, 2007.

Meissner, W.W. *The Cultic Origins of Christianity: The Dynamics of Religious Development.* Collegeville, MN: Liturgical Press, 2000.

Merriam-Webster Online Dictionary. www.m-w.com.

Paine, Mary L., and David J. Hansen. "Factors Influencing Children to Self-Disclose Sexual Abuse." *Clinical Psychology Review* 22 (March 2002): 271–95.

Pearlman, Laurie Ann, and Karen V. Saakvitne. *Trauma and the Therapist: Countertransference and Vicarious Traumatization in Psychotherapy with Incest Survivors.* New York: Norton, 1995.

Phillips, Donald T. *Unto Us a Child: Abuse and Deception in the Catholic Church.* Irving, TX: Tapestry Press, 2002.

Putnam, Frank. *The Diagnosis and Treatment of Multiple Personality Disorder.* New York: Guilford Press, 1989.

Reese, Thomas J. *Inside the Vatican: The Politics and Organization of the Catholic Church.* Cambridge: Harvard University Press, 1996.

Richards, Anne. "Clergy Sexual Misconduct in the Episcopal Church." In *Predatory Priests, Silenced Victims: Sexual Abuse and the Catholic Church*, ed. Mary Gail Frawley-O'Dea and Virginia Goldner. Hillsdale, NJ: Analytic Press, 2007.

———. "Sexual Misconduct by Clergy in the Episcopal Church." *Studies in Gender & Sexuality* 5 (2004) 139–66.

Rose, Michael S. *Goodbye, Good Men: How Liberals Brought Corruption Into the Catholic Church.* Washington, DC: Regnery Publishing, 2002.

Rossetti, Stephen J. *A Tragic Grace: The Catholic Church and Child Sexual Abuse.* Collegeville, MN: Liturgical Press, 1996.

Roth, Susan, and Ronald Batson. *Naming the Shadows: A New Approach to Individual and Group Psychotherapy for Adult Survivors of Childhood Sexual Abuse.* New York: Free Press, 1997.

Ruether, Rosemary Radford. *Sexism and God-Talk: Toward a Feminist Theology.* Boston: Beacon Press, 1989, 1993.

———. *Women and Redemption: A Theological History.* Minneapolis: Fortress Press, 1998.

Russell, Diana E. H. *The Secret Trauma: Incest in the Lives of Girls and Women.* New York: Basic Books, 1986.

Schoenherr, Richard A.; *Goodbye Father: The Celibate Male Priesthood and the Future of the Catholic Church.* Edited with an introduction by David Yamane. Oxford: Oxford University Press, 2002.

Schore, Allan N. *Affect Regulation and the Origin of the Self: The Neurobiology of Emotional Development.* Hillsdale, NJ: Lawrence Erlbaum Associates, 1994.

Schüssler Fiorenza, Elisabeth. *In Memory of Her: A Feminist Theological Reconstruction of Christian Origins.* New York: Crossroad, 2000.

———. *Jesus and the Politics of Interpretation.* New York: Contiuum, 2001.

Shengold, Leonard. *Soul Murder.* New Haven: Yale University Press, 1989.

Sipe, A. W. Richard. *Celibacy in Crisis: The Secret World Revisited.* New York: Brunner- Routledge, 2003.

———. *Sex, Priests, and Power: Anatomy of a Crisis.* New York: Brunner/Mazel, 1995.

Smith, Daniel W., Elizabeth J. Letourneau, Benjamin E. Saunders, Dean G. Kilpatrick, Heidi S. Resnick, and Connie L. Best. "Delay in Disclosure of

Childhood Rape: Results from a National Survey." *Child Abuse & Neglect* 24 (2000): 273–87.

Smith, L. Murdock. "Women Priests and Clergy Sexual Misconduct." In *Predatory Priests, Silenced Victims: Sexual Abuse and the Catholic Church*, ed. Mary Gail Frawley-O'Dea and Virginia Goldner. Hillsdale, NJ: Analytic Press, 2007.

Stein, Ruth. "Vertical Mystical Homoeros: An Altered Form of Desire in Fundamentalism." *Studies in Gender & Sexuality* 4 (2003): 38–58.

Steinfels, Peter. *A People Adrift: The Crisis of the Roman Catholic Church in America.* New York: Simon and Schuster, 2003.

Sugarman, Alan, ed. *Victims of Abuse: The Emotional Impact of Child and Adult Trauma.* Guilford, CT: International Universities Press, 1994.

Urquiza, A., and L. M. Keating. "The Prevalence of Sexual Victimization in Males." In *The Sexually Abused Male.* Vol. 1, ed. Mic Hunter. Boston: Lexington Books, 1990.

van der Kolk, Bessel A. "The Complexity of Adaptation to Trauma: Self-Regulation, Stimulus, Discrimination, and Characterological Development." In *Traumatic Stress: The Effects of Overwhelming Experience on Mind, Body and Society*, ed. Bessel van der Kolk, Alexander C. McFarlane, and Lars Weisaeth, 182–213. New York: Guilford Press, 1996.

———. *Psychological Trauma.* Washington, DC: American Psychiatric Press, 1987.

van der Kolk, Bessel, Alexander C. McFarlane, and Lars Weisaeth, eds. *Traumatic Stress: The Effects of Overwhelming Experience on Mind, Body, and Society.* New York: Guilford Press, 1996.

Waites, Elizabeth A. *Trauma and Survival: Post-Traumatic and Dissociative Disorders in Women.* New York: Norton, 1993.

Walker, Gillian. "Eunuchs for the Kingdom: Constructing the Celibate Priest." *Studies in Gender & Sexuality* 5 (2004): 233–57.

———. "Reflections on Celibacy and the Role of Women in the Church." *Studies in Gender & Sexuality* 5 (2004): 81–102.

Ward, Elizabeth. *Father-Daughter Rape.* New York: Grove Press, 1985.

Weigel, George. *The Courage to be Catholic: Crisis, Reform, and the Future of the Church.* New York: Basic Books, 2002.

———. *Witness to Hope: The Biography of Pope John Paul II.* New York: Cliff Street Books, 1999, 2001.

West, Christopher. *Theology of the Body Explained: A Commentary on John Paul II's "Gospel of the Body."* Boston: Pauline Books and Media, 2003.

Wills, Garry. *Papal Sin: Structures of Deceit.* New York: Doubleday, 2000.

———. *Why I Am a Catholic.* Boston: Houghton Mifflin, 2002.

Wyatt, Gail E. "The Sexual Abuse of Afro-American and White Women in Childhood." *Child Abuse & Neglect* 9 (1985): 507–19.

Magazine, Newspaper, and Television News Articles

Almost every magazine, newspaper, and television article was identified first on the *Abuse Tracker*. Until January 2004, the *Abuse Tracker* was managed by the Poynter Institute of Journalism. The *National Catholic Reporter* then took it over and continues to manage it (www.ncrnews.org/abuse). The *Abuse Tracker* collects media articles on the scandal from across the world and posts summaries with links to the original source.

Arizona Republic

Clancy, Michael. "Anti-Gay Edict Stirs Priest to Step Down." 29 November 2005. www.azcentral.com (accessed 29 November 2005).
———. "Archbishop Promises to Meet Abuse Victims." 24 June 2003. www. azcentral.com (accessed 25 June 2003).
"Diocese Downplays Abuse Scope: Cases Show Patterns of Suppression by Bishop." 10 November 2002. www.azcentral.com (accessed 8 December 2002).
Nelson, Katie. "Victims Network Asks Diocese for 'Concrete Steps.'" 4 July 2003. www.azcentral.com (accessed 5 July 2003).
Reaves, Joseph A. . "Bishop O'Brien Admits Cover-up in Sexual Abuse Cases." 2 June 2003. www.azcentral.com (accessed 2 June 2003).
———. "Unsung Judges Lead Way in Priest Investigations." 23 February 2003. www.azcentral.com (accessed 23 February 2003).
Reaves, Joseph A., and Fred Bayles. "O'Brien's Policies Reversed." 21 June 2003. www.azcentral.com (accessed 23 June 2003).
Roberts, Laurie. "Bishop's Heart Grows Heavy under Weight of Evidence." 7 December 2002. www.azcentral.com (accessed 8 December 2002).
"Text of the Agreement (between Maricopa County Attorney Rick Romley, Bishop Thomas O'Brien and the Roman Catholic Diocese of Phoenix)." 2 June 2003. www.azcentral.com (accessed 2 June 2003).
Wagner, Dennis. "Romley: Bishop Will Be Treated Like Any Criminal Suspect." 17 June 2003. www.azcentral.com (accessed 19 June 2003).

Associated Press

"Abuse is No. 1 Reason Teachers Lose Licenses in W. Va." *Herald-Mail,* 17 October 2005. www.herald-mail.com (accessed 17 October 2005).
Barakat, Matthew. "Priest Indicted on Child Porn Charges." *WTOP Radio Network,* 15 February 2005. www.wtopnews.com (accessed 15 February 2005).
"Bishops Not to Sanction Priest Shown Having Sex in Video." *San Francisco Chronicle,* 6 January 2003. www.sfgate.com (accessed 7 January 2003).
"Bishops Who Quit amid Sex Scandals." *New York Times,* 12 December 2002. nytimes.com (accessed 13 December 2003).
Burling, Lois. "Leading Voice for Abuse Victims Says She was Molested while at the

Air Force Academy." *Star Tribune* (Casper, WY), 15 July 2003. www.trib.com (accessed 17 July 2003).

"Clergy May be Required to Report Child Abuse Claims." *Olympian,* 9 March 2003. www.theolympian.com (accessed 10 March 2003).

"Clergy-Abuse Support Group Ignites Debate: SNAP's Public Tactics, Ties to Lawyers Anger Some Victims." *MSNBC,* 18 December 2004. www.msnbc.com (accessed 18 December 2004).

Eltman, Frank. "Lay Group Leaders Call for LI Bishop's Resignation." *Boston Globe,* 25 July 2003. www.boston.com (accessed 25 July 2003).

"Faithful in Pope's Homeland Press Church to Act on Sex Abuse." *Star Tribune* (Minneapolis/St. Paul), 28 September 2003. www.startribune.com (accessed 29 September 2003).

Farrington, Brendan, Associated Press. "Bill Allowing Lawsuits for Long-Ago Child Abuse All but Dead." *Sun Sentinel,* 10 April 2003. www.sun-sentinel.com (accessed 11 April 2003).

"Focus of Catholic Sexual Abuse Suits Now Includes Nuns." *WAVE 3 News,* 2 August 2004. www.wave3.com (accessed 4 August 2004).

"Former Catholic Priest Sentenced to More than 10 Years' Prison for Child Sex Offenses." *Boston Globe,* 25 May 2003. www.boston.com (accessed 25 May 2003).

"German Bishops OK Sex-Abuse Plan." *Dallas Morning News,* 28 September 2002. www.dallasnews.com (accessed 28 September 2002).

"Globe Wins for Work on Abuse by Clergy." *Boston Globe,* 26 October 2002. www.boston.com (accessed 27 October 2002).

"Group Asks Vatican to Oust N.H. Bishop." *Boston Globe,* 9 November 2003. www.boston.com (accessed 9 November 2003).

"Groups Say Bishops Ignoring Abuse Policy." *Hartford Courant,* 19 December 2003. www.ctnow.com (accessed 19 December 2003).

"Islamic Schools under Scrutiny." *CNN,* 18 September 2005. http://cnn.worldnews.com (accessed 7 October 2005).

Johnson, Carla K. "Advocacy Group Calls in Cardinal George to Resign." *Chicago Tribune,* 25 February 2006. www.chicagotribune.com (accessed 25 February 2006).

———. "Cardinal: Mistakes Were Made." *Chicago Sun-Times,* 28 January 2006. www.suntimes.com (accessed 28 January 2006).

Kole, William J. "Austrians Leaving Catholic Church in Droves after Summer of Scandal." *Canadian Broadcasting News,* 24 September 2004. www.cbc.ca (accessed 25 September 2004).

———. "Child Porn Found at Austrian Seminary." *CNN Netscape News,* 12 July 2004. www.cnn.netscape.cnn.com (accessed 13 July 2004).

"L.A. Church Abuse Testimony to Go Public." *1010 WINS,* 31 August 2005. www.1010wins.com (accessed 31 August 2003).

Lavoie, Denise. "Lawyers for Boston Archdiocese Questions Therapists Who

Worked with Alleged Victims." *Boston Globe,* 17 January 2003. www.boston.com (accessed 17 January 2003).

Mandak, Joe. "Catholic Pastor Resigns over Internet Pornography Charges." *Penn Live,* 9 October 2003. www.pennlive.com (accessed 10 October 2003).

"Paper: Police Helped Hide Abuse Claims." *Wired News,* 31 July 2005. www.wireservice.wired.com (accessed 22 July 2005).

"Parishioners Pack Church for Funeral of Priest Who Apparently Committed Suicide." *Boston Globe,* 3 January 2003. www.boston.com (accessed 4 January 2003).

"Pastor Criticizes Springfield Diocese Handling of Sex Abuse." *Mass Live,* 17 February 2003. www.masslive.com (accessed 17 February 2003).

"Polish Community Raising Money for Accused Priest." *Stamford Advocate,* 6 January 2003. www.stamfordadvocate.com (accessed 7 January 2003).

"Pulitzer Honor Globe's Priest Reporting." *New York Newsday,* 7 April 2003. www.newsday.com (accessed 8 April 2003).

"Researchers Study Gays in Catholic Priesthood." *Boston Channel,* 20 September 2005. www.thebostonchannel.com (accessed 21 September 2005).

Ruff, Joe. "Nebraska Bishop Skips Some Abuse-Prevention Measures." *Corvallis Gazette-Times,* 2 February 2004. www.gtconnect.com (accessed 2 February 2004).

"Some Major Settlements in Catholic Clergy Sexual Abuse Cases." *Salt Lake City National Wire,* 6 August 2005. www.KUTV.com (accessed 6 August 2005).

"Stockton Diocese: Man Didn't Do Enough to Avoid Alleged Molest." *Mercury News,* 15 August 2003. www.bayarea.com (accessed 17 August 2003).

"Text of Bishop Gregory's Remarks." *New York Newsday,* 11 November 2002. www.newsday.com (accessed 13 November 2002).

Winfield, Nicole. "Cardinal Says Gays Shouldn't Be Priests." *Boston Globe,* 6 December 2002. www.boston.com (accessed 8 December 2002).

Wolfe, Charles. "Ky. Bill to Repeal Clergy 'Silent Right.'" *New York Newsday,* 10 January 2003. www.newsday.com (accessed 11 January 2003).

"Worldwide, 21 Roman Catholic Bishops Have Resigned amid Church Sex Scandal Since 1990." *Times-Picayune,* 18 June 2003. www.nola.com (accessed 19 June 2003).

Zoll, Rachel. "Bills on Child Sex Abuse Languish despite Public Anger over Crisis in Catholic Church." *San Francisco Chronicle,* 4 March 2003. www.sfgate.com (accessed 4 March 2003).

———. "Expert: Prosecutor's Deal with Phoenix Bishop Minimizes Damage to Church." *Times-Picayune,* 6 June 2003. www.nola.com (accessed 7 June 2003).

———. "Gay Priests Conflicted as Church Leaders Set to Discuss Restrictions." *The Day,* 13 November 2005. www.theday.com (accessed 13 November 2005).

———. "Keating Says He Was Smeared." *Boston Globe,* 1 October 2003. www.boston.com (accessed 1 October 2003).

———. "O'Brien Resignation Another Blow for Fractured Catholic Church." *San

Diego Union-Tribune, 18 June 2003. www.signonsandiego.com (accessed 19 June 2003).

Boston Globe

Anthes, Emily. "More Join Abuse Suits against Nuns." 18 August 2004. www.boston.com (accessed 19 August 2004).

Belkin, Douglas. "Protesters Aim to Force N.H. Bishop to Step Down." 27 January 2003. www.boston.com (accessed 28 January 2003).

Bullock, Rev. Robert, Rev. Walter Cuenin, Rev. Paul Kilroy, Rev. John McGinty, Rev. Gerry Osterman, Rev. Thomas Powers, Rev. Daniel Riley, and Rev. Dennis Sheehan. "A Forum for Reflection and Study for Priests." 11 April 2002. http://nlnewsbank.com (accessed 5 April 2005).

Carroll, James. "One Cardinal's Old Impulse to Blame Jews." 12 August 2003. www.boston.com (accessed 13 August 2003).

Carroll, Matt. "Bishops' Policy Flawed, Priests Say." 19 October 2002. www.boston.com (accessed 20 October 2002).

Cullen, Kevin. "Lay Group Requests to Engage O'Malley." 29 July 2003. www.boston.com (accessed 30 July 2003).

Davis, Wendy. "End to Time Limits in Abuse Cases Urged." 11 April 2003. www.boston.com (accessed 11 April 2003).

Dezell, Maureen. "A Story of Sisters Who Showed No Mercy: Peter Mullan's 'Magdalene' Dramatizes a Wretched Chapter in Irish Catholic History." 10 August 2003. www.boston.com (accessed 10 August 2003).

Emery, Theo. "Keating Says Church Should Embrace Reform Groups." 4 October 2002. www.boston.com (accessed 5 October 2004).

English, Bella. "'He Was So Angry, Upset, Ashamed, I Know It Affected His Whole Life.'" 18 September 2002. http://nl.newsbank.com (accessed 7 October 2005).

Gedan, Benjamin. "Outspoken Newton Priest Gets Standing Ovation." 9 December 2002. www.boston.com (accessed 11 December 2002).

Globe Staff. "Globe Receives Selden Ring Award." 25 February 2003. www.boston.com (accessed 26 February 2003).

———. "Globe Wins Award for Reporting." 4 February 2002. www.boston.com (accessed 4 February 2003).

Globe Staff and Wire Services. "The World Today: Germany Catholic Church Offers Apology for Sex Abuse." 28 September 2002. www.boston.com (accessed 29 September 2002).

Goodman, Ellen. "A New Chapter in Church Tale." 8 December 2002. http://nl.newsbank.com (accessed 6 November 2005).

Green, Amy. "Clergy Abuse Victims Seek out Some Peace at the Farm in KY: Site Is First Backed by Catholic Leaders." 19 July 2004. www.boston.com (accessed 19 July 2004).

Hall, Kevin, Knight Ridder. "Claim about Charity Leader Rivets Public Argentina." 2 December 2002. www.boston.com (accessed 4 December 2002).

Kurkjian, Stephen, and Walter F. Robinson. "A 'Classic Misuse of Power': Children of Woman Who Died in Affair with Priest Speak Out." 29 December 2002. www.boston.com (accessed 30 December 2002).

Lloyd, Marion. "Priest's Accusers Pose Test for Powerful Institution." 22 December 2002. www.boston.com (accessed 23 December 2002).

Luk, Helen. "Former Priest in Hong Kong Convicted in Sex Abuse Case." 28 January 2003. www.boston.com (accessed 29 January 2003).

MacQuarrie, Brian. "McSorley's Death Recalls a Life Long Lost." 13 June 2004. www.boston.com (accessed 13 June 2004).

McNamara, Eileen. "Opinion: A Matter of Choice." 26 January 2003. www.boston.com (accessed 27 January 2003).

Moore, Leslie. "Sex Abuse Allegations Rock Bastion of Catholicism." 15 September 2002. www.boston.com (accessed 16 September 2002).

Ostling, Richard. "Catholic Bishops' President Defends American Priests after a Negative 'Avalanche' over Abuse." 14 November 2005. www.boston.com (accessed 2 December 2005).

Paulson, Michael. "Abuse Crisis Exploited, Prelates Say." 20 June 2003. www.boston.com (accessed 20 June 2003).

———. "Abuse Specialists Challenge Church Defense Tactic: Assert Depositions Will Betray Victims." 22 January 2003. www.boston.com (accessed 22 January 2003).

———. "Debating the Limits of Forgiveness: Bishop Considers Repentant Abusers." 15 November 2002. www.boston.com (accessed 17 November 2002).

———. "Dislocation, Scrutiny of Priests Raise Fears: Archdiocese Denies Politics behind Moves." 2 October 2005. www.boston.com (accessed 2 October 2005).

———. "Gay Comments Concern Bishops." 10 December 2002. www.boston.com (accessed 12 December 2002).

———. "Gay Seminarian Ban Weighed: Vatican Drafting a Ruling Expected in the Next Year." 6 November 2002. http://boston.com (accessed 8 November 2002).

———. "Lessons Unlearned: Church Struggle Pains LA Region Stung by Abuse in the 80s." 12 June 2002. www.boston.com (accessed 10 August 2002).

———. "Lennon Appeals to Archdiocese for Greater Unity." 16 April 2003. www.boston.com (accessed 16 April 2003).

———. "Push is on to Quell Voice of the Faithful." 7 August 2002. www.boston.com (accessed 8 August 2002).

———. "Resignation Has Not Ended Law's Role in Church." 21 June 2003. www.boston.com (accessed 21 June 2003).

———. "Vatican Warns on Same-Sex Marriage." 1 August 2003. www.boston.com (accessed 10 August 2003).

Pfeiffer, Sacha. "Seminary Ouster of Outspoken Gay Points up Issues: Focus Put on Orientation." 25 November 2002. www.boston.com (accessed 27 November 2002).

Radin, Charles. "A Gay Priest Receives the Sacrament of Acceptance." 6 November 2005. www.boston.com (accessed 6 November 2005).

Ranalli, Ralph. "Church Limits Access to Records on Abuse." 17 September 2003. www.boston.com (accessed 20 September 2003).

Rezendes, Michael. "Church Allowed Abuse by Priest for Years." 15 December 2005. Text emailed by reporter Matt Carroll, 6 January 2006.

———. "Church to Disclose Records of Clergy Accused by Adults." 29 January 2003. www.boston.com (accessed 30 January 2003).

Rezendes, Michael, and Walter V. Robinson. "Church Lawyers to Question Therapists." 17 January 2003. www.boston.com (accessed 17 January 2003).

Robinson, Walter V. "Judge Finds Records, Law at Odds: Lack of Care Seen in Assigning Priests." 26 November 2002. www.boston.com (accessed 27 November 2002).

Robinson, Walter V., and Sacha Pfeiffer. "Nun Placed on Leave after Abuse Allegation." 11 November 2002. www.boston.com (accessed 14 November 2002).

Rosenwald, Michael S. "Cathedral Demonstration: Protesters Vow to Keep It Up." 16 December 2002. www.boston.com (accessed 19 December 2002).

Schiavone, Christopher, with Janice Page. "Broken Vows." 8 December 2002. www.boston.com (accessed 10 December 2002).

Sennott, Charles. "Clerical Abuse Roils Ireland's Church: Allegations against Priests, Cardinal Mirror Boston Case." 11 November 2002. www.boston.com (accessed 11 November 2002).

Viser, Matt. "Priest Was Eyed for Ouster prior to Audit: Timing Enrages Cuenin Supporters." 20 October 2005. www.boston.com (accessed 20 October 2005).

Viser, Matt, and Michael Paulson. "New Pastor Will Leave Embattled Newton Parish." 1 February 2006. www.boston.com (accessed 1 February 2006).

Winfield, Nicole. "Vatican Reaffirms Celibacy for Priests: Church Emphasizes Religious Vocations." 29 April 2003. www.boston.com (accessed 1 May 2003).

Boston Herald

Convey, Eric. "Abuse Victims Learn Settlement Amounts." 21 December 2003. www.bostonherald.com (accessed 21 December 2003).

Herald Staff. "Protest Letter Seeks Resignation." 8 December 2002. www.bostonherald.com (accessed 9 December 2002).

Mashberg, Tom. "Hub Ex-Vicar: Police Gave Church Leeway on Abuse." 29 October 2002. www.bostonherald.com (accessed 29 October 2002).

———. "Priests Eye Call for Law to Quit." 7 December 2002. www.bostonherald.com (accessed 7 December 2002).

Washington, Robin, Eric Convey, and Tom Mashberg. "Victims' Advocates Rip Church over Deposition of Therapist." 17 January 2003. www.bostonherald.com (accessed 19 January 2003).

Weber, David. "Judge at Center of Sad Saga: Catholic Jurist Hailed for 'Shining Light.'" 15 December 2002. www.bostonherald.com (accessed 16 December 2002).

Chicago Sun-Times

Donovan, Lisa, and Frank Main. "Cardinal: I Should Have Done More." 31 January 2006. www.suntimes.com (accessed 31 January 2006).

Falsani, Cathleen. "Contrite Cardinal Offers Answers." 29 January 2006. www.suntimes.com (accessed 29 January 2006).

———. "George: 'Troubled' He Didn't Act Sooner." 3 February 2006. www.suntimes.com (accessed 3 February 2006).

Falsani, Cathleen, and Frank Main. "Nun: I Reported Priest in 2000." 26 January 2006. www.suntimes.com (accessed 26 January 2006).

———. "Source: New Charge for Pastor in Abuse of Boy." 2 February 2006. www.suntimes.com (accessed 2 February 2006).

Greeley, Andrew. "Are Bishops Sorry at All?" 3 August 2003. www.suntimes.com (accessed 4 August 2003).

Chicago Tribune

Brachear, Manya A. "Outsider to Examine Abuse Cases." 16 February 2006. www.chicagotribune.com (accessed 22 October 2006).

———. "Cardinal Faces Angry Parishioners." 30 January 2006. www.chicagotribune.com (accessed 31 January 2006).

———. "Cardinal: Process 'Failed' in Abuse Case." 29 January www.chicagotribune.com (accessed 29 January 2006).

Bush, Rudolph. "End Urged for State's Abuse-Case Time Limits." 11 March 2002. www.chicagotribune.com (accessed 13 March 2003).

Casillas, Ofelia, and Manya A. Brachear. "DCFS Vows New Policy for Priest Abuse Cases." 23 February 2006. www.chicagotribune.com (23 February 2006).

Francisco, Jamie, and Jon Yates. "Cardinal's Supporters Speak Up." 13 February 2006. www.chicagotribune.com (accessed 13 February 2006).

Heinzmann, David, and Manya A. Brachear. "George Takes the Defensive." 27 January 2006. www.chicagotribune.com (accessed 27 January 2006).

———. "Report Blasts Church." 21 March 2006. www.chicagotribune.com (accessed 22 October 2006).

Sheehan, Charles, Margaret Ramirez, and Carlos Sadovi. "George: 'I Take Responsibility.'" 3 February 2006. www.chicagotribune.com (accessed 3 February 2006).

Courier-Journal

Dunlop, R. G. "Abuse by Clergy in Canada is Described: Victims Say that Country Trails U.S. in Dealing with Issues." 23 February 2003. www.courierjournal.com (accessed 23 February 2003).

Hall, Gregory, Peter Smith, Andrew Wolfson, and Deborah Yetter. "Church in Crisis: Alleged Victims Say Incidents Altered Lives." 29 September 2002. http://nl.newsbank.com (accessed 4 November 2005).

Smith, Peter. "Members Protest at Cathedral: Catholic Critics Want Bishops Accountable for Priests' Actions." 24 February 2003. www.courier-journal.com (accessed 24 February 2003).

———. "Online Praise Piles up for Priests." 24 November 2002. www.courier-journal (accessed 26 November 2002).

———. "Petitions Call for Archbishop to Resign: Organizers Fault Kelly's Handling of Abuse Cases." 14 May 2003. www.courier-journal.com (accessed 14 May 2003).

———. "Stories Obscured Facts in Sex Scandal." 6 September 2003. www.courier-journal.com (accessed 7 September 2003).

Smith, Peter, and Debbie Yetter. "Bill Eases Paths for Child Sex-Abuse Suits." 15 January 2003. www.courierjournal.com (accessed 15 January 2003).

Wolfson, Andrew. "Priest's Abuse of Children Was Known for Years: Records Paint a Disturbing Portrait of Daniel C. Clark's Addiction to Child Sex and the Church's Response to It." 4 May 2003. www.courier-journal.com (accessed 5 May 2003).

Dallas Morning News

"DMN Journalists Honored for Legal Reporting." 11 October 2005. www.dallasnews.com (accessed 11 October 2005).

Dunklin, Reese, and Brooks Egerton. "Runaway Priests: When the Law Looks the Other Way: Authorities Allowed Accused Priests to Live Abroad." 4 December 2004. www.dallasnews.com (accessed 4 December 2004).

———. "Vatican Panelists Names Examined: Two Have Advised Bishops not to Report Abusers; Some Fear a Stacked Deck." 24 October 2002. www.dallasnews.com (accessed 25 October 2002).

Egerton, Brooks. "Bishop Letting Priest Work: He Has Admitted to Fathering Child; Diocese Cites Lawsuit Dismissal." 14 May 2003. www.dallasnews.com (accessed 14 May 2003).

———. "Laymen Say Bishop Cut Deal in '97 to Go." 26 January 2003. www.dallasnews.com (accessed 26 January 2006).

———. "Top Catholics Subpoenaed: Lawyer Says Figures Summoned to Grand Jury in Child-Porn Case." 15 March 2005. www.dallasnews.com (accessed 15 March 2005).

Egerton, Brooks, and Reese Dunklin. "Catholic Bishops and Sexual Abuse." 13 June 2002. www.dallasnews.com (accessed 26 July 2002).

———. "Lay Group Says Grahmann Should Go." 20 June 2003. www.dallasnews.com (accessed 20 June 2003).

Hogan-Albach, Susan. "Web Site Supports Embattled Bishop." 2 July 2003. www.dallasnews.com (accessed 3 July 2003).

Sandoval, Stephanie. "Priest's Tip Led to Pastor's Arrest in Porn Case: He Reported Seeing Images of Nude Boys on GP Cleric's Computer." 3 February 2005. www.dallasnews.com (accessed 3 February 2005).

Los Angeles Times

Briscoe, L. "Victim Group Asks Church to Reward Tipsters." 6 July 2003. www.latimes.com (accessed 7 July 2003).

Gottlieb, Jeff. "Molestation Victim Gets Story Told in Churches." 27 January 2003. www.latimes.com (accessed 27 January 2003).

Guccione, Jean, and Doug Smith. "Study Reveals Vast Scope of Priest Abuse." 13 October 2005. www.latimes.com (accessed 13 October 2005).

Hernandez, David. "Sex Abuse Protesters Bring Cross, Photos to Cathedral." 2 June 2003. www.latimes.com (accessed 2 June 2003).

Lobdell, William. "Orange County: He Got Justice, Now Wants to Give It: A Sexual Abuse Victim Who Came to Believe in the Legal System is Sworn in as an Attorney." 5 June 2003. http://pqasb.pqarchiver.com (accessed 7 November 2005).

Stammer, Larry B. "Most Priests Say Bishops Mishandled Abuse Issue: Many Believe that the U.S. Church's Charter, though Protective of Children, is Unfair to Clerics, and Many are Angry at Prelates." 20 October 2002. www.latimes.com (accessed 21 October 2002).

"A Survey of Roman Catholic Priests in the United States and Puerto Rico: June 27–October 11, 2002." 11 October 2002. www.latimes.com (accessed 10 August 2004).

"A Survey of Roman Catholic Priests in the United States and Puerto Rico: June 27–October 11, 2002." 20 October 2002. www.latimes.com/timespoll (accessed 16 March 2004).

Weigel, George. Catholic Church Must Lose Psychobabble." 17 December 2002. www.latimes.com (accessed 17 December 2002).

Milwaukee Journal Sentinel

Heinen, Tom. "Dolan Meets with Petition Organizers: No Discipline Imposed over Letter on Celibacy." 3 September 2003. www.jsonline.com (accessed 3 September 2003).

Heinen, Tom, and Mary Zahn. "Weakland Begs for Forgiveness: Says Earnings Didn't Cover Settlement." 1 June 2002. www.jsonline.com (accessed 3 June 2002).

Jones, Meg. "Details Paint Disturbing Portrait of Priest." 5 October 2005. www.jsonline.com (accessed 6 October 2005).

Kissinger, Meg, and Toni Heinen. "Weakland, Dolan Meet with Victim: Extraordinary Session Focuses on 'Road to Healing' in Abuse." 10 July 2003. www.jsonlinecom (accessed 13 July 2003).

Nichols, Mike. "Media Shared Shame over Silence." 7 June 2003. www.jsonline.com (accessed 3 July 2003).

Rohde, Marie. "Weakland Denied He Abused Man Archdiocese Paid $450,000: Archbishop Asks Vatican to Hasten Retirement." 24 May 2002. www.jsonline.com (accessed 3 June 2002).

Schultze, Steve, and Marie Rohde. "State May Require Clergy to Report Abuse." 10 January 2003. www.jsonline.com (accessed 11 January 2003).

"Tweaking Abuse Legislation." 26 January 2003. www.jsonline.com (accessed 26 January 2003).

Twohey, Megan. "Two Parishes, Two Responses to Sexual Abuse by Priest: One Church Searches for Other Possible Victims." 5 February 2004. www.jsonline.com (accessed 5 February 2004).

National Catholic Reporter

Allen, John L., Jr. "Mexican Cardinal Sees Media Persecution in U.S. Scandal." 12 August 2002. www.natcath.org (accessed 15 August 2002).

———. "Secret Vatican Norms on Abuse Show Conflicts with U.S. Policy." 29 November 2002. www.natcath.org (accessed 3 December 2002).

———. "Sex Abuse in Brazil: Abuser Priest Provides Checklist for Selecting Victims." 21 November 2005. www.nationalcatholicreporter.org (accessed 21 November 2005).

Antiono, William V. "American Catholics from John Paul II to Benedict XVI." 30 September 2005. www.ncronline.org (accessed 30 September 2005).

Bullough, Greg. "Gumbleton's Disclosure Underscores Differences between Survivors, Bishops." 27 January 2006. www.ncronline.org (accessed 26 January 2006).

Cleary, William. "Researcher Studies Why Priests Quit." 23 May 2003. www.natcath.org (accessed 26 May 2003).

Davidson, James D. "Belief in Church as Mediator Slips." 30 September 2005. www.ncronline.org (accessed 5 October 2005).

DiGiulio, Katherine. "Interview of Dr. Leslie Lothstein." 16 August 2002. www.natcath.org (accessed 10 October 2002).

Donovan, Gil. "Priests Say Bishop Issues Gag Order." 14 March 2003. www.natcath.org (accessed 15 March 2003).

———. "Psychologists Dispute Ratzinger's Figures." 10 January 2003. www.natcath.org (accessed 10 January 2003).

———. "Some See Big Reforms on the Horizon." 19 July 2002. www.natcath.org (accessed 20 July 2002).

"Editorial." 1 August 2003. www.natcath.org (accessed 1 August 2003).

"Editorial: Priests' Tough Questions Are a Service to Their People." 9 January 2004. www.natcath.org (accessed 10 January 2004).

Ferder, Fran, and John Heagle. "Time for Bishops to Listen, Take Ordinary Catholics Seriously." 19 July 2002. www.natcath.org (accessed 27 November 2005).

Feuerhard, Joe. "Just How Bad Is It? Priest Shortage Worse than Experts Predicted; Laity, Foreign Priests, Filling in Gap." 17 October 2003, 30–35.

———. "The Real Deal." 19 August 2004. www.nationalcatholicreporter.org (accessed 19 August 2004).

Fox, Tom. "Cardinal Law's New Appointment." 29 May 2004. www. nationalcatholicreporter.org (accessed 31 May 2004).

———. "Web Site Sheds Light on Media Fascination with Abuse Crisis." 12 August 2002. www.natcath.org (accessed 14 August 2002).

———. "A Wondrous Dance of Sex and Spirit." 13 December 2002, 6.

Gautier, Mary L. "Lay Catholics Firmly Committed to Parish Life, Table 8." 30 September 2005. www.ncronline.org (accessed 30 September 2005).

Hoge, Dean R. "Center of Catholic Identity." 30 September 2003. www.ncronline. org (accessed 5 October 2005).

Jones, Arthur. "Abuse Victim in Holy Week Fast outside Los Angeles Cathedral." 17 April 2003. www.nationalcatholicreporter.org (accessed 18 April 2003).

———. "Chaplain's Military Career Ends in Dispute." 29 April 2004. www. nationalcatholicreporter.org (accessed 29 April 2004).

———. "L.A. District Attorney Seeks Access to All Abuse Files." 7 March 2003. www.natcath.org (accessed 8 March 2003).

Kennedy, Eugene Cullen. "Dallas: The Last Remake of Frankenstein." 16 August 2002. www.natcath.org (accessed 17 August 2002).

"Maciel Case Belies Church Promises to Combat Abuse." 23 November 2003. http://natcath.org (accessed 25 November 2003).

Malcolm, Teresa. "Family Assists Others in Memory of Eric." 4 June 2002. http:// ncronline.org (accessed 3 June 2004).

Murnion, Philip J. "Priest: Beyond Employee, to Minister of the Sacred." 27 September 2002. www.natcath.org (accessed 30 September 2002).

Roberts. Tom. "Healing a Betrayed Community." 4 June 2004. www.ncronline.com (accessed 5 June 2004).

Ryan, Dick. "One Bishop's High Cost of Living." 25 October 2002, 6.

———. "Priests Voice Range of Concerns in Effort to Organize in New York." 25 October 2002, 6.

New York Newsday

Breslin, Jimmy. "LI Bishop's Mansion: Biggest Waste of Money, Bar Nun." 8 October 2002. www.newsday.com (accessed 10 October 2002).

Ciolli, Rita. "The Bishop's New Digs." 6 October 2002. www.newsday.com (accessed 6 October 2002).

———. "Experts Lament Unheeded Advice." 10 February 2003. www.newsday.com (accesed 15 December 2003).

———. "A Priest Repents for His Brethren: Oyster Bay Congregants Moved by Gesture." 17 February 2003. www.newsday.com (accessed 20 February 2003).

Ciolli, Rita, Bart Jones, and Erin Rexeira. "Parishioners Lambaste Murphy in Sex Cases." 28 April 2004. www.newsday.com (accessed 29 April 2004).

Eisenberg, Carol. "A Protector or Predator?" 11 February 2002. www.newsday.com (accesed 12 February 2002).

———. "Suit Charges Seminary with Pro-Gay Teachings." 21 January 2003. www.newsday.com (accessed 23 January 2003).

———. "Victims: Abuse Report Not a Fair Picture: New Church Audit, Praised by Bishops, Draws Criticism." 6 January 2004. www.newsday.com (accessed 6 January 2004).

Kelleher, Jennifer Sinco. "Priest Pleads Guilty." 1 October 2004. www.newsday.com (accessed 3 October 2004).

Kimmel, Michael. "Focus on Pedophiles, Not Gays." 14 October 2005. www.newsday.com (accessed 14 October 2005).

Saul, Stephanie. "Alleged Victim Dies." 25 September 2003. www.newsday.com (accessed 25 September 2003).

———. "Judge to Church: Reinstate Principal." 9 April 2003. www.newsday.com (accessed 10 April 2003).

Weissenstein, Michael. "Police: Queens Priest Had Porn, Gun, Nazi Paraphernalia." 8 October 2003. www.newsday.com (accessed 9 October 2003).

New York Times

Belluck, Pam. "Church Seeks Therapy Records." *New York Times,* 17 January 2003. www.nytimes.com (accessed 17 January 2003).

———. "Official Tells Catholics: Fight Abuse with Purse and Feet." 5 October 2002. www.nytimes.com (accessed 6 October 2002).

Davey, Monica. "Milwaukee Priests Seek End to Celibacy Rule." 20 August 2003. www.nytimes.com (accessed 20 August 2003).

Dillon, Sam. "Church's Accounting of Abuse Is Criticized." 8 December 2002. www.nytimes.com (accessed 10 December 2002).

———. "New Hampshire Bishop Embroiled in Abuse Disputes." 22 October 2002. www.nytimes.com (accessed 25 October 2002).

Fisher, Ian, and Laurie Goodstein. "Vatican Punishes a Leader after Abuse Charges." 19 May 2006. www.nytimes.com (accessed 19 May 2006).

Goodstein, Laurie. "Archdiocese of Cincinnati Fined in Sexual Abuse Scandal." 21 November 2003. www.nytimes.com (accessed 21 November 2003).

———. "At Seminary, New Ways for a New Generation." 25 March 2002, A-1 and A-19.

———. "Cardinal Egan Spurns Members of Review Board Studying Abuse." 15 January 2003. www.nytimes.com (accessed 15 January 2003).

———. "Chief of Panel on Priest Abuse Will Step Down." 16 June 2003. www.nytimes.com (accessed 16 June 2003).

———. "Decades of Damage; Trail of Pain in Church Crisis Leads to Nearly Every Diocese." 12 January 2003. www.nytimes.com (accessed 12 January 2003).

———. "For the U.S. Catholic Church, a Mobile Unit of Superhealers." 22 June 2003. www.nytimes.com (accessed 23 June 2003).

———. "Gay Men Ponder Impact of Proposal by Vatican." 23 September 2005. www.nytimes.com (accessed 23 September 2005).

———. "St. Louis Archbishop to Take over Philadelphia Archdiocese." 16 July 2003. http://nytimes.com (accessed 17 July 2003).

Gordon, Mary. "How Ireland Hid Its Own Dirty Laundry." 3 August 2003. www.nytimes.com (accessed 3 August 2003).

Hanley, Robert. "Paterson's Bishop Arrives, Preaching and Politicking." 2 July http://nytimes.com (accessed 7 July 2004).

Kershaw, Sarah. "Rare Kind of Scandal Accord in Spokane Diocese." 2 February 2006. www.nytimes.com (accessed 2 February 2006).

Kocieniewski, David. "In New Jersey, an Archbishop Conservative and Controversial." 30 May 2004. www.nytimes.com (accessed 30 May 2004).

Lambert, Bruce. "L.I. Bishop Meets Priests Critical of His Leadership." 20 January 2004. www.nytimes.com (accessed 20 January 2004).

Lavery, Brian. "New Irish Police Squad to Investigate All Clerical Abuse Cases." 22 October 2002. www.nytimes.com (accessed 23 October 2002).

Lyall, Sarah. "Irish Recall Sad Homes for 'Fallen' Women." 28 November 2002. www.nytimes.com (accessed 29 November 2002).

McFadden, Robert D. "L.I. Diocese Tricked Victims of Sexual Abuse, Panel Says." 11 February 2003. www.nytimes.com (accessed 12 February 2003).

Newman, Andy. "In a Troubled Twilight, a Bishop Speaks." 3 November 2002. www.nytimes.com (accessed 3 November 2002).

Ruethling, Gretchen. "Board Urged Archdiocese to Pull Priest, Official Says." 25 February 2006. www.nytimes.com (accessed 25 February 2006).

Steinfels, Peter. "Analysis: Crucial Issue for Catholics." *New York Times* and *Salt Lake Tribune,* 30 September 2005. www.sltrib.com (accessed 1 October 2005).

———. "Inquiry into Chicago Breaks Silence on Sex Abuse by Catholic Priests." *New York Times,* 24 February 1992. www.bishop-accountability.org (accessed 20 December 2005).

"Tracking Wayward Shepherds." 15 February 2003. www.nytimes.com (accessed 15 February 2003).

Wakin, Daniel. "Bishops Open New Drive Opposing Contraception." 13 November 2003. www.nytimes.com (accessed 13 November 2003).

———. "Cardinal Egan Defends Record in Abuse Cases." 16 August 2002. www.nytimes.com (accessed 17 August 2002).

———. "Catholic Group Asks for Married Priests." 28 April 2004. www.nytimes.com (accessed 28 April 2004).

———. "Catholic Priest Who Aids Church Sexual Abuse Victims Loses Job." 29 April 2004. www.nytimes.com (accessed 29 April 2004).

———. "Praise for a Priest in Abuse Inquiry Angers Victims." 2 March 2003. http://select.nytimes.com (accessed 7 November 2005).

Philadelphia Inquirer

Cusick, Frederick. "Crowd Members Lash out at Cardinal at Villanova." 25 September 2005. www.philly.com (accessed 26 September 2005).

Lounsberry, Emily, and Jim Remsen. "Parishioners Vent Anger at Clergy over Abuse." 27 October 2005. www.philly.com (accessed 28 October 2005).

Murphy, Kevin. "Bishops End Conference without Hearing from Victims." 21 June 2003. www.centredaily.com (accessed 21 June 2003).

O'Reilly, David. "Bishops Vow to Rid Church of Clergy Sex Abuse." 21 June 2002. www.centredaily.com (accessed 21 June 2002).

O'Reilly, David, and Jim Remsen. "Priests Reportedly Chastise Cardinal: Several Clerics in a Private Meeting Are Said to Have Challenged His Defense of the Handling of Sex-Abuse Cases." 28 September 2005. www.philly.com (accessed 28 September 2005.

Phillips, Nancy. "A Past of Hurt, a Mission to Help." 6 October 2002. http://nl.newsbank.com (accessed 6 November 2005).

Phillips, Nancy, Mark Fazlollah, and Craig R. McCoy. "Priest: Silence Ordered on Abuse." 7 August 2005. www.philly.com (accessed 7 August 2005).

Pittsburgh Post-Gazette

McFeatters, Ann. "Church Reforms Needed, Poll of Catholics Show." 14 November 2003. www.post-gazette.com (accessed 14 November 2003).

Rodgers-Melnick, Ann. "Bishops Doing Little on Abuse, Group Charges." 19 June 2003. www.post-gazette.com (accessed 19 June 2003).

———. "Bishop Finds Favor and Faults in Sex Abuse Scandal Coverage." 6 September 2003. www.post-gazette.com (accessed 7 September 2003).

———. "Bishops Lauded for Progress as Conference Ends." 22 June 2003. www.post-gazette.com (accessed 27 June 2003).

———. "Dean Shocked by How Other Dioceses Failed to Discipline Abusing Priests." 19 June 2005. www.post-gazette.com (accessed 20 June 2005).

Seattle Post-Intelligencer

Nicolosi, Michelle. "Man Says Sex with Priest Began at 11: The Cleric, Convicted of Taking Indecent Liberties, Calls Accuser a Liar." 20 August 2004. http://seattlepi.nwsource.com (accessed 20 August 2004).

Nicolosi, Michelle, and Claudia Rowe. "The 11 Abused Cases the P-I Examined." 19 August 2004. http://seattlepi.nwsource.com (accessed 19 August 2004).

Rowe, Claudia. "Archdiocese Hired Lawyer to Reach out to Accusers in Sex Scandal." 27 September 2004. http://seattlepi.nwsource.com (accessed 27 September 2004).

———. "Colombian's 'Adoption' by Priest Too Good to Be True: An Unwanted Name, A Life Not of His Choosing." 20 August 2004. http://seattlepi.nwsource.com (accessed 20 August 2004).

Rowe, Claudia, and Michelle Nicolosi. "Accused Priests Took in Minors: When Fathers Acted as Fathers, Complaints Often Followed." 19 August 2004. http://seattlepi.nwsource.com (accessed 19 August 2004).

Toledo Blade

"Authorities Abetted Diocese in Hiding Sexual-Abuse Cases." 31 July 2005. www.
toledoblade.com (accessed 31 July 2005).

Erb, Robin. "Secret Archives at Heart of Abuse; Group Says Files Hold Key to
Abuse." 6 March 2003. www.toledoblade.com (accessed 6 March 2003).

Sallah, Michael D., and David Yonke. "Believers Betrayed." 2 December 2002.
www.toledoblade.com (accessed 2 December 2002).

———. "Shame, Sin and Secrets." 1 December 2002. www.toledoblade.com
(accessed 1 December 2002).

Yonke, David. "Toledo Diocese Orders Limit on Victim Therapy." 4 September
2004. www.toledoblade.com (accessed 4 September 2004).

Washington Post

Cooperman, Alan. "Bishop Says Priest Abused Him as Teenager." 11 January 2006.
www.washingtonpost.com (accessed 11 January 2006).

———. "Kennedy Rebukes Santorum for Comments: Republican Repeats Remark
Linking Scandal to Boston 'Liberalism.'" 14 July 2005.www.washingtonpost.
com (accessed 14 July 2005).

———. "One Diocese's Early Warning on Sex Abuse: '50s Records Reflect Bishops
Taking Risks." 22 April 3003. www.washingtonpost.com (accessed 25 April
2003).

Dionne, E. J., Jr. "Rebuked by Rome." 22 October 2002. www.washingtonpost.com.

Rosin, Hannah. "Conflict—and Then Some. . . ." 21 July 2002. www.
washingtonpost.com (accessed 21 July 2002).

Williams, Daniel, and Alan Cooperman. "Vatican Letter Denounces 'Lethal Effects'
of Feminism." 1 August 2004. www.washingtonpost.com (accessed 31 July
2004).

Other Magazines, Newspapers, and Television News

"80-Year-Old Marist Brother Jailed." *Herald and Weekly Times* (Durham, NC), 29
November 2002. http://heraldsun.com (accessed 30 November 2002).

Allen, Darren M. "Clergy Added to List of Mandatory Reporters." *Times Argus*
(Barre/Montpelier, VT), 30 April 2003. www.timesargus.com.

Ancer, Jonathan. "Church in Moral Crisis, Says New Archbishop." *Mercury*
(KwaZulu-Natal, South Africa), 20 June 2003. www.themercury.co.za (accessed
21 June 2003).

"Archdiocese of Cincinnati Guilty of Failing to Report Child Sexual Abuse by
Priests." *Dayton Daily News,* 20 November 2003. www.daytondaily.com
(accessed 20 November 2003).

"Archdiocese's Plea Deal: A Cleansing Act." *Cincinnati Enquirer,* 21 November
2003. www.enquirer.com (accessed 21 November 2003).

"Argentine Priest Reveals Sex Life." *BBC News,* 10 June 2004. www.newsvote.bbc. co.uk (accessed 12 June 2004).

Arney, Steve. "Judge: Church's Response to Report Disappointing." *Pantagraph,* 24 April 2004. http://nlnewsbank.com (accessed 16 November 2005).

Arrelano, Gustav. "The Army of God: How a Monk, an Altar Boy, and a Sex-Abuse Victim Joined Forces to Battle Their Common Enemy: The Catholic Church." *Orange County Weekly,* 13–19 August 2004. www.ocweekly.com.

Barba-Martin, Jose. "Ladies and Gentleman of This Committee on Human Rights: Text to Be Read at the Hearing Session of the Human Rights of Children and Youth Committee of the United Nations in Geneva on October 9th, 2002." *Chiesa Newsletter,* 4 April 2003. www.chiesa.org (accessed 6 April 2003).

Barbarisi, Daniel. "Mass. Prosecutor Lists Names of 21 Alleged Abusive Priests: Dist. Atty. Paul F. Walsh Also Announces the Indictment of a Priest Accused of Sexual Abuse." *Providence Journal,* 27 September 2002. www.projo.com (accessed 28 September 2002).

Barrick, Daniel. "Lawmakers: Clergy Are Not Exempt: Confessional Secrecy Is Focus of Sex Abuse Bill." *Concord Monitor,* 12 February 2003. www. concordmonitor.com (accessed 13 February 2003).

———. "State Aims for Tougher Abuse Laws." *Concord Monitor,* 5 March 2003. www.concordmonitor.com (accessed 5 March 2003).

Barrow, Bill. "Bill: Clergy Must Report Abuse." *Everything Alabama,* 9 April 2003. www.al.com (accessed 9 April 2003).

Bearden, Michelle. "Pride in a Pulpit." *Tampa Tribune,* 6 October 2002 www.info. mgnetwork.com (accessed 6 October 2002).

Beyerlein, Tom, and Jim DeBrosse. "Catholic Leader Urged to Resign: Lay Group Says Pilarczyk No Longer Effective." *Dayton Daily News,* 26 November 2003. www.daytondaily.com (accessed 27 November 2003).

Briggs, David. "Catholics Urged to Stay Vigilant in Battle against Child Sex Abuse." *Cleveland Plain Dealer,* 3 March 2003. www.cleveland.com (accessed 3 March 2003).

———. "Mistrust Lingers after Sex Abuse Scandal." *Charlotte Observer,* 4 December 2004. www.charlotte.com (accessed 5 December 2004).

"British Cardinal Calls for Church Honesty." *Catholic News,* 24 October 2002. www.cathnews.com (accessed 25 October 2002).

Brodsky, Robert. "Tragic End for Ridgewood Man Who Claimed Abuse by Priest." *Queens Chronicle,* 2 October 2003. www.zwire.com (accessed 3 October 2003).

Brooks, Scott. "NH Priest Praised by Church Victims Group." *Union Leader/New Hampshire Sunday New*s, 13 November 2003. www.theunionleader.com (accessed 13 November 2003).

Brown, Hilary, and Matt McGarry. "Ireland's Dirty Laundry." *ABC News,* 26 January 2003. www.abcnews.com (accessed 20 June 2003).

Buchanan, Patrick J. "An Index of Catholicism's Decline." *World Net Daily Commentary,* 11 December 2002. www.worldnetdaily.com (accessed 20 December 2002).

Byron, Ken, and Bill Leukhardt. "Priest Held in Sex Assault: Polish Visitor Says He Was Giving Girl Rape Counseling." *Hartford Courant,* 27 December 2002. www.ctnow.com (accessed 28 December 2002).

Call, Maureen. "Tests Confirm Priest Fathered 2." *Enterprise,* 28 October 2003, http://enterprise.southofboston.com (accessed 28 October 2003).

Capeloto, Alexa, and Patricia Montemurri. "Group Raises Funds to Help Some Priests Accused in Sex Cases." *Detroit Free Press*, 23 September 2002. www.freep.com (accessed 25 September 2002).

"A Cardinal without Credibility." *Hartford Courant,* 16 June 2003. www.ctnow.com (accessed 17 June 2003).

Carroll, Terrence. "Transparency Still Lacking in Catholic Sex Scandal." *Seattle Times,* 3 August 2005. www.seattletimes.nwsource.com (accessed 3 August 2005).

"Catholic Priest Sentenced in Chile for Sexual Abuse." *Voice of America,* 24 June 2002. www.voa.com (accessed 25 June 2003).

Chadwick, John. "Members Say Lay Group Not Anti-Catholic." *North Jersey News,* 12 October 2002. www.bergen.com (accessed 15 October 2002).

"Child-Abuser Monk Commits Suicide." *BBC News,* 17 May 2005. http://newsvote.bbc.co.uk (accessed 7 October 2005).

"Church in Europe Getting Ready to Fight Clergy Sex Abuse." *Catholic News*, 30 August 2002. www.cathnews.com (accessed 1 September 2002).

"Church's Moral Clout Eroding." *Manila Times,* 4 June 2002. www.manilatimes.net (accessed 5 June 2002).

"The Church on Trial: Part 1." *CBS News,* 12 June 2002. www.cbsnews.com (accessed 7 November 2005).

"Church Seeks Database on Abusers." *Sunday Times* (South Africa), 5 June 2003. www.sundaytimes.co.za (accessed 6 June 2003).

Clarke, Jim. "Speak Out on the Catholic Church Scandal." *Canton Journal* (MA), 5 June 2003. www.towonline.com/canton/ (accessed 5 June 2003).

Collit, Raymond, Reuters. "Brazil Priest Sentence Fuels Pedophilia Scandal." *San Diego Union-Tribune,* 23 November 2005. http://signonsandiego.printthis.clickability.com (accessed 24 November 2005).

Craig, Gary. "Priest Nabbed in Porn Inquiry: FBI Says Cleric Had Hundreds of Pictures of Children on Computer." *Democrat and Chronicle* (Rochester, NY), 11 March 2005. www.democratandchronicle.com (accessed 11 March 2005).

Crosbie, Sarah. "Kicking out Sex-Molester Priests Called 'a Recipe for Disaster.'" *Kingston Whig-Standard* (Ontario), 26 April 2003. www.thewhig.com (30 April 2003).

Cruz, Isagani. "Culprits in the Cloister." *Inq 7 News,* 27 September 2003. www.inq7.net (accessed 28 September 2003).

Curti, Elena. "High Price of Broken Trust." *Tablet,* 9 July 2005. www.thetablet.co.uk (accessed 10 July 2005).

Dahlby, Fr. Charles. "Scandal in the Roman Catholic Church." *Catholic Citizens of Illinois,* 28 October 2003. http://catholiccitizens.org (accessed 29 October 2003).

"Damning Anglican Sex Abuse Report Revealed." *Australian Broadcasting Company,* 31 May 2004. www.abc.net.au (accessed 31 May 2004).

Diamant, Jeff. "Victims Group Denounces Firing of Priest." *Star Ledger,* 28 May 2003. www.nj.com (accessed 28 May 2003).

Dickey, Christopher, and Rod Nordland. "Precious Suffering." *Newsweek,* 28 February 2005, 26.

Dogliosa, Felix, Jr. "Ex-Priest Kills Self with Gun." *Rocky Mountain News,* 23 September 2005. www.rockymountainnews.com (accessed 23 September 2005).

Dowd, Mark. "Gays in the Priesthood." *Tablet,* 15 May 2001. www.thetablet.co.uk (accessed 3 May 2002).

Drake, Tim. "Catholics Are 'Blogging' on the Internet . . . to Evangelize." *Catholic. net,* 12 June 2002. www.catholic.net (accessed 13 June 2002).

Duin, Julia. "Silenced Priest Warns of Gay Crisis." *Washington Times,* 15 November 2004. www.washingtontimes.com (accessed 15 Noember 2004).

———. "Victims' Group Hits Church Audit." *Washington Times,* 6 January 2004. www.washingtontimes.com (accessed 6 January 2004).

Egelko, Bob. "Court: Whistle Blower Priest Can Sue San Francisco Archdiocese." *San Francisco Chronicle,* 3 January 2003. http://beliefnet.com (accessed 2 January 2006).

Elias, Marilyn. "Is Homosexuality to Blame for Church Scandal?" *USA Today,* 15 July 2002. www.usatoday.com (accessed 20 July 2002).

"Fear in the House of God." *All Africa News,* 24 May 2003. www.allafrica.com (accessed 25 May 2003).

Filteau, Jerry. "Former Sex Abuse Panel Head Says He Was Subject of Smear Campaign." *Catholic News Service,* 2 October 2003. www.catholicnews.com (accessed 3 October 2003).

———. "Study Says Two-Fifths of U.S. Nuns Suffered Some Form of Sexual Abuse." *Catholic News Service,* 8 January 2003. http://catholicnews.com (accessed 11 January 2003).

Finger, Stan. "Group Helps Victims of Clergy Discuss Past." *Wichita Eagle,* 3 February 2002. *www.kansas.com* (accessed 4 February 2003).

Fischer, Howard. "Bill Adds to Scrutiny for Sexual Offenders." *Arizona Daily Star,* 27 February 2003. www.azstarnet.com (accessed 27 February 2003).

Fowler, Daniel. "Jury Indicts Priest." *New Bedford Herald,* 18 December 2004. www.zwire.com (accessed 5 December 2004).

Frank, Jon. "Former Nun Sentenced for Molestation 35 Years Ago." *Virginian-Pilot,* 22 September 2004. http://home.hamptonroads.com (accessed 22 September 2004).

Fraser, Stephen. "Catholic Church Appoints Protection Director." *Scotland on Sunday,* 27 April 2003. www.scotlandonsunday.com (accessed 28 April 2003).

Freund, Charles P. "Madrassas Molesters." *Reason,* April 2005. www.findarticles.com (accessed 7 October 2005).

Frogameni, Bill. "Victims' Advocate." *Toledo City Paper,* 24 April–9 May 2004. www.toledocitypaper.com (accessed 10 May 2004).

Gadoua, Renee K. "Moynihan Apologizes for Abusive Priests." *Post-Standard*, 31 October 2003. www.syracuse.com (accessed 1 November 2003).

Gibson, Gail, and Laura Vozzella. "In Catonsville, A Parish Copes with Disclosures From Its Past: Archdiocese List Named 56 Accused of Sex Abuse; 6 Had Served at St. Mark." *Baltimore Sun,* 13 October 2002. www.sunspot.net (15 October 2002).

Gledhill, Ruth. "Church Pays Hush Money to Sex Abuse Victims." *Times* (London), 20 November 2002. www.timesonline.co.uk (accessed 22 November 2002).

Gloudon, Barbara. "Children's Bodies on the Auction Block." *Jamaica Observer,* 23 January 2004. www.jamaicaobserver.com (accessed 24 January 2004).

Goldwyn, Ron. "Priest Pleads Guilty to Kiddie-Porn Charges." *Philadelphia Daily News,* 24 August 2004. www.philly.com (accessed 25 August 2004).

Goni, Uki. "Sex Priest Stuns Argentina with Love Memoirs." *London Observer,* 20 June 2004. www.guardian.co.uk (accessed 20 June 2004).

———. "Young Fogeys." *Atlantic Monthly,* January/February 2002. www.theatlantic.com (accessed 5 March 2002).

Green, Ashbel S., and Steve Woodward. "Judge Says Archdiocese Owns Parishes, Schools." *Oregonian,* 30 December 2005. www.oregonlive.com (accessed 30 December 2005).

Grossmith, Pat. "Allegations Revealed in Manchester Diocese Settlement." *Union Leader,* 13 October 2002. www.nl.newsbank.com (6 November 2005).

Gupta, Charu, and Christopher J. Kelly. "Demonstrators Picket Timlin." *Scranton Times-Tribune,* 3 February 2003. www.scrantontimes.com (accessed 4 February 2003).

Hahn, Scott. "The Paternal Order of Priests." *Lay Witness,* May/June 2003. www.catholiceducation.org (accessed 12 February 2006).

Hamilton, Elizabeth, and Eric Roth. "A Predator Blessed with Charm." *Hartford Courant,* 15 September 2002. http://pqasb.pqarchiver.com (accessed 5 November 2005).

Hamilton, Marci. "Will State Legislatures Stand up to the Catholic Church and Pass Strong Anti-Child Abuse Laws?" *FindLaw,* 24 February 2003. www.findlaw.com (accessed 24 February 2003).

Hantschel, Allison. "Priest: I Can't Stop Molesting Children." *Daily Southtown* (IL), 10 December 2002. www.dailysouthtown.com (accessed 12 December 2002).

"Hardly Krishna." *The Age,* 2 June 2003. www.theage.com (accessed 7 October 2005).

Harter, Kevin. "Judge: Priest Was Funeral Home Killer." *Pioneer Press,* 4 October 2005. www.twincities.com (accessed 6 October 2005).

Heneghan, Tom. "Popular French Priest Confesses Sin, Backs Reform." *Reuters,* 27 October 2005. http://today.reuters.com (accessed 27 October 2005).

Hogan, Tom. "My Turn: Is It Too Late to Save the Catholic Church?" *Newsweek,* 30 June 2003. www.msnbc.com (accessed 3 July 2003).

Horn, Dan. "Archdiocese Found Guilty of Failing to Report Abuse: No Contest

Plea Ends 2-Year Church Investigation." *Cinicinnati Enquirer,* 21 November 2003. www.enquirer.com (accessed 21 November 2003).

Hughes, Gary. "Church Abuse: The Full Picture." *The Age,* 25 May 2003. www.theage.com (accessed 25 May 2003).

Ickes, Barbara. "Parish Writes Bishop about Abuse Concerns." *Quad-City Times* (Davenport, IA), 2 January 2002. www.qctimes.com (5 November 2003).

"In News: Nuns Were Victims Too." *St. Louis Post-Dispatch,* 7 January 2003. www.stltoday.com (accessed 8 January 2003).

"Interview with Rev. Thomas Doyle." *Religion and Ethics Newsweekly,* 27 January 2002. www.pbs.org/wnet/religionandethics (accessed 29 January 2003).

"Investigation of Accused Priest Widening." *CBS 2,* 22 February 2006. http://cbs2chicago.com (accessed 23 February 2006).

"Italian Priest Arrested for Prostitution, Pornography." *A (Australia) BC News,* 7 May 2003. www.abc.net (accessed 7 May 2003).

Johnson, Erica. "Priest Pleads Guilty in 5 Sex Cases." *Las Vegas Sun,* 2 January 2002. www.lasvegassun.com (accessed 4 January 2003).

"Joint Protocol between Archdiocese, DCFS." *CBS 2,* 22 February 2006. http://cbs2chicago.com (accessed 23 February 2006).

Jones, J. Harry. "Ex-Pt. Loma Pastor in Child Porn Case is Given Probation." *San Diego Union Tribune,* 11 March 2005. www.signonsandiego.com (accessed 11 March 2005).

Junge, Ember Reichgott. "Jeffrey R. Anderson: Fighting for the Rights of Sex-Abuse Victims." *Minnesota Lawyer,* 27 January 2003. www.minnlawyer.com (accessed 28 January 2003).

Keating, Frank. "The Last Straw: Quitting the Bishops' Review Board." *Crisis Magazine,* 1 October 2003. www.crisismagazine.com (accessed 1 October 2003).

Kelly, Matt. "Mixed Blessings." *Boston Magazine,* July 2004. www.bostonmagazine.com (accessed 27 July 2004).

Kelly, Mike. "Abuse Victim Suffered to the End." *Record,* 16 October 2003. www.northjersey.com (accessed 18 October 2003).

Kelsey, David H. "Redeeming Sam: The Difference Jesus Makes." *Christian Century,* 28 June 2005, 24.

Kemen, Maya. "Rodimer Draws Critic's Praise." *North Jersey News,* 13 November 2002. www.northjerseynews.com (accessed 13 November 2002).

Keneally, Thomas. "Cold Sanctuary: How the Church Lost Its Mission." *New Yorker,* 17 June 2002. www.newyorker.com (accessed 1 July 2002).

Kennedy, Dan. "Rome Cast Its Ballot (continued)." *Boston Phoenix,* 8–14 August 2003. www.bostonphoenix.com (accessed 14 August 2003).

Kenny, Jack. "Jack Kenny: Did Police Aid Church's 'Abettors'?" *Union Leader/New Hampshire Sunday News,* 9 March 2003. www.unionleader.com (accessed 9 March 2003).

Kesich, Gregory D. "Ex-Priest Breaks Code of Silence." *Press Herald/Maine Sunday Telegram,* 31 July 2005. www.pressherald.mainetoday.com (accessed 31 July 2005).

Kingsley, Jennifer. "Schuyler Attorney to Testify about Sex Abuse." *Ithaca Journal,* 20 May 2003. www.theithacajournal.com (accessed 21 May 2003).

Klimkiewicz, Joann, and Bill Leukhardt. "Priest Released after Group Raises Bail." *Hartford Courant,* 18 January 2003. www.ctnow.com (accessed 18 January 2003).

Knapp, Krystal. "Priest Sex Victims Want No Statute of Limitations." *Everything Jersey,* 5 December 2002. www.nj.com (accessed 7 December 2002).

Kole, William J. "Austrians Leave Catholic Church in Droves after Summer of Scandal." *CBC News,* 24 September 2004. www.cbc.ca (accessed 24 September 2004).

LaCamera, Paul. "The Immorality of Subpoenaing the Therapists of Victims of Clergy Abuse." *Boston Channel,* 1 February 2003. http://thebostonchannel.com (accessed 2 February 2003).

Lampman, Jane. "A Church Culture Draws Scrutiny." *Christian Science Monitor,* 10 December 2002. www.csmonitor.com (accessed 12 December 2002).

———. "A Married Priesthood? A Shortage of Roman Catholic Priests Has Led Some Clergy to Call for Celibacy to Be Optional. Though Controversial, 'Rent-a-Priest' Helps Fill Gap for Some Catholics." *Christian Science Monitor,* 4 September 2003. www.csmonitor.com (accessed 10 September 2003).

Lee, Grace. "L.A. Cardinal under Fire: Prosecutors Say Sex-Abuse Proof Withheld." *Los Angeles Daily News,* 2 November 2002. www.dailynews.com (accessed 2 November 2002).

"Levada Urges Gay Priests to Remain in the Closet." *Catholic News,* 28 February 2006. www.cathnews.com (accessed 28 February 2006).

Levine, Jay. "Church Place Some Blame on DCFS in Sex Scandal." *CBS 2,* 22 February 2006. www.cbs2chicago.com (accessed 23 February 2006).

Levitz, Jennifer. "Holy War: Three Lawyers Risk Their Careers and Their Faith to Win Justice for Children who Had Been Sexually Abused by Their Priests." *Providence Journal,* 29 December 2002. www.projo.com (accessed 30 December 2002).

Ligomeka, Brian. "Monsignor Tamani Supports Sexual Abuse." *Malawi Standard,* 2 January 2003. www.allafrica.com (accessed 3 January 2003).

Linker, Damon. "Fatherhood, 2002." *First Things,* November 2002, 8.

Lombardi, Kristin. "Law's Disgrace." *Boston Phoenix,* 20 December 2002. www.bostonphoenix.com (accessed 22 December 2002).

Long, Paul A. "Church: We're Not Blaming Victims." *Kentucky Post,* 28 February 2003. www.kypost.com (accessed 3 March 2003).

———. "Diocese to Abuse Victims: Tell Church." *Kentucky Post,* 23 April 2003. www.kypost.com (accessed 7 November 2005).

Louwagi, Pam. "A Family's Faith Was Shaken after Their Sons Were Abused." *Star Tribune,* 29 September 2002. www.startribune.com (accessed 29 September 2002).

Lyons, Daniel. "Paid to Picket." *Forbes Magazine,* 15 September 2003. www.forbesmagazine.com (accessed 18 September 2003).

McAleer, Peter. "Victims: Church Violates Privacy." *Press of Atlantic City*, 20 October 2002. www.pressofatlanticcity.com (accessed 22 October 2002).

McArthur, David. "Abuse Victims Meet with Archbishop." *World News Now*, 31 October 2003. http://wave3.com (accessed 1 November 2003).

McBrien, Richard P. "The Office of Bishop." *Tidings*, 2 August 2002. www.the-tidings.com (accessed 4 August 2002).

———. "The Popes and Wal-Mart on Labor Union." *Tidings*, 13 December 2002. www.the-tidings.com (accessed 15 December 2002).

McGraw, Carol. "Charge against Plesetz Echoed: Woman in Irvine Says She, Too, Had a Child by Former Catholic Priest Assigned to Dana Point Church." *Orange County Register*, 23 September 2003. www2.0cregister.com (accessed 1 October 2003).

Mandelaro, Doug. "Lawyer Advocates for the Abused." *Democrat and Chronicle*, 18 February 2003. www.democratandchronicle.com (accessed 19 February 2003).

Marinay, Manny B. "Venomous Ratzi Rattles Gay Flock." *Manila Times*, 22 June 2005. www.manilatimes.net (accessed 11 July 2005).

Marchocki, Kathryn. "Files: Church Understood Priest Abuse in 1950s." *Union Leader/Sunday News*, 6 March 2003. www.theunionleader.com (accessed 7 March 2003).

———. "Group's Petition Seeks Resignation of Bishop." *Union Leader/New Hampshire Sunday News*, 25 July 2003. www.theunionleader.com (accessed 26 July 2003).

Matteson, Stefanie. "Bishop Says Outreach is Key to Church's Future." *Courier News* (Bridgewater, NJ), 7 November 2005. www.c-n.com (accessed 7 November 2005).

Mattingly, Terry, Scripps Howard News Service. "Top 10 Religion Stories for 2002." *Florida's Treasure Coast and Palm Beach News*, 28 December 2002. www.tcpalm.com (accessed 29 December 2002).

Maurer, Karl. "Rev. Joseph Fession, S.J.: Bishops' Dereliction Made This Spiritual Crisis Possible." *Catholic Citizens of Illinois*, 18 September 2002. www.catholiccitizens.org (accessed 20 September 2002).

Michaels, Paul. "Don't Dare to Speak Its Name." *Tablet*, 24 September 2005. www.thetablet.co.uk (accessed 2 January 2006).

Miller, Michael. "Priests Seek Probe of Bishops." *Peoria Journal Star*, 6 June 2004. www.pjstar.com (accessed 6 June 2004).

Milote, Gregg M. "Accounts Conflict over Diocese's Cooperation." *Herald News*, 27 September 2002. wwww.heraldnews.com (accessed 29 September 2002).

Monsour, Theresa. "Priest Abuse Victims Ask Area Faithful to Help Push for Talk." *Pioneer Press*, 12 January 2003. www.twincities.com (accessed 12 January 2003).

Montemurri, Patricia. "Bishop, Diocese Dispute Efforts." *Detroit Free Press*, 16 January 2006. www.freep.com (accessed 16 January 2006).

———. "Church in Jeopardy of More Suits: Bill Would Provide No Time Limit for Alleged Victims to Act." *Detroit Free Press*, 12 August 2003. www.freep.com (accessed 12 August 2003).

Moore, Pat. "Priest's Resignation Tied to Online Sex Purchases." *Palm Beach Post,* 24 September 2004. http://palmbeachpost.com (accessed 24 September 2004).

Morin, Brad. "UNH Expert Unveils Report on Sexually Abusive Priests." *Foster's Daily Democrat* (Dover, NH), 9 October 2002. www.fosters.com (accessed 10 October 2002).

Munz, Michelle. "Group Takes Its Message on Clergy Abuse to Ballpark." *St. Louis Post-Dispatch,* 22 June 2003. www.stltoday.com (accessed 22 June 2003).

Myers, Steve. "Woman Says Counseling Halted in Retaliation." *Mobile Register,* 5 November 2003. www.al.com (accessed 5 November 2003).

Neuhaus, Richard John. "The Meaning of Apostolic." *First Things,* November 2003, 77.

———. "The Public Square: Scandal Time III." *First Things,* August/September 2002, 93.

———. "Seeking a Better Way." *First Things,* October 2002, 84.

Neumayr, Geroge. "Cardinal Stonewaller." *Spectator,* 27 May 2003. www.spectator.org (accessed 30 May 2003).

"New Phoenix Bishop Orders Priests to Dissasociate from Gay Document." *Life Site Daily News,* 28 April 2004. www.lifesite.net (accessed 28 April 2004).

"New York Cardinal Accused of Snubbing Bishops' Lay Review Board." *Catholic News,* 17 January 2003. www.cathnews.com (accessed 18 January 2003).

Newell, Mike. "'Thy Kingdm Come, Thy Will Be Done: A True Believer, a Victim's Tale, and Wine and Spirits on the Day the New Archbishop Takes Over." *Philadelphia Weekly,* 19 October 2003. www.philadelphiaweekly.com (accessed 20 October 2003).

O'Leary, Stephen. "A Tangled Web: New Media and the Catholic Scandals." *USC Annenberg Journal Review,* 6 August 2002. www.ojr.org (accessed 6 August 2002).

O'Neill, Tim. "Scandal Rocks the Church, but Faith Remains." *St. Louis Post-Dispatch,* 21 June 2003. www.stltoday.com (accessed 21 June 2003).

Owen, Richard. "Priests and Teachers on Trial in Italy over 'Paedophile' Ring." *Times* (London), 19 October 2004. www.timesonline.co.uk (accessed 20 October 2004).

Pagnozzi, Amy. "Priest Still Waiting for Cronin's Answer." *Hartford Courant,* 6 September 2002. www.ctnow.com (accessed 10 September 2002).

Parker, J. Michael. "New Archdiocese Says It Settled Sex Suit to Protect Plaintiff." *San Antonio Express-News,* 21 February 2003. www.mysanantonio.com (accessed 22 February 2003).

Patinio, Ferdinand. "34 Catholic Priests Suspended." *Manila Times,* 19 September 2003. www.manilatimes.net (accessed 20 September 2003).

Patinio, Ferdinant, and AFP. "In Rulebook for Priests: Two Kids and You're Out." *Manila Times,* 20 November 2003. www.manilatimes.com (accessed 29 November 2003).

Paulson, Michael. "Outrage at Vatican's US Hunt for Gay Seminarian." *Sydney Morning Herald,* 17 September 2005. www.smh.com.au (accessed 17 September 2005).

Pigott, Robert. "Vatican to Reinforce Catholic Orthodoxy." *BBC News,* 8 January 2003. www.bbc.uk.co (accessed 10 January 2003).

"Police, Fire, Courts." *Peoria Journal Star,* 19 December 2003. www.pjstar.com (accessed 21 December 2003).

"Priest Admits Child Porn Charges." *BBC News,* 17 December 2004. www.newsvote.bbc.co.uk (accessed 18 December 2004).

"Priest Addresses Sex Crimes from Pulpit." *Donegal News,* 8 November 2002. www.donegalnews.com (accessed 11 November 2002).

"Priest Arrested for Child Abuse." *News 24,* 31 May 2003. www.news24.com (accessed 1 June 2003).

"Priest Calls for Cardinal's Resignation." *NBC 5,* 7 February 2006. www.nbc5.com (accessed 8 February 2006).

"Priest Pleads Guilty to Charges of Child Porn Possession." *San Diego 10 News,* 10 February 2005. www.10news.com (accessed 10 February 2005).

"Priest Says People, Not Clergy, Will Prevail." *Hartford Courant,* 19 November 2002. www.ctnow.com (accessed 21 November 2002).

"Priest Sentenced." *2 News,* 11 March 2005. www.wgrz.com (12 March 2005).

Ramos, Linette C. " 'Strict Rules' for Papa Priests." *Philippines Sun Star,* 21 November 2003. www.sunstar.com (accessed 29 November 2003).

Rams, Bill, Fermin Leal, and Greg Hardesty. "Ex-Priest Left Note." *Orange County Register,* 28 May 2003. www.ocregister.com (accessed 29 May 2003).

"Report: Cardinal Warned of McCormack's Abuse." *NBC 5,* 24 February 2006. www.nbc5.com (accessed 25 February 2006).

"Retired Bishop is Seeking Rome's Permission to Marry." *Total Catholic,* 1 January 2003. www.totalcatholic.net (accessed 1 January 2003).

Reuters. "Cardinal Makes Apology for British Priest Case." *Boston Globe,* 21 November 2002. www.boston.com (accessed 22 November 2002).

Rivera, John. "Keeler Letter Reveals Abuse: Cardinal Says 83 Priests Accused over 7 Decades; 'Spiritual Equivalent of Murder'; $4.1 Million in Settlements Go to 8 Victims in 20 Years." *Baltimore Sun,* 25 September 2002. www.baltimoresun.com (accessed 27 September 2002).

Roberts, Chalonda. "Priest in Court on Child Pornography Case." *WHAM TV,* 14 March 2005. www.13wham.com (accessed 15 March 2005).

Rom, Louis. "Devotion and Deceit." *Times* (Lafayette, LA), 28 August 2002. www.timesofacadiana.com (accessed 28 August 2002).

Rosario, Ruben. "Childhood Sex-Abuse Liability: House Votes to Extend Time Limit for Lawsuits." *Pioneer Press,* 14 May 2003. www.twincities.com (accessed 14 May 2003).

Rosenblatt, G. "A Rabbi Accused of Sexual Abuse Seeks to Reinvent Himself." *Jewish Journal of Greater Los Angeles,* 1 October 2004. www.jewishjournal.com (accessed 7 October 2005).

Ross, Brian. "Priestly Sin, Cover-Up: Powerful Cardinal in Vatican Accused of Sexual Abuse Cover-Up." *ABC News,* 26 April 2002. www.abcnews.com (accessed 13 May 2002).

Rubin, Better Miller. "Resignation: 'A Great Day for Survivors.'" *Chicago Tribune,* 14 December 2002. www.chicagotribune.com (accessed 14 December 2002).

Schembri, Karl. "Police Investigate Priests for Alleged Paedophilia in Church Institution." *Malta Independent,* 28 September 2003. www.independent.com (accessed 30 September 2003).

Schimke, David. "True Believer: St. Paul Attorney Jeff Anderson Had Already Made Millions 'Suing the Shit' out of the Catholic Church. Now All He Wants Is Another Reformation and Credit for Time Served." *City Pages* (Minneapolis/St. Paul), 16 August 2003. www.citypages.com (accessed 16 August 2003).

Schulte, Bret. "Struggling to Keep the Faith." *US News & World Report,* 27 December 2004. www.usnews.com (accessed 27 December 2004).

Schwab, Charlotte R. *Sex, Lies, and Rabbis.* Bloomington, IN: AuthorHouse, 2002.

Schwartz, Noaki. "Miami Archbishop Criticized for Friendship with Child Abuser." *Miami Sun-Sentinel,* 4 September 2002. www.sun-sentinel.com (accessed 5 September 2002).

Scott, Stephen. "Minnesota: Victims Extend Time to File Suit." *Pioneer Press,* 1 February 2003. www.twincities.com (accessed 2 February 2003).

"Sex Abuse Victim Wants Archbishop to Step Down." *NBC 15,* 13 May 2003. www.wpmi.com (accessed 14 May 2003).

"Sex Shame of Priests." *Yorkshire Post Today,* 25 November 2005. www.yorkshiretoday.co.uk (accessed 25 November 2005).

Shaw, Kathleen A. "A Push Is on for Sex Crimes Bill." *Worcester Telegram & Gazette* (MA), 19 November 2002. www.telegram.com (accessed 20 November 2002).

Shook, Dennis. "Archdiocese Supports Bill on Mandatory Reporting: Priests Expected to Reveal Instances of Sexual Abuse." *Waukesha Freeman* (WI), 17 June 2003. www.gm.today.com (accessed 19 June 2003).

Siegel, Jim. "State Aim: Curb Priest Sex abuse." *Marion Star* (OH), 17 June 2003. www.marionstar.com (accessed 17 June 2003).

———. "State May Try to Curb Sex Abuse Secrecy." *Telegraph-Forum* (OH), 14 June 2003. www.bucyrustelegraphforum.com (accessed 14 June 2003).

Silk, Mark. "Catholic Controversy II: Handling Pedophilia." *Religion in the News,* Fall 1998. www.trincoll.edu (accessed 10 December 2002).

Smith, Bill. "Nuns as Sexual Victims Get Little Notice." *St. Louis Post-Dispatch,* 4 January 2003. www.stltoday.com (accessed 5 January 2003).

"St. Poelten Scandal Sees Hundreds Leaving the Catholic Church." *Die Presse* (Vienna), 20 August 2004. http://diepresse.at (accessed 21 August 2004).

Steinfels, Peter. "Excerpt: A Church at Risk." *Sojourners,* July–August 2003. www.sojo.net (accessed 15 July 2003).

Stern, Gary. "Legionaries Not without Its Critics." *Journal News* (NY), 4 June 2002. www.nyjournalnews.com (accessed 4 June 2003).

Studd, Helen, Ruth Gledhill, and Claire McDonald. "Child Abuse 'Hotspots' Uncovered in Five Catholic Dioceses." *Times* (London), 21 November 2002. www.timesonline.co.uk (accessed 22 November 2002).

Sussman, Dalia. "Church Losing Confidence: Poll Finds Image at Its Worst since

Sex-Abuse Scandal Broke." *ABC News,* 18 December 2002. www.abcnews.com (accessed 18 December 2002).

Thomas, Fr. Gerard. "A Source of Scandal: The Vatican's Document on Gays in the Priesthood Represents a Purge. A Gay Priest Asks: Where Is the Message of Jesus in It?" *Beliefnet.* www.beliefnet.com (accessed 2 February 2006).

Tod, Sweeney. "Six Courageous Priests Praised by Abuse Victims." *Religious News,* 25 November 2003. www.sweenytod.com (accessed 24 Novembver 2003).

Toth, Sara. "Catholic Investigator Says Lay People Are Key to Recovery: Former Head of Board that Looked into Child Abuse Speaks at ND." *South Bend Tribune* (IN), 21 January 2005. www.southbendtribune.com (accessed 22 January 2005).

Tu, Janet I. "Legislation to Protect Minors Introduced: Statute of Limitations on Sex Abuse Would End." *Seattle Times,* 17 January 2003. www.seattletimes.com (accessed 18 January 2003).

———. "Victims' Advocates Argued that Bill Must Be Retroactive." *Seattle Times,* 22 January 2003. www.seattletimes.com (accessed 22 January 2003).

Tu, Janet I., and Jonathan Martin. "Spokane Churches Can Be Sold to Pay Debt, Judge Rules." *Seattle Times,* 27 August 2005. www.seattletimes.com (accessed 27 August 2005).

Turner, Maureen. "Calling Church Leaders to Task." *Valley Advocate* (MA), 1 January 2004. www.valleyadvocate.com (accessed 2 January 2004).

"Utica Priest Formally Charged with Child Porn." *Local 4 Click on Detroit News,* 11 June 2003. www.clickoondetroit.com (accessed 11 June 2003).

Van Fleet, Jonathan. "Church Officials Asked Police Not to Charge Priest after Sex Incident with Teen." *Telegraph* (Nashua, NH), 3 March 2003. www.nashuatelegraph.com (accessed 3 March 2003).

Vogel-Short, Maria. "Swift Action Restores Trust at Daytop." *Observer-Tribune* (NJ), 6 January 2005. www.zwire.com (accessed 7 January 2005).

Wahid, Zaheera. "Ex-Priest Faces Sex Charges: He Is Alleged to Have Fathered a Child with a Teenager While He Was at St. Edward Catholic Church in Dana Point." *Orange County Register,* 25 September 2002. www2.0cregister.com (accessed 3 October 2002).

Westcott, Scott. "Rebuilding Trust 2: What Becomes of Abusive Priests?" *Times-News* (Erie, PA), 1 July 2003. www.go-erie.com (accessed 5 July 2003).

"Whistleblower Wants Apology from Church." *Prague Post,* 2 April 2003. www.praguepost.com (accessed 15 April 2003).

Wiener, J. "An End to Denial." *Jewish Journal of Greater Los Angeles,* 7 September 2001. www.jewishjournal.com (accessed 7 October 2005).

Williams, Karin. "Priest Abuse Discussed." *Phoenixville News,* 30 September 2005. www.phoenixvillenews.com (accessed 30 September 2005).

Wineke, Bill. "Arrogance of Bishops Is Appalling." *Wisconsin State Journal,* 20 April 2004. www.madison.com (accessed 22 April 2004).

Wolfe, Warren. "Angered by 'Disrespectful' Agenda, Flynn Cancels Meeting with SNAP." *Star Tribune* (Minneapolis), 5 April 2003. www.startribune.com (accessed 5 April 2003).

———. "Archbishop Flynn to Meet with Sex-Abuse Victims Group." *Star Tribune* (Minneapolis), 14 January 2003. www.startribune.com (accessed 29 January 2003).

"Woman Sues Priest." *CBC News,* 18 February 2003. www.pei.cbc.ca (accessed 14 May 2003).

Woodward, Steve. "Archdiocese of Portland Parishes Will Join Dispute: Legal Action over Asset Ownership Can Proceed Now that Bankruptcy Judge Allows a Class of Defendants." *Oregonian,* 1 July 2005. www.oregonlive.com (accessed 1 July 2005).

———. "Lawyer Asks for Church Counseling Aid after Third Suicide by Sex-Abused Claimant." *Oregonian,* 17 August 2005. www.oregonlive.com (accessed 17 August 2005).

Zagier, Alan Scher. "Priest Scandal Depresses Dioceses Budget Already Hurting from Feeble Economy." *Naples Daily News,* 20 July 2003. http://cgapps. naplenews.com (accessed 21 July 2003).

Zajac, Bill. "Diocese: Church Alleges Conflict: The Plaintiffs' Lawyers Filed a Motion to Have Superior Court Judge Constance M. Sweeney Rule on First Amendment Issues." *Mass Live,* 12 February 2003. www.masslive.com (accessed 14 February 2003).

———. "Gay Priests in Barely Closed Closet." *Mass Live,* 29 February 2004. www. masslive.com (accessed 1 March 2004).

———. "Priest Sees Redemption in Change." *Mass Live,* 23 October 2002. www. masslive.com (accessed 25 October 2002).

———. "Scahill Chosen 'Priest of Integrity.'" *Mass Live,* 4 June 2004. www. masslive.com (accessed 4 June 2004).

———. "Sex Abuse Suits Last Resort, 2 Say." *Mass Live,* 24 September 2003. www. masslive.com (accessed 24 September 2003).

Reports

Abraham, Lynne. *Report of the Grand Jury in the Court of Common Pleas, First Judicial District of Pennsylvania, Criminal Trial Division.* 15 September 2005. www.bishop-accountability.org (accessed 20 December 2005).

Bonaventure, Roseanne. *Grand Jury Report, CP2 § 190.85 (1).* 17 January 2003. Suffolk County Supreme Court Special Grand Jury, May 2002, Term ID. www. bishop-accountability.org (accessed 20 December 2005).

"The Catholic Charities Network at a Glance." *Catholic Charities Information.* www. catholiccharitiesinfo.org/news/statistics.htm (accessed 16 December 2005).

The Catholic Church in America. United States Conference of Catholic Bishops, December 2003. www.usccb.org (accessed 16 December 2005).

Catholic Educators Announce School and Enrollment Statistics. National Catholic

Educational Association. 16 March 2005. www.ncea.org (accessed 16 December 2005).

Conference of Major Superiors of Men. *Improving Pastoral Care and Accountablity in Response to the Tragedy of Sexual Abuse.* 10 August 2002. www.Cmsm.org (accessed 10 August 2002).

Heed, Peter W., N. William Delker, and James D. Rosenberg. *Report on the Investigation of the Diocese of Manchester.* 3 March 2003. Office of the Attorney General, Concord, NH. www.bishop-accountability.org (accessed 20 December 2005).

John Jay College of Criminal Justice. *The Nature and Scope of the Problem of Sexual Abuse of Minors by Catholic Priests and Deacons in the United State*s. Washington, DC: United States Conference of Catholic Bishops, 2004.

Keeler, William Cardinal. *A Public Accounting.* Archdiocese of Baltimore, September 2002. www.archbalt.org (accessed 27 September 2005).

Reilly, Thomas P. *To the People of the Commonwealth of Massachusetts.* 23 July 2002. www.bishop-accountability.org (accessed 20 December 2005).

United States Conference of Catholic Bishops. *Report on the Implementation of the Charter for the Protection of Children and Young People.* February 2005. www.usccb.org (accessed 1 August 2005).

Vatican Documents

Benedict XVI. *Deus Caritas Est: Encyclical Letter of the Supreme Pontiff to the Bishops, Priests and Deacons, Men and Women Religious, and All the Lay Faithful.* Vatican, 25 December 2005. www.vatican.va (accessed 25 January 2006).

Grocholewski, Zenon Cardinal. *Instruction: Concerning the Criteria of Vocational Discernment Regarding Persons with Homosexual Tendencies in View of Their Admission to Seminaries and Holy Orders.* Vatican, 4 November 2005. www.vatican.va (accessed 28 December 2005).

John XXIII. *Pacem in Terris: Encyclical of Pope John XXIII on Establishing Universal Peace in Truth, Justice, Charity, and Liberty.* Vatican, 11 April 1963. www.vatican.va (accessed 2 December 2002).

John Paul II. "Address of John Paul II to a Group of 120 Newly Appointed Bishops from 33 Countries." *Speeches of John Paul II.* Vatican, 22 September 2002. www.vatican.va (accessed 3 November 2003).

———. *Evangelium Vitae.* Vatican, 25 March 1995. www.vatican.va (accessed 19 April 2003).

———. *Sacramentrium Sactitatis Tutela.* Vatican, 20 April 2002. www.vatican.va (accessed 15 November 2002).

Paul VI. *Gaudium et Spes: Pastoral Constitution on the Church in the Modern World.* Vatican, 7 December 1965. www.vatican.va (accessed 2 December 2002).

———. *Humanae Vitae: Encyclical of Pope Paul VI on the Regulation of Birth.* Vatican, 25 July 1968. www.vatican.va (accessed 2 December 2002).

Pius X. *Pascendi Domenici Gregis: Encyclical of Pope Pius X on the Doctrine of the Modernities.* Vatican, 9 August 1907. www.vatican.va (accessed 2 December 2002).

Miscellaneous

Adamec, Bishop Joseph. "Decree." Altoona-Johnson Diocese, 2 September 1999. www.dioceseaj.com (accessed 2 December 2002).

Appleby, Scott. "The Church at Risk." Paper presented at the United States Conference of Catholic Bishops Spring Meeting, Dallas, 13 June 2002. www. usccb.org (accessed 15 June 2002).

Bishop-Accountability.org, Inc. Website. www.bishop-accountability.org.

Catholic Online. Website. www.catholic.org.

Clohessy, David. Personal Communication. September 2005.

Erwin, Rev. Mike. Personal Communication. October 2005.

France, David. Personal Communication. February 2006.

Gensler, Daniel. "Entitlement, Temptation, and Betrayal from a Psychoanalytic Perspective." Paper presented at Sexual Betrayal and Scandal in the Catholic Church: Psychoanalytic, Religious, and Social Perspectives, New York, New York, 13 November 2004.

Gregory, Bishop Wilton. "A Catholic Response to Sexual Abuse: Confession, Contrition, Resolve." Paper presented at the United States Conference of Catholic Bishops Spring Meeting, Dallas, 13 June 2002. www.usccb.org (accessed 14 June 2002).

Hammer, Sherrel L. "Chapter XX.I. Puberty.*" Case Based Pediatrics for Medical Students and Residents.* Department of Pediatrics, University of Hawaii, March 2002. www2.Hawaii.edu (accessed 1 July 2005).

The Healing Alliance: Discovering Life beyond Abuse. Website. www.thelinkup.org (accessed 15 August 2005).

Irish Independent. www.unison.ie/irish_independent.com. Archives can be searched for numerous reports of Catholic sex scandal in Ireland.

Jones, Kirby Parker. "The Beginning and End of Reproductive Life: Pubertal and Midlife Changes." University of Utah Medical School, 1997. www.medstat.med. utah.edu (accessed 1 July 2005).

McBrien, Richard P. "Obligatory Celibacy." *Essays in Theology,* 22 April 2002. http://129.74.54.81/rm (accessed 16 July 2002).

———. "On Being a Pastoral Bishop." *Essays in Theology,* 18 May 1998. http://129.74.54.81.rm (accessed 16 July 2002).

———. "Reformers and Restorationists." *Essays in Theology,* 1 May 2000. http://129.74.54.81.rm (accessed 13 July 2003).

Martin, Rev. James, S.J. Personal Communication.

Martin, Thomas. Personal Communication.

Papesh, Rev. Michael. Personal Communication. February 2006.

Pflomm, Msgr. Personal Communication. October 2005.

"Philosophy of Healing at the Farm." Healing Alliance. www.thelinkup.org (accessed 15 August 2005).

Reynolds, Rev. William. Personal Communication. December 2002.

"SNAP Mission Statement." Survivors Network of Those Abused by Priests. www. snapnetwork.org (accessed 15 August 2005).

Sipe, A. W. Richard. Personal Communication. October 2004.

SurvivorsFirst. Website. www.survivorsfirst.org.

Terry, Karen. Personal Communication. January 2005.

Index